Everyday Preparation for JESUS' RETURN

Rocky Veach

i·m·y·n
In y ame
Boldly publishing the Gospel message!

A division of
T.O.R.CH. Ministries
Mark 13:10

Copyright © 2011 Rocky Veach

ISBN-13: 978-0615505657 (IMN (In My Name))
ISBN-10: 0615505651

Everyday Preparation for JESUS' RETURN
365 Ways to Stay Ready
© 2011 by Rocky Veach
First Edition: 2011

IMN (In My Name). A division of T.O.R.CH. Ministries
P.O. BOX 27
Southbury, CT 06488
www.rockyveach.com
rockyveach@gmail.com

ISBN-13: 978-0615505657 (IMN (In My Name))
ISBN-10: 0615505651

Editorial Consultant: Ginger Bisanz
Layout and Cover Design: Rachel Adams, Raylyn Designs

ENDORSEMENTS

Unless the roots grow deep, the plant or tree will wither and die in the heat of the summer and drought of water! So in life the true follower must be deeply rooted in 'The Word' mixed with the glorious infilling of the Holy Spirit and a living passion for Jesus.

This book full of scripture and wisdom deals with real life and how to live in the Way of God. For many there is sudden zeal, a desire to live for Jesus and share Jesus with others. Then in time often the fire dies and one's life is only filled with dreams and wishes but not power and fruit bearing as a living witness for Jesus.

Now, I challenge you to take a daily journey in following Jesus for the next year. I can assure you that your life will be powerfully transformed with the infilling of the love of God and a desire to share Jesus with others. You will be filled with the glorious expectancy of Jesus' Return.

Rocky Veach is a personal friend but much more a true man of God. A man Jesus is raising up to carry the torch of biblical knowledge and wisdom mixed with evangelism and witness. As I grow older and my time is shorter I am thrilled to read this book and know the great hope we have for the Gospel to go forth to all the world in the generation now and to come. Rocky is a powerful voice in this fresh new wave of the Glory of God sweeping the earth. I wholeheartedly recommend "Everyday Preparation for Jesus' Return!"

The greatest Preparation for Jesus Return is to know Him personally and then to grow like a tree planted by the waters...

God bless you on your journey.

A cross carrying pilgrim follower of Jesus,
Arthur Blessitt
Luke 18:1
www.blessitt.com

Rocky Veach is a friend and a true son in the faith. I don't want to recommend this book as much as I want to recommend him! My wife, Nance and I have traveled around the world with Rocky and his family, spent weeks at a time in their home, ministered alongside them and studied him as a person. Because I KNOW Rocky I can wholeheartedly assure you that this book will be a blessing to your life. Look beyond the words, read between the lines and you will find the kind of treasure that shines through the heart of a man who has been touched by the heart of Jesus! God is using men like Rocky Veach to raise up champions for His cause in these challenging times. May the Lord bless and prepare you in your pursuit of Him through these pages!

Neil Miers,
Founder, Global Connexions, www.neilmiers.com
President of COC International 1990-2010
Brisbane, Australia

DEDICATION

My wife, Bobbi is the greatest gift God has given me in this life! She has been there everyday for the past 27 years, helping prepare me for Jesus' return! Her dedication to Him, support for her family and perseverance in the ministry has been a powerful example to many and a constant source of inspiration to me. Therefore, I dedicate *Everyday Preparation for Jesus' Return* to her…I love you sweetheart, your name should be on the cover!

I would also like to thank the faithful team of friends and associates who helped me through the grueling process of layout and publishing. Rachel, Jim, Lori, and Ginger you are the best! Thank you guys!!

PREFACE

A funny story might be the best way to introduce a serious subject. On the final day of 2008 it seemed the Lord impressed me to spend the following year writing something that would help remind others of His soon return. So, I spent every day of 2009 compiling scriptural passages from the Bible and commenting on them as a means of helping people remember to get ready to meet Jesus Christ. Gleaning fresh revelation daily and trying to sum up many of the things God had taught me in my 20 plus years of ministry, while balancing the duties of pastoring a local church and traveling to speaking engagements demanded my full attention.

At the same time, I also happened to have a precious elderly widow in my church that spent much of her time in prayer. One day she recounted how Jesus had suddenly and unexpectedly appeared in her bedroom during her devotional time! Now, her advanced age demands that we question whether her experience was completely genuine or partially imagined but it certainly served to reinforce the need for me to write this book. At the very moment this sweet little church lady saw the Lord, she suddenly exclaimed in a frightful tone, "Jesus Christ"!!

It was all I could do not to laugh but she was so sad in telling me how a little bit of the "old (wo)man" had just "slipped" out of her mouth when she least expected it. To make matters worse, she said Jesus simply looked at her lovingly but with obvious disappointment in his eyes and disappeared! It was not how she hoped to be found by the One she was trying to live out her last days for. Such a natural reaction in the biggest spiritual moment of her life illustrated for me again how surprisingly unaware we can be of our frail human condition.

All of us are more like this woman than we may realize. The world, and especially the Church today which has so much of the world inside it, need to be reminded that Jesus truly IS coming! It will be just as sudden as this story, but not nearly as funny – especially if we are the ones caught off guard. So, the purpose of this book is found in its title. Doing a little biblical forward thinking each day will help us be more prepared for the suddenness of the Last Day!

I have chosen Acts 1:9-14 as my starting point because these verses reveal how God focused the earliest disciples' attention on the need to live and serve with an expectation of the Second Coming. Upon hearing the angels' words, they immediately "DEVOTED" themselves, as the Amplified version of the Bible says. Everything we read afterward in this same New Testament book is simply the result of God working out His plan, according to His Word, through their daily lives (as promised in Mark 16:20)!

This kind of devotion is the same basic requirement for those in every generation who want to be found faithful. Proximity to God is what keeps us in a true state of *faithfulness, usefulness* and *readiness*. These terms are the themes of this book – things I believe He wants every Christian to think more about. It is designed in a devotional format so you can use it for either personal reading or as starting points for studying provocative subjects to teach others. Regardless of how you proceed, let this humorous little story keep you serious about expecting Jesus to show up!

TABLE OF CONTENTS

BEFORE YOU BEGIN

MAKE THE MOST IMPORTANT DECISION OF YOUR LIFE!

Sincerely inviting Jesus Christ into your life is the number one thing you must to do in order to be prepared for His return. This is extremely personal and public at the same time but it is all by divine design!

The Bible says we must all believe in our heart that God raised Jesus from the dead and confess with our mouths that He is Lord (Romans 10:9-10). It is in the doing of both things that we are saved. God desires a personal relationship with you but he also demands a public recommendation from you! If you are willing to do both, it proves you are serious. If not, you probably won't be willing to accept the full invitation of Jesus to "FOLLOW" Him.

Take the time to consider what is being asked of you. A Christian is called to break with the past and go forward into God's future. This requires "repenting" or turning away from sin and then receiving the pardon Jesus died on the cross to purchase for you. Salvation is costly because it is precious. Serving Jesus is not always easy outwardly but the freedom, peace and joy you will experience inwardly cannot be valued in limited human terms. The eternal rewards are even greater. Not only are you saved from the unending punishment of hell but more importantly you are destined to spend forever in a heavenly state of being!

So, before moving further, whether you are unsaved or simply not in a right place with God, stop and ask Jesus to forgive you right now and become the Lord of your life. Then take up your cross and follow Him...you will never regret it!

JANUARY 1…DAY 1
FINISHING WHAT JESUS STARTED

"…but you shall be baptized with the Holy Spirit not many days from now… you shall receive power when the Holy Spirit has come upon you; and you shall be witnesses to Me in Jerusalem, and in all Judea and Samaria and to the ends of the earth." Acts 1:5, 8 NKJV

Jesus' strategy for building the Church in His absence is notably straight-forward, simplistic and meant to be viewed as continuous from the day He left until the day He returns. The same approach He used in ministry He now gives to those who follow His call. Remaining immersed "in" what the Holy Spirit initially pours "upon" us is our primary objective. This ensures that we will personally experience the Spirit to spirit connection, life, and power before we try to pass it on or explain it to someone else.

Next, we learn our practical approach to delivering Christ's message. It is carried by "witnesses", or literally according to the Greek martyrs. Only the dead can truly carry life. It will be these who finish what Jesus started, extending His cross by carrying their own to both the farthest reaches and final moments of planet Earth…which is what the term "end of the earth" means.

JANUARY 2…DAY 2
HOW TO PASS THE TEST OF TIME

"Then He spoke a parable to them that men always ought to pray and not lose heart, saying: There was in a certain city a judge who did not fear God nor regard man…And he would not for a while;…and shall God not avenge His own elect who cry out day and night to Him, though He bears long with them?"
Luke 18:1-2, 4a, 8 NKJV

Our biggest obstacle is handling inactivity. It is what we do when we don't know what to do that makes all the difference with God. In this parable (a fictitious similitude that symbolizes the Truth), Jesus tells us plainly that God operates on His own timetable. His seeming inactivity often makes no sense to us whatsoever, yet He remains right on schedule!

When you feel like this widow in your relationship with God do not stop praying, and you will maintain the control and courage of your heart for your circumstances. You will pass a gigantic test with God and stay ready for His coming if you continually keep approaching Him now, especially when you feel far away! This is a heart matter…if you remind yourself how much you need the Lord now nothing will shake your faith later!

JANUARY 3…DAY 3
IF SHE CAN DO IT YOU CAN TOO

Now there was widow in that city; and she came to him, saying, 'get justice for me from my adversary.' Luke 18:3 NKJV

The word "widow" literally means deficient or lacking. This lady had no resources to leverage, nothing to barter except her own weakness. The list of things she did not have was extensive. No authority to speak for her, no helper to do the hard work, no voice in society to get public support, no natural hope for the future. Yet somehow this widow found the one thing she did have to tender…herself!

Jesus is teaching us the secret of bringing ourselves to God. It is the heart of the Gospel and it works every time. Like Jesus, the most useful thing we have to offer is our own life. Give it away for the Lord and it comes back 100 times greater! Hold onto it and you lose it completely in the end.

Be like this widow and keep your perspective not on what you can or cannot do, but rather on what the just Judge can do for you...if only you refuse to quit. This is one way in the end of days, when the Adversary looks like he is winning, we will get final justice!

JANUARY 4…DAY
BRING YOUR OWN PRESSURE

"…but afterward he (the unjust judge) said within Himself, 'Though I fear not God nor regard man, yet because this woman troubles me I will avenge her, lest by her continual coming she weary me.' Then the Lord said, 'Hear what the unjust judge said.'" Luke 18:4b-6 NKJV

One important thing you need to know about God is that He keeps things "close to His vest" so to speak. He knows exactly what He is doing at all times, yet reserves the right to change His course of action according to our willingness to interact with Him. How many times did Jesus nearly pass people by in the Gospels until they did something that changed His direction?

The specific game-changer in this story is the "trouble" the woman was bringing. The Greek defines this word as "the cut or pain caused by one who stays near awaiting an occasion!" That means we must be the ones who bring the pressure to bear, not those who fold under it. Let's stay near to God now...in the end we will have our optimum occasion!

JANUARY 5...DAY 5
RELENTLESS VENGEANCE

"...Avenge me from my adversary'...'because this widow troubles me I will avenge her'...'And shall God not avenge his own'...'I tell you He will avenge them speedily.'"
Luke 18:3b, 5a, 7a, 8a NKJV

Believers have a very real "adversary" against whom we make our stand in Christ. It is interesting to me that this word in the Greek language means an adversary in a lawsuit, and is specifically referring to Satan.

Jesus is teaching us here that our Father takes the adversary's attacks on the people of God, and the matter of executing the legal vengeance we need very seriously. It doesn't always seem that way. We may have to keep stating our case, based on our rights in Christ. Sometimes it looks like a lost cause, but He will avenge us in our spiritual battle; immediately, eventually, or ultimately.

Notice that the term, "avenge" is used in this parable four times! The word simply means vindication, retaliation or revenge. God is not an unjust judge but a righteous one. He knows the scope of Satan's jurisdictions and the limitations of his legal rights to harass a believer. If we know our rights and the power of relentless prayer, vengeance on our behalf will not only come...it will come "speedily!"

Remember the Lord's language here as you prepare for life in the last days. If "I will," then "God shall," and surely "He will." We need to be confident in our salvation, knowing that God is always ready to rescue us from satanic devices!

JANUARY 6...DAY 6
SEEING THE END IN THE BEGINNING

"Then the Lord said, 'Hear what the unjust judge said.
And shall God not avenge His own elect who cry out day and night to Him, though
He bears long with them? I tell you that He will avenge them speedily.'"
Luke 18:6-7 NKJV

Whenever Jesus tells us to "listen up" in the Bible it is a good idea to pay special attention. If we do hear what He tells us, we will learn which principles are particularly important in developing a working relationship with God.

What did the unjust judge say that is so important for us to understand? Again, it is the relentlessness he sees in the widow that causes him to relent! This gets more interesting when you look at the meaning of the Greek word, "continual" in verse five. It literally means "to approach something with the end in mind!"

Managing our actions with this kind of goal-oriented thinking pays off with God, and it teaches us why we must keep the end of time in our sights as we live for God today. Most of us tend to get distracted in life trying to do too many things at once. We either don't do any of them to the best of our ability, or we miss the goal God has set for us completely.

Remember Jesus' words in this passage. God is a righteous judge who wants you to succeed and you will...if you are willing to see the end in the beginning and keep working towards it no matter what!

JANUARY 7...DAY 7
WHO WILL LET THE DOGS OUT?

"Then the Lord said, 'Hear what the unjust judge said. And shall God not avenge
His own elect who cry out day and night to Him, though He bears long with them? I
tell you that He will avenge them speedily. Nevertheless, when the Son of Man comes,
will He really find faith on the earth?'"
Luke 18:6-8 NKJV

"Then it happened, as He was coming near Jericho, that a certain man sat by the
road begging. And hearing a multitude passing by, he asked what it meant. So they
told him that Jesus of Nazareth was passing by. And he CRIED OUT, saying, 'Jesus, Son
of David, have mercy on me!' Then those who went before warned him that he should

be quiet; but he CRIED OUT ALL THE MORE, 'Son of David, have mercy on me!'...Then
Jesus said to him, 'receive your sight; your faith has made you well.' And
immediately he received his sight and followed Him..."
Luke 18: 35-43 NKJV

Did you notice how Jesus closes the parable of the widow by asking two questions in its last two verses? This is significant. The first one, posed in verse seven, is about God and the second in verse eight, is about us.

Today let's deal with the first question. Regarding the affairs of His "elect," Jesus proves beyond question before the chapter is finished, that as far as God is concerned He will act "speedily" for those willing to "cry out!" He proves His point by stopping for the blind beggar near Jericho, who did exactly what the relentless widow did in the parable he had just related in Jerusalem. The blind man refused to lose heart and quit.

When they told him to shut up he just got louder. You could say he howled. The term "cry" is the word "halloo" in the Greek, meaning "to incite dogs to chase!" This tells us we have to "let the dogs out" for God if we want to see His power displayed on our behalf!! He will move in any situation, if in our desperation we proceed like we really believe He is the answer! If you want to be ready for last days' living, you have to know that God will respond to those who respond radically to His presence. Try it...go ahead, let your dogs out!!

JANUARY 8...DAY 8
THE LAST MEN STANDING

"Then the Lord said, 'Hear what the unjust judge said. And shall God not avenge
His own elect who cry out day and night to Him, though He bears long with them? I
tell you that He will avenge them speedily. Nevertheless, when the Son of Man comes,
will He really find faith on the Earth?'"
Luke 18:6-8 NKJV

I asked you yesterday to consider the two questions with which Jesus ends the parable of the widow. We looked at the first one, found in verse seven, and proved God's willingness to act on behalf of His "elect."

Today I want you to look with me at the second question, which is directed towards us and proves who the "favorite, selected ones" (elect) of God really are. The answer to verse eight seems like a "no-brainer" but it should bother us a bit because it's a question – implying there is no precise answer! We tend to think, "Of course people will be holding to the faith when Jesus returns. Since He has shown His goodness and promised to intervene against our adversary there will certainly be multitudes lined up to meet the Lord!" But shockingly, this scripture is posed as a rhetorical question for a reason. Jesus wasn't seeking our opinion He was divulging the outcome!

In the language of the text, this part of speech is known as an interrogative particle. It implies both anxiety and impatience on the part of the questioner, (Jesus), and presumes a negative answer on the part of the one being questioned (us)! Ah, oh!! Jesus is telling us that even though God is so good, most people won't respond to Him in the end! The Bible is clear that the last days are going to be hard times to believe in God (2 Thessalonians 2:3)! Christianity isn't going to be an easy religion to half-heartedly follow as it is in so many places today. So, this really is an open ended question.

It remains for each of us to decide how we will answer. Every non-believer, believing Christian, and existing church of any size should consider their answer now...so they will really be ready when our answers count! Many are called but few are chosen. Better to cry with courage now than to cry with regret later!

JANUARY 9...DAY 9
READ A LITTLE FURTHER TO BE READY

"Also He spoke this parable to some who trusted in themselves that they were
righteous and despised others."
Luke 18:9 NKJV

Looking at the parable of the widow as preparation for building a solid last day's lifestyle, we are compelled by the writer (Luke) to remain longer in this chapter. The following parable, which gives the contrast of two men praying at the temple, is written in a way that connects the two parables. Notice the phrase, "...He spoke..." In my studies I found that this happens to be a primary particle with a "copulative" and sometimes a "cumulative" force. All that means is that this next parable is tied together with the first in Jesus' teaching, and that it is probably meant to build upon its meaning.

When you put verse 1 and verse 9 together, we then get a wider view of what God considers to be a proper approach to a godly lifestyle. The first parable teaches that if we learn the importance of continuous prayer we will find the secret of being blessed by God. The second focuses on keeping our hearts pure in the process of prayer by looking away from self, and letting God become our righteousness.

The two principles of persistence and humility go together in our groundwork and training for the end times. The two outcomes, vengeance and exaltation will be our reward! There is much to be said for not stopping short even in our Bible reading...the additional Word we read now, the further ready we will be at that needed time!

JANUARY 10...DAY 10
THE FOUNDATION OF ANY TEAM

"Also He spoke this parable to some who trusted in themselves that they were righteous and despised others."
Luke 18:9 NKJV

We have already seen how the widow in the previous parable was commended for acting alone in persistent faith. In this second parable, which is really a continuation of the first, Jesus highlights the fact that there is another central issue in our approach to God. Our preparation for His RETURN also hinges on our own consistently righteous APPROACH to Him now!

Please note how "righteous" is defined in this context by its connection with the words, "trust" and "others." There is a looking away from self that is required to properly view others who are also trying to connect with God. On God's scale even the Pharisee cannot understand spiritual matters without keeping a godly perspective of the sinful Publican, or tax collector! In our trusting God we must learn to trust His workings in others at the same time, for He is measuring us by this "golden rule."

The Publican is ultimately justified in this story, having committed HIMSELF honestly into the hands of the only one who can save, without even a glance of judgment toward his cold-hearted religious leader. At the end of the day, we learn how vital our opinions of others are. In many ways, all who approach God are on one big team. And, trust is the foundation of any successful team, especially for the one (Church) who awaits Jesus' return!

JANUARY 11...DAY 11
THE "HALF OFF" CHURCH PRINCIPLE

"Two men went up to the temple to pray, one a Pharisee and the other a Publican...I tell you this (one) man went down to his house justified rather than the other." Luke 18:10, 14 NKJV

There is a clear distinction between the kind of person who connects with God and the one who does not. As a pastor, I'm sure this line is not nearly as distinct as it needs to be in today's Church World. If you care to make the connection, notice how this parable is simply an extension of Jesus' larger discussion of end times leading up to the end of Luke chapter 17. In both places Jesus indicates to his disciples that when He returns there will be a 50% separation…and will it be among their ranks?

When I read this I immediately think of the ten virgins in Matthew 25. Again, half (5) of them were considered wise and the other half foolish, because they did not fully know what was expected of them while waiting for the one who's approach was imminent. This gap in time exposed their true condition much like the Pharisee's prayer disqualified him from God's justification. It seems probable that as many as half of us think more about ourselves than we do about God! Scary!!

JANUARY 12…DAY 12
THE STANCE OF A GODLY MAN

"The Pharisee stood and prayed thus with himself…And the Publican, standing afar off, would not so much as raise his eye to heaven, but beat his breast…"
Luke 18:11-13 NKJV

The ground on which we stand makes a gigantic difference to God. Just as Moses was told to remove his shoes at the burning bush, we learn in this parable that our feet and heart are connected. Being a religious leader, the Pharisee made the mistake of standing with HIMSELF on the ground of mere scriptural knowledge. Meanwhile the Publican, knowing he was far away from the graces of God and man, stood in a manner that honored the truth. Here are two individuals close in terms of physical proximity within the Temple grounds but far apart with respect to Holy ground!

Everything the Pharisee leaned on was true only within his own perspective. In reality he was a "taker," unjustified, a spiritual adulterer and even a tax collector in his own heart. His fasting and tithing were nothing more than outward acts of custom, because they did not reflect the attitude of generous giving which God expects from a believer. The Publican's secret was that he recognized that God already knew everything from shade to light about him.

We will not harbor or project any delusions about ourselves or others when we take this approach. We naturally open our heart when we humbly stand at a distance until God bids us come closer. Moses' shoes were stained with 40 years of hiding, after doing his own thing didn't work. The Pharisee's shoes carried the contamination of doing things according to the world system and calling it religion. The Publican did not presume to know anything except the fact that he needed help, and God was the Great helper!

Always "beat your breast" before God…this stance will keep you free from the snares of both failure and success and ready to meet the Lord when He bids you come near.

JANUARY 13…DAY 13
REMEMBER LOT'S WIFE

I tell you, this man went down to his house justified rather than the other; for everyone who exalts himself will be humbled, and he who humbles himself will be exalted…Remember Lot's wife. Whoever seeks to save his life will lose it, and whoever loses his life will preserve it."
Luke 18:14; Luke 17:32-33 NKJV

Have you ever considered the huge importance of this tiny sentence of Jesus, "Remember Lot's wife?" It is a warning to those through whom He would build the New Testament church. It's about the need for His people to constantly be focused on following Him without regret. By "Remembering Lot's wife" we thoughtfully maintain the highest Old Testament principle of putting God first. Called to His attention, we can stay ready for every step we will take along the highway of preparing the world for His return!

I have connected the statement Jesus made about the Tax Collector with this previous one about Lot's wife to make an important point. Saving your life is the same as exalting yourself in God's eyes, while losing it is equated with humility. When we take these two things together we understand that "choosing to lose" is the best way to gain with God! Self always wants to look back, to recollect, to hold onto and to go back to save itself; and will do so if allowed, at the cost of pressing on toward the goal for the prize of the higher or upward Call of God in Christ Jesus! (Phil. 3:14) Dying to ourselves is a prerequisite to living for the Lord…Remember Lot's wife!"

JANUARY 14…DAY 14
WHEN LIGHTNING STRIKES

"And they will say to you, 'Look here!' or 'Look there!' Do not go after them or follow them. For as lightning that flashes out of one part under heaven shines to the

9

other part under heaven, so also the Son of Man will be in His day."
Luke 17:23-24 NKJV

When lightning strikes in the Bible it is usually a sign of God doing something of tremendous spiritual importance! For example, take Jesus' statement about Satan's fall from heaven in Luke 10:18, or when the Lord descended on Mt. Sinai before the Israelites in Exodus 19-20. Ezekiel received a vision from the Lord where he saw the emergence of four living creatures from a storm as lightning (Ezekiel 1:13-14). John also notes several times in the book of Revelation (4:5, 8:5, 11:19, 16:18), that he witnessed lightning "flashing" from the heavenly Throne. God Himself being described as a "consuming fire," displays the directed explosiveness of lightning as one of His key attributes.

We understand this more clearly when we remember Moses' second ascent on Sinai. While the Israelites only saw the glory that Moses was engulfed in as a "consuming fire" on the top of the mountain, the man of God himself descended from the "cloud" of God's presence with his face and skin shining from an inward transfiguration. Jesus experienced the same thing with his three closest disciples, teaching us to recognize both the external shock and the internal awe of the Almighty!

Before Jesus returned at his resurrection, an angel was sent forward to roll away the stone. Matthew says, "His countenance was like lightning..." When Jesus returns again He cautions us to look for the same indicator...it will be the real thing only when that identical matching lightning strikes again!

JANUARY 15...DAY 15
THE QUICKEST FIX

"And they will say to you, 'Look here!' or 'Look there!' Do not go after them or follow them. For as lightning that flashes out of one part under heaven shines to the other part under heaven, so also the Son of Man will be in His day."
Luke 17:23-24 NKJV

Even in our day I am amazed how easily Christians will follow all the wrong things! What others state is "Jesus" one day so often turns to have only been their misguided perceptions or false expectations the next day! Human beings are foolish that way...which is precisely why Jesus issued this warning! It's like the old saying, "you've got to stand for something or you'll fall for anything." What are you standing for and upon today? Is it the Truth of God's own Word, or the loose opinions of others?

The Church has to bring to a halt being so easily distracted by outward appearances, whether "here" or "there." We can only accomplish authenticity by "looking unto Jesus, the author and finisher of our faith." He is not an issue, nor a cause, or thing about which to discuss or conjecture. He is THE Way, THE Truth and THE Life Himself!!

We often prefer God's benefits rather than the reality of knowing His face and heart. We can never assume to act or presume to know His farthest reach or every detail of His strategy or timing. He is perfect, judicious, omniscient and not flawed from the Fall as we are. This was the tendency of the mainstream religious leaders of Jesus' day. They were prone to presumptuous errors such as looking at the outside of inward truths and, as a result, missing the point.

When we compare verse 21 and 24, we can clearly see the Lord's warning not to follow those who would mislead people toward a false Christ is aimed directly at the Pharisees! In the last days you will not be able to trust in religious establishments or the men who oversee them. Just keep your focus on Him…everyday. When you comprehend that you have strayed, move quickly back to Him. Train yourself to be quick about it, for He is coming quickly!

JANUARY 16…DAY 16
FIRST THINGS FIRST

"The days will come when you will desire to see one of the days of the Son of Man and you will not see it…But first He must suffer many things and be rejected by this generation." Luke 17:22-25 NKJV

Before Jesus would come to end all the suffering of humanity, exercise punishment on a disobedient world, and take complete rule and reign on earth, He must first execute something quite the opposite!

Those promises He will accomplish in a later generation. He was letting his disciples know that of necessity He must first taste the cruelty of their own day and time!

Events run their course according to a divine plan in God that is higher than we can fully comprehend. If Jesus had to suffer restraint before He could bring release, it stands to reason that we as His followers should apply the same principle. We are often prepared to perform what we think needs to be done, long before we have arrived at the time and place God has appointed for those things to be enacted. As believers we find ourselves sometimes calling for sacrifice now for what we must bear later! Don't get ahead of God's timetable. It was the suffering of Christ at the proper appointed time, which allows us to stand today, in preparation for our part in God's will be done on earth Kingdom tomorrow.

Jesus will come in an hour when many do not expect Him. However today is always the day of Salvation, a time when we must give our lives for others. So, put first things first and you will be a living sacrifice in the hand of God in your day. A pure Bride, able to go out and meet Him in that soon arriving day!

JANUARY 17...DAY 17
THE DAYS OF NOAH #1

"Then He said to the disciples, "The DAYS will come when you will desire to see one of the DAYS of the Son of Man, and you will not see it...And as it was in the DAYS of Noah, so shall it be also in the DAYS of the Son of Man: They ate, they drank, they married wives, they were given in marriage, until the DAY that Noah entered into the Ark..." Luke 17:22, 26-27 NKJV

In preparation for the last days we must recognize the importance of particular words in the Bible inked in red, which signify they come straight from the mouth of God! In this passage Jesus specifically makes a distinction between the words, "Days" and "Day." The use of the plural tells us that He is talking about something that will happen over a longer period of time, while the singular describes a more specific point in time.

The disciples had to be prepared for the long haul of an over comer. They were going to have to be ready to experience the ups and downs of following Jesus during the days leading all the way up to the final day on God's calendar of New Testament events. We also live in the extended "DAYS of the Son of Man" wherein the resurrected Lord is working through His own Body of believers. What Jesus started He will finish, but there is a specific danger in this era that will ensnare us if we do not heed His words.

Two men are mentioned as examples, Noah being the first. What is it about his days which are so important with regard to this dispensation between the first and second coming of the Lord?

Several good things are mentioned that are common to all generations; eating, drinking, marrying and enjoying life. Being natural in origin, these are the blocks upon which the "world" system has been built. The lust of the eyes, the lust of the flesh and the pride of life, will be a constant source of distraction for people right up until the final "DAY" of the Lord! Even through judgments and tribulation the tendency of man will be to try and feed his carnal nature, just as they did in the "Days of Noah." Now is the time to learn to "detach" from the subtle things that can prevent our final entrance into the ark of God's presence.

JANUARY 18…DAY 18
THE DAYS OF NOAH #2

"UNTIL the day Noah entered the ark, and the flood came and destroyed them all."
Luke 17:27 NKJV

"Then the Lord saw the wickedness of man was great in the earth, and that every intent of the thoughts of his heart was only evil continually…
But Noah found grace in the eyes of the Lord."
Genesis 6:6-8 NKJV

Why is it we say "Pay day always comes," but act like judgment day will never come! Do we love the world more than the Bible! Noah was a real man who lived in a real bad time. The people were wicked and consumed by sin…they thought about self, they were motivated by lust and they built their lives around the sin nature of this world! This is when what is known in Christian terms as the "World" system was formed. It was perhaps the Devil's peak hour, but God and one righteous man put a sudden stop to it!

Like water finding a fissure, the sin nature in Noah's family eventually gave way again; but only after judgment had come for everyone else. Remember, this description of Noah and his family is part of the end-times scenario Jesus foretold so we wouldn't be caught off guard. Until the end of time The Lord is continually gazing at our affairs and He knows the pool from the puddle, weighing the shallow, from the deep end of the water. Our days are similar to Noah's where one righteous man (Jesus) has made a much bigger difference for God, and the big picture is playing out in exactly the same way.

This world culture Satan has redeveloped through our complicit and tacit agreement is hopelessly broken. The only way of escape is in the lifeboat (Church) Jesus is building with our cooperation, according to His instructions! Since the days we are living in are an extension of Jesus' first coming, replete with all the victory He purchased and persecution He suffered, we can expect the same end He described in the scriptures above.

On the DAY Jesus returns there will be another closing of the door that will separate believers from unbelievers, with the same kind of finality described in Genesis 6. Will you be ready? The only way to be certain is to be like Noah, working under the favor and ability of God to accomplish your part to save all the creatures God is calling to salvation!

JANUARY 19...DAY 19
THE DAYS OF LOT #1

"Then He said to the disciples, "The DAYS will come when you will desire to see one of the DAYS of the Son of Man, and you will not see it...Likewise as it was also in the DAYS of Lot: They ate, they drank, they bought, they sold, they planted, they built"
Luke 17:22, 28 NKJV

Lot is the second person Jesus mentioned as a Biblical example of a perilous last days lifestyle. Although there are similarities in the lists of things highlighted from both Noah and Lot's generations, there are also a few interesting differences. In Noah's day the emphasis was on individual's overindulgence in personal interests and relationships, in Lot's day the sin was more commercial in nature. One society was rural, the other urban. One was attached to simple pleasures, the other exotic. Yet they both incurred God's wrath and received total destruction. The former was Satan's system developing in the undefined world outside of God's garden; the latter was an extension of Satan's more defined pagan Babylon into the boundaries of God's Promised Land!

Jesus is painting a picture for us of a last generation that will increasingly gratify itself in all of these indulgences! Again, what really stands out about Jesus' comments regarding both periods is that the activity is not exclusively sinful but worldly in scope. Normal worldly practices will abnormally characterize the very end of the church age.

How caught up are people today in foods, fashion, status, class, commerce, music, jargon, politics, dead or false religion and sensational success? We live in a heightened state of awareness of all these things at the same time!! It is difficult to picture believers anxiously awaiting Jesus' return when they have been so practically detached from Him in multiple and various facets of their everyday lifestyles.

As appalling as it was in Noah's day, Lot's era was worse due to extreme worldliness of the culture in Sodom. This godly but tainted man could barely save only some of his own family...how many last days' believers will be like Lot's wife?!

JANUARY 20...DAY 20
THE DAYS OF LOT #2

"But on the day that Lot went out of Sodom it rained fire and brimstone from heaven and destroyed them all." Luke 17:29 NKJV

"...and turning the cities of Sodom and Gomorrah into ashes, condemned them to destruction, making them an example to those who afterward would live ungodly" 2 Peter 2:6 NKJV

A further look into the circumstances surrounding Lot's generation gives us even more clarity about conditions prior to the Lord's return.

Ezekiel tells us plainly that God saw fit to destroy Sodom for obvious reasons. Specifically, pride, fullness of food, a prosperous ease and their failure to help the poor and needy are outlined (chapter 16:49-50). Along with Gomorrah and the surrounding areas, Sodom serves as an ultimate example of the kind of hazardous behavior, which always results in establishing cultures and standards that reject the authority of God.

How similar is the world today? The same system that has been at work since the days of Babel was employed then, and is globally networked today! When we consider the root of the outward evils of society we must remember to check within. The practice of things God calls "abominable", spring from the love of self. The Sodomites loved themselves above anything or anyone else. This gives us insight into why Lot ended up in that place after departing from Abraham. He simply went where it was most comfortable or convenient for his compromised lifestyle!

Although he was rescued physically, we can see the tremendous toll living there took upon him and his family in the end. Peter says, everyday Lot literally tortured and wore down his own righteous soul by the things he heard and saw. Let us be careful to protect ourselves from wrong attachments to the world, and even more importantly to monitor the indulgences and conditions of our own hearts!

JANUARY 21…DAY 21
IN THAT DAY

"Even so will it be in THE DAY when the Son of Man is revealed.
In THAT DAY…" Luke 17:30-31a NKJV

There is a definite day coming when Jesus will return. His references to both Noah and Lot describe conditions that will be prevalent in the era preceding His return, but his use of one word draws our attention to a central thought in the mind of God.

In each story there was a process leading up to a critical point in time. Noah only predicted the rain up until a certain day, and then God shut the door of the Ark and it began to rain. Lot lived under grace for a designated period until God inspected the situation, and then met with Abraham to work out the "terms" of Sodom's destruction. After much procrastination on Lot's part, the angels finally pushed him and his family out of town; but then the fire fell, on a certain day.

Jesus uses these pictures to prepare us for another definite day that will not fail to come. Just as in Noah's time, God will bear long with that final generation giving them every opportunity to repent. As in Lot's time, He will hold back and work with His own people to get them in the appointed places of deliverance.

The day will surely come! What kind of day will it be? Jesus specifically calls it a day of "revelation" (verse 30). That is interesting to me because this is the same Greek word John uses for the vision he had of Jesus in the book of "Revelation." It means, a disclosure or uncovering, thus a day when things will turn sharply into the light. Today we see and know God, but in a very obscure and limited way (1 Corinthians13:12). In that certain and definite day everyone, every one of us, will know exactly who He is, including we His Church.

Hold onto your salvation and don't let anyone shake your faith in Jesus, but understand that much of what you think you know in totality is incomplete. Many will miss Jesus at His return because they tagged onto and chased something else that came from someone other than Him! Stay in the Word, keep your heart in communion with Him and you will live in revelation all the way up to THAT DAY when He is completely unveiled!

JANUARY 22...DAY 22
WHEN GOD CHECKS IN

"But the Lord came down to see the city and the tower which the sons of men had built. And the Lord said, 'Indeed the people are one and they all have one language, and this what they begin to do; now nothing that they propose to do will be withheld from them. Come let us go down and confound the(m)'"
Genesis 6:5-6 NKJV

"And the Lord said, 'Because the outcry against Sodom and Gomorrah is great, and because their sin is very grave, I will go down now and see whether they have done altogether according to the outcry against it that has come to Me; and if not, I will know.'"
Genesis 18:20-21 NKJV

I always found it interesting that throughout the Old Testament God checks in on people and situations in a very personal way. However, just because we live on the other side of the Cross doesn't mean He has stopped doing so.

The New Testament says at all times remain hospitable because when we do, we sometimes unknowingly entertain angels! It seems like God has unusual methods of keeping tabs on people, situations and circumstances! The bottom line is that God wants us to be aware that He often does things we are unaware of!

Notice how the Lord personally scattered and confused the people who originally conspired to build the satanic world system at the Tower of Babel. In the case of Sodom and Gomorrah He consulted with His friend, Abraham, about His intentions to obliterate an entire culture. God personally wrestled the Jacob out of Jacob, and thereby changed the course of Israel's future. He confronted His own servants several times in scripture, sometimes with a drawn sword! Gideon learned to work with the Lord..."the Sword of the Lord and Gideon!" In the book of Revelation, John saw Jesus with flames of fire in his eyes and a sharp word in His mouth! His instructions are telling..."write down what you see and send it to the churches." Don't think God is not watching the world and closely monitoring the progress of His Church. Jesus is checking in on us...are we checking in with Him?!

17

JANUARY 23...DAY 23
LOSING YOUR STUFF

"In that day, he who is on the housetop, and his goods are in the house, let him not come down to take them away. And likewise the one who is in the field, let him not turn back. Remember Lot's wife. Whoever seeks to save his life will lose it, and whoever loses his life will preserve it."
Luke 17:31-33 NKJV

In order to continue ready at all times to meet the Lord we must critically deal with our natural love for "things." Here Jesus gives us a simplistic way to gauge our preparedness for living in the last of the last days. By using the terms "house" and "field" He alerts us to pay attention to our most basic, central sphere of life. In our homes we store the "goods" we have accumulated by working in our career fields.

There is an interesting play on words here in that this word, "goods", refers not only to the things that a man has but also figuratively to his wife, as she relates to the using and care of those things! I don't think the Lord was saying for men to abandon their wives in that day, but rather that believers must be willing to leave behind all people places and things holding them back from following Him. This is probably why Jesus interjects Lot's wife immediately into our view. Her story represents both a longing for the lifestyle God was making her put behind, and an example of one who actually became a component of the bitterly leftover landscape that resulted from the divine judgment of Sodom.

We too are warned to wean our hearts from "coming down" to get our worldly goods and "turning back" to preserve a life that is destined for destruction. We must maintain a forward pursuit of our higher call in Christ. In the end, the only way to save your self is to lose your stuff...willingly!

JANUARY 24...DAY 24
WHEN NIGHT FALLS

"I tell you, in that night there will be two men in one bed: the one will be taken and the other will be left. Two women will be grinding together: the one will be taken and the other left."
Luke 17:34-46 NKJV

Here the Lord reiterates His point about distinguishing the places and people found in the very last days leading up to His return. They will be both in their homes (beds) and at their jobs, because His coming will be a global event. Unlike our annual New Year's celebrations graduated by the earthly rising and setting of the sun, there will come a moment when He will return suddenly in every time zone at the same time.

Notice Jesus uses the word, "Night" this time instead of "day." It is the same word translated "midnight" in Matthew 25 in the parable of the wise and foolish virgins. Although His return will happen quite literally during the night time in half the world, this is also figurative language.

We are being warned of a "midnight hour" in history that will take everyone by surprise...except those with ears to hear what Jesus is saying! And what is the basis of separation between these people?

Verse 33 tells us the difference is their attitude toward self. Are you in a place of readiness? If you are "getting up" now before the midnight hour and buying oil, not for selfish purposes but spiritual ones, you will be taken or chosen by the Son of God. If you lag backwards, whether He comes in your night or day, you will be left to your own sparse schemes!

JANUARY 25...DAY 25
EXPECT IT WHEN YOU LEAST EXPECT IT

"Watch therefore, for you do not know what hour your Lord is coming. But know this that if the master of the house had known what hour the thief would come, he would have watched and not allowed his house to be broken into. Therefore, you also be ready, for the Son of Man is coming at an hour you do not expect."
Matthew 24:42-44 NKJV

How strange is it for us to endlessly speculate about the details of Jesus' coming, and not guard our "homes" from the ultimate break in?! The only way to "know" anything important about eschatology is to approach the subject in a state of readiness for its manifestation. God is seeing to it that we will not completely comprehend what our enquiring minds would love so dearly to know! Jesus punctuates this point with the last verse by restating the first verse in more direct language. When He finally comes it will not seem like the expected time.

Today, so many Bible teachers estimate Jesus' return according to their perception of world events and Bible prophecy. Although this may be helpful in terms of general timeframes it is not on what we are to base our readiness. If we do, we are making the common mistake of assuming God is too much like us. I say examine the signs on both sides of these predictions, those that make His return seem imminent and those that do not. In other words, constitute an "expect it when you least expect it" mentality!

JANUARY 26...DAY 26
KNOW THE END BY THE BEGINNING

"Now after Jesus was born in Bethlehem of Judea in the days of Herod the king, behold, wise men from the East came to Jerusalem saying, 'Where is He who has been born King of the Jews? For we have seen His star in the East and have come to worship Him'...and behold, the star which they had seen in the East went before them, till it came and stood over where the young Child was. And when they had come into the house, they saw the young Child with Mary His mother, and fell down and worshipped Him. And when they had opened their treasures, they presented gifts to Him: gold, frankincense, and myrrh. Then, being divinely warned in a dream that they should not return to Herod, they departed for their own country another way."
Matthew 2:1-2, 9b-12 NKJV

Understanding the birth of Christianity is very important to our correctly perceiving its latter days. Recorded further in this same Gospel of Matthew (24:22) Jesus Himself warns us that before He returns, it will get so horrific in the world that God in His mercy will shorten time! If He did not, every person would be lost! So it seems that both advents of the Lord's coming, beginning and end of the Church, are both attended by just a few brave souls! In between these posts many have and will come to Lord, but the end is going to be very similar to its beginning.

The "wise men" are an accurate example of the kind of people that will endure that last generation. They found Jesus only because they had discernment of the scriptures and understanding of the times. When they found him, they honored him appropriately because they also had excellence of spirit.

There is an interesting connection to the prophet Daniel here. These men were called "Magoi" (like "wizards" in the sense of having great wisdom, see Jeremiah 39:3, 13). Daniel had been supernaturally appointed as leader over this designation of wise men centuries before under four Babylonian kings. A lowly Jewish captive, he had been promoted to the very top of that kingdom. When Daniel translated Nebuchadnezzar's dream he gained great respect and left his prophetic writings for succeeding generations of wise men to explore. This is why the wise men were expecting Jesus at his birth!! Daniel also predicted how in the end times there will be another people who will rise and shine because of their wisdom.

Follow these wise men's example. As you look with expectancy for Christ's return, study, seek, worship and present your treasured gifts to the King...such people will supernaturally GPS (God Presiding System) the way to meet Him at his coming!!

JANUARY 27...DAY 27
THE SIN OF CAIN #1

"...And the Lord respected Abel and his offering, but He did not respect Cain and his offering. And Cain was very angry, and his countenance fell. So the Lord said to Cain, 'Why are you so angry? And why has your countenance fallen? If you do well, will you not be accepted? And if you do not do well, sin lies at the door. And its desire is for you, but you should rule over it."
Genesis 4:3-7 NKJV

Mention the name Cain and almost everybody remembers he was the first murderer. How many people understand the actual sin that led to his crime? The name Cain means "to be fixed and sure", while Abel comes from a term meaning "vain or less than desirable." This tells us that Cain was a natural in the natural world, and Abel was one who probably had to struggle living in his older brother's shadow. It is another account of God choosing the younger over the older, but with some clear indicators to show us why. When we get to the part of the story where God inexplicably accepts Abel's offering and not Cain's, we should consider that this was most likely a huge role reversal for the sons of Adam.

It can seem as if God was not fair when we do not stop to consider that He looks upon the heart of the matter. In these two brothers we find what is also true in each of us...the natural wars against the spiritual. Cain's problem was that he did not respect God, and so God did not respect him! He brought his offering on his terms, out of his own sureness or righteousness.

Because of his personal state of weakness Abel was probably a little more sensitive of and dependent upon what God required. Maybe he remembered how God sacrificed an animal to cover his parents' nakedness after their fall in the garden. Surely Abel put extra effort into what he offered. He went that extra mile that causes our hearts to inquire what God wants! More than anything, the last days are about going the distance.

JANUARY 28...DAY 28
THE SIN OF CAIN #2

"...And the Lord respected Abel and his offering, but He did not respect Cain and his offering. And Cain was very angry, and his countenance fell. So the Lord said to Cain, 'Why are you so angry? And why has your countenance fallen? If you do well, will you not be accepted? And if you do not do well, sin lies at the door. And its desire is for you, but you should rule over it."
Genesis 4:3-7 NKJV

If step one in Cain's transgression was disrespect, step two was anger. An old saying says, "Danger" is just one letter away from "anger." The word for anger here means to glow or blaze up. This reminds us that emotions get involved when we begin to feel wronged. If not managed, these sensations will then compel us to further sin. Cain did not spontaneously decide to kill Abel on the day he surprise attacked him in the field. Murder had first formed in his heart from unchecked escalations of anger!

Because the last days are seen in scripture to be times of upheaval on the earth and high pressure among men, this principle applies to our topic. If we can train ourselves to walk in the awareness of God's presence, cultivating His peace and becoming comfortable with being uncomfortable we will prepare ourselves for Jesus' return. When the Bridegroom calls we will be ready to go out to meet Him...not glowering, but aglow with a joyful face!

JANUARY 29...DAY 29
THE SIN OF CAIN #3

"...And the Lord respected Abel and his offering, but He did not respect Cain and his offering. And Cain was very angry, and his countenance fell. So the Lord said to Cain, 'Why are you so angry? And why has your countenance fallen? If you do well, will you not be accepted? And if you do not do well, sin lies at the door. And its desire is for you, but you should rule over it."
Genesis 4:3-7 NKJV

So far we have looked at the steps Cain took toward the eventual murder of Abel. In our study of how to prepare for the second coming Jesus said it is imperative to know how to "possess our souls in patience."

Cain initially showed both arrogance and disrespect toward God and his brother. That root then grew into a seething anger that he was unable to bury. The Bible makes note of something I find very significant. God remarked to Cain, (and had it recorded more than once for our instruction), that his "countenance fell."

In the nearly two and half decades I have served in ministry I have rarely, if ever, known someone with a habitual sour face overcome the tests and trials specific to their personal journey. Many have been successful in some capacity, but that is very different from thriving in the arena God has called that person to. When preaching I often take note of the eyes which look away, or the resentment etched on the faces of some who attend my services. This is usually indicative of a deep seated issue in their lives, and a signal they are thrashing blindly at their circumstances. Now we all fit into that category at times, but remember I'm talking about people who habitually struggle with these issues. If we have any score to settle with man or God, it's best to take them up with the Lord before He returns!

JANUARY 30...DAY 30
THE SIN OF CAIN #4

"...And the Lord respected Abel and his offering, but He did not respect Cain and his offering. And Cain was very angry, and his countenance fell. So the Lord said to Cain, 'Why are you so angry? And why has your countenance fallen? If you do well, will you not be accepted? And if you do not do well, sin lies at the door. And its desire is for you, but you should rule over it."
Genesis 4:3-7 NKJV

Regrettably, Cain ultimately killed his brother Abel. Afterward God "marked" him to keep others from repeating his actions. In the last days Satan will mark all those like him who choose to wander the world, far from God! Pride, anger, negative body language, aggression; that is the spiraling list of traits illustrated in Cain's life and defined as sin by God. Since we, in Christ, are called to walk in the way of Abel and avoid falling into the curse of Cain, let us look closely at the lessons to be learned in this story.

Notice above that God leaves us a tool to utilize in locating sin. The key is in knowing where sin hides...at the door of the one who contemplates wrong when he knows how to do right. Here God reveals His fairness in not accepting Cain's offering. Cain did not do what he knew to do, and then was enraged at someone else for the outcome!

Today Christians know it is certainly wrong to murder, but there are multitudes that habitually practice the first three steps of arrogance, disrespect and anger without realizing how close sin is to knocking down the door and invading their lives at an unparalleled level! Abiding in the light that we have and walking in its unfolding revelation keeps us right with God and "accepted" or elevated; at our highest and best. Jesus has clarified the necessity of "doing well" and ruling over our emotions by paying the price and purchasing the grace for God's Spirit to lead us to obey Him from the heart. Yet for a little while, we too must consider our ways before the Lord and keep the door closed to sin...until He comes again and wipes away every tear!

JANUARY 31...DAY 31
THE AFTER-EFFECTS OF SIN

"Then the Lord said to Cain, 'Where is Abel your brother?' He said, 'I do not know. Am I my brother's keeper?' And He said, 'What have you done? The voice of your brother's blood cries out to Me from the ground. So now are you cursed from the earth, which has opened its mouth to receive your brother's blood from your hand. When you till the ground, it shall no longer yield its strength to you. A fugitive and a vagabond you shall be on the earth.' And Cain said, 'My punishment (iniquity) is greater than I can bear! Surely you have driven me out this day from the face of the ground; I shall be hidden from Your face; I shall be a fugitive and a vagabond on the earth,'...And the Lord set a mark on Cain, lest anyone finding him should kill him."
Genesis 4:9-15 NKJV

What is the punishment for someone who sins, enjoys it, mocks God, and has no feelings of guilt for his wrongdoing? Using the terminology of the world, this person is very close to being either a psychopath or sociopath or both! God's punishment for the behavior listed here is called a "curse", and it literally means to pronounce evil upon!

Notice, the multiple effects this pronouncement has on Cain. First, the earth itself now rejects him. Even though he was by trade a "tiller of the ground", he would no longer be able to get the ground to yield its fruit to him! The ground is pictured as literally being affected by the blood of Abel. It was "crying out" or shrieking to God!

Second, not only was Cain driven from the welcoming face of the ground, he was also hidden from the favorable face of God! A curse cuts a person off from having a relationship with God even from a distance. This explains Cain's miserable life afterwards, wandering because he is estranged from God and building a city because the ground will not bless him.

Finally, the third result of Cain's punishment is to be cut off from acceptance before the face of people. If not for God's grace extended by "marking" or putting an evidence/signal upon him, he would also have constantly been prey.

As the writer of Hebrew says, (Heb. 12:24), Jesus' blood now speaks better and louder than Abel's in the realm of the spirit and touching earth. So let's make sure we do not refuse God's grace while there is still time to receive it. There are serious consequences for mishandling the things of God, yet overwhelming forgiveness available for humbling ourselves before Him!

FEBRUARY 1...DAY 32
HOW GOD'S PEOPLE ACT AROUND HIM

"After these things I looked, and behold, a great multitude which no one could number, of all nations, tribes, peoples, and tongues, standing before the throne and before the Lamb, clothed with white robes, with palm branches in their hands and crying out with a loud voice, saying, 'Salvation belongs to our God who sits on the throne and to the Lamb'...'These are the ones who come out of great tribulation and washed their robes and made them white in the blood of the Lamb.'"
Revelation 7:9-10, 14 NKJV

We communicate by two types of language, our speech and our body language. Pay attention to both languages used by those with whom God surrounds Himself! We find God gathering these particular people around Him from the four corners of the earth. They are those believers who "come out" of great tribulation having been killed for the faith. From the description of events in the previous chapter, we know that it is going to get terrible when the Lord, the Lamb of God, unseals the seven forms of judgment in the last days. Yet, here this diverse group is found in the very throne room of God, taking the posture of those who celebrate great victories! They are standing, waving their hands and shouting to the Father and the Lord Jesus. God's crowd selection at this important moment in the book of Revelation tells us a lot about Him! We are given a glimpse into our own potential future in the response of these martyrs to God; remarkably after their having died for the Gospel. It is one of absolute honor and praise! A defining people for a defining moment, declaring the salvation or sure rescue of God in heaven, as an interlude between two scenes of great judgment and destruction on earth!

If God will so favor such action at that time, how should we be responding right now in preparation for such a great day? Let's not wait until we totally understand it all (if there is such a time on this earth) to act like the people of God. Let's find ways to demonstrate His praises, by faith today...if it's the last thing we do!!

FEBRUARY 2...DAY 33
WHAT GOD'S PEOPLE SAY ABOUT HIM

"(and) all the angels stood around the throne and the elders and the four living creatures, and fell on their faces before the throne and worshiped God, saying: 'Amen! Blessing and glory and wisdom, thanksgiving and honor and power and might, be to our God forever and ever. Amen."
Revelation 7:11-12 NKJV

Not only do we find believers in heaven in the midst of the coming "Great Tribulation" period demonstrating the greatness of God, we also find them amongst angelic beings and great men of God from history. In fact, we see the latter saying 'amen' to God's purposes in having used these martyrs as His testimony on earth, and then gathering them to Himself. Not only is there tremendous body language in this scene, but also powerful speech. After this heavenly host fall on their faces in worship, they utter seven specific words all servants of God should become familiar with:

1. Blessing speaks of largeness and fine reverential speaking. The Greek word is "Eulogia," used in English when a great man is "eulogized" at his funeral.

2. Glory speaks of the very apparent dignity of God. Literally, it means the highest thought one can have!

3. Wisdom is a word meaning "Clear" and speaking especially of practical skill or acumen, not just discretion or intelligence.

4. Thanksgiving is used to express one's gratitude for what another has done for them. It means to be grateful from the heart.

5. Honor is a word with which we show the great value of something and the high esteem that must be expressed for it. It literally means "money paid."

6. Power is the recognition of God's supernatural Force. It is miraculous in nature. This word is also used for a miracle itself.

7. Might is the ability to enforce and apply forcefulness. This is recognition of God's supreme authority and our submission to Him.

These are not words reserved for the future they are used by all who wish to be in God's presence anytime, anywhere! In preparation for the Lord's return we must learn to speak the language God wants to hear. He always draws closer to those who are serious about their approach to Him. Use these words in your conversation and in prayer. You may find yourself caught up in heavenly places now!

FEBRUARY 3...DAY 34
REMEMBER WHERE YOU CAME FROM

"Then one of the elders answered, saying to me, 'Who are these arrayed in white robes, and where did they come from?'...'These are the ones who come out of great tribulation and washed their robes and made them white in the blood of the Lamb. Therefore, they are before the throne of God, and serve Him day and night in His temple. And He who sits on the throne will dwell among them. They shall neither hunger anymore nor thirst anymore, the sun shall not strike them, nor any heat; for the Lamb who is in the midst of the throne will shepherd them and lead them to living fountains of waters. And God will wipe away every tear from their eyes.'"
Revelation 7:13-17 NKJV

The reason many are not in active fellowship with God's people today is that they do not remember "where" they came from. John saw a vision of the last days that pictured the events in heaven and earth as one intertwined drama. This is why you cannot afford to look at the end-time happenings in a narrow, religiously compartmental way. Events and the heavenly multitudes around God's throne and in His Church flow together! Our relationship to His heavenly habitation and our service are forever connected. They cannot be separated for our convenience, or we will miss the blessing of living in unity with God both now and then. These martyrs enjoy the literal presence of God for eternity, because they have come out of something very real during their lifetime.

Who are they, the heavenly narrator asks? Then he emphasizes, 'those who have come out of or completed great tribulation.' The Greek dictionary tells me this means they have successfully undergone intense pressure, anguish, affliction, persecution and/or trouble! Their blood has been spilled, which enables them understand the value of Jesus' sacrifice all the more. In a special way, they have shared His suffering and therefore enjoy the pure love of His person. They cannot be moved - forever! God is with them in every way and will never leave them. Did Jesus not promise us this same thing?

Have you experienced a real walk with Jesus? If so, you know exactly where these people are coming from...and you know where to find that secret place around God's throne!

FEBRUARY 4...DAY 35
THE ULTIMATE WORSHIP SERVICE

"...I looked and behold a great multitude...standing before the throne and before the Lamb, clothed with white robes, with palm branches in their hands and crying out with a loud voice, saying, 'Salvation belongs to our God'...All the angels stood around the throne, and the elders and the four living creatures, and fell on their faces before the throne and worshiped God, saying, 'Amen!'...they are before the throne of God day and night and serve Him in His temple."
Revelation 7:9-12; 15 NKJV

This is one of the all-time ultimate worship "services" that will ever take place and we are pre-viewing it through John's eyes! When you compare this scene with those in the days of the Acts of the Apostles, there is no real confusion about what services should resemble in our churches. They should be preparation for as many people as possible to be part of this "big one" which will surely come!

The key is to learn the lesson being taught here, and see how heaven and earth intermingle through and in God's people. Notice how, when the martyrs in this scene PRAISE God before His throne in Spirit, the heavenly host respond by WORSHIPING around that same throne in truth. This is the beauty of a people who know the realms of the spirit. "Deep calling unto deep" is how David describes this principle (Psalm 42:7). Solomon says, "The words of a wise man's mouth are like deep waters..." and again, "Counsel in the heart of man is like water in a deep well, but a man of understanding draws it out." (Proverbs 18:4; 20:5)

Be wise in understanding and in your faith at this late hour. Let the profound deep calling of God touch and draw out the depths in you. When you do, then you will learn what it means to truly "serve" him both now and forever. The world is waiting for such people...ones who lay their lives down for the pleasure of a God who is real...churches who resonate with a heavenly echo of praise and worship!

FEBRUARY 5...DAY 36
THE UPSIDE OF THE LAST DAYS

"And it shall come to pass in the last days, says God, That I will pour out of my Spirit on all flesh; Your sons and your daughters shall prophesy, Your young men shall see visions, your old men will dream dreams."
Acts 2:17, (Joel 2:28) NKJV

The last days are particularly marked for an outpouring of the Holy Spirit upon the whole world! How interesting that we should expect supernatural revelation to accompany the darkest days, but that is what this verse says.

Since the time I was a new believer, I have had a knack for revelation. Many times I have been shown things in advance through a dream or a prophetic word about a particular situation. I have also had the experience of another coming into my life to speak something only God would distinguish that I needed to know.

I've learned a lot by the Spirit, and have come to expect this kind of activity to surround my life. For me, it's always just a matter of time before my next encounter with God! We all have different gifts, talents and abilities, but we should all experience the anointing of the Holy Spirit. If we are called to accomplish our tasks for the Lord in good times...how much more in hard ones?! Learn to lean into God further as the time grows shorter. Talk to Him and listen for His voice. The closer we come to His return the louder it will be for those who are so inclined.

FEBRUARY 6...DAY 37
GET IN THE WATER

"...Your old men will dream dreams, Your young men shall see visions."
Joel 2:28b NKJV

"Let no one deceive you by any means, for that day will not come
unless the falling away comes first..."
2 Thessalonians 2:3 NKJV

I'm not sure what the age of distinction is between young and old, but I have had many dreams and a few visions. They are often hard to distinguish because, for me, they both usually come in the night. Several of the things I have seen in my "night visions" have had to do with the last days, and the condition of the Church.

In 2003 I dreamt I was entering a large mall-like building. Everything was very organized and busy as I walked down a large corridor into an open common area, where three different sections of this great complex came together. In the core was a retail center, business park, and hospital and a huge waterfall was on display. Everyone was hurriedly moving from place to place, but would slow down in awe as they passed the waterfall. As I approached I instinctively knew and heard myself say, "I must get in the water!" Immediately the scene changed, and I was at the top looking down from what appeared to be about a three-story waterfall. I purposefully stepped over the edge plunging down through the opening in the floor where the water disappeared.

Again the scene changed and I was now in an outer hallway looking back into the building where I had been before. I noticed that there was a bluish-black mist in the air that I didn't notice while inside and it was dangerously toxic. God had showed me the state of the Church in these last days as a warning. It is not safe to stay in the man-made church only where they worship around the Holy Spirit but never get wet!

These are deadly days! Do not be deceived. We must "fall into" the center of God's river in order to experience real Christianity...not "fall away" from it!

FEBRUARY 7...DAY 38
CHOOSE YOUR RIDE

"...Your old men will dream dreams, Your young men shall see visions."
Joel 2:28b NKJV

"Then one said to Him, 'Lord, are there few who are saved?' And He said to them,
'Strive to enter through the narrow gate, for many, I say to you will seek to enter and
will not be able...And indeed there are last who will be first,
and there are first who will be last.'"
Luke 13:23-24, 30 NKJV

After seeing the toxic mist inside the modern church in my lucid 2003 dream, there was one more final scene. It teaches the biblical concept of the first-rate but remnant believers who will be going against the current of the world in the last days.

The next thing the Lord showed me was a set of doors which exited the building into a valet parking area. Completely on the outside of this large religious complex, where believers were duped into perceiving themselves and their business as something other than the world cloaked in religious activity, I noticed two available automobiles. They were entirely different in every way except their era of origination, and it was for me to choose one. The first was a '60 something Pontiac GTO, black with all the chrome. The other was also a '60's model, similar to a Plymouth Valiant, dull and boring in appearance. I obviously wanted the muscle car but knew I must opt for the economy alternative! That was a good choice, because when I slipped into the driver's seat I was aware that Jesus was next to me in the passenger's seat. As a kaleidoscope multiplies images, I then turned to look at the back seat and it seemed as if there were endless back seats!! When I turned around again to look ahead I noticed other people also coming out of the (church) building, some staggering, others sitting on the curb to catch their breath, but all needing help. I knew I was to drive around the walkway and collect the ones the Lord directed me to. The dream ended as I began doing this.

The Bible reveals that in the last days there will be both a great falling away from the true church and a great outpouring of the Holy Spirit upon the relatively few who escape the world's imitation. Which will you be? I'm just an old '60's model guy (born in 1965). Which model are you? In any case, we all will have to come out of the world's (imitation) church and choose wisely to find God's guidance and follow His directions in these end times.

FEBRUARY 8...DAY 39
THE SPIRIT OF THE BIBLE

"'On that day I will raise up The Tabernacle of David, which has fallen down, and repair its damages; I will raise up its ruins, and rebuild it as in the days of old; that they may possess the remnant of Edom and all the Gentiles who are called by My name,' says the Lord who does this thing."
Amos 9:11-12 NKJV

"And with this the words of the prophets agree, just as it is written; After this I will return and will rebuild the tabernacle of David, which has fallen down; I will rebuild its ruins, and I will set it up; So that the rest of mankind may seek the Lord, Even all the Gentiles who are called by My name, says the Lord who does all these things.' Known to God from eternity are all His works."
Acts 15:13-18 NKJV

It is expressly important to grasp the "spirit" of the Bible. In reading these two passages, I noticed how James interprets Amos' words about the last days to be specifically referring to the opening of the Gospel to the non-Jewish world instead of only a literal "possessing" of its nations.

Why did he take such liberty with the Old Testament text, and how does it relate to our theme of preparing for the last days? Throughout the Bible, and especially encrypted in its prophetic writings, there is the surface meaning of information and also various depths of revelation.

As it was in the first coming of Jesus, there is an immense distinction to be gleaned between WHAT God is going to do and HOW He actually does it. If God's plan was patently obvious the religious world would have been waiting for Jesus in Bethlehem. Instead, His way was so obscure that only the wisest of spiritual men from the east, (who were by the way, most likely followers of the prophet Daniel and his "sealed" revelation), could recognize the majestic moment! What and who is forefront in the spirit of the teaching you follow?

FEBRUARY 9...DAY 40
WORD-PLAY

"'On that day I will raise up The Tabernacle of David, which has fallen down, and repair its damages; I will raise up its ruins, and rebuild it as in the days of old; that they may possess the remnant of Edom and all the Gentiles who are called by My name,' says the Lord who does this thing."
Amos 9:11-12 NKJV

"And with this the words of the prophets agree, just as it is written; After this I will return and will rebuild the tabernacle of David, which has fallen down; I will rebuild its ruins, and I will set it up; So that the rest of mankind may seek the Lord, Even all the Gentiles who are called by My name, says the Lord who does all these things.' Known to God from eternity are all His works."
Acts 15:13-18 NKJV

"When Amos said, "...possess the remnant of Edom..," there is a play on words in the Hebrew that a mere intellectual reading of the passage can miss. "Possess" is very similar in its Hebrew spelling to "seek" and "Edom" is equally similar to "Adam" (or "man"). Literally, it appears to speak of the capturing of the nations for the service of the Lord, which will ultimately be the case. The prophetic view, however, often takes a wider scope and sees the hidden meaning of God's obscure design. Here the Spirit has guided James and Peter into a realization that it is the Lord's intention that all kinds of people are going to come to know Him through a Church age of grace! The seeking will lead to possession, and Adam will ultimately include Edom but not in the way most men would think! We must learn this principle as well. God's Word is so true that often we cannot understand it with only surface information. We need the guidance of the Holy Spirit even in the study of the Bible. The end of the last days will be similar to the beginning of Jesus' ministry...we will have to have ears to hear what He is saying!

FEBRUARY 10...DAY 41
DON'T FEED THE BEAST

"We are in danger of believing ourselves advanced towards perfection in proportion to our knowledge of the way. But all our beautiful theories, far from assisting in the death of self, only serve to nourish the life of Adam in us by a secret delight and confidence in our illumination."
Francois Fenelon

"Then I stood on the sand of the sea, and I saw a beast rising up out of the sea...and all the world marveled and followed the beast"
Revelation 13:1-3 NKJV

The devil seeks to destroy us by stirring up what is already in us! He uses us against ourselves, which is why Jesus was so pointed about the need to die to self in order to really live. Think about it, finishing even a practical venture requires taming the "beast within" our carnal nature that screams at us to quit before time. This is what the whole world is facing in the second coming of Christ. Can we keep turning away from our own drives, delinquencies, and desires long enough to overcome?

We often think of the need to take action for the Lord, but do we understand the power of simply not acting at the right times? Our natural inclination is to bend the way of things to our satisfaction, but in the spirit realm Jesus is "THE WAY." We are to follow him based on His preferences until our self has been virtually replaced by His self. We don't lose our identity we just become filled with Him!

The more you study Jesus the more you insulate yourself from end time delusions occurring on a smaller scale today! The self-satisfying will always follow the beast that rises up out of the world system. Beware of the seductive self-gratifying thinking found in the sea of humanity. The secret is in learning to turn to Jesus continually. When you realize that you have strayed, whether in thought or deed, simply come back. This conditions your heart to follow and serve him. As you do, you will naturally begin to recognize the Lord's hand and train yourself to sniff out the foul subtle schemes of Satan!

FEBRUARY 11...DAY 42
GET THE DUST OUT OF YOUR EYES

"Foolish one, what you sow is not made alive unless it dies. And what you sow, you do not sow that body that shall be, but mere grain...And as we have borne the image of the man of dust, we shall also bear the image of the heavenly Man."
1 Corinthians 15:36-37, 49 NKJV

From a human standpoint, the greatest reason for preparing ourselves for the return of the Lord is the payoff! Where can you get a return on an investment like the one God promises those who sow their lives into His service?!

In this letter written to the church in Corinth, Paul reminds us of the highest plane of the law of sowing and reaping. Many believers are more conscious of the fact that if they give money or service to God's Kingdom they will be blessed, than they are of the ultimate prize. Giving our lives to Him will result in a whole new image on "that day" in the future!

The Bible says when we see Jesus at His return we will be like Him and know Him even as we are known by Him! (1 Cor. Chapter 13:12) The Promises of God certainly apply to us in this life, but that cannot be compared to what is awaiting the faithful. Now, there is still a lot of "dust" in our eyes, but then there will be such a heavenly clarity...even in the way we see ourselves!

FEBRUARY 12...DAY 43
HOW TO OVERCOME ANYWAY

"But thanks be to God, who gives us the victory through our Lord Jesus Christ. Therefore, my beloved brethren, be steadfast, immovable, always abounding in the work of the Lord, knowing that your labor is not in vain in the Lord."
1 Corinthians 15: 57-58 NKJV

As it is with every promise in scripture, our "victory" has a spiritual side and a practical application. A believer or a church has to be absolutely in no doubt that they are an over comer in this present hour, based on what Jesus has done for us previously. If that confidence in Jesus' victory is not overriding it will be much harder to stay focused on doing what it takes everyday to actually be found "steadfast, immovable, and always abounding" at the hour of the Lord's return.

This is why the three adjectives in verse 58 are so important. They give every serious Christian an outline or road map to follow in every circumstance they encounter. "Steadfast" means to be firm and settled. It is the stand that we must take against every adversity if we want practical success in any spiritual venture. "Immovable" is a similar word with subtle distinctions. Where steadfastness causes you to hold your ground, being immovable will not allow anyone else to shove you off your position! It is being so settled that even if your body is captured, your focus never can be. Finally, we find the phrase, "always abounding." This is the clincher for actual victory in any arena; literal (as in the Roman Coliseum, where Christians were once fed to the lions) or metaphorical (like the pressure to quit we all face when attempting to succeed). The definition here means, to be in excess and to rise above.

We have a serious adversary who does not want us to welcome Jesus at His second coming. With these verses in mind, still, we will hail Him and greet Him nevertheless!

FEBRUARY 13...DAY 44
KNOW YOUR JOB DESCRIPTION

"This is now the third time Jesus showed Himself to His disciples after He was raised from the dead. Jesus said to Simon Peter, 'Simon, son of Jonah, do you love Me more than these?' He said to Him, 'Yes, Lord; You know that I love You.' He said to him, 'Feed My lambs.' He said to him again a second time, 'Simon, son of Jonah, do you love Me?' He said to Him, Yes, Lord; You know that I love You.' He said to him, 'Tend My sheep.' He said to him the third time, 'Simon, son of Jonah, do you love me?' Peter was grieved because He said to him the third time, 'Do you love Me?' 'And he said to Him. 'Lord, You know all things; You know that I love You.' Jesus said to him, 'Feed My sheep.'"
John 21:15-17 NKJV

When God repeats Himself in the Bible He is underlining something of importance. Two examples are the case of Moses at the burning bush and Samuel as a child, when God called their names multiple times. Each was being groomed for positions of spiritual leadership over the nation of Israel, so God urgently interrupted their lives to get their attention.

In this case, Jesus repeats Himself to Peter three times! Scripturally speaking, this is immensely significant. Jesus prayed three times in the Garden of Gethsemane (Mark 14:41), and Paul sought the Lord three times for help regarding an attack from Satan (2 Cor. 12:8). The number three seems to represent the "sealing" of a thing, which is what I believe we find here.

Peter is not only being restored from his denial of Jesus at His arrest, he is also being prepared for the journey God has mapped out for him. Peter has what most of us have, both a shaky past and a daunting future to consider. It would be easy for him to get frustrated and draw back again, so Jesus walks him through the job description that will keep him settled every day until the last day!

What are you called to focus on each day? Take the time to sit with Jesus and find out, because time spent with Him is the bond that will hold you steady in the will of God until Jesus returns.

FEBRUARY 14...DAY 45
EAT YOUR HEAVENLY BREAKFAST

"So when they had eaten breakfast, Jesus said to Simon Peter, 'Simon, son of Jonah, do you love Me more than these?' He said to Him, 'Yes, Lord; You know that I love You.' He said to him, 'Feed My lambs.' He said to him again a second time, 'Simon, son of Jonah, do you love Me?' He said to Him, Yes, Lord; You know that I love You.' He said to him, 'Tend My sheep.' He said to him the third time, 'Simon, son of Jonah, do you love me?' Peter was grieved because He said to him the third time, 'Do you love Me?'And he said to Him. 'Lord, You know all things; You know that I love You.' Jesus said to him, 'Feed My sheep.'"
John 21:15-17 NKJV

Remember when Jesus told His disciples that he had meat to eat that they knew nothing about (John 4:32)? He went on to reveal that this food was His willingness to do the will of God! It is easy to let the terminology remain poetic in our thinking and not contain the real substance it does.

On at least two occasions Jesus received angelic assistance to strengthen Him in performing God's will, once in the Wilderness of Temptation and again in the Garden of Gethsemane. We don't know the specifics of what transpired in either of these instances but they sound similar to Elijah's experience after he ran from Jezebel. 1 Kings 19:5-8 describes literal heavenly substances, a cake and a bottle of water that angels fed to Elijah in order to prepare him for a difficult journey ahead!

I find it interesting here that Jesus Himself prepared food for his disciples and then discussed, at least with Peter, important details about the will of God for his life. It could be in the last days we will need this same kind of assistance to accomplish our tasks. Let's not underestimate the lengths to which Jesus will go in order to prepare us for His second coming!

FEBRUARY 15...DAY 46
KEEP JESUS CONNECTED TO HIS PEOPLE

"Jesus said to Simon Peter, 'Simon, son of Jonah, do you love Me more than these?' He said to Him, 'Yes, Lord; You know that I love You.' He said to him, 'Feed My lambs.' He said to him again a second time, 'Simon, son of Jonah, do you love Me?' He said to Him, Yes, Lord; You know that I love You.' He said to him, 'Tend My sheep.' He said to him the third time, 'Simon, son of Jonah, do you love me?' Peter was grieved because He said to him the third time, 'Do you love Me?' And he said to Him.

'Lord, You know all things; You know that I love You.' Jesus said to him, 'Feed My sheep'".   John 21:15-17 NKJV

Why did Jesus say those specific things to Peter? God always deals with us as individuals, and so gives each of us the details we need for our calls. He also deals with us as His own "Body," commanding that we lay our lives down for each other as we do for Him. Both of these directives are seen clearly in this passage. The reason for the repeated question about Peter's love for Jesus is because without His love and compassion we can never properly care for His people. Our service for God must be a direct result of our love for Him.

Although it seems that Jesus is asking Peter the same exact question three times, in reality it is the same general thought being asked in three distinct ways! The first time it is, "pasture my little lambs." Next, "supervise and tend my sheep and/or sheepfolds." Finally, the wording means to "pasture my sheep and/or sheepfolds."

Simon Peter was the "son of" somebody here on earth as well as a son of God. Jesus is emphasizing the importance of remembering to not only be a leader, but both a son and a father in the process of overseeing the Church. When Jesus returns He will demand an account of how we dealt with both Him and His people.   In your preparation for His return, keep your covenant to God and your agreement with God about tending His flock jointly in your faith!

FEBRUARY 16...DAY 47
FAITH THAT SAVES YOUR SOUL

"'For yet a little while, and He who is coming will come and will not delay. Now the just shall live by faith; but if anyone draws back, My soul has no pleasure in him.' But we are not of those who draw back to perdition, but of those who believe to the saving of the soul."
Hebrews 10:37-39 NKJV

When you consider this scripture it becomes clear that faith and the end times are connected. In order to be prepared for the return of the Lord, we should learn everything we can about living by faith and touching the miraculous now.

I have found eleven particular cases in the New Testament where people experienced miracles as a direct result of their faith. In each instance the miracle performed was attributed directly to the faith of the individual in need. They believed, but it was because they had someone (Jesus) manifest to believe in. While all creation awaits His return, until then, we are those who stand visibly in His place.

Notice how there is a clear distinction between a coming specific time when Jesus will return and "now." This tells us that the only lifestyle that will prepare a believer for the sudden return of the Lord is a faithful one. This faith does not "draw back" or cower. It is a verb. Faith doesn't just perceive something impending tomorrow, it acts today! While we are waiting on the Lord to return there is a continual process of aligning our thoughts and actions with God's. It is miraculous, it pleases God and it is literally "saving our souls."

FEBRUARY 17...DAY 48
FAITH FOR THE LAST DAYS...
#1 FAITH'S CHAIN OF COMMAND

"The centurion answered and said, 'Lord, I am not worthy that You should come under my roof. But only speak a word, and my servant will be healed. For I also am a man under authority, having soldiers under me. And I say to this one, 'Go,' and he goes; and to another, 'Come,' and he comes; and to my servant, 'Do this,' and he does it.' When Jesus heard it, He marveled and said to those who followed, 'Assuredly, I say to you, I have not found such a great faith, not even in Israel!...Then Jesus said to the centurion, 'Go your way; and as you have believed, so let it be done for you.' And his servant was healed that same hour."
Matthew 8:8-10, 13

Not even an Israelite, this Roman military leader is distinguished as having the greatest faith Jesus encountered!

The Lord had already said He would come and heal his paralyzed servant, yet the details of the centurion's further actions teach us the benefits of going the extra mile with God. If he thought it important for Jesus to know that he understood both authority and submission, should we think differently? Because the centurion was in authority, he recognized that his position to Jesus was nothing more commanding than being the Lord's servant! The root of his "great faith" was vast vision, honor, and execution. Notice how this military mind handled his faith as a chain of command! The centurion first measured the situation properly and deemed himself "unworthy" or incompetent compared to Jesus, even though Jewish elders had said otherwise (Luke 7:4). He next honored the Lord by magnifying the power of His word alone to resolve the situation. Finally, this man became instantly subservient to and compliant with anything Jesus might say.

This is truly a picture of laying down all. It was not faith...it was Great Faith, exactly the kind that will be needed in the days leading up to Jesus' return!

FEBRUARY 18...DAY 49
FAITH FOR THE LAST DAYS...
#2 A FEW GOOD FAITH FRIENDS

"When Jesus saw their faith, He said to the paralytic, 'Son, be of good cheer, your sins are forgiven you'...then He said to the paralytic, 'Arise, take up your bed, and go to your house.'"
Matthew 9:2, 6 NKJV

In the New Testament, there is a place of unity among believers that creates powerful results. When we believe God together, we minimize our weaknesses and maximize our strengths. Think about it. Because these five friends (Mark 5:3) pooled their resolve, one of them received the answer he needed. Not only was he healed of his paralysis, more importantly he was forgiven of his sins!

It is easy to focus on the healing that occurred and miss the greater revelation contained in this famous Bible story. Sin and sickness come from the same root source. It is the fall of man that has corrupted all things upon the earth and, where faith is found and the will of God is known, the Son of Man can resolve any of its effects. Jesus exposed two things to us that day. One, if sin is honestly addressed in a person's heart other external limitations can be removed as well. Two, religious people have a harder time believing in forgiveness than an ordinary group of guys looking for an answer for their hurting friend!

In the last days we may not have time to argue doctrine...but we will need the kind of friends that can tear the roof off of Jesus' house for us!

FEBRUARY 19...DAY 50
FAITH FOR THE LAST DAYS...
#3 INTERRUPTED FAITH

"Now a woman, having a flow of blood for twelve years, who had spent all her livelihood on physicians and could not be healed by any, came from behind and touched the border of His garment. And immediately her flow of blood stopped. And Jesus said, 'Who touched Me?...Somebody touched Me, for I perceived power going out from Me.'...and He said to her, 'Daughter, be of good cheer; your faith has made you well. Go in peace.'" Luke 8:43-45a, 46, 48 NKJV

There is a time when your faith must be interruptive to secure God's blessings. It goes against the grain of one side of our human nature to do this. Most people would not be bold enough to run the risk of the possible humiliation and rejection this woman confronted. She "blind-sided" Jesus, driven by something very deep that urged her to touch his garment.

What did she know that we may not? Maybe she realized that Jairus' daughter was the same age, twelve, as the length of her own infirmity. She might have reasoned that if Jesus was saying yes to one twelve year old situation he surely would to another as well?! This unnamed lady might also have know that the garments of a man of God were made to reinforce the covenant God had with His people (Numbers 15:38). She may have been aware that clothing can sometimes retain the anointing God puts on such a man Himself (Matt. 14:34-36, Luke 6:17)! In any case, her "touch of faith" got Jesus' attention, because it literally drew power from Him!! The Church will have to interrupt deep corruption and evil in the last days...let's press into Jesus and get in touch with a bolder level of raw faith in God now!

FEBRUARY 20...DAY 51
FAITH FOR THE LAST DAYS...
#4 UNINTERRUPTED FAITH

"And behold, there came a man named Jairus, and he was a ruler of the synagogue. And he fell down at Jesus' feet and begged Him to come to his house, for he had an only daughter about twelve years of age, and she was dying. But as he went, the multitudes thronged Him...While He was still speaking, someone came from the ruler of the synagogue's house, saying to him, 'Your daughter is dead. Do not trouble the Teacher.' But when Jesus heard it, He answered him, saying, 'Do not be afraid; only believe, and she will be made well'...and they ridiculed Him, knowing that she was dead. But He put them all outside, took her by the hand and called, saying, 'Little girl, arise.' Then her spirit returned, and she arose immediately."
Luke 8:41-42, 49-50, 53-55 NKJV

If the woman who delayed this religious ruler's miracle proves there is a time to interrupt God with your faith, then Jairus himself teaches us there is also a time to remain steadfast in believing no matter what happens! You could say there is a faith that must be uninterrupted. Put yourself in his shoes for a moment. You have a twelve year old child near death, who is also your only daughter. If you are a normal father there is nothing you won't do to help her, nothing! So then, the pressure in this kind of situation is to push in your own strength to make something happen. This is when your faith has to keep you focused on the goal.

Notice how Jesus reassured Jairus with a three-fold piece of "miracle advice." "Do not be afraid." This tells him what to guard against. "Only believe." This keeps him aligned with the Lord's stated will. "She will be made well." This reinforces the divine intention. God always has a plan...we merely have to grasp it, guard it and see it through to its end. Easier said than done, but easier started today so that no matter what happens between now and the day of Jesus' return, we will still be on task and ready to finish our course!

FEBRUARY 21...DAY 52
FAITH FOR THE LAST DAYS...
#5 FAITH THAT STOPS GOD IN HIS TRACKS

"...As He went out of Jericho with His disciples and a great multitude, blind Bartimaeus...sat by the road begging. And when he heard that it was Jesus of Nazareth, he began to cry out and say, 'Jesus, Son of David, have mercy on me!' Then many warned him to be quiet; but he cried out all the more, 'Son of David, have mercy on me!' So Jesus stood still and commanded him to be called. Then they called the blind man, say to him, 'Be of good cheer. Rise, He is calling you.' And throwing aside his garment, her rose and came to Jesus. So Jesus answered and said to him, 'What do you want Me to do for you?' The blind man said to Him, 'Great One, that I may receive my sight.' Then Jesus said to him, 'Go your way; your faith has made you well.' And immediately he received his sight and followed Jesus on the road."
Mark 10:46-52 NKJV

I always love to read how this beggar "threw aside" his garment when Jesus called for him. In the Greek it literally means "to throw something off and walk away from it." It summons the visual of completely letting go of something!

There is a facet of pure faith that is comparable. It can rise up in you when your soul reckons your chance for contact with God. It first calls to Him in desperation when it senses He is near then responds with abandon when He answers back!!

Do you sense the nearness of the coming of the Lord? Now is the time for the Church to be like Bartimaeus more than ever...cry out and then respond when the Lord stands still for His people. Maybe we don't think we have anything we need to cast off? Bartimaeus did. His very name meant "Son of the unclean!" He was also blind and helpless on the side of the road he was meant to travel. This is a picture of the last days church; dirty, blind and living to the side and beneath its promise! According to the Apostle Paul, much of the church will be in a fallen position instead of faithfully anticipating the return of the "Great One" (2 Thess. 2:3). But today, I hear the Lord calling the blind man again and saying, "Be of good cheer! What do you want Me to do for you?"

FEBRUARY 22...DAY 53
FAITH FOR THE LAST DAYS...
#6 FAITH THAT CAN'T SHUT UP

*"...two blind men followed Him, crying out and saying, 'Son of David, have mercy
on us!' And when He had come into the house, the blind men came to Him. And Jesus
said to them, 'Do you believe that I am able to do this?' They said to Him, 'Yes, Lord.'
Then He touched their eyes, saying, 'According to your faith let it be to you.' And their
eyes were opened. And Jesus sternly warned them, saying, 'See that no one knows it.'
But when they had departed, they spread the news about Him in all that country."*
Matthew 9:27-31 NKJV

"Do you believe that I am able to do this?" Let this same question Jesus asked the
two blind men find its way into your heart today.

In discussing the last times we must locate our faith. If we want the identical results
of these two blind men, we must be willing to act on the impossible when it's called
for. In the darkest of days we too may not have the vision to find our own way. Based
on scripture it is safe to assume before Jesus returns that many Christians must do
exactly what these guys did...or suffer the consequences!

What was their act of faith? Notice how besides pursuing Jesus and crying out in an
abnormally bold way, they specifically said what Bartimaeus also voiced in Mark 10:46.
The appellation "Son of David" referred to the Jewish scriptural belief which taught that
the Messiah would be King David's descendant. These blind men had the right kind of
insight! They approached the true King with the appropriate honor. They couldn't
help but shout their convictions. That is what faith really is. You believe something
God has said in your heart then you let it pour out of your mouth! Even after Jesus
told them to keep the miracle quiet, they still spread the news of Him everywhere.
They couldn't contain the faith they had.

In the last days, the darkness will not be able to contain the light found in those
who remain miraculously faithful to the end!

FEBRUARY 23...DAY 54
FAITH FOR THE LAST DAYS...
#7 NOTORIOUS FAITH

"And behold, a woman in the city who was a sinner, when she knew that Jesus sat at the table in the Pharisee's house, brought an alabaster flask of fragrant oil, and stood at Hs feet behind Him weeping; and she began to wash His feet with her tears, and wiped them with the hair of her head; and she kissed His feet and anointed them with the fragrant oil...Then He turned to the woman and said to Simon (the Pharisee), '...her sins, which are many, are forgiven, for she loved much. But to whom little is forgiven, the same loves little.' Then He said to her, 'Your sins are forgiven...Your faith has saved you. Go in peace.'"
Luke 7:37-38, 44a, 47-48, 50 NKJV

"Notorious" is generally defined in English dictionaries to mean things like, publicly talked about, evident, or known to one's disadvantage. This word is nearly always used in an ill sense...This is an accurate description of the woman in this Bible passage. She was a well known town sinner before coming to Jesus, but she has been a well known woman of faith ever since that time!

If you know the Word of God even a little bit, you know that the last days are going to be days of unbridled sin in the world. We have seen how Jesus compared that time to the notoriously sinful days of Lot in Sodom and the notoriously sinful days of Noah before the flood. Here we can learn how to handle such days by following this woman's example. She escaped her condition by becoming more worshipful and honorable than sinful! Because she knew how great Jesus was, she was able to recognize how unbounded her forgiveness could be. Her hope in Him caused her to pour herself out on Jesus in a very lavish way; much the way God demonstrates His love to us.

It has been speculated that this alabaster flask of perfume was worth the equivalent of a year's wages, and yet she held nothing back. She gave completely, even using her own tears, hair and kisses to wash the Lord's feet! Jesus then contrasted the inaction of the self-righteous religious leader in whose home this occurred with this woman's deed, straightforwardly telling him that his love was insufficient for such levels of faith and forgiveness!

We have an opportunity to go above and beyond the "normal standards" for God in these last days. Let's be notoriously passionate believers in anticipation of Jesus' return!!

FEBRUARY 24...DAY 55
FAITH FOR THE LAST DAYS...
#8 FAITH THAT GETS WHAT IT WANTS

"And behold, a woman of Canaan came from that region and cried out to Him, saying, 'Have mercy on me, O Lord, Son of David! My daughter is severely demon-possessed.' But He answered her not a word. And His disciples came and urged Him, saying, 'Send her away, for she cries out after us.' But He answered and said, 'I was not sent except to the lost sheep of the house of Israel.' Then she came and worshiped Him saying, 'Lord, help me!' But He answered and said, 'It is not good to take the children's bread and throw it to the little dogs.' And she said, 'Yes, Lord, yet even the little dogs eat the crumbs which fall from their masters' table.' The Jesus answered and said to her, 'O woman, great is your faith! Let it be to you as you desire.' And her daughter was healed from that very hour."
Matthew 15:22-28 NKJV

In my years of ministry I have found there to be very few people who can overcome what I call the "Three strikes and you're out" rule. I am referring to the principle this foreign lady taught us how to defeat. Jesus all but said, "No!" to her three times, yet she ended up getting what she wanted from him anyway. Most people just cannot handle that level of direct rejection without becoming hurt, angry or offended. There will be a good deal of disillusionment within the end-times Church. Believers will be tempted to buy into the theory that nothing has changed since the days of the early church. "Every generation thinks they are living in the last days," will be a popular theme for scoffers who are truly living in the last days (2 Peter 3:3-4)!! This woman, on the other hand, displayed no such weakness. She shook it off when Jesus said nothing to her. She shook it off when He insinuated that her race disqualified her from God's blessings. She shook it off when Jesus told her in no uncertain terms that she was a "dog!"

She reminds me of the widow in Luke 18 and so many others who got what they wanted because their faith could not be broken! Her ancestors, the Canaanites, were the primary people God targeted when He sent the Israelites into the Promised Land. That did not seem to deter this woman in the least! Next to the Roman centurion, this little Canaanite lady is recognized by Jesus as having the greatest faith of all!! She stands as an example for people from every nation as one who knew how to receive from God.

Will you still be standing in your batter's box after strike three has been called? If so, you'll be ready for anything the last days can throw at you!

FEBRUARY 25...DAY 56
FAITH FOR THE LAST DAYS...
#9 FOLLOW THROUGH FAITH

"Then as He entered a certain village, there met Him ten men who were lepers, who stood afar off. And they lifted up their voices and said, 'Jesus, Master, have mercy on us!' So when He saw them, He said to them, 'Go, show yourselves to the priests.' And so it was that as they went, they were cleansed. And one of them, when he saw that he was healed, returned, and with a loud voice glorified God, and fell down on his face at His feet, giving Him thanks. And he was a Samaritan. So Jesus answered and said, 'Were there not ten cleansed? But where are the nine?' Were there not any found who returned to give glory to God except this foreigner?' And He said to him, 'Arise, go your way. Your faith has made you well.'"
Luke 17:12-19 NKJV

Once again, we find the kind of faith we need to follow illustrated in the words and actions of a foreigner! As a preacher, I find it to be much the same today. Genuine, heart-felt trust in the Lord (and His promises) is more often discovered outside the walls of churches. When reading this story, I automatically think about how "Samaritans" are referred to several times in the Gospels. They were originally a group of foreigners who were moved into the region between Judea and Galilee by the Assyrians when God used them to disperse the northern ten tribes into captivity (2 Kings 17:22-24). In Jesus' day these people were seen as "half-breeds" at best, with a substitute brand of religion. Jesus told the parable about the "Good Samaritan" in Luke 10:33. It teaches the principle of doing the right thing when presented the opportunity regardless of who you are. In John chapter four, Jesus himself traveled to Sychar, a city of Samaria to speak to the woman at Jacob's well. This was unheard of among the Jews, but the result was much of the town came to believe on Him! In Jerusalem, the Pharisees in their hatred even accused Jesus of being a demon-possessed Samaritan!

I think this Samaritan leper makes the point best of all. He not only approached Jesus against all the racial barriers he faced, but he also followed through and came back to seal his faith, thanking Him for the healing he received. As we consider our preparation for Jesus' return let us remember the Lord's puzzled response, "...where are the nine!?"

FEBRUARY 26...DAY 57
FAITH FOR THE LAST DAYS...
#10 EXORCISE YOUR FAITH

"Then one of the crowd answered and said, 'Teacher, I brought You my son, who has a mute spirit. And wherever it seizes him, it throws him down; he foams at the mouth, gnashes his teeth, and becomes rigid. So I spoke to Your disciples, that they should cast it out, but they could not.' He answered him and said, 'O faithless generation, how long shall I be with you? How long shall I bear with you? Bring him to Me'...And he (the father) said...,'if you can do anything, have compassion on us and help us.' Jesus said to him, 'If you can believe, all things are possible to him who believes.' Immediately the father of the child cried out and said with tears, 'Lord, I believe; help my unbelief!'...When Jesus saw the people came running together, He rebuked the unclean spirit, saying to it: 'Deaf and dumb spirit, I command you, come out of him and enter him no more!' Then the spirit cried out, convulsed him greatly, and came out of him..."
Mark 9:17-19, 21-26 NKJV

Christians have the same real arch-enemy Jesus had, and it takes faith to overcome him. The closer we get to the Day of the Lord the more apparent this will become and the more crucial it is going to be that we know how to deal with him. To teach us, Jesus corrected this father in the essentials of his faith.

The prerequisite for healing was confidence directed in Jesus' ability to restore the man's son. If you read the entire account you realize what this meant. First, when the man brought his son to Jesus the spirit in him immediately sent him into a seizure. This it-looks-worse-in-the-natural-before-it- gets-better situation would tempt an unsteady believer to doubt that anything was going to change. Second, the fact that Jesus asked and found out that these seizures had been occurring since childhood tells us that there were other deep-seated issues involved beyond the son's physical condition. Finally, this was also a particular "kind" of case according to Jesus (verse29). It was not just demonic oppression but a certain type, evidently more tenacious than most others.

If you are serious about dealing with the devil, you have to get serious in your faith. The last days are going to be a time where even never met "new" kinds of demons will be released. So, let's learn now what it means to put our trust fully in the Lord, look the devil in the eye and exorcise evil spirits!

FEBRUARY 27...DAY 58
FAITH FOR THE LAST DAYS...
#11 VISUAL FAITH

"...And in Lystra a certain man without strength in his feet was sitting, a cripple from his mother's womb, who had never walked. This man heard Paul speaking. Paul, observing him intently and seeing that he had faith to be healed, said with a loud voice, 'Stand up straight on your feet!' And he leaped and walked."
Acts 14:8-10 NKJV

All of our faith sketches over the last several days have been intended as biblical examples of how we should act as believers, especially when preparing for the last days. Today's final profile, however, is even more explicit in showing us that faith can truly be observed by and encouraged in those watching.

Because of what he saw in this crippled man notice how Paul spoke with bold confidence himself. True faith is like that, it is visibly illustrative and/or substantial when it surfaces in a person. We are not told exactly what Paul saw just that it was recognizable faith. When Paul coupled his own faith with this man's the result was miraculous.

This reminds me of a similar incident, recorded in Acts 3, where Peter and John "fixed" their eyes on another crippled beggar. They too saw something in the man, touched that circumstance in Jesus' name and beheld the exact same result!

1 Corinthians 12:9 lists an aspect of the Divine called a "manifestation" of the Spirit. Studying the scripture allows this kind of faith to make more sense. The word manifestation means an exhibition, or in other words, a visual display. There are nine particular kinds of these "expressions" and one of them is faith. So at times a superlative type of faith can manifest as we follow God. When we recognize these openings, we need to go with the flow of the Spirit and work with the Lord in building His Kingdom. These are part of the "perks" for being faithful.

Learn to use the faith you have and expect times when extraordinary levels of it come into your line of sight. If you do, you will be ready for anything...even the darkest hour of history!

FEBRUARY 28...DAY 59
MODERN MISINFORMATION

"Now about the spiritual gifts (the special endowments of supernatural energy),
brethren, I do not want you to be misinformed. You know that when you were
heathen, you were led off after idols...Therefore I want you to understand that no one
speaking under the power and influence of the [Holy] Spirit of God can really say
'Jesus be cursed'; and no one can really say 'Jesus is my Lord,' except by and under
the power and influence of the Holy Spirit."
1 Corinthians 12:1-3 AMP

Ignorance is possibly the greatest enemy of Christianity's spiritual well being. In saying that God's people were destroyed for "lack of knowledge" the prophet Hosea distinctly voiced God's displeasure that Israel had rejected spiritual knowledge.

There are many logical thinkers today who simply do not want to investigate spiritual mysteries, if they even believe God exists! Many believers are not willing to be pressed to discover the ways of The Spirit. In their zeal, others foolishly propel themselves without any operational knowledge into counterfeit pseudo spiritual realms without God's invitation or guidance.

This has led modern churches into a classic tactical disadvantage on the spiritual battleground described in Ephesians 6. The two extremes of traditionalism and fanaticism in the Christian world, long embraced as the only visible choices for the average seeker, has made the option of authentic and balanced spirituality seem too "idealistic." Consequently, Satan easily tempts most to choose the comfortable middle ground of ignorance, when it comes to the only thing that really matters in true Christianity...God!

"Fundamentalism" offers a misplaced religious identity, by refocusing on knowledge and away from the God who established biblical foundations, and Who then expects Christians to mature beyond those elemental spiritual fundamentals. (Hebrews 6:1)! Today's Church has "camped out" between these two extremes and created a "Christian" draw toward the spiritual vacuum they don't realize they live in! When we are not willing to listen when the Lord speaks by His Spirit, our faith is reduced to a monotonous set of precepts and rules that can lull otherwise sound men and women into a dangerously passive religious state (see Isaiah 28:11-13 in the Amplified Bible)!

Faithful believers, however, stand upon an entirely different kind of middle ground. Radically real Christianity trusts exactly what the Lord has said, keeps learning about it and knows the virtue of putting it into practice! The Word of Truth will not allow us to accept anything less than the certainty, accuracy, and precision of the Holy

Spirit! It also won't let us take the quick fix of hyper-spiritualism in place of Him, or languish in the mediocrity that ends up reducing Him down to our own level!

The very words of the Apostle Paul in our text demand that we study the genuine characteristics of the Holy Spirit and His works. Our job is to become familiar with the variety of expressions and personality traits He uses to reveal Jesus to the world...let's not waste His time and ours by settling for the old and stale, sensationalizing the new and nutty, or safely performing our faith!

FEBRUARY 29
SCARING THE HELL OUT OF PEOPLE

"But you, beloved, building yourselves up on your most holy faith, praying in the Holy Spirit, keep yourselves in the love of God, looking for the mercy of our Lord Jesus Christ unto eternal life. And on some have compassion, making a distinction; but others save with fear, pulling them out of the fire, hating even the garment defiled by the flesh." Jude 20-23 NKJV

I am intensely interested in saving people from hell. The biggest obstacle to my mission is that so many people either don't really know what that means, or they don't believe it is factual. There are many reasons why people are challenged in their faith. Here, our scripture makes a distinction between two types of people, but the Amplified translation (of verses 22 -24) shows there are actually four conditions that exist within those who do not believe.

Some simply like to argue, we are to refute them with conviction. Others waver and doubt, with them we extend more mercy and patience in our instruction. Then there are people who are overly sensual who demand that we, out of pity, warn them sternly about the dangers of continuously pleasuring the flesh. Finally, there are some who are just "hell-bent" in their approach to this life, needing forceful confrontation. All of these categories are in danger of the "fire", and it is any Christian's job to sound a clear alarm to them.

Notice, however, the emphasis in this passage is first upon our own conduct! It reminds me of the emergency instructions I hear every time I fly, "...first secure the oxygen mask around your own head and face, then do the same for any children or others in need of help around you." If we want to be of any value to those who are spiritually dead we must be spiritually full of life! This means being full of faith because we are building our lives through real communication with the Holy Spirit. It means keeping our hearts firmly immersed in the first-hand experience of God's love. It means having an outlook that is aware of the Lord's mercy upon our own sins and past lives. When we walk like this the message we send will be distinct. More than what we say, it will have become who we are.

In the earth's darkest hour, our lights will need to shine the brightest!

MARCH 1...DAY 60
WHAT YOU ALLOW TODAY,
YOU WILL LIVE WITH TOMORROW

"An astonishing and horrible thing has been committed in the land: The Prophets prophesy falsely, and the priests rule by their own power; and my people love to have it so. But what will you do in the end?"
Jeremiah 5:30-31 NKJV

One of the most tragic statements in scripture goes almost unheard today. At the same time, I see much the same condition existing in the modern Church. It is a great deal more heinous because we represent the nation of God's people under the New Covenant.

God told Jeremiah that his people had surpassed the deeds performed by the wicked! They promoted a belief system that no longer pled the cause of the fatherless, or defended the rights of the needy. They also had developed a defiant and rebellious heart toward the Lord in replacing true worship with deceitful policies and practices. According to James 1:27, this is the definition of a defiled or false, imitation religion that God despises! I don't know if very many are willing to acknowledge this or not, but we need the Jeremiah's again today. Bold spokesmen like this prophet of God, who angered the religious and political establishments of his day by declaring the truth of God's Word. He was persecuted harshly for sharply exposing his fellow prophets and priests in their hypocrisy!

Look around you. We have the same brand of silly prophets who devalue true revelation with their senseless bantering, and self-indulgent pastors exercising dull spiritual oversight while they ascribe high levels of spirituality to themselves! Then look a little deeper into the Word here and you will find a shocking reason for this. "...MY PEOPLE love to have it so." The Church ends up with what it wants even when confessing something else!

God then asks, "But what will you do in the end?" This is the question you and I must hear and clearly define in our times. Where does all "our religion" get us? The answer sometimes is in a worse place than if we didn't believe at all...worse than the world around you! We desperately need the genuine Prophets and Pastors today who will yield to the indisputable living God. What, who do we love? Our answer will make all the difference in the end (times).

MARCH 2...DAY 61
VALID RELIGION

"If anyone among you thinks he is religious, and does not bridle his tongue but deceives his own heart, this one's religion is useless. Pure and undefiled religion before God and the Father is this: to visit orphans and widows in their trouble, and to keep oneself unspotted from the world."
James 1:26-27 NKJV

Before we go and live out our life with or without spots and blemishes we need to define the terms of pure and undefiled religion. For example, some people will tend towards religion while others prefer a secular life. What do these choices mean?

Looking back, I realize that I had tried both lifestyles without really knowing the definition of either. It seemed to me that some people tried to pretend they believed in God and others tried to pretend they didn't believe in Him! I didn't fully understand either position until I met Jesus! That is when I realized there is true religion, false religion and the rejection of religion!

According to Revelation 3:15, did you know God would rather that we were either hot or cold? He prefers we know what the options are, make our choice and then live it like we love what we chose!

If you tend toward religion or "the observance of something outward or ceremonial", then do it in a way that pleases God; not you or some man-made institution or warped ideology.

According to our text, this means three basic things. One, do it His way. Follow Jesus from your heart, not the rules from your head. If not, your religion will be nothing more than a ceremonially Christianized format of false religion or secularism!

Two, be pure about taking up the cause of Christ. It is not enough to confess Him without also doing what He did. Help the needy and the unaided by extending the Gospel to them not only in word but also in deed. Expand yourself to give others what they actually need, not what is most comfortable for you to offer.

Third, maintain a spirituality that is always aware of the Kingdom of God and wary of the World System. These three things were modeled by Jesus Christ and can only be experienced through a real, living faith in Him. The last days will be marked by a world full of religiously blemished believers and mottled, tarnished worldly unbelievers. A true Believer's job is to be distinct from them because they know and chose the One who makes religion vital and valid...JESUS!

MARCH 3...DAY 62
THE FRIENDS OF GOD

"And the Lord said, 'Shall I hide from Abraham what I am doing, since Abraham shall surely become a great and mighty nation, and all the nations of the earth shall be blessed in him? For I have known him, in order that he may command his children and his household after him, that they keep the way of the Lord, to do righteousness of justice, that the Lord may bring to Abraham what He has spoken to him." Genesis 18:17-19 NKJV

"'...Abraham believed God, and it was accounted to him for righteousness.' And he was called the friend of God."
James 2:23 NKJV

"Greater love has no one than this, than to lay down one's life for his friends. You are My friends if you do whatever I command you. No longer do I call you servants, for a servant does not know what his master is doing; but I have called you friends, for all things that I heard from My Father I have made known to you.
John 15:13-15 NKJV

God has friends and He has enemies. Abraham became the father of all those who exercise faith in God (Romans 4:11). He believed beyond natural reason and followed Divine directions. In doing so, he became the "friend" of God!

You can see that God is "fond" (Greek meaning) of those who trust Him when it's not easy to do so. It is interesting how these two concepts, faith and friendship, are connected. Understanding this linkage is vital for anyone preparing for the second coming. Jesus used this exact same terminology to describe those He who followed Him to the end. They were an inner circle of pupils who become his dearest friends! In fact, He was so fond of them that He died for them!

If we are serious about our Christianity, we must be willing to get close enough to the Lord to find out what He wants from us then pursue those things. This is the secret to any strong and lasting relationship. It will also get you on the "inside" track with

God, to the point where He will show and tell you things before they happen (John 16:13). Abraham's "pull" was so great that he even negotiated with God and rescued his nephew, Lot! Be a friend of God...for the Last days will require Abraham's obedience and faith!

MARCH 4...DAY 63
THE ENEMIES OF GOD

"Then the men said to Lot...we will destroy this place, because the outcry against them has grown great before the face of the Lord, and the Lord has sent us to destroy it." Genesis 19:12-13 NKJV

"Adulterers and adulteresses! Do you not know that friendship with the world is enmity with God? Whoever therefore wants to be a friend of the world makes himself an enemy of God."
James 4:4 NKJV

Again, God has his friends and He has his enemies. Which one are you? There is an interesting twist in understanding the difference between the two. In the above scripture God's enemies are simply those who have a particular misplaced friendship! As we saw yesterday, God has chosen to be friends with those who accept His will for their lives. For those who will not, the "world" is the only alternative. This term refers to "an arrangement" or systematic order of things on planet earth that are not necessarily aligned with God's intentions.

When believers align their friendship with the world (system), it naturally works to cancel their relationship with God. Why? Because the world order was initiated (beginning at the fall of Adam and Eve), and is now carried out through Satanic spirits hostile to God and bent toward the seduction of mankind.

The cultural conditions in Sodom and Gomorrah are a clear example of this fallen system in operation. Their extreme levels of sin were due to the fact that they loved the world too much! They stand as a warning to everyone living in the last days. Such people are God's enemies, and will pay the ultimate price if they do not repent!

MARCH 5...DAY 64
THE WORLDLY GOVERNOR AND THE HEAVENLY KING

"Then Pilate entered the Praetorium again, called Jesus, and said to Him, 'Are you the King of the Jews?' Jesus answered, 'Are you speaking for yourself about this, or did others tell you this concerning Me?' Pilate answered, 'Am I a Jew? Your own nation and the chief priests have delivered You to me. What have you done? Jesus answered, 'My kingdom is not of this world. If My kingdom were of this world, my servants would fight, so that I should not be delivered to the Jews; but now My kingdom is not from here.'"
John 18:33-36 NKJV

Here is a picture of two very different casts of men. Pilate is a crafty Roman governor, Jesus, a mysterious heavenly king. They come together in this account, ostensibly for the interrogation of Jesus who could not be legally put to death by the Jews of His day. However, it is Jesus who really does the probing. The Heavenly man analyzes the worldly man. When these two types meet, the lower kingdom cedes to the higher.

To comprehend this you must be observant! Pilate could not understand the spirit of the matter before him, although Jesus did give him opportunity. He referred to another "Kingdom" three times, using language an ambitious politician like Pilate could seize. Each time, Jesus contrasts His own Kingdom with the "world," the system that the Roman government represented.

Pilate had the same opportunity you and I have. He failed to follow Jesus' lead and present any questions of his own. Like most politicians, he wasn't really interested in a kingdom higher or more powerful than his own. Since he wasn't willing to discern Jesus' meanings, His way into the heavenly Kingdom was blocked. He was trapped in the world's way of thinking, alienated from the life and blessings of God. In the end there will be many like Pilate, choosing their own rule and courting the foolish notions of suspicious people to their own demise. Don't be fooled...Jesus is coming!

MARCH 6...DAY 65
THE INCONVENIENT TRUTH

"Pilate therefore said to Him, 'Are you a king then?' Jesus answered, 'You say rightly that I am a king. For this cause I was born, and for this cause I have come into the world, that I should bear witness to the truth. Everyone who is of the truth hears

My voice.' Pilate said to Him, 'What is truth?' And when he had said this, he went out again to the Jews, and said to them, 'I find no fault in Him at all.'"
John 18:37-38 NKJV

If you don't know what truth is you're going to have a hard time recognizing God. If you recognize truth and will not admit it, that's even worse!

Pilate made one of those mistakes that you can never reverse. Here came a one time opportunity for him to respond differently. It would not only have changed his own life, but also would have spoken loudly to others like him. Instead, the Roman governor took the expedient way out, once again. What an all-time blunder!

Before we judge him too quickly though, let's talk about what "truth" means. This word in the original language of scripture means whatever is "right, factual, or real," in an objective sense. It is the standard everything can be measured by to determine its authenticity. Subjectively speaking, this word also can define our personal level of excellence. It is "that candor of mind which is free from affection, pretense, simulation, falsehood or deceit." You could say that when we meet truth it tests the reality in us. Especially when it is spelled with a capital "T," as it was here (John 14:6)! So, in order to be ready to meet God at all times, we must remain "real" in every sense of the word! Ironically in retrospect, Pilate's choice has spoken loudly down the millennia to a whole world full of other people not so different from him. His mistake is one very piercing reason you and I have our own opportunity to choose the inconvenient things...before we meet Jesus face to face at His return!

MARCH 7...DAY 66
WHERE ARE YOU COMING FROM?

"...Jesus answered, 'You say rightly that I am a king. For this cause I was born and for this cause I have come into the world, that I should bear witness to the truth. Everyone who is of the truth hears My voice.' Pilate said to Him, 'What is truth?'
John 18:37b-38a NKJV

Today, I would like to draw your attention to the key word Jesus spoke to Pilate. I believe it contained all the insight he would have needed to really "wash his hands" (Matthew 27:24) of Jesus' death! While Pilate was asking about the Jewish leaders' charge of Jesus claiming to be a king, the Lord answered by disclosing what His real mission was.

I don't think Pilate got it. I'm sure most people today, even many Christians, still don't! If you and I discern it, we will help prepare ourselves to meet with the Lord at any time. Notice, Jesus outlined His purpose in verse 37. He said it was to "bear witness." This word in the Greek means to literally lay your life down as testimony to some fact, the way a "martyr" dies for his cause. Well, Jesus' cause was the truth because He is THE TRUTH! He came to make a distinction between the world system and God, darkness and light.

The world system is, in truth, a lie. It takes the contrasting clarifying light of Jesus set against it to accurately see the nuances and gradations of falsehood from truth.

Look at His life. Listen to His words. Notice anything different? Of course you do, immediately! What is it? It is the essence or origin of who He is. Did you read the phrase, "Everyone who is of the truth..."? "Who is of," means to "originate from." These have always been the ones who can hear God's voice because they have a heart for Who He is.

Outward appearances begin with inward realities. Pilate couldn't hear Jesus because he was dishonest with himself. Those who were seeking truth recognized Jesus even when He passed by at a distance!! How good is God? Though He knew Pilate wasn't going to listen to the truth at that exchange, He still presented it to him. We're not told if Pilate did respond at a later time in his life, because of this encounter with Jesus.

Herod, on the other hand, didn't even get a word from Jesus (Luke 23:6-12)! All I do know for sure is that, to quote an old hymn, "...Once I was blind, but now I see!" In the end, if we will listen, we will come to perceive the Truth, and it will make us free (John 8:32)!

MARCH 8...DAY 67
CONSPIRACY THEORY?

"Now is the judgment of this world; now the ruler of this world will be cast out. And I, if I am lifted up from the earth, will draw all peoples to Myself.' This He said, signifying what death He would die."
John 12:31-33 NKJV

A Believer must believe the Word of God. One cannot pick and choose what they prefer from among the total body of teaching found in the scripture, especially when it comes to the words of Jesus.

This passage exposes an important truth that many today would rather not face. It clearly identifies two key figures and two central arenas of spiritual battle. The scripture also draws a sharp distinction between them. Notice, there is a "ruler" over this "world" that "Jesus" was sent to the "earth" to confront.

By His death Jesus would put into effect God's master plan of judgment upon a rogue spiritual mastermind, who imposes his subtle but systemic rule over this planet. If you believe Jesus, you have to accept that Satan is His adversary and yours! If you only partially believe what Jesus said, you might misunderstand what He is stating. Like links on a rusty chain, this lack of knowledge and unawareness then become part of the great deception by which this evil ruler secrets his work.

It's daunting! No one really wants to believe there is a great conspiracy behind the scenes seeking to manipulate the thoughts, perspectives and actions of societies everywhere; but there is...according to Jesus. This is not a man-made conspiracy but something far more sinister. It is a collusion of invisible spiritual forces, hiding behind ideologies and using them to delude and destroy people!

The earth belongs to the Lord but the "world" is the "arrangement" within it that has been taken over by Satan and shown itself hostile toward God since the Garden of Eden. Because of Jesus' death and subsequent resurrection, we now have the authority to overcome the world during our time here on the earth.

Whose eyes are you seeing through? The world system is the biggest obstacle to you being ready to meet the Lord at His coming...whether you visualize it or not!

MARCH 9...DAY 68
A TALE OF TWO WORLDS

"Then God said, 'Let Us make man in Our image, according to Our likeness; let them have dominion'...Then God blessed them, and God said to them, 'Be fruitful and multiply; fill the earth and subdue it; have dominion over...every living thing that moves on the earth." Genesis 1:26-28 NKJV

"And they heard the sound of the Lord God walking in the garden in the breeze of the day..."
Genesis 3:8 NKJV

"We know that we are of God, and the whole world lies under the sway of the wicked one." 1 John 5:19 NKJV

Have you ever considered how vastly different the general mentality and perception of the world is now, compared to that which was originally established in Eden? The contrast should be enough to convince us how dangerous it is to just "go with the flow" or "run with the crowd."

In the beginning, God created Adam and Eve in such a way that it was quite natural for them to cooperate with Him. They were made in God's "image" or literally, He made them His spiritual representatives on earth. These first people were made according to God's own "likeness," which meant they were also modeled after Him even in physical form. These two things enabled them "have dominion" or dominate and subdue all other creatures. They were built to govern God's creation and empowered to rule under His direct blessing, but in conjunction with His own presence. This naturally supernatural arrangement meant that they could freely make the decisions necessary to rule, but the real brain behind whatever system they developed would in actuality be the Lord's.

As beautiful as the present earth is, it is far from the paradise it once was. The current intellect behind the thought processes the world system generates is observably unholy in nature! This is because, at the fall, Satan stole much more than Adam and Eve's innocence...he stole their world!

MARCH 10...DAY 69
KNOW NOW WHAT YOU'LL NEED
TO KNOW THEN

"Now the serpent was more cunning than any beast of the field which the Lord God had made. And he said to the woman, 'Has God said...?'"
Genesis 3:1 NKJV

"Put on the whole armor of God that you may be able to stand against the wiles of the devil. For we do not wrestle against flesh and blood, but against principalities, against powers, against the rulers of the darkness of this age, against spiritual hosts of wickedness in the heavenly places."
Ephesians 6:11-12 NKJV

We have been examining different aspects of the world system in order to expose its dangers to the believer. I am no legalist trying to drive people to ascetic behavior for my own twisted religious pleasure. On the contrary, I know God's goodness and I am convinced He wants us to enjoy life and walk in His blessings. At the same time, there are so many Christians today who do not seem to make much of a distinction between what is "of God" and what is "of the world." This leads them, and sometimes the churches they attend, to exhibit an expression of godliness that is really just religious worldliness. What I mean is, they talk kind of like God but act a whole lot like the devil! This is because the devil is very "cunning" in his "wiles" or methods.

Notice, the scripture says we are "wrestling" against something unsuspected and behind the panorama of this world. In fact, the word for "world" when talking about it as an organized, arranged system is the Greek word, kosmos. What is enlightening here in Ephesians chapter six is that the phrase, "rulers of the darkness of this age" is a similar word, kosmokrator.

Along with the other three types of spiritual entities this category of Satan's leadership are specifically in charge of maintaining the dark influence of what we know as the "world around us." Pretty spooky stuff, but we are better off learning to be aware of it now and learning to keep ourselves fixed in the peace of God, because it only gets worse the later the hour!!

MARCH 11...DAY 70
WATCH YOUR FORM

"Pure and undefiled religion before God and the Father is this: to visit orphans and widows in their trouble, and to keep oneself unspotted from the world."
James 1:27 NKJV

"Now we have received, not the spirit of the world..."
1 Corinthians 2:12 NKJV

"For the wisdom of this world is foolishness with God."
1 Corinthians 3:19 NKJV

"For the form of this world is passing away."
1 Corinthians 7:31 NKJV

"And do not be conformed to this world..."
Romans 12:2a NKJV

The "world" will leave its mark on you if you let it. All you have to do is nothing! Notice how the world has a "spirit," its own kind of "wisdom," and "form" that "conforms" you to its shape! This is why James plainly states that religion is a popular target for the forces behind this distrustful network of people, places and things.

There are two words which are very similar in this verse, "undefiled" and "unspotted." Christians and church leaders in particular, need to pay close attention to their meaning in order to prevent the faithful from slipping into a mere "form of godliness" that denies the very power of God (2 Timothy 3:5). These words both mean to remain unsoiled or unsullied. Thayer's definition for undefiled goes on to explain it as meaning, "free from that by which the nature of a thing is deformed and debased, or its force and vigor impaired."

Does that sound like large segments of the modern church world to you? What can we do about it? Beware of the world's ways and exercise your spiritual senses to become more responsive to the Kingdom of Heaven...it is another sure way to be ready for Jesus' return!

MARCH 12...DAY 71
BEND YOUR THINKING

"And do not be conformed to this world, but be transformed by the renewing of your mind, that you may prove what is that good, and acceptable and perfect will of God."
Romans 12:2 NKJV

"Now we have received, not the spirit of the world, but the Spirit who is from God, that we might know the things that have been freely given to us by God."
1 Corinthians 2:12 NKJV

"Transformation" is the radically intrinsic change that flows from the Holy Spirit, through the open hearts of believers as they continually yield to the will of the Lord. It is also the process by which the mold of this world's nature is reconfigured within our minds in order to make them compatible with God's Spirit. Before a believer undergoes this transformational process he cannot recognize or properly test whether the things around him are good, acceptable or complete in God's mind. At best the most an undeveloped Christian can have is a hit-and-miss spirituality. Sometimes they recognize God moving in their lives because their spirits are already renewed in Christ. At other times a believer who has not gone through "renewal of the mind" can be easily mislead into thinking that something which sounds good to their natural, rational thinking is truly good according to God; when it is actually carnal, or even satanic in origin.

You can readily see this superficial Christianity will become even more problematic the closer this world hurtles towards the end times! When all is sound in society, this distinction might be ignored with less peril to the individual or the church, but not under elevated levels of pressure.

The preeminent thing is to discern accurately now that what may sound good to man or the world is not automatically good with God. The only way to do that is through exercising your "mind" in the truths (Word) of God. The church is soon "conformed" to the world today because it has abandoned the "transformation" process of its Lord. Become an attentive believer...bend your thinking and catch the fact that Jesus is coming back, SOON!

MARCH 13
SPIRITUAL SUICIDE!

"And do not be conformed to this world, but be transformed
by the renewing of your mind, that you may prove what is that good,
and acceptable and perfect will of God."
Romans 12:2 NKJV

"But we all with unveiled face, beholding as in a mirror
the glory of the Lord, are being transformed into the same image
from glory to glory, just as by the Spirit of the Lord."
2 Corinthians 3:18 NKJV

The Israelites, who were led out of Egypt by Moses are the ultimate historical illustration of spiritual suicide! They took history's greatest opportunity to know God supernaturally and squandered it. Through selfishness and grumbling they became blinder than they were before He appeared to them! To our human minds and egos their preference seems impossible. Like Peter, we believe that we could never deny the daily reality of a miraculous God we have witnessed up close and personally.

When you read 2 Corinthians 3 in context you find an interesting reversal of fortune in scripture. By using the example of Moses, Paul teaches us the secret of spiritual transformation. The children of Israel had an amazing leader who went into the presence of God for them. Because they were too faithless and insensitive to appreciate the gesture when God beckoned (Exodus 19; 20:18-21; 34:29-35), Moses put a veil on his face when speaking with them to hide the glory which reflected through the skin of his face. Paul tells us this was to keep them from looking upon what they were not worthy to see...the Lord! So, they lost touch with the transformation process that happens when a person is able to look upon the Lord Himself, not just the words written about Him. As a result to this day Old Testament believers cannot understand the scripture unless their heart turns to God in sincerity.

In stark contrast, we who believe in Christ have been restored to a position of "beholding." The "veil" Moses wore is removed in the person of Jesus. We can gaze upon Him, through the Spirit of His Word, in a very real way!! In the last days the Church is going to be tested to see what they prefer to gaze on...Lets look to Jesus now, so we will be ready to meet Him then!

MARCH 14...DAY 73
MORPHING INTO THE NEW YOU

"Now after six days Jesus took Peter, James and John, and led them up
on a high mountain apart by themselves; and He was transfigured before them.
His clothes became shining, exceedingly white, like snow, such as not a launderer on
earth can white them. And Elijah appeared to them with Moses, and
they were talking with Jesus. Mark 9:2-4 NKJV

When I was in second grade our class conducted a butterfly-catching contest. It was something I still remember today partly because the kid who was the best at it also had one of the worst home situations of anyone in our school.

Later in life my friend spent many years in prison, but back then he was free to run and catch beautiful Monarch butterflies and discover an ability inside himself to be a champion! I have often thought of the irony in this little story. Most of us know the butterfly doesn't begin its journey in the same shape in which it finishes. It goes through an almost unbelievable process of transformation on its way to becoming something superior. If it survives the slow crawl of a caterpillar and the complete immobilization of the cocoon, it will soar into skies with a visible beauty greater than our comprehension to understand!

Jesus said the Kingdom of God works similar to the way a child considers. (Matthew 18:2-6; Matthew 19:14). My friend in second grade was the butterfly, an innocent believer in all good things, until the blows of life transformed him into something he was never intended to be. This world molds people, completely altering them into its own image.

As believers we have a second chance at real kingdom life. Jesus and Moses were literally transformed in God's presence to such an extent their skin radiated the glory of a higher realm. We are invited to ascend to this identical place in the Lord when we follow him closely as did Peter, James and John. God is intent on restoring what the influence of the devil has stolen from mankind.

"Transformed" and "transfigured" are the same word in the New Testament, meaning to "change into another form." That is what Christianity really is all about.

Transporting damaged people from darkness back into the light of God's glory...never to be the same again, inwardly or outwardly!!

MARCH 15...DAY 74
TRANSFORMATION VS. TRANSFORMATION

"Now after six days Jesus took Peter, James and John, and led them up on a high mountain apart by themselves; and He was transfigured before them.
Mark 9:2-4 NKJV

"For such are false apostles, deceitful workers, transforming themselves into apostles of Christ. And no wonder! For Satan himself transforms himself into an angel of light. Therefore it is no great thing if his ministers also transform themselves into ministers of righteousness, whose end will be according to their works."
2 Corinthians 11:13-15 NKJV

"Transformation" is a more serious issue than many "nice" preachers and churches are willing to address. It is one of those things that is easier to talk about than to experience, but the rewards for putting yourself through the process are hard to overestimate.

Jesus took his closest disciples up on what became known as the, "Mount of Transfiguration" for a reason. Did you notice how it all seemed so ordinary for Him and Elijah and Moses?! From the look of their conversational approach it is like they had done this before...maybe often!

Jesus didn't need to "shine" in the presence of God for His own sake. He was very familiar with that spiritual state of change. He prayed often, studied the scriptures thoroughly and knew God as His Father. No, this experience is recorded for our sakes, so that we would know how to approach God and come to recognize the value of living in the spiritual realm.

Beware, though, because Satan also knows the power of thorough change. He not only practices a deceptive brand of it himself, he specializes in transforming ministers into religious images that are only outward in their spirituality! According to the Bible this is not going to diminish as we draw closer to the end of time, it is going to increase! In contrast we must shine, inwardly reflecting the image and glory of God until it radically changes us outwardly.

In the last days there will be a great need for people like Peter and John who, when interrogated by ungodly leaders, received this assessment: "They realized that they had been with Jesus" (Acts 4:13). Let's take our faith seriously...those beacons could and should be you and me!!

MARCH 16...DAY 75
GET USED TO TRIBULATION

"...we ourselves boast of you among the churches of God for your patience and faith in all your persecutions and tribulations that you endure, which is manifest evidence of the righteous judgment of God, that you may be counted worthy of the kingdom of God, for which you also suffer; since it is a righteous thing with God to repay with tribulation those who trouble you, and to give you who are troubled rest with us when the Lord Jesus is revealed from heaven with His mighty angels,..."
2 Thessalonians 1:4-7 NKJV

There are two types of "tribulation" mentioned in the New Testament though they both stem from one Greek word. There is what some call the "Great Tribulation," a term referring to that specific period during the end of time when Jesus Himself said (Matthew 24:29) it will be harder for believers than ever before. Keep in mind that tribulation is not something reserved exclusively for the last days. It is an everyday likelihood if you are a true Christian!

Both of these concepts are described in our text for today. Verse 3 describes the everyday variety of tribulation, and verse 6 the coming period of intensified tribulation. In preparation for a challenging future, we should familiarize ourselves with this word and its implications ahead of time or "pre-trib!"

In other areas of scripture this term is also translated as "affliction," "trouble," "burdened" and "persecution." It reflects the sufferings a Christian must endure for Christ as a result of the pressure which comes from the world system because he is a justified member of the Kingdom of God.

In John 16:21, this word is also used to illustrate the "anguish" of a woman during childbirth. All of this tells us Christianity should not be approached lightly. It is a costly thing to follow Jesus! Those who will be prepared for the second coming of Christ are the ones who are willing to go all the way through rejoicing, and (1Peter 4:13)"to the degree that you share the sufferings of Christ" now "so that also at the revelation of His glory, you may rejoice with exaltation!"

MARCH 17...DAY 76
NARROWING YOUR VISION

*"Enter by the narrow gate; for wide is the gate and broad is the way that leads to
destruction, and there many who go in by it. Because narrow is the gate and difficult
is the way which leads to life, and there are few who find it."*
Matthew 7:13-14 NKJV

It rubs against our natural inclination to willingly be squeezed into uncomfortable
situations. Yet, this is exactly what the word "narrow" means in these Bible verses. It
describes the difficult passageway a Christian will encounter for the spiritual stance he
takes against the unseen forces of darkness which influence this world system. Let the
picture Jesus draws here impact your choices today.

Following Him demands restraint, patience, faith, a high threshold for pain, and a
willingness to stay focused in cramped circumstances! This is not to say that the
blessings Jesus has paid for and promised us do not far outweigh these discomforts. I
am simply pointing out that we must decide to walk the way of the few, not the many.

While Christianity has become a celebrated philosophy in much of the western
world, many have continued to lay their lives down for Christ daily in many other
places. The first now will be last then and vice-versa. Beware lest you accept a false
version of Jesus' "Good News" on your way to church on Sundays! "Difficult" means
difficult! But God will give us the grace, if we will use our faith and make unselfish
decisions, allowing the Gospel to identify the wide ways of a lost world. Jesus came to
save the world...we're His Body...let's narrow our focus to hold close His vision.

MARCH 18...DAY 77
RUNNING TO WIN THE LAST ELECTION

*"Immediately after the tribulation of those days the sun will be darkened, and the
moon will not give its light; the stars will fall from heaven, and the powers of the
heavens will be shaken. Then the sign of the Son of Man will appear in heaven, and
then all the tribes of the earth will mourn, and they will see the Son of Man coming on
the clouds of heaven with power and great glory. And He will send His angels with a
great sound of a trumpet, and they will gather together His elect from the four winds,
from one end of heaven to the other."*
Matthew 24:29-31 NKJV

There are no less than eight major Christian points of view regarding the exact timing and precise sequence of the events surrounding Jesus' return! If you are interested in studying them further, you can research the subject of "eschatology," delving into the "Rapture," the "Second Coming," and the "Millennium" for yourself. You will uncover more information to sort through than most people know what to do with, but it is worth taking the time to familiarize yourself with the basics of what the Bible says about the end times.

One word of advice, keep the eyes of your heart on Jesus not on all the opinions and speculations of people, no matter how "great" they may be. I also have many opinions, but there is only one thing I can tell you for sure. Jesus Himself said that He is coming back, and before He does there is going to be a time of great shaking on this planet! This "Great Tribulation," as many Bible scholars refer to it, will involve incredible levels of stress on people. There will be cosmic disturbances, a worldwide regret at not having believed in Him beforehand, and a gathering together of those He has "elected" because of their genuine belief in Jesus.

Therefore, remember to keep Jesus as your focal point while it's still today. The most important thing is to make sure you win His election now (Romans 10:9-10)!

MARCH 19...DAY 78
JUST HOW STRANGE ARE GOD'S WAYS TO YOU?

"Because Ephraim has multiplied altars for sinning, they have become to him altars for sinning. Were I to write him my laws by the ten thousands, they would be regarded as a strange thing."
Hosea 8:11-12 ESV

Today, I want to discuss the outlandish fact that it is entirely possible for the select people of God to disqualify themselves from His favor, at least for long periods of time. "Ephraim" was Joseph's youngest son. He received the greater honor when his grandfather Jacob prophesied over him and his elder brother, Manasseh. Though Ephraim was not the firstborn, the family blessing was laid upon him (Genesis 48:1-20).

It is interesting to note that even this boy's name, which meant, "double fruit," carried a God-given distinction. To Ephraim, Jacob ascribed nations in the plural whereas the descendants of his brother, Manasseh, were only promised the greatness of a "multitude." Here we see a person who was certainly chosen, yet in later generations his offspring incurs God's curse through the prophet Hosea! It shouldn't be as hard as it seems to be for modern Christians to understand this principle: It doesn't matter how we start in our faith nearly as much as how we finish! It is very important for believers to pass a genuine, sincere faith down to their children. This is one of the very reasons God gave for sharing some of his purposes with Abraham! He knew he would pass spiritual reality and truth in a strong way to his household enabling them to keep close to God and, accordingly, His promises would come to pass (Genesis 18:16-19).

Ephraim's descendants forgot God in the midst of all their blessings. Once the sin got to the height of their "altars" no amount of godly rules and regulations for righteous living would ever bring them back.

Today, most of professed, organized Christianity regards the details of God's Word as a "strange" or dishonored and a forgotten thing. Jesus is coming back for those who have Him and His laws written on their hearts!

MARCH 20...DAY 79
NO MATTER WHAT

"Then Elihu...burned with anger. He burned with anger at Job because he justified himself rather than God. He burned with anger also at Job's three friends because they had found no answer, although they had declared Job to be in the wrong. Now Elihu had waited to speak to Job because they were older than he...and Elihu...answered and said: 'But it is the spirit in man, the breath of the Almighty, that makes him to understand.'"
Job 32:2-4, 8 ESV

After many years of walking with the Lord the one thing I know is He Himself, and beyond that I don't know very much! God keeps us on a "need to know" basis more often than most religious types can bear to admit. That was the exact problem with Job and his three "good" friends.

Working with God requires that we learn the lesson Elihu taught them, or we just might be tempted to throw in the towel when we run out of explanations for the most difficult circumstances in life. Job was a true man of God, but stubbornly refused to admit that he didn't know everything about spiritual matters. This lead him to justify himself at the expense of honoring God. His friends were lower than Job on the spiritual foundational ladder yet refused to admit their divine ignorance.

All of these guys were guilty of being subtle hypocrites or what is commonly referred to as "religious!" This happens when a Christian doesn't know what he or she doesn't know but keeps acting like they do anyway! The best thing is to always be honest with God, others, and the most demanding, yourself. Because neither Job nor his three friends knew anything about Satan's legal maneuverings in the unseen realm of the spirit (Job 1:6-12), they were ill equipped to deal with the consequences played out in their own back yard!

We have access to the Bible which forewarns us Satan is the "accuser of the brethren" (Revelation 12:10). They didn't have that revelation. The result was they attacked God and accused each other until a "less wise" young man with an understanding of the spirit, spoke up. So, the lesson for us is not to be a hard-headed know-it-all. Trust that Jesus discerns all things and will work it all out for your good...no matter what. If not you may never see Him coming!!

MARCH 21...DAY 80
DON'T GO UNDERCOVER

"Again Jesus spoke to them, saying, 'I am the light of the world. Whoever follows me will not walk in darkness, but will have the light of life.'"
John 8:12 ESV

"You are the light of the world. A city set on a hill cannot be hidden. Nor do people light a lamp and put it under a basket, but on a stand, and it gives light to all in the house. In the same way, let your light shine before others, so that they may see your good works and give glory to your Father who is in heaven."
Matthew 5:14 ESV

Unlike the devil, Christians have been saved from judgment; however, we still must occupy the same planet with the deceiver. He operates through this subtle age-old "world system" that he established. Contrastingly, we abide in the new creation realities of God's Kingdom. This is why Jesus called both Himself and us the "light of the world". He modeled the walk of a Son of God, spreading a heavenly ability to overcome the darkness that envelopes this present world. Through his death, Jesus purchased our salvation and through His resurrection, He empowered us to walk like Him as children of the light, to activate real change by using His example!

History marks that wherever genuine believers have carried the Gospel message it has freed people and replaced their superstitions with the real love and life of God! Nothing could stop Jesus from completing His mission before His time, and the only thing that can stop us before ours is not walking in Jesus' footsteps. To be a believer is to shine! Let the Holy Spirit be your guidance system, inspiring you to say and do the things Jesus did...boldly. The closer we get to His return the more we need to look like Him!

MARCH 22...DAY 81
PUT YOUR MONEY WHERE YOUR MOUTH IS

"For I the Lord do not change; therefore you, O children of Jacob, are not consumed...return to me and I will return to you, says the Lord of hosts. But you say, 'How shall we return?' Will a man rob God? Yet you are robbing me. But you say, 'How have we robbed you?' In your tithes and contributions. You are cursed with a curse, for you are robbing me, the whole nation of you."
Malachi 3:1-9 ESV

One of the most amazing things about God is that He remains consistent in His righteous nature even when we try Him in the most dishonorable ways. In all matters His is a perfectly calculated action or reaction, and for this we should daily be thankful.

The Israelites of Malachi's day were thieves in the Lord's eyes, worthy of being consumed for the level of wickedness they displayed, yet they were not. God has mercy and is faithful to His own promises and timetables. Nevertheless, these people were not going unpunished. They just did not realize the full ramifications of their actions. The Prophet tells them they are "cursed" which means they were on a sinking ship no matter how small the trickle may have appeared for the short term. To be cursed simply means to have the blessings of God removed from one's life.

The entire nation of Israel was founded upon the promise of God's blessing (Deuteronomy 28:1-14). It existed for His reasons, beyond which as a nation, they served no purpose (see Deuteronomy 28:15-68)! For them not to obey the Lord's commands, even with regard to their economy, meant they had reached the end of His mercy in that area and they would certainly suffer the consequences of their actions! According to 1 Corinthians 10:11 their existence serves as our example and for our instruction, especially in light of the fact that the "end of the world" has come upon us! Therefore, in preparation for Jesus' soon return let's be aware of the importance of putting our money where our mouth is...so the blessings of God can flow freely even if the times are tight!

MARCH 23...DAY 82
CONSIDER YOUR BLESSINGS

"Bring the full tithes (tenth) into the storehouse, that there may be food in my house. And thereby put me to the test, says the Lord of hosts, if I will not open the windows of heaven for you and pour down for you a blessing until there is no more need. I will rebuke the devourer for you, so that it will not destroy the fruits of your

soil, and your vine in the field shall not fail to bear, says the Lord of hosts. Then all
nations will call you blessed, for you will be a land of delight, says the Lord of hosts."
Malachi 3:7-9 ESV

As bad as it can eventually get for us when we disobey the Lord, it can be better than best when we do! Malachi had both good news and bad news to deliver to the nation of Israel on God's behalf. After having known the Lord personally for over a quarter of a century, I think the two tend to work together, though. What I mean is, if you know both sides of an issue you can evaluate more completely what you need to do. It was useful for these people to know they were literal robbers in God's eyes. It was even better for them to understand they had an alternative.

So often, Christians serve a version of God they have "created" because they don't know where He stands or where they really stand with him. Instead, they have constructed ideologies that although they may sound good and reasonable, are far from accurate. If these Israelites could not clearly see how they were wronging God they could not have "righted the ship" and learned to walk in His blessings.

To be blessed by God means to have Him involved in everything we do! Even a casual reading of our text today makes it very clear that God's backing is something not to be lightly regarded! As you are considering your condition before Jesus in preparation for His return, seek to bless Him and to be blessed by Him!

MARCH 24...DAY 83
CASHING INTO GOD'S SYSTEM

"Bring the full tithes into the storehouse, that there may be food in my house. And
thereby put me to the test, says the Lord of hosts, if I will not open the windows of
heaven for you and pour down for you a blessing until there is no more need. I will
rebuke the devourer for you, so that it will not destroy the fruits of your soil, and your
vine in the field shall not fail to bear, says the Lord of hosts. Then all nations will call
you blessed, for you will be a land of delight, says the Lord of hosts."
Malachi 3:10-12 ESV

Giving a tenth of your income to support the Lord's work will test you. What many people don't realize is that "tithing" also tests the Lord! Under the nationalized economy of the Old Testament this was God's method of supporting the religious structure through which He originally intended to govern and bless the Hebrew nation. It was a requirement and yet, as we can see by reading this chapter in the Bible, Malachi's generation had given up the practice.

Money is like that for believers. It is a commodity of the world system, which easily lures us beyond the bounds of our faith into areas of compromise. The only way to make finances work for you is to trade it in the Kingdom of God. How do you do that? By giving...according to God's standards. Here we see there are not only "tithes" (required giving) but also "offerings" (selective giving). God gives us both channels as financial means with which to trade our monetary instruments for a kind of unseen currency that will invite His blessings. This is not just a sermonette. God tells us plainly to test this process...and that is not something He normally allows us to do (Luke 4:12)! Look at the rewards in these verses compared to the risks in analyzing whether God is a good investment or not. In the last days, Satan is going to alter the monetary system to his advantage...but that shouldn't matter to those who are already accustomed to cashing into to God's system!

MARCH 25...DAY 84
WHEN IT'S TIME TO GET WILD

"A PRAYER of Habakkuk the prophet, set to wild, enthusiastic, and triumphal music. O Lord, I have heard the report of You and was afraid. O Lord, revive Your work in the midst of the years, in the midst of the years make [Yourself] known!...The Lord God is my Strength, my personal bravery, and my invincible army; He makes my feet like hinds' feet and will make me to walk [not to stand still in terror, but to walk] and make [spiritual] progress upon the high places..."
Habakkuk 3:1-2,19 AMP

When a prophet prays over a person or a church body, the situation is often dissimilar to what the ordinary believer or church would prefer. Chances are if this type of spiritual leader is involved, it is because the ordinary religious course of action will not sufficiently address the problem at hand. Prophets change the setting and tone of our approach to God in order to help us break out of ritual, and re-establish our connection to His presence and power.

The Bible tells us that in preparation for the end times, God has poured out His Spirit in a prophetic way on all his sons and daughters enabling them to carry this same ability (to a degree) to change the climate in and around people's lives everywhere (Acts 2:14-21). When Habakkuk prayed, his purpose was to reinforce the spirit of victory in God's people, paving the way for Him to supernaturally revive the nation. It seems that we need wild displays of bold prayer to shake the atmosphere around us, especially when we have lost the reality of God in our midst. A prophet will tear down the weak ways of the church and build confidence in its place, knowing it will cause the Lord to act powerfully on our behalf! Unfortunately, they often uproot many comfortably "calm" believers at the same time! I say it's time to let the prophets loose, crank up the prayer music and reset the atmosphere in the Church! It's another important factor that will bring us to higher places of spiritual victory in preparation for all that is coming prior to Jesus' return!

MARCH 26...DAY 85
RECOGNIZE THE PROPHETS

"A PRAYER of Habakkuk the prophet, set to wild, enthusiastic, and triumphal music...In wrath [earnestly] remember love, pity, and mercy,...Though the fig tree does not blossom and there is no fruit on the vines, [though] the product of the olive fails and the fields yield no food, though the flock is cut off from the fold and there are no cattle in the stalls, yet I will rejoice in the Lord; I will exult in the [victorious] God of my salvation!
Habakkuk 3:1,2b, 17-18 AMP

Habakkuk was not only an advocate of wild prayer and praise he also called for exuberant rejoicing when there was nothing we would naturally perceive as a cause to celebrate!

The Church needs true prophets to effectively endure the last days because they are part of God's plan for establishing a precise vision in His people. True believers can find the note of victory no matter what happens; that is, until someone with no spirituality takes them to their "church" and programs them how not to! I love the local church but be aware, many churches in the last days will be filled with those who have a form of Godliness but deny the power (or reality) of God (2 Timothy 3:5). This will call for far more powerful men and women of God than we generally see today, who can break the form(at)s and help release the full heart of God back into His people.

Don't be afraid of the true prophets of God...those who know not only God's judgments but also His love and mercy. They often come in unorthodox packages, but have always been a vital part of God's church building blueprint throughout history. We need prophets as we approach the end of the age. Look for them...they will be the wildest praise givers when most need help to merely believe!

MARCH 27...DAY 86
TROUBLE REQUIRES TROUBLEMAKERS

"But the angel of the Lord said to Elijah the Tishbite, 'Arise, go up to meet the messengers of the king of Samaria, and say to them, 'Is it because there is no God in Israel that you are going to inquire of Baal-zebub, the god of Ekron?' Now therefore thus says the Lord, You shall not come down from the [sick] bed to which you have gone up, but you shall surely die.' The messengers returned to the king, and he said to them, 'Why have you returned?...What kind of man was he who came to meet you and told you these things?' They answered him, 'He wore a garment of hair, with a belt of leather about his waist.' And he said, 'It is Elijah the Tishbite'... So He died according to the word of the Lord that Elijah had spoken."
2 Kings 1:3-4, 7-8, 17a ESV

Elijah is the classic portrait of an Old Testament prophet. He defines the makeup more than any other one man of God. His story teaches us not only why prophets are important amongst godly leadership, but how we are to deal with them. It doesn't take long after Elijah is introduced in 1 Kings Chapter 17, before he creates disturbance in the nation of Israel. In fact, it all comes to pass in the first verse!

As I said yesterday, prophets are often unorthodox. Like Jeremiah (chapter 1:10) said, they tear down and build up, usually with the worst coming before the best! The Church prefers to operate according to a system of government that can serve God's interests, but God would rather send direct ambassadors who tell us exactly what He wants done! In the New Testament these messengers are primarily prophets, along with apostles. They are God's form of government and they can look and act stranger than fiction! Like Elijah, they confront mismanagement, expose devilish devices, predict outcomes, don't look very religious and yet God backs them up!!

When you read up on the last days you find a lot of troublesome things happening in the world...the only way to be completely equipped will be to make more room for God's big troublemakers in the Church!

MARCH 28...DAY 87
WHAT A MAN OF GOD LOOKS LIKE

"...What kind of man was he who came to meet you and told you these things?' They answered him, 'He wore a garment of hair, with a belt of leather about his waist.' And he said, 'It is Elijah the Tishbite.'"
2 Kings 1:3-4, 7-8, 17a ESV

"In those days John the Baptist came preaching in the wilderness of Judea, 'Repent, for the Kingdom of heaven is at hand'...
Now John wore a garment of camel's hair and a leather belt around his waist, and his food was locust and wild honey."
Luke 4:1-2, 4 ESV

The further into the last days we go the more crucial it becomes that we know how to discern the true from the false, especially regarding spiritual authorities.

Who would have thought, for example, that in the fall of 2006, one of the leading evangelical authorities in the United States would be exposed as a drug addict with homosexual tendencies?! The correct answer is almost no one because this particular man seemed so "normal!!" If you want to know how to spot a real man of God, take a lesson from the lives of two of the Bible's greatest prophets, Elijah and John the Baptist. What is interesting about these two men is that they had the same spirit, or anointing upon their lives and ministries.

John came to "prepare the way of the Lord," as a type of Elijah, according to Jesus. In Matthew 17:9-13, Jesus also infers that there will be another such figure preparing things spiritually before He comes again (also see Malachi 4:5). Notice how both Elijah and John looked; hairy guys in leather, doing wild things! In other words, not normal everyday church folk! Be careful what you think Christianity should look like. What we tend to incline to will be exactly what real prophets are sent to straighten out!

MARCH 29...DAY 88
THE KIND OF MAN THAT CALMS A STORM

"And when he got into the boat, his disciples followed him. And behold, there arose a great storm on the sea, so that the boat was being swamped by the waves; but he was asleep. And they went and woke him, saying, 'Save us, Lord; we are perishing.' And he said to them, 'Why are you afraid, O you of little faith?' Then he rose and

rebuked the winds and the sea, and there was a great calm. And the men marveled,
saying, 'What sort of man is this, that even winds and sea obey him?'"
Matthew 8:23-27 ESV

There is a big difference between the way we normally react to catastrophic situations and the way Jesus responded. In this scripture, however, we can see that he expects us to become more like Him!

Notice the two things He said to His disciples here. The first is a question, "Why are you afraid?" It should make us think about what answer Jesus was seeking. Our immediate reaction might be surprise, if not anger. How could someone say something so contrary to all reason? Why would they? Maybe because Jesus knew it was the only way to get the spectacular results that such defining moments require.

The situations both God and the devil hurl at us often seem to be unreasonable. If we are locked into a natural way of thinking, which only allows us to reason logically, we will not be able to maneuver in the realm of faith.

This is why the second thing Jesus says is a statement about that subject, "O you of little faith!" He was actually giving them the answer to His preceding question. We are lacking faith on any level if we are afraid. Fear is the opposite of faith in God. Trust is an action in faith; it is walking on the water and putting legs to that faith.

His disciples knew He could change their circumstances. They did not know Him well enough to recognize that they too could speak and change the atmosphere because He was with them! That is a good definition of faith and it is the thing that sets true men of God apart from others. The closer we get to the end of all things, the more we are going to need to become the sort of men...who can speak authoritatively to the winds and the waves of life in Jesus' Name because He is continuously with us!

MARCH 30...DAY 89
PUTTING THE "D" BACK IN EVIL

"Be sober (self-controlled), be vigilant (watchful); because your adversary the
devil walks about like a roaring lion, seeking whom he may devour. Resist him,
steadfast in the faith, knowing that the same sufferings are experienced by your
brotherhood in the world. But may the God of all grace, who called us to His eternal
glory by Christ Jesus, after you have suffered a while, perfect, establish, strengthen,
and settle you. To Him be the glory and the dominion forever and ever. Amen.
1 Peter 5:8-11 KJV

Modern Christianity has allowed Satan to disappear back into the darkness he has used throughout the ages to mask himself and his works. Historically, even the Church often chooses not to look beneath the carpet of its own affairs for fear of stirring up the dirt devils! It tends to be content to look for the good in the extreme, and by doing so often fails to unearth God or His adversary.

This approach to reality will always fall short because it fails to locate the problem! Notice how Peter points out the fact that we have an evil adversary, and then tells us exactly who he is! I want you to notice the similarity of two Bible words, "evil" and "devil." It is as if the Lord highlighted the connection between the two for those of us who speak the English language. By adding one letter ("d") to the name of the one who is behind all wickedness (evil), it makes a lasting impression upon our memory.

We must not dwell on evil but rather be willing to touch it with the blood of Jesus and resist its author, in the Name of Jesus! By exposing satanic activity in this way, we limit his ability to continue to work out his deceptive strategies uncontested. We enforce the judgment and victory Christ executed on the Cross, and begin to draw a sharp contrast between "Satan's System" and "God's Ground." So, let's not be uneasy when we interface with evil. Allow God scope to use us to reverse its influence. This will surely mean some suffering for us now but, according to Peter, it will glorify God for eternity!

MARCH 31...DAY 90
TOUCHING EVIL FOR GOOD

"Then his brothers also went and fell down before his face, and they said, 'Behold, we are your servants.' Joseph said to them, 'Do not be afraid, for am I in the place of God? But as for you, you meant evil against me; but God meant it for good, in order to bring it about as it is this day, to save many people alive. Now therefore, do not be afraid; I will provide for you and you little ones.' And he comforted them and spoke kindly to them." Genesis 50:18-21 NKJV

There is an interesting reversal of terms found here at the end of the book of "beginnings" (Genesis). In its opening chapters we find the serpent using the "Tree of the Knowledge of GOOD and EVIL" to coerce mankind into a sinful fall, here at the close we see God transposing these exact terms as an exclamation point to His own greater plan for reconciliation.

In fact, the life story of Joseph seems to me to be a prophetic foreshadowing of how God intends to use the Church at the end of time to walk in the blessing of Christ's own triumph over the author of evil. We, like Joseph's brothers, are called to first accept and then display His forgiveness in order to ultimately extend the goodness of God to all humanity! Joseph ascended to the right hand of Pharaoh and saved the world of his day from the evils of famine, even though his own brothers tried to kill him. Jesus has ascended to the right hand of God the Father in heaven and saved the world of our day from the satanic oppression and spiritual hunger, even though we (metaphorically) killed him! In the end, however, God meant it for good!! Jesus was willing to touch the devil around us for God's good plan of salvation to be realized within us.

Egypt was a type of this world, yet God cared for and blessed this family in that land until the day came for their deliverance. Our day will also come in the very end of days, amidst a similar kind of tribulation that the Israelites faced (see Exodus chapters 1-14). Until then let's remember the story and example of Joseph...so we will be ready!

APRIL 1...DAY 91
TIME AND TIMING

"For everything there is a season, and a time for every matter under heaven: a time to be born and a time to die;...a time to break down and a time to build up;...a time to embrace, and a time to refrain from embracing;...a time to keep silence, and a time to speak;...a time to love and a time to hate..."
Ecclesiastes 3:1-2a, 3b, 5b, 7b, 8a ESV

Most people seem to have an inborn, constant need to know what time it is. Is it because we are created on God's timetable, whether we realize it or not?

When you think about what King Solomon was saying in the above scripture, you begin to catch a glimpse of his God-given wisdom. First, he had wasted much of his own effort on things that did not please God, so Solomon knew how precious time itself was and still is. Second, as a result of having accomplished some of the greatest feats in history the wisest king who ever lived also knew just how crucial "timing" is in this life!

Keep these two things in mind the next time you find yourself asking, "what time is it?" If you know the value of time, you will remember how little of it you really have been allotted. Remind yourself to find and obey God's will for your life. If you know the importance of timing, you will avoid doing things on your own, with your natural strength and native wisdom, and you will seek the Lord's help as you obey Him. Solomon realized his own failure in these areas even as he wrote them down for us to learn and bring to remembrance.

It may have been too late for Solomon in part, but there is still time for us. Our time to love, honor and serve God is now, and the wisdom for success is available to us through His Holy Spirit. Jesus is coming soon…don't underestimate the lateness of the hour or the importance of being ready to meet Him when it comes! Time and timing are essential.

APRIL 2…DAY 92
ONE MAN'S TIMING

"For everything there is a season, and a time for every matter under heaven:…a time to plant, and a time to pluck up what is planted; a time to kill, and a time to heal;…a time to weep, and a time to laugh; a time to mourn, and a time to dance; a time to cast away stones, and a time to gather stones together;…a time to seek, and a time to lose; a time to keep, and a time to cast away; a time to tear, and a time to sew;… a time for war, and a time for peace."
Ecclesiastes 3:1, 2b, 3a, 4, 5a, 6, 7a, 8b ESV

The Russian author, Leo Tolstoy, is one of history's best writers. His personal story is even better than his fiction. He wrote the novel, "War and Peace," which fits nicely with the last verse of our scripture for today. He is also famous for another novel, "Anna Karenina."

In his autobiography, "A Confession," Tolstoy recounts his journey into the Christian faith. He relates how after achieving fortune, fame and high standing, there came a particular TIME in his life when he came to question if life was meaningless.

He began a quest to find purpose. This led him to study philosophy, science and to pursue many higher avenues of learning. He found these side streets contained no real answers and decided religion must be the reason for life.

He examined and quickly ruled out both Islam and Judaism, only to find that most of the Christians in his circle were living no more purpose filled lives than his own!

It wasn't until he looked a little lower that he found the higher truth he sought, in the lives of the Christian peasants of his day! Among them he witnessed a kind of true faith in Jesus Christ, which kept their hearts full of joy and gave them a purpose for living in spite of the hardships they faced! These Christians lived the truth they professed to such a degree that Tolstoy himself gave up everything he had to live the rest of his life among them!

It is an amazing testimony to the TIMING of a man's life. Maybe you haven't yet found the higher life you've been looking for. This could be your time to discover the same Jesus Leo Tolstoy was missing! You're best story is about to be written...while "time" is still on your side!

APRIL 3...DAY 93
WHO NOT TO BE

But understand this, that in the last days will come (set in) perilous times of great stress and trouble [hard to deal with and hard to bear]. For people will be lovers of self and [utterly] self-centered, lovers of money and aroused by an inordinate [greedy] desire for wealth, proud and arrogant and contemptuous boasters. They will be abusive (blasphemous, scoffing), disobedient to parents, ungrateful, unholy and profane. [They will be] without natural [human] affection callous and inhuman), relentless (admitting of no truce or appeasement); [they will be] slanderers (false accusers, troublemakers), intemperate and loose in morals and conduct, uncontrolled and fierce, haters of good. [They will be] treacherous [betrayers], rash, [and] inflated with self-conceit. [They will be] lovers of sensual pleasures and vain amusements more than and rather than lovers of God. For [although] they hold a form of piety (true religion), they deny and reject and are strangers to the power of it [their conduct belies the genuineness of their profession]. Avoid [all] such people [turn away from them]. 2 Timothy 3:1-5 AMP

Sometimes the best way to learn what something is, is to take a close look at what it is not. That is exactly what this passage does for us. It identifies how dangerous the last days will be and how far people, CHRISTIAN PEOPLE, will have strayed from the truth of the Gospel!

I purposely copied the Amplified version of today's scripture for you to see the various shades of meaning in the specific behaviors listed here.

There are nineteen types of deviant Christian conduct arranged in the text, beginning with the initial category of "self-centered." I believe this serves as a general description under which all these other aberrant Christian characterizations fall, while the last one, those who "hold a form of godliness but deny its power" (New King James Version), sums up them all.   When you put the totality of these characteristics together you have a list of "who not to be" any time as a believer; especially not in the last times! Sadly, this behavior is found in the church today, and will only increase as time goes forward. So, scrutinize, examine your attitudes and allegiances closely and give your whole heart to Christ...that you might be found in the opposite condition of the above scripture, checking your behavior and holding fast to the living God!

APRIL 4...DAY 94
GET INTO SHAPE

"But know this, that in the last days perilous times will come: for men will be lovers of themselves, lovers of money, boasters, proud, blasphemers, disobedient to parents, unthankful, unholy, unloving, unforgiving, slanderers, without self-control, brutal, despisers of good, traitors, headstrong, haughty, lovers of pleasure rather than lovers of God, having a FORM of godliness but denying its power.
And from such people turn away! For of this sort are those who creep into households and make captive of (the) gullible..."
2 Timothy 3:1-6a NKJV

In the same way an athlete must be in the right kind of shape to compete effectively in a particular sport, Christians will have to be in top "form" in order to be ready for the end times. In our text for today the apostle Paul tells his protégé, Timothy, exactly what that means.

First, commit to "sweating" a little everyday by remembering that the description "perilous" means very troublesome and stressful times will come. It is always easier to handle hardship if you see it coming, because you remove the shock factor.

Second, to get fit for the end of time we have to eat right and stretch properly now. A steady diet of studying God's Word, coupled with a constant regimen of praying in His Spirit, and sincerely interacting with His People will keep us strong and flexible, spiritually.   Finally, once we are in shape we have to stay in shape!

The nineteen types of behavior listed here reveal that the last days' church at large is not going to be in keen, competitive shape, even though to many it will look like it is! The problem: They will have a "form of godliness" but their denial of God's power (the presence of God) will keep others from reaching the finish line!

Even today, there are many churches and believers who have only a formatted Christianity because they have strayed from the God of their faith! For this reason, the Bible tells us to check (what something looks like can be deceiving) and make sure we are in the faith (2 Corinthians 13:5)...Jesus is coming back for a fit bride!

APRIL 5...DAY 95
REARRANGED

"...having a FORM of godliness but denying its power. And from such people turn away! For of this sort are those who creep into households and make captive of (the) gullible...Now as Jannes and Jambres resisted Moses, so do these also resist the truth: men of corrupt minds, disapproved concerning the faith; but they will progress no further, for their folly will be manifest to all, as theirs also was."
2 Timothy 3:1-6a NKJV

"And be not conformed to this world, but be TRANSFORMED by the renewing of your mind, that you may prove what is that good and acceptable and perfect will of God."
Romans 12:2 NKJV

There is an interesting connection between these two capitalized words, "form" and "transformed." In the Greek language, the word translated "form" is "morphe" meaning a thing's shape, fashion or appearance. The word, "transformed" contains this same Greek word plus another prefix, (metamorphosis) which, when you put them together, means to change into another form. This is the same word, "transfigured" is used in Matthew 17:2 to describe Jesus on the mountain with Moses and Elijah, when His face and clothing reflected the light of God.

So, stop and think about it today; the difference between these two words is that only one requires change! The church in the last days will have a "form" not produced by the power and life of God. But our command is to be "transformed" by a process that changes both heart and appearance.

Reality for a Christian comes down to those who are willing to change! Refusing to be totally rearranged by God leaves religious people trying to look like something they are not. We must turn away from those who resist the Lord's progress...so that, in the end their folly, and not our own, will become obvious to everyone.

APRIL 6...DAY 96
SPIRITUAL DENIAL

"But know this, that in the last days perilous times will come: for men will be lovers of themselves...having a form of godliness but denying its power. And from such people turn away! For of this sort are those who creep into households and make captive of (the) gullible..."
2 Timothy 3:1-2a, 5-6a NKJV

According to my Bible dictionary, the word, "denying" means contradicting, disavowing or rejecting. In the context of our reading for today you can see the pivotal position in which Paul chooses to insert these meanings. In his shocking behavioral sketches of "the last days" believer, the Apostle sums them all up by emphasizing that these traits will ultimately flourish in an environment where the form of the faith is placed above its object of worship. We must be so careful even today when selecting churches to attend, or preachers to follow because of this very fact. (If I had to guess how close the return of Christ is, just based upon this one verse alone, I would have to say it is upon us!) Let's get back to our word "denying."

Maybe the most revealing aspect of all is the literal meaning of the compound Greek word here. It is one word with two parts, or a combination of two other words, which when you put them together mean literally, "say not." Deny = say not.

This is the battle that has been waged in the church since its inception and will find its climax at the very end. The pressure to say not who God really is (a sovereign omnipotent God who is mighty to save and deliver from every evil force) draws a dividing line between those who are true Christians and those who are not!

When someone is in this particular "religious denial" they can say one thing and act in a contrary manner. They can live like the devil and act like they love God, because they never authentically embrace all of God! Instead, they leave the power (explosive, miraculous) part of God out because it doesn't display itself easily (without genuine faith behind it). Miracles, signs, and supernatural wonders do not fit neatly into a natural, convenient, comfortable, un-taxing everyday life.

Beware, the only alternative true believers have for such people is to "turn away" from them...or to be the gullible ones who are deceived by them! Take another look at your spiritual surroundings...the last days may be closer than you think.

APRIL 7...DAY 97
CALM, COOL, AND STEADY

"I charge you therefore before God and the Lord Jesus Christ, who will judge the living and the dead at His appearing and His kingdom: Preach the word! Be ready in season and out of season. Convince, rebuke, exhort, with all long-suffering and teaching. For the time will come when they will not endure sound doctrine, but according to their own desires, because they have itching ears, they will heap up for themselves teachers; and they will turn their ears away from the truth, and be turned aside to fables. But you be watchful in all things, endure afflictions, do the work of an evangelist, fulfill your ministry."
2 Timothy 4:1-5 ESV

The Apostle Paul wrote this second letter to Timothy at the very end of his life at a time when Christianity was being severely persecuted by the psychotic Roman Emperor, Nero. It is a touching, but very serious, script from a spiritual father to his son.

Between Paul's warning to Timothy about the condition of the last days church (chapter 3: 1-9) and his personal farewell address (chapter 4:6-8), he issues this "charge." He uses the solemn language of a courtroom testimony to remind Timothy how to be prepared for Jesus' return.

Because the undercurrent of the world's way of thinking leaks into the church we, like this young minister, need to remember the importance of staying rock-solid in our faith. This is the antidote for both persecution and error. Both stand directly between you and your destiny, and will intensify as the end draws nearer.

Paul's advice to Timothy was to continue preaching the pure Gospel message regardless of the times, and confronting those who turn away from the truth favoring their own preferences.

The Amplified translation then says to be "calm and cool and steady" under difficult circumstances, willing to exert the pressure to win souls instead of lying down under it. This is the secret to "fulfilling" the ministry, or call of God that He has placed upon our lives. Don't shrink from the end...charge toward it just as Paul did!

APRIL 8...DAY 98
THE PRESSURE POINTS YOU FEEL
WHEN GOD'S HAND IS UPON YOU

"Then his brothers also went and fell down before his face, and they said, 'Behold, we are your servants.' Joseph said to them, 'Do not be afraid, for am I in the place of God? But as for you, you meant evil against me; but God meant it for good, in order to bring it about as it is this day, to save many people alive.
Genesis 50:18-21 NKJV

"...'God resists the proud, but gives grace to the humble.' Therefore humble yourselves under the mighty hand of God, that He may exalt you in due time, casting all your care upon Him, for He cares for you."
1 Peter 5:5b-6 NKJV

When God puts His hand upon you it is the highest honor you can receive, and a sure sign that incredible things are ahead. However, if the life of Joseph (and many other biblical characters) is any indicator, things could get worse before they get better! You must learn how to always keep your eye on the bigger picture when walking out the purpose God has for your life.

Almost everyone knows the end of Joseph's story. It is the ultimate "rags to riches" tale of how he rose above all the adversity he faced on his journey from the pit his cruel brothers cast him in, to Pharaoh's palace. Too often, though, we fail to look at the points along the way, which God used to make Joseph "the man" in Egypt.

For the next couple of days, I want to remind you of the Five Pressure Points you will feel when the Hand of God is heavy upon your life by examining the life of Joseph. If you can recognize these "threshold moments" and work through them with the help of the Holy Spirit, you too will be exalted by God in your "due season"...regardless of which hour in history you live.

APRIL 9...DAY 99
GOD'S INDEX FINGER...PRESSURE POINT #1

"Now Joseph had a dream, and he told it to his brothers; and they hated him even more...Then he dreamed still another dream...so he told it to his fathers and his brothers; and his father rebuked him...And his brothers envied him, but his father kept the matter in mind..."
Genesis 37:5-11 NKJV

"The steps of a good man are ordered by the LORD, though he fall, he shall not be utterly cast down; for the LORD upholds him with His hand.
Psalm 37:23-24 NKJV

The First Pressure Point you will feel when God's hand is upon your life is His "index finger", and He uses it to point us out early in life.

In the biblical account of Joseph's life (Genesis 37-50) it is obvious from the beginning that God has singled out this young man for a specific divine purpose. From our perspective the childhood favoritism his father Jacob showed this son may seem unfair, but it was only a revelation of God's perspective towards Joseph.

God had chosen Joseph as the person ordained to effectively handle the assignment necessary to save the world in that generation from a future catastrophic famine. Even Joseph's name, meaning "may he add," and the coat of many "pieces" Jacob made for him were indicative of the heavenly authority that rested upon his shoulders.

His early encounters with God through his dreams further revealed a difference between the purposes God had instilled in him as opposed to his brothers and family. Because his brothers weren't spiritually minded, Joseph's excitement about these revelations only served to incite their jealousy and commence God's version of his "true life" story.

So, how has the Lord pointed you out in life? Where do you stick out from the crowd? How are you made different in the light of God? It pays to find out. His intention is to get your attention in the beginning...and use your cooperation to spread His blessing in the end!

APRIL 10...DAY 100
GOD'S THUMB...PRESSURE POINT #2

"And Israel said to Joseph...Please go and see if it is well with your brothers...Now when they saw him afar off, even before he came near them, they conspired against him to kill him. Then they said to one another, 'Look, this dreamer is coming! Come therefore, let us now kill him and cast him into some pit;...So it came to pass, when Joseph had come to his brothers, that they stripped Joseph of his tunic, the tunic of many colors that was on him. Then they took him and cast him into a pit...and sold him to the Ishmaelites for twenty shekels of silver. And they took Joseph to Egypt."
Genesis 37:13-28 NKJV

The second pressure point Joseph felt because the hand of God was upon him came in the form of a spiritual "thumb!" When the time came for God's maturation process for Joseph to begin, it was as if suddenly a heavenly hand tapped him on the shoulder and introduced him to a harsh new reality.

Like Joseph, we are usually surprised by the timing of God, and initially feel overwhelmed. No one at the start feels equal to the task before them, because the burden of our call appears to leave us with no way out.

When the "bottom drops out" and our dreams seem shattered we truly experience what it means to be "thumbed" by the hand of God, coming to realize that His call is indeed a heavy one. It is a sobering place deep inside the pit, stripped of everything we have become comfortably familiar with. But it is there we first learn to truly depend on God and God alone. In this humbling attitude, we can only be sure He will exalt us in the long run when we find ourselves with nowhere else to turn!

Nothing can happen to a believer because he is following the call of God that would be more difficult than running away from the call of God! It is a good thing to feel as if you cannot escape the hand of God instead of dreading something as undefined as the last days.

APRIL 11...DAY 101
GOD'S MIDDLE FINGER...
PRESSURE POINT #3

"And his master (Potiphar) saw that the LORD was with him and that the LORD made all he did to prosper in his hand. So Joseph found favor in his sight, and served him. Then he made him overseer of his house, and all that he had he put under his authority...But it happened...that she (Potiphar's wife) caught him by his garment, saying, 'Lie with me.' But he left his garment in her hand, and fled and ran outside. And so it was, when she saw that he had left his garment in her hand and fled outside, that she called to the men of her house and spoke to them, saying, 'See, he has brought in to us a Hebrew to mock us. He came in to me to lie with me, and I cried out..." Genesis 39:3-4, 11-14 NKJV

Potiphar's house is the place where we learn to make difficult decisions in life. It was there the long "middle finger" of God's hand exerted a higher third level of pressure upon Joseph. Although he was a slave, he was recognized by the captain of Pharaoh's guard and exalted to a high degree. From his position there I can imagine Joseph almost beginning to see the light at the end of the tunnel, and how all of this could end up working out for his own good after all! Just when he may have been tempted to think it was "safe to go back into the water" of depending on his own gifts and talents to gain success, a dangerous and desperate housewife stepped in between his renewed dreams and their certain fulfillment.

This finger of God is just long enough to bless us, and at one and the same time prevent us from settling for our egotistic ideas of success. In this pressure place, the Lord confronts us with a life changing choice...the temptations of the world or the true riches of heaven! Remember God can reach you in any circumstance, so be a Joseph whether in good times or bad and you will be exalted due course!

APRIL 12...DAY 102
GOD'S LITTLE FINGER...PRESSURE POINT #4

"So it was, when his master heard the words which his wife spoke to him, saying, 'Your servant did to me after this manner,' that his anger was aroused. Then Joseph's master took him and put him into the prison,...But the LORD was with Joseph and showed him mercy, and He gave him favor in the sight of the keeper of the prison. And the keeper of the prison committed to Joseph's hand all the prisoners who were in the prison; whatever they did there, it was his doing. The keeper of the prison did not look into anything that was under Joseph's authority, because the LORD was with him; and whatever he did, the LORD made it prosper."
Genesis 39:19-23 NKJV

The fourth stop on destiny's road to achievement introduces us to the "smallest finger" on God's hand. The pressure it exerts is just enough to keep us humble and patient, but not so much that we lose our own personality.

Joseph never seemed to despair even though everything he started out with appeared hopelessly lost. In prison for doing a good deed that others called evil, this true man of God showed unnatural maturity. He resigned himself to doing right no matter what because that is who he was in God. Better he thought to suffer for righteousness' sake, than to be in the company of the wicked enjoying the pleasures of sin for a season!

When we come to the end of our strength we discover the beginning of God's power. Interestingly, our littlest finger has the biggest gripping power of all our fingers because it is designed with a locking mechanism. When every other hold God has on us seems broken, His little finger remains sure. We cannot fall! Knowing this, Joseph became comfortable with the pressure he felt, and even dependent upon the weight of God's hand on his life. As you will see tomorrow, he was finally right where God needed him to be!

APRIL 13...DAY 103
GOD'S RING FINGER...PRESSURE POINT #5

"Then the chief butler spoke to Pharaoh, saying, "I remember my faults this day...Now there was a young Hebrew man with us there...And we told him, and he interpreted our dreams for us...and it came to pass, just as he interpreted for us, so it happened'...Then Pharaoh sent and called Joseph and they brought him quickly out of the dungeon...So Joseph answered Pharaoh, saying, 'It is not in me; God will give Pharaoh an answer of peace.'"
Genesis 40:9-16 NKJV

"And Pharaoh said to his servants, 'Can we find such a one as this, a man in whom is the Spirit of God?' Then Pharaoh said to Joseph, 'Inasmuch as God has shown you all this, there is no one as discerning and wise as you. You shall be over my house, and all my people shall be ruled according to your word; only in regard to the throne will I be greater than you.' And Pharaoh said to Joseph, 'See, I have set you over all the land of Egypt.' Then Pharaoh took his signet ring off his hand and put it on Joseph's hand; and he clothed him in garments of fine linen and put a gold chain around his neck."
Genesis 41:38-42 NKJV

The fifth and final finger in the story of Joseph carries only the pressure of position.

The "ring" finger is to be adorned, being dependent of the fingers around it for much of its motion! God directed Pharaoh to put his own ring on Joseph's hand! As the new ruler of Egypt, he was finally in the right position to fulfill the purpose of God.

Instead of being the center of his own dreams, Joseph had learned to be an instrument in the center of God's will! All of his dreams came true as he walked in the authority God had given him, but it was for the sake of the rest of the world that he fulfilled the responsibilities of that office.

Famine came but a godly man with spiritual wisdom and vindicated discretion saved the day. He also saved his own family and extended a forgiveness that still brings tears to my eyes when I read his story!

APRIL 14...DAY 104
THE PRESSURE IS WORTH ITS
WEIGHT IN GOD

"And he had him ride in the second chariot which he had; and they cried out before him, 'Bow the knee!' So he set him over all the land of Egypt. Pharaoh also said to Joseph, 'I am Pharaoh, and without your consent no man may lift his hand or foot in all the land of Egypt.' And Pharaoh called Joseph's name Zaphenath-paneah....Joseph was thirty years old when he stood before Pharaoh King of Egypt. And Joseph went out from the presence of Pharaoh, and went throughout all the land of Egypt."
Genesis 41:43-46 NKJV

Just like Joseph, we need the hand of God in our lives, families, churches and nation. It is interesting to note that God's hand in Joseph's life caused opportunities to be continually poured into his hands. Read the story for yourself and you will find that when we let God work in us and through us we never really lose. It is constant gain in the areas of wisdom, discretion, experience, character, spirituality, maturity and momentum towards destiny! We are being groomed for greatness, and the world is depending on our ability to withstand the pressure of our call.

Joseph was given an interesting name by the Pharaoh. Zaphenath-paneah means "the revealer of secrets, or the man to whom Secrets are revealed. What we learn through Joseph is that in "due season," "full recognition" comes to those who trust in the dreams of God! So, don't despair during the journey, even when all seems lost. Be a Joseph and put yourself in God's hand so he can exalt you, and use you to help save your generation! The hour is late...let's make the pressure of God's call count!

APRIL 15...DAY 105
TAKING ANOTHER LOOK AT YOUR TAXES

"Now behold there was a man named Zacchaeus who was a chief tax collector, and he was rich. And he sought to see who Jesus was, but could not because of the crowd, for he was short of stature. So he ran ahead and climbed up into a sycamore tree to see Him, for He was going to pass that way. And when Jesus came to the place, He looked up and saw him, and said to him, 'Zacchaeus, make haste and come down, for today I must stay at your house.'"
Luke 19:1-5 NKJV

It is amazing how many times taxes and tax collectors are mentioned in the life story of Jesus. In fact, it was an occasion during which the Roman government held a worldwide census for the purpose of taxing its empire that Joseph and Mary were brought to the prophesied destination of the Lord's birth in Bethlehem (Luke 2, Micah 5:2)!

Tax collectors were despised in Israel in those days. They were viewed as the antithesis of "righteous" people, especially in the eyes of the religious establishment. Yet, Jesus ate with them and used them as examples (both good and bad) in His teachings and parables. He even chose one, Matthew, to be numbered among His twelve disciples! Luke says that "a great company" of them gathered to listen to Jesus after Matthew had left the "business" to follow the Lord (chapter 5:29).

This generosity angered the leading religious figures present, proving both God's great love for sinners and His great difficulty convincing those who professed to own the greatest spiritual knowledge!

And then there is Zacchaeus, whose name interestingly enough means "pure of heart." He was a high level tax man, which probably made him the worst kind of sinner in his society. He was also short in stature, with a hidden goodness about him that perhaps only the Lord could see. He is a beautiful picture of how God does things differently than we do.

Remember that when the tax man comes to your house. His blessings come in strange packages and at surprising times. Zacchaeus, the taker, GAVE half of his belongings to the poor that night and vowed to repay everyone he had cheated fourfold, according to the Law of Moses! He is a lesson that every negative is an opportunity for the Gospel, even when it comes to those who take your money!

APRIL 16...DAY 106
DR. JESUS WILL SEE YOU NOW

"As He passed by, He saw Levi (Matthew) the son of Alphaeus sitting at the tax office. And He said to him, 'Follow Me.' So he arose and followed Him. Now it happened, as He was dining in Levi's house that many tax collectors and sinners also sat together with Jesus and His disciples; for there were many, and they followed Him. And when the scribes and Pharisees saw Him eating with the tax collectors and sinners, they said to His disciples, 'How is it that He eats and drinks with tax collectors and sinners?' When Jesus heard it, He said to them, 'Those who are well have no need of a physician, but those who are sick. I did not come to call the righteous, but sinners, to repentance.'"
Mark 2:14-17 NKJV

This is a familiar scene. We have the Pharisees and the Tax collectors grouped together in a setting very similar to the parable Jesus told in Luke 18:9-14. Since this story of the gathering at Matthew's house is also found in Luke chapter 5, we understand that the parable came afterward. That means Jesus' words were not only an illustration of how spiritual things can get warped among religious people, it was based on facts! Both things teach us the importance of never taking God's Word for granted.

The Pharisees were a sect (denomination) of believers who sought distinction and praise by their outward forms of piety and ceremonial rituals, often going beyond the written law and adding many oral traditions to their legalistic observances. The tax collectors of that day were a parallelic contrast to them, also going beyond the legal limits of their job and exacting more money from people than they owed. Generally speaking, both groups were equally guilty before God but it is always easier for the self admitted sinner to recognize their need for the Savior! The Pharisees were often severely rebuked by Jesus for their politically ambitious religious motives.

On Judgment Day there will be many people who "think" they are right with God only to find out they are not! Recognize that you miss the mark in many ways and let the Great Physician tend to your life now!

APRIL 17...DAY 107
DO YOU REALLY KNOW JESUS?

"But to what shall I liken this generation? It is like children sitting in the marketplace and calling to their companions, and saying: 'We played the flute for you, and you did not dance; we mourned to you, and you did not lament.' For John came neither eating nor drinking, and they say, 'He has a demon.' The Son of Man came eating and drinking, and they say, 'Look, a glutton and winebibber, a friend of tax collectors and sinners!' But wisdom is justified by her children."
Matthew 11:16-19 NKJV

It is super important to grow up in our understanding of God and self in preparation for end time living. I have found that we often get them (God and self) confused, and then have a hard time staying ready for Jesus' return. It is simply too difficult to look very seriously or accurately into the things of God while you continue filtering all the information you learn about Him through your own emotions.

The multitude Jesus was addressing in our text for today got an ear full of the best safeguarding revelation available. Notice how He points out their "childishness," which is not to be confused with the necessary quality of "child-likeness" He talked about in

Luke 18:16. They mistakenly acted as if God was at their disposal, waiting for them to decide which tune to play, what instrument to use and when!

Christians often make this same mistake in our generation. Many people assume that God is so interested in their blessing and happiness that He will overlook their immature and erroneous judgments about who He is and what He is doing!

As a whole, that generation got Jesus and John the Baptist all wrong. They allowed the leading religious figures of their day to transpose their own ideas of who these two messengers really were with God's idea and identification of them in His Word. You must be careful and open at the same time. Just when you figure out a John the Baptist, his call, his style and idiosyncrasies, God will throw a Jesus at you!! These are two totally different approaches to ministry, but the same plan of God working in them both.

Jesus was harder to read than anyone ever before or since. As a complete spiritual man, He knew who He was AND who God was...that made Him ready and able to finish His course!

APRIL 18...DAY 108
EAT IT ALL

"...On the tenth day of this month every man shall take for himself a lamb...for a household...Your lamb shall be without blemish, a male of the first year...Then the whole assembly of the congregation of Israel shall kill it at twilight. And they shall take some of the blood and put it on the two doorposts and on the lintel of the houses where they eat it...You shall let none of it remain until morning, and what remains of it until morning you shall burn with fire. And thus you shall eat it: with a belt on your waist, your sandals on your feet, and your staff in your hand. So you shall eat it in haste. It is the LORD's Passover."
Exodus 12:3-11 NKJV

The God of Israel has an "all or nothing" personality. His very name alludes to the fact that He alone is the self-existent One, above all others. That being true, there is no excusable reason (besides complete ignorance of this fact) for any person to serve any other being or figure. To knowingly resist the Lord or to half-heartedly obey His commands puts one on dangerous ground. Even though His nature is to be merciful, and He knows that we are imperfect creatures, God expects us to walk respectfully before Him with a humble attitude according to the degree of enlightenment we possess. When we do, He always makes the way open before us.

Our scripture for today illustrates the greatest way God has ever made for us, symbolically foreshadowing Jesus as the Passover Lamb slain for the world! The Israelites were given detailed word pictures pinpointing Messiah, each a different aspect of Who Jesus is/was, what He would come to do, and how they and we are to receive Him.

You can research the Hebrew Seder meal for more insight regarding the significance of Passover which foreshadows the sacrifice of Jesus and His exchange for our lives, but make one note for today - the personality of God remains changeless. The Israelites had to eat the entire lamb at one time in anticipation of an immediate deliverance. For Christians, our salvation is exactly the same. Take all of Jesus...so that when times get tough and the wrath and judgment of God fall on this world, He will command His angels to "pass over" you!

APRIL 19...DAY 109
A LAST TEMPTATION OF CHRIST

"But you are those who have continued with Me in My trials (temptations).
And I bestow upon you a kingdom, just as My Father bestowed one upon Me, that
you may eat and drink at My table in My kingdom,
and sit on thrones judging the twelve tribes of Israel."
Luke 22:28-30 NKJV

"Because you have kept My command to persevere, I also will keep you
from the hour of trial (temptation) which shall come upon the whole world,
to test those who dwell on the earth. Behold I am coming quickly!
Hold fast what you have, that no one may take your crown."
Revelation 3:10-11 NKJV

It seems someone famous is always trying to depict Jesus as having fallen into sin as a false messiah. Devaluing the person and purpose of The Lord by using a false historical perspective of the facts surrounding His life is just a cheap attempt at over valuing one's self!

Try as these people might, Jesus Christ stands as the most popular person ever and is exactly who He said He was. This being true, He will return to set the facts straight one second coming soon day. According to the biblical information God has given us, we should live like His return could be today!

Before Jesus' second coming, there will be one last "Temptation of Christ". Like most spiritual revelation it is not as lineal thinkers would suppose. True Christian believers are corporately called the "Body of Christ," being the spiritual extension of His life (in the Godhead), and occupying the earth as His ambassadors until He comes again.

Jesus made the initial stand, overcoming Satan and restoring the dominion of mankind in the earth. As Jesus' representatives we are called to make the final stand, (by His power and grace); overcoming the world by our faith in Him until He returns to finalize everything as He promised!

This is no movie...it is real life in the end times! Hold fast and stay close to Jesus...He will keep those who persevere in power and perfect peace in Him!

APRIL 20...DAY 110
JESUS WANTS TO BE YOUR JONATHAN

"Now when he had finished speaking to Saul, the soul of Jonathan was knit to the soul of David, and Jonathan loved him as his own soul."
1 Samuel 18:1 NKJV

Four months and twenty days into the turn of this century, the Lord woke me up at five o'clock in the morning to notify me of my job description for the next season of my life and ministry. I was living in Denver (and realized later that day was the first anniversary of the Columbine school shooting) when He said to me, "Rocky, tell my people that I want to be their Jonathan!"

Until I read the first several verses in 1 Samuel chapter eighteen, the whole experience sounded kind of strange. The scripture brought understanding of how David was a type of true corporate Christianity in scripture. The anointing he received from the prophet Samuel represented a shift in God's plan for the nation of Israel. David was called to be the next king, and what he lacked only Jonathan could give! The willing sacrifice of one in a greater position of authority, power and provision was all that was needed in David to begin his development into the role God had for him. After much persecution, David became the ultimate prototype of the modern church, functioning as a Prophet, Priest and King and leading the church of his day into previously unknown dimensions of worship and service to God.

Jesus is preparing His people today for a similar calling. He, like Jonathan, has already given us everything necessary for us to rule in His kingdom here on earth (see verses 2-5), and to be cared and provided for at the King's table. Now, He is calling us onward in our advancement into the next season of God's plan for our generation.

Where we are exactly on His Kingdom timetable I do not know, and that is not primarily what we need to find out. What I do know is that there is a greater heavenly dimension available to those who will trust God, walk humbly, and not grab for themselves what only heaven can bestow.

I think it is quite likely that we are at a critical place in history, and the Lord is raising up a greater 'spiritual leadership' that will help the Church find its heart again and lead it toward God's master stage of heavenly development.

As a new era of terrorism has infiltrated our world during this past decade, the "Prince of Peace" has told me to remind you to focus on His plans for ultimate conquest. So today, be encouraged in your pursuit of God. He wants to BE your "Jonathan," so BE His David and let Him "knit" your soul to His own…in preparation for Jesus' return!

APRIL 21…DAY 111
WEIGHING HEAVY DECISIONS…
LIFE'S 7 MOST IMPORTANT QUESTIONS

"Now the serpent was more subtle and crafty than any living creature which the LORD God had made. And he [Satan] said to the woman, 'Can it really be that God has said, You shall not eat from every tree of the garden?'"
Genesis 3:1 AMP

Before you read today's article let me invite you to find a Bible and also read Genesis 1:28, 2:15, 19-20, 3:2-10 if you would like a more complete background. These verses recount the biggest decision any person has ever had to make. They also reveal, among other things, the source of one of the most common conditions that continues to cripple the human race. We have all experienced both the paralyzing effects of INDECISION and the painful disappointments associated with wrong decisions. So, in order to make better decisions in life, let's learn to identify and avoid the same kinds of mistakes Adam and Eve made.

Like a master technician, Satan used a subtle process of manipulation to strip Eve of her confidence in the place and position God had given her beside Adam in His creation. Piece by piece, he removed each pillar of Truth in the foundation that their relationship with God stood upon, until he was able to deceive them into the ultimate wrong choice. His aim with them, as it is with us, was to bring them to a place of complete vulnerability in the spiritual arena and then expose them to its darker realities.

I want you to particularly notice how that before he usurped their authority and replaced their dominion in this world with his own, he first systematically destroyed their decisiveness. Satan did far more than simply give them all the wrong answers; rather he enticed them to question all the right ones! Instead of standing firm in who they already were in God and what they possessed because of His love for them, they began to speculate about alternative possibilities.

The process of stripping a person of divine destiny begins with an attack on their human reasoning. Adam and Eve fell because they did not answer the 7 Basic Questions of Life properly. They became confused about: 1. WHO they trusted, 2. WHAT they knew, 3. WHEN they would benefit, 4. WHERE they stood, 5. WHY it really mattered, 6. HOW wrong information affected them, and 7. WHAT THEN would be the outcome. These same questions are always the difference between good decisions and bad ones in our lives. Now it becomes our responsibility to answer them appropriately if we want to avoid the trap Adam and Eve fell into. If we can, we will become 'spiritually decisive' and go further with God and man.

APRIL 22...DAY 112
LIFE'S 7 MOST IMPORTANT QUESTIONS
QUESTION #1...WHO DO YOU TRUST?

"And Satan said to the woman, can it really be...
Gen. 3:1 AMP

The first question we must ask ourselves in order to eliminate the kind of speculation that erodes our faith in the Lord is simply are we presently trusting GOD, MAN OR OURSELF?

Eve was living in such a naturally supernatural state with God that she had never considered the possibility of turning to another source of authority in making her decisions. As a result of her "self-discovery," the rest of us find the ability to rebel against God to be a very natural inclination that must be actively opposed on a deeper level than just mental reasoning. We must purpose to trust in the Lord with all of our heart, not 'leaning' on our own understanding. Once we first acknowledge Him in all of our ways, God's Spirit can then teach us His ways and make our paths straight (Proverbs 3:5).

Remember that you must stand firm in your position in God's Garden! We begin from a place of victory because of the fact that Jesus Christ came as our "second Adam" and, after making all the right decisions (that Adam didn't make), exchanged His life for ours! Like that first couple in the Garden of Eden we now have the ability to say, "This is the garden God created for us and we will guard and keep it!"

There are 3 Specific things you need to remember at this point in the process of becoming a more decisive servant of God. First, in order to truly trust God, you must learn to trust the instincts He built into your spirit or 'inner man.' Two, learn to seriously distrust your own reasoning and perception of things as you see them right now. If you are not open to spiritual realities how can you come to understand things from Gods' perspective? Finally, don't let the devil surprise attack you. Expect him to intrude into your 'garden' and be ready to answer his every move with the truth of what God has spoken over your life and family!

APRIL 23...DAY 113
LIFE'S 7 MOST IMPORTANT QUESTIONS
QUESTION #2...WHAT DO YOU KNOW?

"...can it really be that God has said..?"
Gen. 3:1 AMP

The second step in becoming a spiritually decisive Christian goes hand in hand with the former. It can also be learned through Adam's and Eve's mistake.

We must come to rely on 'Revelation Knowledge' as opposed to WHAT we know by calculating the sum of things around us. A believer has to be able to distinguish between the sources and meanings of the information to which they have access. Things are not usually as they first appear from a deductive mental glance. Our minds, although very complex and incredibly capable, are finite and subject to error. Our spirits on the other hand, when awakened to God through a rebirthing encounter with Jesus, are cleansed by His blood and infinitely able to receive information from God. Our spirits can then relate to Him and appropriately monitor our thoughts, feelings and actions.

We are commanded in the Bible to "Walk in the spirit," which means learning to weigh our intuitive perception about matters even before we began to reason them out in our minds. The old saying, "It's not what you know but who you know" is true when it comes to spiritual decisiveness. What we know is important and our mental capacities are important AFTER we are in the safety of a right relationship with God. From there we can then trust our instincts about things and make much better decisions.

According to the Bible, our mind actually becomes "renewed" as we follow this course of action. There are three things you must remember about WHAT you know. First, begin to explore and learn the difference between your spirit and your soul. Remember to check the source of the information your mind processes by asking yourself if it is coming from within or without, then follow the inner guidance system God has built into you (1John 20-27).

Second, know your Scriptural Boundaries. Many mistakes can be avoided in the arena of decision making if you having a good working knowledge of what God has already said to others. Remember, this also means going beyond just what the Bible says into the 'spirit' of what it teaches.

Finally, learn to recognize the demonic strategies that tempt you to follow anything other than God. Much if not most of the modern Christian world ignorantly substitutes mental understanding for spiritual revelation, thinking they are making intelligent decisions. The wisdom of this world, or the prevailing thought patterns of society at large, represent foolishness to God and will ultimately lead believers into error (1 Corinthians 1:18-28).

APRIL 24...DAY 114
LIFE'S 7 MOST IMPORTANT QUESTIONS
QUESTION #3...WHEN DO YOU BENEFIT?

"For God knows that in the day you eat of it..." Gen. 3:6 AMP

A person can have a revelation of God, learn to cultivate an intuitive perception of the inward movements of His Spirit, begin to experience a kind of supernatural Christian lifestyle that causes others to take notice that something is different in their life...and still get sidetracked!

Even as their spiritual life is on the rise, the issue of timing can cause many to fall because of false expectations! We must be careful about what WE think God should do both today and tomorrow! Satan was able to get Eve's focus off of the day she was living in and onto another time in the future. Although vision is important, nothing is ever as critical to a believer's mindset as 'staying in the moment' locked into what is happening right now.

Jesus personally instructed us to not worry or take excessive thought about tomorrow because when we make it our aim to seek God TODAY, He causes our future to work out according to a higher set of plans than our own (Matthew 6:33-34). From

God's vantage point in the spiritual realm timing is a very different issue than what we understand it to be. In absolute godly reality there is little difference between today and a thousand years from now in many ways. (2 Peter 3:8)

The Bible speaks about certain divine events unfolding in our dimension in the "fullness" or "maturity" of time (Galatians 4:4, Ephesians 1:10 & Acts 2:1). Accordingly, we must step outside our own timelines in order to properly view spiritual things. Jesus told his own brothers (John 7:6) that, from their unspiritual points of view, "the time was always ready" to do whatever they found convenient. He, on the other hand, viewed time as something God laid out for divine opportunities to unfold. They must be waited for then seized at the right moment.

Ambition is a hazardous detour for many people as they attempt to travel the road God places before them. Any manipulation on our part to hasten the arrival of something that God destines for our tomorrow is a dangerous attempt at rearranging time. Experience teaches that what we do today determines much of what happens to us tomorrow! God designed it that way so we would remain focused on our present tense one day at a time NOW relationship with Him instead of lapsing into following Jesus just to get what we want from Him on our timetable! Our pursuit and focus is Christ alone with or without the Christmas presents; which a true relationship with Him always brings. Time is a tool God uses to build maturity into our lives.

No doubt there was a perfect place in God's timeline for learning more about the Tree of the Knowledge of Good and Evil, but Eve just couldn't wait to find out about "in that day" the Devil placed in her head. What a crucial mistake for her and for us!

APRIL 25...DAY 115
LIFE'S 7 MOST IMPORTANT QUESTIONS
QUESTION #4...WHERE DO YOU
PRESENTLY STAND?

"...your eyes will be opened, and you will be like God..."
Genesis 3:6b AMP

Yesterday's and today's questions are closely connected. Together they form a deadly combination for many Christians. In fact, if most believers could get these two concepts down they would overcome many of the obstacles that prevent them from accurately interpreting much of the spiritual information made available to them.

The When and Where of things usually provide enough warning indicators to alert us that we are close to making a big mistake and need help. If we are not where we are supposed to be it is usually a good indication that we are also not in the right timing of things, and are probably not listening to the right voices! How many believers attempt to change their location instead of simply believing God where they are even if it is uncomfortable, letting Him take care of them and their frustrating situations?

Eve was still in control of her situation at this point in Genesis and so are we. If we can just locate ourselves on the spiritual map long enough to ask what in the world we are doing talking to a questionable creature about the unquestionable nature of The Creator, we have a shot at stopping the bleeding and recovering ourselves from the snare of the enemy!

Adam and Eve were already like God where they were. He had created them in His own image. God breathed the breath of life into them. On top of that He came around daily in the 'wind' of the day to reinforce the closeness of their relationship! When we are walking with God we don't need to go anywhere else or project ourselves too far into our future. God enjoys being our 'everything' and proving His love for us where we are. However, if the Devil can convince you that there is that ever illusive 'more' just for the picking out there for you, you will not only forfeit what you already have but also fall from the security of where God has placed you right now!

When Moses stood before the impassable Red Sea with the Egyptian army behind him God adamantly asked him "why do you cry to Me?" The command was to "go forward" using what God had already placed in his hand. Moses simply put forth the Rod that had already been used miraculously and opened up another opportunity for God to create yet another miracle! This is what Adam and Eve needed to do, trust that God had already given them all that they needed for that season. We must also use the priceless treasures that God has already placed in our hands to protect that 'Garden Relationship' we enjoy with the Lord.

APRIL 26...DAY 116
LIFE'S 7 MOST IMPORTANT QUESTIONS
QUESTION #5...WHY DOES IT
REALLY MATTER?

"...you will be like God, knowing the difference between Good and Evil..."
Genesis 3:5 AMP

The devil loves to emphasize the intellectual differences among God's people, and at the same time capitalize on their ignorance to separate and divert them from the things that really matter.

As I stated earlier, God obviously had a greater plan for the Tree of the Knowledge of Good and Evil and the lessons it contained than simply using it as a gauge to test Adam and Eve's obedience. By pointing out that there were unknown factors hidden within its branches, Satan was able to seduce Eve into separating the thought processes of her soul from the spiritual "Word of Truth" that the Lord has spoken to her and Adam. As long as they remained united under God's authorization, Adam and Eve held the delegated power to keep that tree untouched and the rest of the Garden protected.

I find it very interesting, and revealing that Satan used their sense of curiosity to begin a process of dividing them as a means of removing their spiritual authority. First he subtly targeted the woman, who had originally been separated from the innermost recesses of Adam's own being. Next he isolated her, and tricked her into speculating about decisive issues on her own. Then Satan used her wrong decision to paralyze Adam with enough indecision about his true loyalties until, incredibly, he did nothing to stop the bleeding!

This is a very important point in our effort to gain an understanding of how the enemy strategizes against God's people today, especially Christian couples. To the serpent's assertion that greater knowledge and understanding awaited the one who would eat of its fruit, Eve should have simply answered that it really did not matter! She might instead have grilled him about the virtues of the Tree of Life and questioned his unwillingness to talk about it! We must learn to always "choose life" in the spirit because the more of it we have the more capable we become of handling the knowledge which automatically grows out of our maturation process. Outside of God what is really worth knowing, anyway? Just like Adam and Eve, we usually come to this realization only AFTER we have made the wrong spiritual decisions. Spiritual people leave the "WHYS?" to God and get on with enjoying the Paradise that His Presence affords them. For you "know-it-alls" this one is a "no-brainer!" Jesus is coming soon...let each one of us keep our faith in His Word!

APRIL 27...DAY 117
LIFE'S 7 MOST IMPORTANT QUESTIONS
QUESTION #6...HOW WILL WRONG
INFORMATION AFFECT ME?

"...and when the woman saw...she took...she gave...they ate...then the eyes of them both were opened and they knew..."
Genesis 3:6-7

Have you ever regrettably looked back on a wrong decision you made and thought, "If I had only known?" Adam and Eve surely felt this way as they were introduced to the sudden new reality of life where the mind, will and emotions exalt themselves in the absence of a finely tuned spirit. They had no way of truly knowing, in the spiritually selfless state they existed in, how a self-conscious perception would affect them.

We also struggle to realize what it fully means to live life in the spirit as Romans chapter 8 describes, because of the affect that our heightened awareness of natural realities (this physical world) has had on us. God is a spirit according to John 4:24 and He is constantly seeking those who are willing to worship Him in a truly spiritual way. That means not worshipping God the way 'we think' it should be done or expecting others to follow our religious traditions and procedures. Our versions of Christianity are often developed by several generations of ministerial leaders who have lost the original spiritual perception that created a passionate magnetism to the God that their predecessors once enjoyed. When we aimlessly follow such blind leadership we end up equally blind and as spiritually destitute as Adam and Eve after they were driven out of the Garden.

Because of our fallen human nature, we must be reminded periodically of our need for the presence of God and the dangers of any information developed wholly outside that environment. Wrong perceptions lead to wrong realities for innocent people. It is better for us as believers to remain innocently ignorant, if necessary, than to fall into the devil's strategy of thinking we know (or need to know) more than we do! Let the scholars and philosophers (those who can't control their need to know) do the rigidly logical reasoning, arguing and debating so you can linger and abide in the presence of God!

When we let God govern our thinking we remain cloaked and covered with the authority He has given us, safely headed toward the destiny He has called us to! Keep your "why's" and "how's" sheltered in God. He knows how to answer all your questions...even about end time concerns...as you continue to seek HIM first.

APRIL 28...DAY 118
LIFE'S 7 MOST IMPORTANT QUESTIONS
QUESTION #7...WHAT THEN WILL MY OUTCOME BE?

"...And the Lord God said to the woman, 'What is this you have done?'"
Genesis 3:13 NKJV

The final question I have for you is not one the devil wanted Eve to think about. What will the decisions we make in our minds manifest in the spirit? Had Eve been more focused on her relationships with God and Adam she could have asked herself, "Have I used my mind appropriately and thought completely through all my actions until my innermost being has had a chance to express itself in God?" Our outcomes in life depend on this kind of spiritual thinking. How different things really would have been if only Adam and Eve had done this. They would have gone on to unknown natural and spiritual levels, and we would never have had to learn these same hard lessons. We would effortlessly and straightforwardly walk as spiritual men and women with awesome mental capacities in that physical paradise God created to be a heaven on earth.

Thank God Jesus came as the "second Adam" according to First Corinthians chapter 15, verses 45 through 49. He has restored the ability for mankind to live in the Spirit again by following through with the call of God where Adam failed. Jesus' life was all about the submission of His soul to the Spirit of God. As a result he completely fulfilled and finished the superior plan of God for mankind. His sacrifice was one of soul and body for the freedom of the spirit of man. He did nothing from his own design. Everything Jesus did was purely spiritual in that it was God formatting His every move; and thus absolutely perfect.

If the first couple had thought these questions through and not fallen under the power of sin, they would still have encountered Christ the Lord, because man and woman created by God will always behold and realize their total need to depend on the Godhead, (The Three in One.)

We only lack the perfect physical and mental environment Adam and Eve had originally. I believe our spiritual capacity is potentially even greater than theirs. We now have the opportunity to experience God's plan for our lives through the person and power of Christ Jesus, even though we have all already eaten of the forbidden fruit! Beyond that we have the further opportunity to reflect a degree of the likeness of God to every person we come in contact with. We actually become the physical and mental representation of the Lord to those who so desperately need to encounter Him on a personal level...until He returns!

APRIL 29...DAY 119
TILLING YOUR SPIRITUAL GROUND

"Then to Adam He (God) said,'Because you have heeded the voice of your wife
(who heeded the voice of the serpent), and have eaten from the tree of which
I commanded you...Cursed is the ground for your sake;
in toil you shall eat of it all the days of your life..."
Genesis 3:17 NKJV, (parenthesis mine)

So, let's think it through as we finish our series of devotions on spiritual decisiveness. Adam sinned and we all identify with him in our struggle to throw off the carnal nature. Jesus did not sin, and we can now identify with Him and overcome every obstacle preventing us from returning to a Garden experience of walking in the very image of God!

Ask the right questions in life and you will not only start getting the right answers, but you will also reverse the curse of spiritual death. What is next for you? Where are the consequences of your present actions going to take you? This is the ultimate question for mankind to seriously ponder for the sake of the eternal outcome we will all face one day. All of the questions we find in the story of Adam and Eve are important to a believer who is preparing himself for Jesus' return. Question number 7, "What then will my outcome be?" is the most important step to becoming a spiritually decisive person along the way.

Notice what Jesus said to the Apostle John at the end of the Book of Revelation: "Behold I am coming soon, and I shall bring My wages and rewards with Me, to repay and render to each one just what his own actions and his own work merit. I am the Alpha and the Omega, the First and the Last (the Before all and the End of all). Blessed are those who cleanse their garments that they may have the authority and right to [approach] the tree of Life and to enter through the gates into the (heavenly) city."

This is your chance to get a fresh start. Why not quit working so hard in the "naturally tough" soil we have been killing ourselves to produce from, and start tilling the spiritual ground God originally made to "produce for us." It yields much better results!

APRIL 30...DAY 120
WALK IN THE SPIRIT

"Do you not say, 'There are still four months and then comes the harvest?'
Behold, I say to you, lift up your eyes and look at the fields,
for they are already white for harvest!"
John 4:35 NKJV

Why not give someone the chance to let God radically change their life today by introducing them to Jesus Christ as the One Who forgives and saves. It is a truly "heavy decision" yet we should constantly be giving people the option to "weigh out."

I have found that one of the best ways to maintain clarity in my own spiritual decision making process is to give away the Truth to others. Since spirituality is not something we can just "know" and hoard but rather something we must demonstrate and "walk" in, soul-winning is among our highest responsibilities as believers. It gives us the opportunity to pass along the best of Christianity; the love, hope and faith found in Christ, which are also the eternal ingredients necessary for any heart to find salvation.

Today's nugget of wisdom is a "try it before you buy into it" thing. Now that you've considered the scripture and my comments on the subject, wherever your life takes you for the rest of this day try it out. Look around you for those in God's harvest fields and find openings to tell them about Jesus. The Holy Spirit will do the rest! Some will be takers, most will listen, and a few might even show a little hostility but everyone will be the better for it including you. Test it out after sharing Jesus with someone, and see if you're not feeling better and spiritually stronger yourself.

When it comes to being prepared for the end times there is no better way to keep well equipped than to help someone else find Jesus now!

Rocky Veach

MAY 1...DAY 121
GOD WANTS YOU TO BE WELL!

*"How God anointed Jesus of Nazareth with the Holy Ghost and with power:
who went about doing good, and healing all who were oppressed of the devil;
for God was with Him."*
Acts 10:38 NKJV

God wants you to be well. This is a simple fact of the Christian faith that is seldom taught in many pulpits today. What a shame that Jesus is so clearly portrayed in scripture as the healer of those He encountered, yet so many of His modern followers suffer with sicknesses of every kind. Some even imagine it is God's will under normal conditions to be sick! Even though we are only human and our bodies interact with the diseases that fill this world we live in, Jesus has never changed. He still heals even the most hopeless cases, and if you are suffering you can be sure that He wants to do something about it. What you must do is position yourself to receive what God wants to give you, and you will be able to overcome the obstacles we all face in this life. There are several steps one needs to take in order to do that.

I want to discuss the first step with you today. You must first know the facts and then establish your belief system around God's revealed will. If you are critically ill you cannot afford to accept someone else's word about divine healing, you have to know God's perspective on healing for yourself. Then, you can think and believe properly. Never blindly follow a church that is so satisfied with maintaining a 'nice' congregation that the preacher is afraid to proclaim the truth! Follow the Bible and believe what it says if you want to recover.

Notice how Peter described Jesus' ministry in our text. From this one verse we can begin to understand God's attitude towards oppression and sickness. It is obvious that they go together, and that God is all about eradicating them. He purposefully contrasted Himself with the devil, the oppressor, author of misfortune and perpetrator of illness, by dismissing those enslavements from people's lives. As we draw closer to the end of days health will become a major issue for people on planet earth...make sure you know where you stand by remembering Jesus' stand and His stripes!

MAY 2...DAY 122
JESUS CAN AND WILL HEAL YOU

"...for this purpose the Son of God was manifested,
that He might destroy the works of the devil."
John 3:8 AMP

In the four Gospels there are 41 specific cases of healing which record God's will about sickness and oppression. If you read them all you can only come to one conclusion: God wants people healthy!

Healing was one of the primary ways Jesus destroyed the work of Satan while ministering here on earth. He continually freed people from the clutches of sin, sickness and oppression for the purpose of contrasting the kingdom of darkness against the will and goodness of God's Kingdom before mankind.

When it comes to spiritual realities, we must keep the boundaries clear about who does what, or we run the risk of being deluded and misled as so many will be in the church just prior to the return of the Lord! Today, I want you to notice a particular difference in two biblical cases of healing.

In Mark 1:40-41, a leper approached Jesus begging on his knees and saying, "...If you are willing, you are able to make me clean. And Jesus, moved with compassion, put forth his hand and touched him and said to him, I am willing, be made clean!" In Mark 9:22-23, another man brought his demonized epileptic son to Jesus and, after describing his condition said, "...But if you can do anything, do have pity on us and help us. And Jesus said, [You say to me], If you can do anything? [Why,] all things are possible to him who believes!"

Do you see the difference here? One man knew Jesus could, but wasn't sure if he would. The other had heard that He would but was not sure if Jesus could handle his particularly difficult case. We have to comprehend both characteristics of the Lord. He can and will heal, we simply need to be certain of it.

Both men eventually received what they needed from Jesus, and we have their stories recorded for us in the Bible. We can be in no doubt of God's will. When it comes to illness, all we need is correct information and the faith to believe it!

MAY 3...DAY 123
GET SERIOUS ABOUT YOUR HEALTH

"And He went about all Galilee, TEACHING in their synagogues,
and PREACHING the Gospel of the kingdom, and HEALING all manner of sickness and
all manner of disease among the people."
Matthew 4:23 AMP

The next step in order to overcome ill health is exercising faith after reflecting on what Jesus has said and done in the scriptures regarding this subject. It is one thing to believe God wants to heal you, and another thing to continue believing regardless of what circumstances are thrown your way.

There are many factors in life we cannot control, but there are some we definitely can. Faith is one of them. We need to get God's Word inside our hearts until it begins to flow back out!

If you are sick you simply need to listen to God until you begin to think like Him! Often, however, we are so shallow in spiritual issues we have little or no power over the works of the devil. It will help us to look at our text for today and remember how Jesus conducted His ministry.

Notice that He usually proclaimed Healing before performing it. According to this verse, it seems He did at least twice as much speaking as He did healing! It follows that we will have to do at least twice as much listening to, agreeing with and reiterating those same declarations to encourage belief.

Several people who were healed during Jesus' ministry were helped as a direct result of their own faith. Since the Bible tells us that faith comes by repeatedly hearing God's Word (Romans 10:17), we need to stay in a listening position if we are serious about receiving healing. Notice Luke 5:15. "...and great crowds kept coming together to hear Him and to be healed by Him of their infirmities."

It seems many Christians today would rather be sick than have to 'keep coming' to the Lord or to services designed to fill them with the faith they need to be healed! If you are serious about healing you have to be serious about listening to what Jesus has already said about it...this is the same prescription necessary for being found well and able at His return.

MAY 4...DAY 124
HEALING VS. MEDICINE

"He said to them, 'God, show yourselves to the priests.'
And so it was that as they went they were cleansed."
Luke 17:14 NKJV

Step number three on my list of things you need to do in order to touch the healing power of God is: Don't be stupid! No one should deny the reality of sickness and disease. They are very real killers, who show no partiality. At the same time, we should not deny the reality of God's Word.

According to the Bible (especially the Hebrew and Greek texts), Jesus paid the price necessary for our complete salvation; spirit, soul and body. We are partakers in that salvation, in part while we live on earth and in fullness when Jesus returns. Healing is just an extension of our salvation in Christ and to deny it on the basis of our own personal persuasions or experiences is to be untruthful to scripture.

We can all get stuck in what is familiar to us and miss the higher truths of life. For example, it is not a 'lack of faith' to see a doctor, as some religious extremists preach, unless you are depending on that doctor in a way that puts him or her in the place of God in your life! In the Bible, God obviously condones the use of medicinal treatments to help alleviate the suffering of mankind. He takes exception when someone puts more faith in any idol than in Him.

In the case of the ten lepers, Jesus instructed them to go and get a physical examination by the priests as an obedience to the instructions of the Law and as a proof of the authenticity of their healing (Luke 17:14). In the parable of the Good Samaritan, the Lord commends the fact that this man "treated" the wounds of the beaten stranger he encountered on his journey (Luke 10:34). Doctors often treat many of the physical symptoms we wrestle with and if you have ever been seriously ill you know how necessary their job is. Medicine and divine healing should not stand in opposition to one another. They quite naturally go together since their aim of helping hurting humanity is one and the same. The higher truth, though, is that God alone can treat the spiritual causes behind the physical symptoms we sometimes face. No doctor is able to effectively treat a 'Spirit of Infirmity' (Mark 9:14-29). You will need some prayer, fasting and the leading of God's Spirit for that!

MAY 5...DAY 125
SALVATION VS. HEALING

"When evening came, they brought to Him (Jesus) many who were under the power of demons, and he drove out the spirits with a word and restored to health all who were sick. And thus He fulfilled what was spoken by the prophet Isaiah, 'He Himself took our weaknesses and infirmities and bore away our diseases [Is. 53:4].'"
Matthew 8:17 NKJV

Physical healing is not divided from our spiritual salvation. If you can put together the connection between the two then you should be able to accept the fact that God will heal you. This fact is proven several times in scripture. Get your Bible out and read Isaiah 53:4-5, which is a prophetic look forward to the atonement of Jesus Christ for the sins of mankind. Isaiah refers directly to the One who would bear our "grief and sorrows," being "wounded with stripes that we would be made whole."

The two places in the New Testament which cover the fulfillment of this prophecy in Jesus' life and death tell us everything we need to know about God's idea of healing.

In our text you can see how Jesus brought 'fulfillment' to Isaiah's prophecy about grief and sorrows by physically healing their bodies and casting demons out of their souls! Jesus was not referring to this prophecy as being entirely fulfilled, because the Greek word used for "fulfilled" here is in the Aorist tense which is used to indicate "momentary completed past action" AND "to express future events which must certainly happen"[1]

It is the same word used in Matthew 12:17 where Jesus refers to the fulfillment of another of Isaiah's prophetic utterances concerning the Messiah's anointing to reach and save the Gentile world. The Hebrew language draws no sharp line of distinction between diseases of the soul or mind and those of the body; neither does God nor should we today! Tomorrow, we'll look at the second New Testament proof text.

MAY 6...DAY 126
HIS STRIPES = YOUR HEALING

"Surely He has borne our griefs and carried our sorrows;
Yet we esteemed Him stricken, smitten by God and afflicted.
But He was wounded for our transgressions, He was bruised for our iniquities;
the chastisement of our peace was upon Him, and by His stripes we are healed."
Isaiah 53:4-5 NKJV

"He personally bore our sins in His own body on the tree cross),that we might die to sin and live to righteousness. By His wounds you have been healed."
1 Peter 2:24 NKJV

Yesterday we looked at the first New Testament connector to Isaiah 53:4-5. Here is a second foundational scripture which proves the unmistakable connection between salvation and healing. Not surprisingly, this is another passage that opponents to physical healing use to "prevent" people from believing God in this area.

The problem for that perspective is that 1 Peter 2:24, like Matthew 8:17, is a direct reference to Isaiah 53:4-5. Therefore, we have another passage of scripture with emphasis on our spiritual salvation. But when you look a little closer it has a deeper meaning for us to realize.

According to early twentieth century Greek scholar, Dr. T.J. McCrossan, the word used for healing cannot be taken to mean only salvation. It is the "1st Aorist passive, 2nd person plural of the deponent verb *iaomai* a word that always in the New Testament refers to physical healing.[2] Now, I am no linguistic scholar myself, but I can certainly study and examine the works of those who are. Bible lexicons also tell me that it is the same tense used in other passages which refer to our salvation, such as Romans 5:6 and 1 Corinthians 15:3. This proves that not only did Christ's redemptive work make it possible for God to save every sinner who will meet the needful conditions of repentance and faith in God, but He also made it possible for every sick person to be healed by praying the prayer of faith.

Don't let sickness keep you from meeting the Lord at His coming...stay saved AND healed AND complete!!

MAY 7...DAY 127
THE HONEST APPROACH TO THE LAST DAYS

"And He was teaching daily in the temple. But the chief priests, the scribes, and the leaders of the people sought to destroy Him, and were unable to do anything; for all the people were very attentive to hear Him."
Luke 19:47-48 NKJV

To arrive where God wants to take us, we must first accurately determine where we now are. The religious leaders of Jesus' day could not see their need for salvation or healing, and as a result the Lord passed them by in favor of those who knew they needed a savior and physician. Their 'religious' convictions alone could not help them connect with the life and power of the Spirit, which flowed out from the Son of God.

We must be careful to not make the same mistake of letting our viewpoint hinder us from recognizing and receiving the blessings He has promised us! To thoroughly discuss healing we have to place down a foundation of honesty. In the church world today there are no lack of opinions and allegiances. I have found that most believers, (and especially their leaders), find it daunting to wander any distance outside the organizations they serve. Their teachings mimic their teachers instead of the Great Teacher, creating doctrines that lean on the letter of the Bible but fatally lack the Spirit of His Word.

The primary context of scripture is its spiritual underpinning. Holy men of God wrote the Bible through the inspiration of the Holy Spirit. Today's wannabe holy men scrape God's heart out of the Word by stirring the importance of logic and reason.

If you read your entire Bible, which will put you in a very select company, you will find that by far the majority of it is not written in language that is appealing to the natural human mindset. No matter how intelligent you are or how much you pride yourself on your diligent study, you will still need the Holy Spirit to REVEAL the deep hidden meaning of the material and how it applies to your life. No wonder the church in America has recently gone through a long period statistical non-growth! We try to reach the hearts of 'big-time' sinners with 'small-time' anemic academic messages. Be honest with yourself today...that approach won't cut to the heart of the matter in the last days!

MAY 8...DAY 128
GOD'S LAST LOOK

"And Jesus went into Jerusalem and into the temple.
So when He had looked around at all things, as the hour was already late,
He went out to Bethany with the twelve."
Mark 11:11 NKJV

What was so important that Jesus was willing to travel into Jerusalem and browse around the temple courts in the late afternoon or early evening...only to leave and return the next day bringing punishment? Notice the verse says that He didn't just glance around but checked out "all things!"

Although He already knows the ramifications, it seems God is interested in minutely examining suspicious situations. This is what He did when He sent angels down to check out Sodom and Gomorrah (Genesis 18:21). Why is this?

I think He goes the extra mile to allow us more time, or exceptional grace to spin ungodly activities around. Could it be that before final judgment comes for a person or place God enters the scene in some manner to allow an acknowledging response to His Presence and a decisive behavioral adjustment?

By direction of the Holy Spirit, Peter gave both Ananias and his wife Sapphira last minute opportunities to repent, though neither chose to do so. Through Moses, God exerted ten miraculous plagues in advance of Pharaoh's total destruction!

God is truly good, but let's not forget that Jesus returned to the temple in striking mode and "cleaned house." In Mark 13:2, He prophesied its total destruction which was fulfilled in 70 A.D.

I see an end-time parody being played out in the last few days of Jesus' life as a warning to all future generations. "THE HOUR WAS ALREADY LATE," reads the next phrase in Mark 11:11 but the moneychangers and their politically inclined religious leader/brokers did not realize it. They were beaten and driven out of God's courts for missing God's final appraisal...let's invite Him instead inside to examine our temples, help us clean up our act and not make the same mistake in our generation!

MAY 9...DAY 129
THE LINE YOU CAN'T CROSS

"This I say, therefore, and testify in the lord, that you should no longer walk as the rest of the Gentiles walk, in the futility of their mind, having their understanding darkened, being alienated from the life of God, because of the ignorance that is in them, because of the blindness of their heart, who, being past feeling, have given themselves over the lewdness, to work all uncleanness with greediness. But you have not so learned Christ..."
Ephesians 4:17-20 NKJV

There are many lines laid out for us in scripture that serve as reminders to identify those things that are in and out of bounds. Verse seventeen serves as one clear boundary for every Christian. Stay on one side of it and you will not only find your way into God's will for your own life, but you will also fit into His master design as He builds His people together into an ever-increasing expression of Himself!

On this "church" (Greek meaning: Those called out together into a public forum) side you will find five different kinds of gifts Jesus has conferred to those who represent aspects of Himself, the Great Teacher. These preachers and leaders (verse 11) train the people of God, equipping them to grow and develop into an extension or "Body" of the Lord. Jesus Himself serving as their head and heart.

On the other side of this line, however, there are also five things mentioned that are often displayed in a "borderline" believer's life, which are clearly not learned from the Lord. Darkness, alienation, ignorance, blindness and callousness are all to be found on the wrong side of the scriptural tracts. Each is an extension of the confusion that comes from not knowing Jesus. The line itself is demarcated in our thinking, determined by whether we choose to walk inside or outside the limits of a personal relationship with the Lord.

As the end-times draw nearer there will be an increase of churched people choosing to live outside the boundaries of true spiritual life. Let's learn righteous things, from the right representatives, now. Be saved and walk completely out of your past...while it's still today,. . .while the lines, at least in your Bible, are still to be found legible and defined!

MAY 10...DAY 130
THE LINE WORTH WALKING

"I, therefore, the prisoner of the Lord, beseech you to walk worthy of the calling with which you were called, with all lowliness and gentleness, with longsuffering, bearing with one another in love, endeavoring to keep the unity of the Spirit in the bond of peace."
Ephesians 4:1-3 NKJV

"This I say, therefore, and testify in the Lord, that you should no longer walk as the rest of the Gentiles walk, in the futility of their mind, having their understanding darkened, being alienated from the life of God, because of the ignorance that is in them, because of the blindness of their heart, who, being past feeling, have given themselves over to the lewdness, to work all uncleanness with greediness. But you have not so learned Christ..."
Ephesians 4:17-20 NKJV

Did you notice how Paul chose the word "walk," first at the beginning, and then again in the middle of this important Bible chapter? His choice identifies the overarching theme for this section of his letter to this local church.

These believers needed to conduct their lives in a purposeful manner, like a man does when he is "walking." It is the same Greek word in both verse one and seventeen, meaning to "tread all around." This illustration served to describe how there are two ways a believer can occupy his time and build a lifestyle. In other words, however we consistently walk is the true indication of who we really are. For these Christians, the Apostle who once led them to the faith was drawing a line of distinction between the way they had previously walked and the way in which their lifestyles would be worthy of the Lord. Notice, he begins his list of expectations for everyday godly behavior by first referring to himself as the Lord's "prisoner." Paul connects our ability to serve the Lord appropriately to the required position of being an absolute servant.

No one will walk very far with Jesus who has not made Him the "Lord" or master of their life(style). Only then can we remain humble, teachable, patient, peaceful and in harmony with other believers. Without this spiritual mindset, our entire process of thinking will gradually slip back to a world-based way of viewing things through the dark (futile or vain, verse 17) lens of self. In view of the end times, we will need all the light we can get!

MAY 11...DAY 131
THE GREAT MAKEOVER

"But you have not so learned Christ, if indeed you have heard Him and have been taught by Him, as the truth is in Jesus: that you put off, concerning your former conduct, the old man which grows corrupt according to the deceitful lusts, and be renewed in the spirit of your mind, and that you put on the new man which was created according to God, in true righteousness and holiness."
Ephesians 4:20-24 NKJV

There is an "old man" to put off and a "new man" for every Christian to put on. In between there is this all important process of "mind renewal," by which a person can be transformed from a state of unrighteousness to righteousness, ungodliness to holiness. I like to call this the "Great Makeover."

Since I have five daughters, I am way too aware of how many fashion shows are on TV. One of them is about extraordinary makeovers, or cases where they take a very plain looking and poorly dressed person and upgrade them into the world of modern fashion. The catch is whether or not this person can adapt and be flexible enough to learn new ways of expressing themselves. In other words, they put off their old man and put on a newer version...same as our text today!

The hardest part of any kind of renewal is the decision to make a change. In order to "reform" (Greek synonym for "renewed") spiritually one has to work on the disposition or "spirit" of their mind and then keep working at it! The benefit of being born again is that you have a recreated spirit deep within your being to draw from, whereas the unbeliever has a darkened understanding and a blinded heart.

The best thing you can do to prepare for the end times is to get saved, if you question your salvation or never have given your life over to Christ. Keep putting on that garment of salvation if you are saved! You are going to need a daily makeover until Jesus comes to reveal the completed you. Until that day, make sure you reapply "learning" so you will continually become the latest greatest model of the ever renewing you!!

MAY 12...DAY 132
THREE KINDS OF PEOPLE
#1 NATURAL MAN & SPIRITUAL MAN

"But the natural man does not receive the things of the Spirit of God, for they are foolishness to him; nor does he know them, because they are spiritually discerned. But he who is spiritual judges all things, yet he himself is rightly judged by no one...And I, brethren, could not speak to you as spiritual people but as to carnal, as to babes in Christ."
1 Corinthians 2:14-15; 3:1 NKJV

Paul mentions three kinds of people every believer must be alerted to. The funny thing is that you will not only find them all around you, but you can find them all inside you!! Knowing who is who on this list will help you figure yourself out spiritually. It will also allow you to grasp where others are coming from. The less you know the more vulnerable you are to dysfunction, deception and danger, especially in light of our subject of end-times living!

Paul first points out the "natural" man. This is the guy (or gal) who cannot receive or appreciate spiritual things, primarily because they have not been saved and made new in the innermost part of their being or spirit. One of the shades of meaning for the word "receive" in verse fourteen is "to grant access as to a visitor." An unsaved person cannot receive the things of God because they are spiritual in nature (John 4:24), and they have never granted God's Spirit the initial access to themselves that is required for salvation.

Secondly, there is the "spiritual" man referred to in verse fifteen. This person is saved and has experienced the movement and communication of the Holy Spirit within himself. This intimate knowledge causes him to respond to the truth and, through God's communication with him, to be able to develop in the life-long process of spiritual maturity. Such a man or woman is able to actually tap into the "mind of Christ" (1 Corinthians 2:16) as he or she walks with the Lord. They are also able to discern the will of God, through a kind of extraordinary spiritual sensitivity.

Tomorrow, we'll discuss the most dangerous of all...number three on our list, the "Carnal" man!

MAY 13...DAY 133
3 KINDS OF PEOPLE...
#2 THE CARNAL MAN

"And I, brethren, could not speak to you as spiritual people but as to carnal, as to babes in Christ." I fed you with milk and not with solid food; for until now you were not able to receive it, and even now you are still not able; for you are still carnal. For where there are envy, strife, and divisions among you,
are you not carnal and behaving like mere men?"
1 Corinthians 3:1-3 NKJV

"For everyone who partakes only of milk is unskilled in the word of righteousness, for he is a babe. But solid food belongs to those who are of full age, that is, those who by reason of use have their senses exercised to
discern both good and evil."
Hebrews 5:12-14 NKJV

Inside every true Christian there is both an "old" or natural man, and a "new" or spiritual man. Even though a person is saved he still has to contend with the old nature which works through his "flesh" or sensory appetites.

When a believer continually yields to those physical instincts instead of the spiritual nature God has given him at his "new birth"(salvation), New Testament writers refer to him as "carnal." He is saved but in his preferences, desires, and emotions he is living as though he is not. As this category of believer continues deeper into this condition, he is described (Hebrews 6) as becoming more and more dangerous to himself and others!

Notice today, how the Bible specifically defines a "carnal" Christian for us. These verses say they are sectarian in their affiliations, childish in their tastes and capacity for spiritual things, unstable in their emotions and divisive troublemakers in their behavior! The most telling thing of all, they are unskilled in the Word of God, valuing human opinion above truth!

These verses can be used as a checklist to rate our own current spiritual foundation level, with a goal towards building a more godly lifestyle. Beware of the carnal Christian. They are growing in number as we approach the last days. It seems they are everywhere today...have you checked your own backyard?!

MAY 14...DAY 134
WHEN THE LORD TURNS TO TALK TO YOU

"From that time Jesus began to show to His disciples that He must go to Jerusalem, and suffer many things from the elders and chief priests and scribes, and be killed, and be raised the third day. Then Peter took Him aside and began to rebuke Him, saying, 'Far be it from You, Lord; this shall not happen to You!' But He turned and said to Peter, 'Get behind Me, Satan! You are an offense to Me, for you are not mindful of the things of God, but the things of men.'"
Matthew 16:21-23 NKJV

When Jesus "turns" around in scripture to address someone, it is either remarkably good or extremely bad! We find this happening on at least nine separate occasions throughout the four Gospels. The statistics are interesting. Four times, Jesus turned to speak to someone for the purpose of rebuke or correction, twice involving Peter! Another four instances were to give encouragement or approval. In two cases Jesus noted the importance of a person's faith in receiving a miracle from Him!

In Luke 7:44, the Lord did both. Jesus rebuked the religious leader (Simon, a Pharisee) for not doing enough to honor him as a guest in his house, while simultaneously accepting the worship of one of that town's most famous sinners and forgiving her for her sin!!

My main point today is this friendly reminder - the last days are a good time to think about getting God's attention even if it means being "straightened out" by Him first! The Bible is clear in teaching how God corrects those He loves, sometimes rather severely, because he is a Father.

Calling out Satan right in the midst of a conversation with Peter is a perfect example! It must have been hard on Peter's psyche but it paid dividends later when, after he blatantly denied Jesus, he was able to make a "RE-TURN" and lead the early church in the footsteps of the Lord.

No one is called to be perfect, we all make mistakes, sometimes really big ones, but we are expected to pick ourselves up and keep following God...especially in the end of days, when the world will need to see examples of people who have looked the Lord in the eye and lived to tell about it!

MAY 15...DAY 135
PSUCHE VS. ZOE

*"I am the door. If anyone enters by Me, he will be saved, and will go in and out and find pasture. The thief does not come except to steal, and to kill, and to destroy. I have come that they may have LIFE and that they may have it more abundantly. I am the good shepherd. The good shepherd gives his LIFE for the sheep...As the Father knows Me, even so I know the Father; and I lay down My LIFE for the sheep...Therefore My Father loves Me because I lay down My LIFE that I may take it again...My sheep hear My voice, and I know them, and they follow Me.
And I give them eternal LIFE, and they shall never perish;
neither shall anyone snatch them out of My hand."
John 10:10-11, 15, 17, 27-28 NKJV*

I have highlighted the word "life" in the five places it is found in this segment of scripture to make our point for today.

In the English language it appears as the same word in every instance, but in the original language of the New Testament there are two separate words with distinct literal and connotative differences. The first one, found in verse 10, is the Greek word, "zoe," which describes the essential vitality that physically animates a person. To the one who chooses salvation, Jesus promises to take this to an abundant (v. 10) and eternal (v. 28) level! Then there is the second word, "psuche," found in verses 11, 15 and 17, from which we get the English word, "psyche." This word is often translated, "soul" and refers to life more in the sense of the mind, will and emotions of a person.

The way it is used in our text shows how Jesus specifically laid down His life. He gave His soul or power of choice, feeling and intelligence, completely over to death for the salvation of people's most intrinsic life quality. So, Jesus traded "psuche" or His personal idea of life (awareness of self), for something deeper, "zoe" or life itself! As we will see tomorrow, this is what we are also called to continue to do ...until Jesus comes again!

MAY 16...DAY 136
THE TASTE OF DEATH

"Then Jesus said to His disciples, 'If anyone desires to come after Me, let him deny himself, and take up his cross, and follow Me. For whoever desires to save his life will lose it, but whoever loses his life for My sake will find it. For what profit is it to a man if he gains the whole world, and loses his own soul? Or what will a man give in exchange for his soul? For the Son of Man will come in the glory of His Father with His angels, and then He will reward each according to his works. Assuredly, I say to you, there are some standing here who shall not taste death till they see the Son of Man coming in His kingdom.'"
Matthew 16:24-28 NKJV

Right after Jesus rebuked Peter for having a "mind full" ("mindful," verse 23) of the devil we uncover an expose on true life. I find it very revealing that the Lord uses the same basic word, "come" in verse 24 and "coming" in verse 28 to teach us one of the most important principles of the Christian faith. Essentially He was foretelling that His three closest disciples, Peter, James and John, were about to witness a vivid representation of the highest expression of supernatural life on the "Mount of Transfiguration" seven days later...and that those who were willing to go through God's process of "tasting death" could experience a similar kind of life transformation themselves! Jesus was "setting them up" to "come" to God in the right mode then experience the influence of the Holy Spirit to an unusual degree.

Notice that you find the words "life and soul" used four times in our text. These are all from the word, "psuche" in the Greek language. Jesus is talking about the part of a person that is most aware of and concerned about self. The Lord puts into words, in verses 24 through 27, the process of dying to self He Himself exemplified in His own everyday life. The explosions of miraculous life we see in the ministry of Jesus were simply expressions of the fact that his normal human life was totally engaged in the service of God. Not only Jesus' death but also His life teaches us that if we are first willing to taste death we will enjoy the fullness of eternal life, even while we are living on planet earth!

MAY 17...DAY 137
THE PROCESS OF LIFE

"Then Jesus said to His disciples, 'If anyone desires to come after Me, let him deny himself, and take up his cross, and follow Me. For whoever desires to save his life will lose it, but whoever loses his life for My sake will find it. For what profit is it to a man if he gains the whole world, and loses his own soul? Or what will a man give in exchange for his soul? For the Son of Man will come in the glory of His Father with His angels, and then He will reward each according to his works.'"
Matthew 16:24-27 NKJV

As we discussed yesterday, there is "process" of self death Jesus' disciples are called to suffer that produces eternal life. The Lord Himself was the living example of this lesson, teaching us how a person can really live his or her life wholly for God. It is important to understand the prime hindrance to this process is revealed to Peter before Jesus tells us what it is.

Tomorrow we will discuss the most important word in verse 23, "offense." Today let's look at the four steps every person who has a desire to follow God's plan for their life must take. Step one is "the denial," found in verse 24. A Christian intent on being prepared for Jesus' return, must deny HIMSELF. You cannot serve two masters. It is impossible to live for you and God at the same time!

Step two, found in verse 25, is "the death." Jesus called this the "cross" and told His followers they must carry it even before He physically did so on the way to his literal death! It is not nearly as thorny to die as a martyr for the Lord (and this will be a requirement for many end times saints), if you are already dying for Him in the desires and choices of daily life.

Step three is, "the deal," found in verse 26. An exchange is necessary...God's life for your soul. In other words, we trade in our love for this world for the firsthand experience of God's love for us!

Finally, step four is "the dividends." Jesus promises two kinds of rewards to those who practice this lifestyle...the ultimate blessings of an eternity spent enjoying the realms of heaven, and the transformation into a reflector of God's light and glory even while serving His interests here on earth!

MAY 18...DAY 138
AVOID THE DEVIL'S TRAP

"But He turned and said to Peter, 'Get behind Me, Satan! You are an offense to Me, for you are not mindful of the things of God, but the things of men."
Matthew 16:23 NKJV

There are so many good things ahead of the believer who lays down his life for the Lord. But they will only happen if we get our biggest problem behind us! What is our biggest dilemma? We could blame it on the devil, and he is obviously part of the equation according to our scripture for today. We could also blame it on ourselves as we find the word, "Me" in this sentence more than once.

The hidden factor, however, is neatly packaged right there between these two words. It is that ordinary little unassuming word, "offense." This is an interesting Greek word referring to the trigger of a trap, the particular mechanism which when tripped causes an unsuspecting victim to be ensnared.

One thing you can't afford in the last days is to get caught off-guard as a result of ignorance of the devil's devices or overconfidence in yourself! You must know that Satan combines these two conditions in formulating his custom-fitted plan of attack against you. As with Peter, he will often use our strengths against us by baiting us into an emotional arena where we will automatically employ our weaknesses. The purpose is to get your attention and energy misdirected towards the things that are meaningful to men instead of God.

When this happens a person actually begins to think they are being righteous when, in fact, they are exemplifying just the opposite. Jesus was much too smart for this simple deceptive approach. It usually takes time and practice for us to discern. Keep Satan and your weaknesses behind you by learning to remain "offense free." If you do it now, you will avoid end-time traps in the future that could be coming up to bring you down!

MAY 19...DAY 139
TAKE THE GATE...ESCAPING OFFENSES

"Then He said to the disciples, 'It is impossible that no offenses should come, but woe to him through whom they do come! It would be better for him if a millstone were hung around his neck, and he were thrown into the sea, than that he should offend one of these little ones. Take heed to yourselves. If your brother sins against you, rebuke him; and if he repents, forgive him. And if he sins against you seven times in a

day, and seven times in a day returns to you, saying, 'I repent,' you shall forgive him.'
And the apostles said to the Lord, 'Increase our faith.'"
Luke 17:1-5 NKJV

My pastor, Neil Miers, has often made a statement, both in private and from the pulpit that speaks loudly in my ears whenever things get ugly in the ministry. In his native Australian inflection he will say, "If you're going to take offense, mate, make sure you take the gate (of the "fence") with you to let yourself out later!" True wisdom, spoken in everyday terms by a true man of God, that will help you stay sweet when things turn sour, especially as a believer.

Most Christians never imagine they will encounter worldly problems in the church until it happens. There is a reason the New Testament spends so much time explaining how to behave in the house of God. Paul goes to great length in his letters to the churches he founded (i.e. Corinthians, Galatians, Thessalonians etc.) to warn them about lapsing into carnal sins such as envy, jealousy and strife. Why? Because these will "fence" the "sheep" into dangerous territories and stop a "flock" from finding the lush pastures or peaceful waters God has intended.

Notice Jesus commands us to "take heed to yourselves" in our text for today. This means to "hold these thoughts in your mind" or pay close attention. Offenses are hurt feelings, resentments and the anger that grows in our hearts as a result of negative relational issues. They are guaranteed to sinner and saint alike in this fallen world and the only way out of one is through the gate of honesty, humility and forgiveness. Don't be caught without a way of escape! Check your heart and do whatever is necessary, and possible, to make things right with your brother...in order to be ready to meet your heavenly Father!

MAY 20...DAY 140
THE RIGHT "SLANT" ON DISCIPLESHIP

"Therefore gird up the loins of your mind, be sober, and rest your hope fully upon the grace that is to be brought to you at the revelation of Jesus Christ; as obedient children, not conforming yourselves to the former lusts, as in your ignorance; but as He who called you is holy, you also be holy in all your conduct, because it is written, 'Be holy, for I am holy.'"
1 Peter 1:13-16 NKJV

I recently read about an interesting group of public schools called the KIPP (Knowledge Is Power Program) schools, a national network of 99 public charter schools in 20 states and Washington, DC. They originated as a single school in one of the poorest neighborhoods in Houston, Texas during the mid 1990's. Their vision is to help inner-city kids learn the skills necessary to qualify for first-rate colleges and beyond.

The result has been that these minority and reduced income kids do as well by the eighth grade as other children across America from more affluent neighborhoods; especially in mathematics. The thing that caught my attention was the founder's simple yet highly effective code of behavior, which drives these students to success. It is packaged in the acronym, "SLANT" and should be memorized by any student wanting to prepare for the next level of life...including Christians wanting to be ready for Jesus return! Here is what it stands for: Smile and Sit up, Listen, Ask questions, Nod when being spoken to, and Track with your eyes.

How amazing is that? Isn't this what most civilized people should have been taught in school from a very young age? More importantly, this is what the Bible teaches about honor and respect. This system has a profound effect upon a person's ability to break free of the restrictions of their environment!

The Apostle Paul taught his disciples to be imitators of both God and himself (as he followed God). Jesus modeled the same approach in training His closest disciples to literally "follow" Him.

What works as a KIPP school kid's ticket to a better life will also work as your voucher to the next life...so SLANT yourself toward Christ's return!! (The above information on KIPP was taken from the book, "Outliers," by Malcolm Gladwell; 2008, Little, Brown and Company. All KIPP schools are public schools and are non-secular).

MAY 21...DAY 141
SUPERNATURAL TECHNOLOGY

"Those who are wise shall shine like the brightness of the firmament, and those who turn many to righteousness like the stars forever and ever. But you, Daniel, shut up the words, and seal the book until the time of the end; many shall run to and fro, and knowledge shall increase...Although I heard, I did not understand. Then I said, 'My lord, what shall be the end of these things?' And he said, 'Go your way, Daniel, for the words are closed up and sealed till the time of the end. Many shall be purified, made white and refined, but the wicked shall do wickedly; and none of the wicked shall understand.'"
Daniel 12:3-4, 8-10 NKJV

The Bible tells us that there will be a generation of end-time believers who will experience an 'unsealed' walk with the Lord and will do extraordinary things, (even by Biblical standards) as a result of their understanding and familiarity with His ways. Christians should live in expectation of the return of the Lord because spiritually it will be our finest hour!

The Bible educates and trains us for this walk in two important ways. One is the reality of God. His Word is, by its very nature, above and beyond what is usual or normal from our human perspective. It is a collection of spiritually inspired revelation handed down through history for the enlightenment and salvation of each successive generation. In a word it is 'supernatural.'

Secondly, inspired scripture is a tool for advancement. It is also a method by which we achieve the practical purposes God has designed for our lives. By studying the Bible we begin to recognize the patterns of intelligent obedience that have made others great and as a result, learn to be great in God ourselves.

It only stands to reason that end-time Bible believers will be more 'high-tech' than any other previous generation. So, start getting ready for a master display of the fruit of the two trees that God placed in the original Garden of Eden. The culmination of everything that has been sown in the history of mankind will climax in the days just before Jesus' return.

There will be a harvest of righteousness, and of unrighteousness! The technology of the Tree of the Knowledge of Good and Evil and the technology of the Tree of Life will come to their ultimate fruition. Both "technologies" will continue to escalate among mankind, with the clash between the two pushing the planet to the brink of extermination before Jesus returns. So, let's get back to an understanding of the things of God today...so we can start shining before the seals are broken. (Revelation 5-11).

MAY 22...DAY 142
CONSCIOUS OF GOD?

"But sanctify the Lord God in your hearts, and always be ready to give a defense to everyone who asks you a reason for the hope that is in you, with meekness and fear; having a good conscience, that when they defame you as evildoers, those who revile your good conduct in Christ may be ashamed."
1 Peter 3:15-16 NKJV

The Bible says much about the importance of a person's conscience and its role in effectively walking with God. However, the modern world is crammed with an ever-increasing variety of available distractions that damage the moral compass of mankind. By taking a closer look at what 'conscience' is and what scripture teaches about it, we can learn how to steer clear of spiritual danger and more consciously follow God's will for our lives.

My Oxford's Dictionary defines conscience as, "a moral sense of right and wrong, especially as felt by a person and affecting behavior, or an inner feeling as to the goodness or otherwise of one's behavior." Isn't it amazing that all people, even the scholars among us, recognize the existence of this instinctive feeling or sixth sense, which lies deep within us? Yet, in spite of this, many Christians today often seem bent on ignoring it! According to its very definition, our conscience exists to tell us not only what is wrong, but also what is right and, most importantly, the difference between the two!

The Greek word for conscience is "suneidesis." It literally means "co-perception", or "co-knowledge" with one's self. This tells us that we are not left totally on our own. God put a little something else within us in order to help us make good decisions. When we get to the bottom of conscience, we find that we are truly more than just another animal on this planet. We have an inner security system into which God has breathed a portion of His own Spirit. Whether we explore deep enough to locate what God is saying within and learn to work with Him is up to us, but God definitely designed us to have the option.

Despite what many think, a minister's job is not primarily to tell people what to do or make decisions for them. Their conscience within them already does that. A Pastor's job is to reinforce one's functioning conscience, encouraging and warning believer's to be mindful of and ready to meet the Lord!

MAY 23...DAY 143
IS YOUR CONSCIENCE CLEAR?

"Then Paul, looking earnestly at the council, said, "Men and brethren, 'I have lived in all good conscience before God until this day.'"
Acts 23:1 NKJV

"Therefore I exercise and discipline myself [mortifying my body, deadening my carnal affections, bodily appetites, and worldly desires, [endeavoring in all respects] to have a clear (unshaken, blameless) conscience, void of offense toward God and toward men." Acts 24:16 AMP

If a man of the Apostle Paul's spiritual stature puts this echelon of importance on conscience, it is equally important for our spiritual development and success. Let's highlight other scriptures in this devotional that give us further insight on the need for a healthy inner perception of right and wrong.

1 Timothy chapter one warns us that our Faith can be "shipwrecked," our love stunted, and our heart tainted if we are not firmly founded with a good and strong conscience. Even in Christianity's earliest days some men rapidly "swerved" from this truth and were divided by rejecting the warning signals of their consciences.

Chapter three and verse nine of this same New Testament book lists one of the main qualifications of future church leaders as "holding the mystery of the faith in a pure conscience." The fourth chapter of 1 Timothy verse one cautions us about the culture we will find in the last days. Verse 2 then tells us why there will be a great departing from the faith. Seducing spirits and demons that teach false doctrines will literally find their way into the church through people who "Speak lies in hypocrisy; having their conscience seared (like) with a hot iron…!"

Romans 2:15 teaches us that all men will answer to God based on whether their own individual consciences accuse or excuse their responses and actions now. 1 Corinthians chapters eight and ten reveal that conscience can be weak or strong based on a person's individual knowledge. The scripture demands we be careful not only to protect our own conscience, but also those of others. According to Hebrews chapters nine and ten, only the blood of Jesus, as it is applied through repentance and faith, can cleanse and purge people's tainted consciences and restore a state of "God-consciousness" to them.

We all need to examine our conscience periodically to make sure we are doing the right thing in life…it is a key to being ready for Jesus when He returns!

MAY 24…DAY 144
LISTEN AND LEARN

"I still have many things to say to you, but you cannot bear them now. However, when He, the Spirit of Truth has come, He will guide you into all Truth; for He will not speak of His own authority, but He whatever He hears He will speak; and He will tell you things to come. He will glorify Me, for He will take of what is Mine and declare it to you."
John 16:12-14 NKJV

Have you ever wondered how much vital information you may be missing simply because you cannot hear God clearly when He speaks to you? According to the Bible this is a common problem which can affect anyone, but can be overcome by those who are willing to learn how to listen.

If we want to hear and are able to adjust to His way of communication, God will give us the answers and ideas we need to excel in life. The secret to hearing God's voice is found in tuning our ears to the source of all truth. Many times in the four Gospels Jesus commands those who have ears to 'listen', in a higher sense of the word, to gain understanding about what is available to them. More often than not, though, the very people He spoke to directly were the ones who could not understand what He was talking about! They were only listening with their natural minds and thus were prevented from receiving the supernatural instruction they needed. Simultaneously, other less 'learned' listeners would seemingly emerge from the crowds and effortlessly receive the miracles they so desperately needed. The latter heard the spirit of what Jesus was saying and were empowered to receive the full authority of His words.

Remember we saw this same condition in 1 Corinthians 3:1. And then in Hebrews 5:11 we found the exact same problem again! (See May 12 & 13) Spiritual "dullness" is a common problem in any church or era, but will be at its apex just before Jesus returns...make sure you are an uncommon believer if you want to be ready!

MAY 25...DAY 145
FOLLOW THE LEADER TO
LEAD THE FOLLOWERS

"However, when He, the Spirit of Truth has come, He will guide you into all Truth; for He will not speak of His own authority, but He whatever He hears He will speak; and He will tell you things to come. He will glorify Me, for He will take of what is Mine and declare it to you."
John 16:13-14 NKJV

According to our text, the Holy Spirit is the heavenly messenger and tour guide for our spiritual expedition throughout this life. His job is to 'lead' us into all truth and our job is to 'follow' as we are being groomed to be Jesus' "body" or His spiritual leadership on the earth. The problem is that too many believers want to lead before they know how to 'be led!'

It is a very real and present danger that so many churches are occupied by unspiritual people with carnally oriented leaders, all trying to convince unbelievers to obey the God they do not listen to themselves! In this way the church shames itself without even realizing it, giving society a license to label it as outdated and hypocritical.

We can only become light to humanity by first learning to be enlightened by the Holy Spirit. Notice how the Spirit of God was provided in the absence of Jesus Himself to equip believers with everything needed to successfully navigate through this life for God.

The word 'guide' here literally means that God's Spirit has been given to us as our 'conductor' or 'route leader.' If we are willing to follow and do things His way, the Bible tells us that He will take us where we need to go in order to fulfill our destiny; which is God's will. He will helm and pilot the business of the church in such a way to cause it to be a conductor of His business!

"Learning to be led" becomes your life's map through this lost world, and a marker of God's hidden treasures for other seeking souls!

MAY 26...DAY 146
THREE FACETS OF SPIRITUAL LEADERSHIP

"However, when He, the Spirit of Truth has come, He will guide you into all Truth; for He will not speak of His own authority, but He whatever He hears He will speak; and He will tell you things to come. He will glorify Me, for He will take of what is Mine and declare it to you. All things that the Father has are Mine. Therefore I said that He will take of Mine and declare it to you."
John 16:13-15 NKJV

There are three specific areas of knowledge the Holy Spirit wants to introduce into us for purposes of leadership. Firstly, He guides us into the proper expression of God. He doesn't speak on His own behalf or with the warped, confused and selfish ambition of evil spirits. Because He too is an adept follower, He can expertly convey precisely what Jesus wants communicated to His church. Just as the Lord spoke to His followers when He was incarnate, so He still speaks clearly to us today when we listen to the inner urgings of the Holy Spirit.

Secondly, Jesus said the Spirit would foster accurate understanding of the deep, secret things God has reserved for us. When God decides to speak and we determine to listen with our heart, we attain the ability to know what is ahead of us.

In Matthew 16:18 Jesus said the disclosure of hidden spiritual information is the very foundation on which He would build the church and empower it to prevail.

Thirdly, the Holy Spirit's purpose is to glorify, or to exalt and honor Jesus Christ. Have you ever tried to pray directly to the Holy Spirit? He will always redirect and point our focus to Jesus. He does this by taking the Lord's words and transmitting them to us. The result is that we have access to consistent answers for every circumstance that Jesus confronted while on earth and that we presently face. We become His extension in this world, saying what He said, doing what He did while giving Him all the credit. The literal job description of the church is to keep the spiritual cycle of godly honor going! He honors us so we will honor Him so He can continue to honor us so we can continue to honor Him...until there is so much Jesus worship in His church that it creates an environment where His Presence abides to the extent that there is no visible separation between Christ and His body!!

MAY 27...DAY 147
THREE AVENUES OF SPIRITUAL INFLUENCE

"However, when He, the Spirit of Truth has come, He will guide you into all Truth; for He will not speak of His own authority, but He whatever He hears He will speak; and He will tell you things to come. He will glorify Me, for He will take of what is Mine and declare it to you."
John 16:13-14 NKJV

The role of spiritual leadership is a serious concern for any Christian. The Holy Spirit's job is to guide us into absolute Truth by taking who/what Jesus is/has then transferring these characteristics and dynamics to us. As a result we gain something real which is spiritual in origin to offer and to help lead others. The more proficient we become at following God, the more able we are to influence others for Him. This is spiritual leadership.

According to our scripture, Jesus subtly tells us there are three general avenues by which the Holy Spirit influences believers. Notice that He specifically helps us to first RECOGNIZE the voice of the Lord. He then moves to RELAY what Jesus is saying to His followers. Finally, the Holy Spirit REVEALS the meaning of what has been said. If you want to be someone who goes beyond lip service to fulfill the will of God for your life, then you must learn the language of the Holy Spirit, follow His lead, and lead others to follow Him.

Modern computer technology is based on the concept of 'Pattern Recognition.' The higher the capability a computer model has of recognizing the patterns that are encoded in various kinds of software, the more useful it is to its owner. In the same way the more sensitive we are to the Holy Spirit and His patterns of leadership the more useful we become at training, mentoring and supervising other believers who are less qualified than ourselves. We have to realize ahead of time that The Holy Spirit is going to speak to us in ways that are often foreign to the way we think, and introduce us to experiences we have never had before.

God is a spirit and so are we, but this mind and body we are encased in while on earth orients us toward relying on reason and logic rather than Spirit and absolute Truth. In scripture, the Holy Spirit is often compared to such free-moving elements as wind, water and fire. If we want to truly understand God's voice we must realize that it is more about the recognition of how He speaks than the rationalization of what we think He should say! This is a most important distinction for every believer to make in preparation for last day surprises!

MAY 28...DAY 148
TWO WAYS GOD LEADS

"Then Jesus, being filled with the Holy Spirit, returned from the Jordan and was led by the Spirit into the wilderness, being tempted for forty days by the devil."
Luke 4:1-2a NKJV

"Immediately the Spirit drove Him into the wilderness. And He was there in the wilderness forty days, tempted by Satan, and was with the wild beasts; and the angels ministered to Him."
Mark 1:12-13 NKJV

The Holy Spirit urged Jesus into the wilderness to be tempted by Satan immediately after He was baptized in the river Jordan and commissioned for ministry. It is interesting to note, though, that Luke and Mark used two different words to describe the method by which our Lord was directed. In Luke 4:1 the word is 'led' which means, to induce as in the birthing process. Here we see the gentle side of God's nature in that He leads by coaxing us lovingly from one stage of maturity to the next. He leads us as a shepherd caringly leads his sheep to the green pastures and still waters to restore peace and increase strength.

In contrast, the word used in Mark 1:12 is 'drove' which almost creates a paradox. This word literally means to eject or throw from within, as when a person vomits! What the Bible is telling us is that there is another side to God's nature. Not only does He lead us gently at times, but He also compels us when necessary to go forward into our destiny! Jesus, like us, had to encounter His chief adversary in order to complete His earthly life lesson. He would have to be particularly obedient to His Father to fulfill the biblically predicted description of the Messiah. That meant being pushed along the way to confront those circumstances which were contrary to his incarnate nature for the sake of all mankind!

Like Saul of Tarsus on the Damascus road, there are times when we may need to get knocked to the ground by the intensity of God's own Presence, in order to obtain a complete perspective of what we should truly be involved in...to prepare us to endure what we may suffer in the end!

MAY 29...DAY 149
TWO EFFECTS OF BEING LED BY GOD'S SPIRIT

"For as many as are led by the Spirit of God, these are the sons of God."
Romans 8:14 NKJV

"But if you are led by the Spirit, you are not under the law."
Galatians 5:18 NKJV

There are two specific New Testament rewards you should expect as you embark upon this spiritual lifestyle. The first is a sense of 'son-ship,' which repositions our mindset from thinking we can serve God on our own, and in our own way. In Romans 8:14 the Bible makes clear our place in the household of God, and the privileges we share as His sons and daughters. The scripture tells us that we have a full inheritance in Christ, and that all of creation is waiting for the children of God to mature into their Kingdom capacity. Yes, even nature needs our help to be released from the bondage sin has placed upon it through mankind, so that everything can once again function from the original spiritual position it possessed in the Garden of Eden! We carry a responsibility to inherit all God has for us by being led by His Spirit!

Besides the heavenly status we receive and the spiritual resources God grants us for becoming His sons and daughters there is another major effect that comes from following the Holy Spirit. Galatians 5:18 clarifies what it means to be free from the weight of the 'Law.' Perhaps the greatest aspect of The Holy Spirit is the fact that He is a part (the Spirit) of God Himself and thus perfect. He can work in us to keep the commandments of God's law, which are perfect in themselves, while also revealing our imperfections!

The Bible teaches that the legal aspects of God's Old Testament covenant with us can only be kept through the New Testament sacrifice of Jesus Christ. We are simply unable to please God without faith in His Son, or without maintaining a continual relationship with Him via the Holy Spirit. The bottom-line is that we don't have to 'do religion,' instead we get to 'know' the Lord firsthand! There is all the difference in the world between attending a church where God is in every service, and one where others are there only to opine what God would have you do! In the last days there may not even be a 'church' to attend, so seek and be led to the true seats of fellowship now!

MAY 30...DAY 150
THE FLESH PROBLEM

"For those who live according to the flesh set their minds on the things of the flesh, but those who live according to the Spirit set their minds on the things of the Spirit...those who are in the flesh cannot please God."
Romans 8:5, 8 ESV

To effectively finish life's race there is one big obstacle every Christian must overcome. It is outlined for us here by the use of a little word in the Bible with a big-time meaning, 'FLESH'. We must all come to terms with it before we can further discuss spiritual leadership.

This word speaks of our carnal nature or unspiritual tendencies. It is listed as a direct enemy to God and His Spirit in our quote, in Galatians 5, and various other scripture. The flesh, or the combination of our natural physical desires and the untamed thoughts, feelings and purposes of our souls, literally opposes the Spirit of God and desires the opposite of what He wants for us. The Bible tells us that we cannot please God in that condition, because we will constantly choose what is comfortable and pleasing to us. We will 'grieve' and 'quench' the Holy Spirit as we recklessly demand our own way, and even attack His purposes when we cannot comprehend His influence in our own or other's lives.

The Church today bears the marks of having tried in vain to serve a God who is Spirit, by offering itself to Him in the flesh! Meanwhile, the world around us is more desperate than ever for spiritual answers. People are often disappointed and detoured toward false religions when they look into our churches for help, only to discover how we have reinvented a God who more reflects a mere natural image not much different than their own!

This is the day for Christianity to shake itself and come to its true spiritual senses before the crises of the last days arrives on its own front doorstep! Let's focus our minds and thoughts on the things of God and set our affections there. Then put the information you receive from Him into practice and stay tuned to the Holy Spirit for further instructions. Not only will you get more out of God...He will get more out of you!

MAY 31...DAY 151
GIVING GOD SPACE TO WORK

"I call heaven and earth to witness this day against you that I have set before you life and death, the blessings and the curses; therefore CHOOSE LIFE that you and your descendants may live. And may love the Lord your God, obey His voice, and cling to Him. For He is your life and the length of your days..."
Deuteronomy 30:19-20

One of the greatest gifts God has given to mankind is the power of CHOICE. This human resource is so subtle that believers often overlook its importance on their way up the "ladder" of Christian success. However, it is the key difference between those who end up at the top of God's ladder, walking victoriously above life's obstacles and those who succumb to the pressures, and finish on the lower rungs of spirituality.

Most of us do not purposefully choose to become a victim in life, but we can still miss the thrill of the climb by failing to make our choices with purpose. I have learned that it is what I do in that little space in time called "choice," which decides the outcomes in my life. As our scripture indicates, the opening between what we consider in our mind and what we decide in our heart is the Holy Spirit's "work-space." Every situation holds both right or wrong. If we give the Lord room to lead us, right choices will overtake wrong decisions. As we choose to do the right things our character develops and the power of our life goes far beyond our words. Every time we stop and choose rightly we suffer a little, and lose another bit of our inborn selfishness. The pain of this process works to break down our egocentricity, making us both stronger and wiser along the way. We learn to consistently say no to self and yes to some One greater. As a result, we are headed toward ever-increasing levels of rightful success, avoiding the temptation to settle for less than what is best along the way!

You are destined to be a winner in Christ, so choose not to be a victim to the very circumstances you were called to overcome! The most basic way to ensure your spiritual success is by giving God the space in your life to work all out that concerns you to His good pleasure.

JUNE 1...DAY 152
LEADERSHIP PRINCIPLES OF THE
HOLY SPIRIT

"Truly, truly, I say to you, whoever believes in me will also do the works that I do; and greater works than these will he do, because I am going to the Father...And I will ask the Father, and He will give you another Helper, to be with you forever, even the Spirit of truth, whom the world cannot receive, because it neither sees Him nor knows Him. You know Him, for He dwells with you and will be in you."
John 14:12, 16-17 ESV

"Little children, you are from God and have overcome them, for He who is in you is greater than he who is in the world."
1 John 4:4 ESV

In the New Testament, the Holy Spirit is the "Greater One" Who has been authorized to lead us into "Greater Works" on the Lord's behalf. What Jesus was in everyday life to His disciples, the Spirit is to believers today. He continues to display the reality of God through contemporary believers in the same way He did over 2000 years ago through the life and ministry of Jesus Christ. Our responsibility is to be today's disciples! That means keeping close company with the Lord and especially obeying those things He teaches and trains us to do.

If you examine what Jesus and His Disciples state in scripture about the Holy Spirit, you will find a concrete set of principles by which God guides those into spiritual greatness who are serious about serving Him. You could call these guidelines "Leadership Principles of the Holy Spirit," as they are the essence of true Christian leadership. Scripturally speaking, note how He is referred to as the Spirit of:

1.	CONSOLATION	(John 14:16)
2.	RECOGNITION	(John 14:17)
3.	COMMUNION	(John 14:21-23)
4.	INSTRUCTION	(John 14:26)
5.	RECOLLECTION	(John 14:26)
6.	CONFIRMATION	(John 15:26)
7.	CONVICTION	(John 16:8)
8.	REVELATION	(John 16:13)
9.	DIRECTION	(John 16:13)
10.	TRANSMISSION	(John 16:14)
11.	DEMONSTRATION	(Acts 2, 1 Corinthians 2)
12.	EDIFICATION	(Jude 20)

By becoming more and more familiar with these various ways the Holy Spirit expresses God/Himself we can trust to be led by Him and reflect the kind of leadership found in the Bible. The last days will to call for at least the same spiritual level of guidance found in the earliest days of the church, and doubtless more. The more familiar we get with the different characteristics listed here the more we will understand about how God "moves".

Let's learn all we can about the "Greater One"...in preparation for the "great and terrible day of the Lord!"

JUNE 2...DAY 153
THE SPIRIT OF CONSOLATION

"And I will ask the Father, and he will give you another HELPER, to be with you forever, even the Spirit of Truth, whom the world cannot receive, because it neither sees Him nor knows Him. You know Him, for he dwells with you and will be in you. I will not leave you as orphans; I will come to you."
John 14:12, 16-17 ESV

These "Leadership Principles of the Holy Spirit" will help you learn how to face the end-times, and all time's of your life, God's way. In fact, this first lesson will eliminate the fear of facing anything on your own! I use the word, "principles," because it speaks of fundamental truths or codes of conduct, things that are absolute but not necessarily obvious or easily manipulated. These are Biblical descriptions of the Holy Spirit's person and work in the New Testament, as outlined primarily by Jesus himself in the fourteenth, fifteenth and sixteenth chapters of John's Gospel. They delineate Who He is and how He "operates." Depending on the degree of awareness, belief, and obedience to the Lord a person exercises, these principles are the basic ways by which the Holy Ghost leads.

The first one, "consolation," is a synonym for "helper" in our text and can also be translated as "comfort." Here it literally means "one called alongside to help", or an assistant who will aid in the all things that concern a disciple of Christ. God's Spirit is a supernatural counselor given to help His people through the process of Christian development and service. He "counsels" us when we are unsure how to think or feel. He is our "back-up" to lean on when things get difficult...one who "strengthens" and empowers us to press forward in the grace of God. The Spirit comforts us when we need encouragement and pushes us when we need drive.

Notice the text says "another Helper." His job is to take the place of Christ for us just as he did for the Apostles as they transitioned into taking Jesus' message to the world on His behalf. The Holy Spirit is our advocate, standing with us like a defense attorney in the courtroom of life. The closer we move toward Christ's return, the more we are going to need His spiritual comfort and counsel.

JUNE 3...DAY 154
THE SPIRIT OF RECOGNITION

"The Spirit of Truth, whom the world cannot receive, because it neither sees Him nor knows Him; but you know Him, for He dwells with you and will be in you."
John 14:17 NKJV

The second Christian leadership principle I want to discuss is that the Holy Spirit is an agent of "recognition." This is very important because without an initial awareness of a thing there can be no deeper understanding of it. Since God's essence is spirit (John 4:24), we must develop a familiarity with spiritual things to have any interaction or experience with Him.

How interesting is it that in the Person of the Holy Spirit the highest link has been made as our personal "connector" with God?

Jesus explained to his disciples that they were separate from the everyday unspiritual populace because the Holy Spirit was dwelling "with" them. By virtue of their relationship with Jesus, they were also in a position of nearness to God's Spirit. He was the One who had originally stirred their hearts when the Lord called them to follow Him. After they responded, He was the One that kept prompting them to continue listening to Jesus' directions and pursuing His directives.

Apart from the Spirit, our hearts grow dull to the reality of spiritual things, blinded to their source, or the origin from which they spring. How many Christians today know the Bible but do not recognize the Holy Spirit when He begins to stir their hearts or their churches? You can see how critical He is to the everyday life of the believer...how much more to those who find themselves living in the last of the last days?

Until Jesus came the Holy Spirit was "with" those who followed God, but His death ushered in a new closeness. This is what Jesus meant when He said, "and will be in you." God's Spirit literally took up residence within those He "came upon" on the day of Pentecost (Acts 2:1-4)!

A new day required a new way. Jesus paid a price worthy not only of the removal of our sins but also of the improvement of our relationship with God. As a result we now see and know the Spirit from a different vantage point. Before Jesus' death and resurrection men knew God from the perspective of a leading influence, now they may see Him through His own eye, peering from the windows of their own inner man!

Because of this distinction we are equipped to see things as they really are, from God's absolute vantage point. The Spirit of Truth leads us into a personal recognition of spirit and truth...an advancement that will make all the difference in the end.

JUNE 4...DAY 155
THE SPIRIT OF COMMUNION

"He who has My commandments and keeps them, it is he who loves Me. And he who loves Me will be loved by My Father, and I will love him and manifest Myself to him. Judas (not Iscariot) said to Him, 'Lord, how is it that You will manifest Yourself to us, and not to the world?' Jesus answered and said to him, 'If anyone loves Me, he will keep My word; and My Father will love him, and
We will come to him and make Our home with Him.'"
John 14:21-23 NKJV

This one is a mind-blower! Through the connection of the Holy Spirit, Jesus promises to "appear" to the believer who keeps His commandments or teachings. The word, "manifest" used in this verse means to, exhibit, disclose, appear or declare openly. The incredulity of this powerful statement caused Judas to ask for clarification. Just as it is hard for us to imagine Jesus literally appearing to us and communicating personally with us after his death and resurrection, so Judas struggled to understand how the Lord would need to!

The disciples enjoyed a deep personal relationship, or state of "communion" with the Lord, and feared that it was about to be stripped from them. We struggle to rationalize how we could ever experience what they had. Through the Holy Spirit both things are possible. Jesus said He and the Father would "come and make Our home with" one who followed the true definition of spiritual love. That means doing what He taught not just acting religious.

Modern Christianity is far from the level of the early church in many ways. When we read the "Acts of the Apostles" we see that after they were filled with the Holy Spirit they continued to have the same purpose, presence and power around their lives and churches that Jesus had when He walked among them.

What is different today? We just don't grasp and/or believe passages like the one above. Jesus said He is coming to commune with us by the presence of the Holy Spirit abiding within our hearts, but we reason ourselves out of it. The problem is we love the world more than God most of the time, and it steals His place in our hearts.

The spiritual realm is a real place too, and we have the greatest friend and ally, the Holy Spirit, connecting that realm to each believer on earth. Look up today...ask Jesus to identify and come into your secret place...so you never fall away from the reality of God!

JUNE 5...DAY 156
THE SPIRIT OF INSTRUCTION

"These things I have spoken to you while being present with you, but the Helper, the Holy Spirit, whom the Father will send in My name, He will teach you all things, and bring to your remembrance all things that I said to you."
John 14:25-26 NKJV

Notice this is the second time we find the word "Helper" in the various texts where Jesus discussed the personality and leadership characteristics of the Holy Spirit. What's more as we study these ten basic aspects of spiritual leadership, we'll see it used two further times! It is so important that Jesus highlighted it four times in three chapters of John's Gospel.

By using the Greek word, "parakletos," He is telling us that the Holy Spirit's primary job is as One "summoned to our side for assistance" in specific kinds of ways. In our verses for today, we find the first way that He helps us is by teaching us. How often do we not know exactly what to do or how to do it regarding God's purposes for our lives? This is when the Spirit of God comes to our aid. In fact, Romans 8:26 (in the Amplified Bible) says exactly that: "So too the [Holy Spirit] comes to our aid and bears us up in our weakness; for we do not know what prayer to offer nor how to offer it worthily as we ought, but the Spirit Himself goes to meet our supplications and pleads on our behalf with unspeakable yearnings and groanings too deep for utterance."

This is an unusual approach to teaching but remember we are discussing spiritual matters. There are times when we have said and done all we know to do and yet still sense things are incomplete. This is when the Holy Spirit will begin to move with us in prayer to align our understanding with God's will.

The phrase, "He will teach us all things," speaks of the Spirit's ability to move beyond natural boundaries to instruct, train and enlighten us in the ways of God's

Kingdom. Of course the Lord teaches us many practical things along the way but our main classroom is always in the school of the spirit, where it is too deep and unreachable for the unspiritual to attend.

If you "want to know" God let His Spirit enroll you now to prepare you for the degree of wisdom needed to finish your course!

JUNE 6...DAY 157
THE SPIRIT OF RECOLLECTION

"These things I have spoken to you while being present with you, but the Helper, the Holy Spirit, whom the Father will send in My name, He will teach you all things, and bring to your remembrance all things that I said to you."
John 14:25-26 NKJV

If you are like me, you forget more stuff everyday than you care to remember. Many things need to be forgotten and left in the past so we can move forward. God uses change to develop us spiritually. For that reason I allow casual information that moves across my mind through the day to vanish with the night. This keeps me free to track God's continuous infilling information.

Some things, however, not only need to be remembered but valued and cherished. For example, we are instructed to "bind" the Word of God around our necks and write it upon the tablets of our hearts" (Proverbs 3:1-3), (2 Corinthians 3:3)! According to the Bible, the renewal of our minds is the key to our spiritual transformation (Romans 12:1-2, Ephesians 4:23). I am very thankful that the Holy Spirit is the One alongside me to help remind me of that Word...particularly the things Jesus has already taught me that I might have forgotten to apply, at any given time. He is commissioned to "bring to your remembrance" all those things Jesus spoke.

Notice that this promise was made to the disciples in particular. By being closely associated with the Lord, the implication is that they had already heard Jesus' words or The Word. How else could the Holy Spirit remind them of it?

We are Jesus' disciples today. We too need His Word to abide in our hearts. It is more valuable than any other single resource, especially if we end up being the generation faced with walking faithfully through the last days!

Learn to depend on the Holy Ghost for spiritual recall. There are many things we have had written upon the tablets of our hearts in the past, which the Lord needs to call back into our conscious awareness if we are going to overcome. Small understandings, big lessons, but anything the Lord wants you to remember is important. Listen for the voice of the Spirit and don't be surprised when He simply reiterates prior information. He is turning it into revelation and understanding...inscribing it on your heart until you are established in the purposes of God for your life!

JUNE 7...DAY 158
THE SPIRIT OF CONFIRMATION

"But when the Helper comes, whom I shall send to you from my Father, the Spirit of truth who proceeds from the Father, He will testify of Me. And you also will bear witness, because you have been with Me from the beginning."
John 15:26-27 NKJV

There is that word, "Helper," again! According to the Amplified Bible's translation, the Holy Spirit is totally geared toward "counseling, helping, advocating, interceding, strengthening," and "standing by" us! In this particular case He does all this by testifying OF Jesus through our life as a disciple.

In past lessons we pointed out how the Spirit of God teaches and reminds us what Jesus has said, but today let's examine the purpose of those tasks. God wants to work deeply in us so He can reach further through us! The Holy Spirit Himself testifies of Jesus when He develops a disciple. There is an impartation beyond the information given. In other words, something is received from His nature that can be carried. This is also called an "anointing" or ability similar to His own with which to catch other people's attention and touch their lives.

Mark 16:19-20 recounts the end result of the Apostles three and a half years spent in Jesus' personal boot camp! "So then, after the Lord had spoken to them, He was received up into heaven, and sat down at the right hand of God. And they went out and preached everywhere, the Lord working with them and confirming the word through the accompanying signs. Amen." How did the Lord work with these guys since He was at the right hand of God? It was through the person of the Holy Spirit. Jesus was and still is able to "confirm" His Word through those who: 1) have been with the Him long enough to have received something more than information and; 2) believe that what He said about signs following them (verses 15-18) was true!

Many Christians don't believe in divine demonstrations today, and as a result don't carry much of Jesus' confirming power. All of us could use an increase ...especially in light of the darkness ahead! The key is having been with Jesus before we go everywhere for Him...coming days will demand this!

JUNE 8...DAY 159
THE SPIRIT OF CONVICTION

"Nevertheless I tell you the truth. It is to your advantage that I go away; for if I do not go away, the Helper will not come to you; but if I depart, I will send Him to you. And when He has come, He will convict the world of sin and righteousness, and of judgment: of sin, because they do not believe in Me; of righteousness, because I go to My Father and you see Me no more; of judgment, because the ruler of the world is judged."
John 16:7-8 NKJV

Okay, if you don't get that the Holy Spirit wants to "help" you by now I can't help you! Seriously though, this is a big one on our list of spiritual leadership principles. He has to assist us when it comes to reaching the world for Christ because we cannot influence lost people in the three areas listed here without heavenly help. This is why Jesus told His disciples in no uncertain terms that it was an absolute must that He "go away!" He knew the only way they would be able to do the same things He Himself had done was by being immersed in the same Spirit...and that required Jesus' death and resurrection!

The word "convict" used here means, to convince or prove a person's true condition. If your experience is anything like mine, you know just how hard it is to convince another person of their faults if they are unwilling to see them. Even after salvation we can easily get stuck in our natural tendency to rationalize good and bad (sin), right and wrong (righteousness), guilt or innocence (judgment). Every Gospel preacher knows he needs a "spirit of conviction" to open the hearts of men and women and expose them to the Truth. Without a heart of awareness, our knowledge of spiritual things is limited to only the rational mind; which means most heavenly realities won't make sense to us.

How many non-Christians struggle to understand the Bible when they choose to read or study it? Only the Holy Spirit can bring someone to a recognition that they: 1) do not believe in the Savior, 2) need to exchange their life for His, 3) will face a certain day of reckoning along with the devil, whom Jesus has already defeated and judged. The Bible says these tenets are sheer absurdity to the world (1Corinthians 1:18), but it is the power of God to those of us who are being saved and prepared everyday to meet the Lord with a clear conscience!

JUNE 9...DAY 160
THE SPIRIT OF REVELATION

"I still have many things to say to you, but you cannot bear them now. However, when He, the Spirit of truth has come, He will guide you into all truth; for He will not speak on His own authority, but whatever He hears He will speak; and He will tell you things to come."
John 16:12-13 NKJV

Doesn't it seem strange that Jesus would tell his disciples they would be in a better position to receive His own message after He was gone?! The era of the Holy Spirit's ministry within the church is so important because it allows Jesus to be everywhere all the time, distributing His message on a much larger scale than when He originally spoke it. On top of that is the timing factor. After the Spirit was poured out upon those first disciples you can immediately see the growth in them. Peter sounds like a new man in Acts 2 delivering his first sermon, not to mention the results were Jesus-like with 3000 converts!

What those guys could not understand when Jesus first said it to them, they later were able to move in with God's guiding Spirit feeding them the right messages at the needed moments.

The Holy Spirit is a master distributor. Notice the text says He "guides" us into the truth. He often reveals things as they are about to unfold. He illustrates outcomes before they come, for the purpose of keeping us "flowing" with God. This is very different than the way we are used to operating and it takes a little getting used to on our part!

Think of Jesus as He went about doing good and healing all that were oppressed of the devil (Acts 10:38), under the anointing of the Holy Spirit. Peter mentions this as he is preaching to the first non-Hebrews that converted to Christianity. Why? Because this is what it takes to move with the Holy Spirit, and as long as the disciples were with Jesus they would never completely learn how to rely on the Lord's secret source of power.

Revelation means you know now by the light of the Spirit that which you could not comprehend before. It means learning to listen and feel for the wind and then moving with it. Jesus pointed this out to Nicodemus in John 3:8. It is what those early believers and preachers did, and the book of Acts evidences the results. They replicated Jesus' acts because they had the same Spirit revealing God's will to them that He had while on earth.

We have the same Spirit today, working in us to touch the world the same way...until Jesus comes again!

JUNE 10...DAY 161
THE SPIRIT OF DIRECTION

"I still have many things to say to you, but you cannot bear them now. However, when He, the Spirit of truth has come, He will guide you into all truth; for He will not speak on His own authority, but whatever He hears He will speak; and He will tell you things to come."
John 16:12-13 NKJV

Leadership principle number nine brings us back to the beginning of our study. The Holy Spirit is, above all things, our guide or leader. In this role He is our ultimate example. By examining His activities we find that it is impossible to be a spiritual leader without first learning to be led. The Spirit of God does not do anything on His own. He is a part of the greatest team in this or any God created universe, and stays accountable to the authority structure of the "Trinity." He says only the things He hears, yet He moves with a fluid spontaneity, distributing a liberating kind of regulation to all He touches. Without this foundation our guidance of self and others will ultimately veer away from God, regardless of how spiritual our actions may look, sound or feel. This is the case in many of our religious organizations today. Ministers have been taught leadership principles without learning to first be led by the Spirit. As a result, they can proffer direction that congregants will follow, but not always in the most spiritual, important or beneficial way.

The Holy Spirit's aim is to guide us into "truth." The Greek word means "reality" and speaks of things as they really are, not as they seem to be. This is the forward path God is everlastingly leading us on. He desires to dip us deeper into the source of life, not just the 'better lifestyle' shallow end of a manmade pool. This temporal life will be over one day soon, and from there on out spirit will be the same concentric reality for us all.

The will of God is to direct and transform our lives now, developing in us a solid sense of spirit and truth. It is from this vantage point that God seeks His own to worship Him (John 4:23). So, let's start giving Him what He requires while it is our choice...before He returns to demand it!

JUNE 11...DAY 162
THE SPIRIT OF TRANSMISSION

"He will glorify Me, for He will take of what is Mine and declare it to you.
All things that the Father has are Mine. Therefore I said that He will
take of Mine and declare it to you."
John 16:14-15 NKJV

"Now concerning spiritual gifts, brethren, I do not want you to be ignorant...There
are diversities of gifts, but the same Spirit...But one and the same Spirit works all these
things, distributing to each one individually as He wills."
1 Corinthians 12:1, 4 NKJV

It makes Jesus more famous every time the Holy Spirit relays information to us from Him. The Lord sums up His comments on the subject of "spiritology" here in John's Gospel, by "boiling down" the Spirit's job description for us.

We see how the Spirit "transmits" Jesus' intentions to His people. Each time He does so, the Lord's popularity increases in two worlds. Jesus gets more and more personal credit when those who follow Him do the kinds of things He Himself did through the Spirit He accomplished them with! He is honored and His name is magnified through this process in both heaven and on earth.

Like a modern "WIFI" signal, which relays information from the internet to a personal computer, the Holy Spirit distributes various kinds of signals to the "Body of Christ" from its Head or Leader. Because Jesus won a great spiritual victory over the god of this world (Satan, 2 Corinthians 4:4), "ALL" things have been placed under His control. Since it is the Holy Spirit who carries out the will of God, it is His natural inclination to now equip and inspire true believers with any resource necessary to accomplish everything Jesus wants done.

Now you know why not everything we say and do happens the way we want it to! Much of the Church's activity is about its own purposes. The Holy Spirit is not obligated to back up anything outside of God's will. When we are disconnected from the signals that distribute the Word and will of Jesus, and when what we do does not truly make Jesus more famous, we are on our own. Anything less than a cooperative relationship with the Holy Spirit is living under our own spiritual provenance...not exactly where we want to be found when He comes again!

JUNE 12...DAY 163
THE SPIRIT OF DEMONSTRATION #1

"When the Day of Pentecost had fully come, they were all with one accord in one place. And suddenly there came a sound from heaven, as of a rushing mighty wind, and it filled the whole house where they were sitting. Then there appeared to them divided tongues, as of fire, and one sat upon each of them. And they were all filled with the Holy Spirit and began to speak with other tongues, as the Spirit gave them utterance."
Acts 2:1-4 NKJV

This principle refers not to something Jesus said directly but rather something that He did. Both His life and ministry were rock-solid demonstrations of the reality of the Holy Spirit. He was miraculously conceived by the Spirit's power to demonstrate God's overwhelming love for mankind. Though He was God Himself in human form, His ministry was a secondary demonstration of how man is to live under the influence and direction of the Holy Spirit. After His baptism, where the Spirit descended upon Him and separated Him to his work, Jesus immediately followed the Spirit and did not do or say anything from that point forward without first receiving direction from God the Father!

We have the Lord's complete life as an example of our need to allow the Holy Spirit to demonstrate the goodness and power of God. In Acts 10:38, Peter reminds the first Gentiles he preached the Gospel to of, "how God anointed Jesus of Nazareth with the Holy Spirit and with power, who went about doing good and healing all who were oppressed by the devil, for God was with Him." Then in verse 44, the Bible records that while Peter was speaking, the Holy Spirit fell on all those who heard these words. Cornelius' family members were all filled with the Spirit and spoke in tongues in Caesarea, exactly as the disciples had in Jerusalem on the Day of Pentecost. Once Jesus' followers have the Holy Spirit in and upon them, God uses them as spiritual demonstrators wherever they go under His direction!

Christianity was never meant to be a philosophy or doctrine, but a living illustration of the reality of the Gospel message. As believers, we have a responsibility to carry something more than testimonies and sermons. With the view of the last days on our horizon, more than ever we need to be empowered to lead people into dramatic and dynamic encounters with the Lord...before the last great "act" plays out with His soon return!

JUNE 13...DAY 164
THE SPIRIT OF DEMONSTRATION #2

"And I, brethren, when I came to you, did not come with excellence of speech or of wisdom declaring to you the testimony of God. For I determined not to know anything among you except Jesus Christ and Him crucified. I was with you in weakness, in fear, and in much trembling. And my speech and my preaching were not with persuasive words of human wisdom, but in demonstration of the Spirit and of power, that your faith should not be in the wisdom of men but in the power of God."
1 Corinthians 2:1-5 NKJV

Jesus was "God on display" for the 33 plus years he lived and worked in Israel and Egypt. Since that time His most serious followers have taken their roles in His heavenly production, playing to audiences all around the world!

The problem is many Churches have long ago lost the true living biblical drama and become merely clubs retelling spiritual history. Before we judge too strictly, however, let's remember that this lack of demonstrating power can puncture the best of our hot air balloons. All that is necessary is for the Person of the Holy Spirit to be excluded from or reduced in our events, operating procedures and methods of leadership training (discipleship). In fact, this happens quite automatically when we lower the standard to meet our own human levels of understanding, value and comfort.

This is why Paul gives us a template to follow in 1 Corinthians 2 that will produce the same results Peter experienced in Acts 2 and Acts 10. He knew his process would work for us because it worked for him, and he wasn't even one of the original disciples. The believers in the city of Corinth also knew these principles had first affected them through Paul's ministry, and then succeeded by building their church in the midst of one of that era's most pagan cities.

Notice first, he tells us how NOT to behave. Excellent speech and human wisdom will not produce the demonstrating power of the Holy Ghost. Although this is what many churches are familiar with today, these qualities will not equip a minister to lead people very far, spiritually speaking. The Gospel cannot be delivered merely using our mental knowledge, our strength of confidence or our persuasive speeches! A Christian has to come to a place of exchange to experience the life of God, and a minister must come to the same place again to allow the Holy Spirit to demonstrate Jesus' message. Giving God complete control and following Him in a way that fears the absence of His Spirit is what establishes people in the faith. If it were easy, every preacher and church would be doing it, but this kind of radical Christian approach to ministry will become increasingly mandatory the closer we get to the Lord's return!

JUNE 14…DAY 165
THE SPIRIT OF DEMONSTRATION #3

"And I, brethren, when I came to you, did not come with excellence of speech or of wisdom declaring to you the testimony of God. For I determined not to know anything among you except Jesus Christ and Him crucified. I was with you in weakness, in fear, and in much trembling. And my speech and my preaching were not with persuasive words of human wisdom, but in demonstration of the Spirit and of power, that your faith should not be in the wisdom of men but in the power of God."
1 Corinthians 2:1-5 NKJV

Does your lifestyle demonstrate the reality of Jesus Christ to the world around you? Do you know too much about all the wrong things? What do you really bring to the spiritual table?

These are uncomfortable but valid questions for the person seeking to be ready to meet the Lord at His second coming. They are also the same concerns Paul addressed to these Corinthian Christians in our scripture for today. If you read this entire book of the Bible you will find that they excelled in matters of spiritual ability, yet they needed serious correction when it came to using their blessings for the right reasons.

They were not much different from us. We can all get stuck in our own perceptions of reality. We can then reduce God's gifts into reasons to divide, insulate ourselves from, and even injure the brothers and sisters He has given us in Christ. The devil loves to take what God meant for good and turn it into opportunities for people to believe that He doesn't even exist!

As believers, we are called to fight the good fight of faith for the Kingdom of God, but we must not use carnal or human methods if we want to see Christ's victory demonstrated among those around us. Instead of trying to be powerful himself, the Apostle Paul taught us to give place to a powerful God by yielding our lives to the Holy Spirit. The words, "weakness," "fear," and "much trembling" speak of an extreme state of dependency on God. Paul had learned that the miraculous aspect of the Gospel is released when one acknowledges weakness. Through our weakness He reveals His strength. As Paul said in 2 Corinthians 12:9, the kind of grace that is sufficient to empower us for anything we face is always found at the end of ourselves!

This may be why he said in verse twelve that the "signs of an apostle" were accomplished in his ministry first through "perseverance," then with "miracles and wonders and mighty works." When we are truly broken in ourselves, we discover a supernatural connection with God...the kind a world that is lost, dim and hurting can begin to see!

JUNE 15...DAY 166
THE SPIRIT OF DEMONSTRATION #4

"However, we speak wisdom among those who are mature, yet not the wisdom of this age, nor of the rulers of this age, who are coming to nothing. But we speak the wisdom of God in a mystery, the hidden wisdom which God ordained before the ages for our glory, which none of the rulers of this age knew; for had they known, they would not have crucified the Lord of glory...But God has revealed them to us through His Spirit. For the spirit searches all things, yes, the deep things of God."
1 Corinthians 2:6-10 NKJV

It was Satan's devilish rulers in the spirit world who produced the plot against Jesus, using human potentates to kill Him. They would never have done it if they knew what kind of heavenly egg it was going to hatch here on earth! God chooses to use the foolishness of this world to expose both the futility of the demonic realm and the glory of His own kingdom. What the devil didn't realize, God relished! Only He knew that something as worthless as a wooden cross would produce a spiritual chain reaction in this world if handled properly. Jesus was abandoned there and men were saved everywhere! Jesus gave up His spirit there and the Holy Spirit has filled people everywhere! Jesus was disgraced there and the power of God's grace has exploded everywhere...for over 2,000 years and continuing!

Jesus was the seed of God planted back into His garden which is growing and multiplying more rapidly the nearer we get to the end of His "human reconciliation plan." Because of what Jesus has done, you and I have become carriers of the same Spirit He carried. We are God's invasion plan for planet earth, not just preaching the Gospel and displaying it the same way, but in more places around the world. Jesus Himself said (John 14:12) that we would do even greater things than He did, if we simply "believe."

Everyone knows this world needs help. Maybe you haven't realized that you yourself are the answer, if you are filled with the Holy Spirit. If you are not, just ask for the Lord to overshadow and immerse you today. Then expect a new presence and power around your life and expect to make a difference everywhere you go. Satan sought to kill one man, Jesus. The devil knows now Christ's followers are multitudinous reproductions of Himself, but he is hoping you never do!

JUNE 16...DAY 167
THE SPIRIT OF EDIFICATION

*"But you, beloved, building yourselves up on your most holy faith, praying in the
Holy Spirit, keep yourselves in the love of God, looking for the mercy of our
Lord Jesus Christ unto eternal life."*
Jude 20-21 NKJV

*"He who speaks in a tongue edifies himself, but he who prophesies edifies the
church. I wish you all spoke with tongues, but even more that you prophesied; for he
who prophesies is greater than he who speaks with tongues, unless indeed he
interprets, that the church may receive edification...for if I pray in a tongue,
my spirit prays, but my understanding is unfruitful."*
1 Corinthians 14:4-5, 14 NKJV

Here we have a controversial, but nevertheless crucial principle by which the Holy
Spirit leads Jesus' disciples. It is the principle of "edification" or "building up" found in
these different passages of scripture. Both English translations are taken from the same
root word in biblical Greek and simply mean "to build, or raise an edifice." This is a
perfect illustration describing what happens spiritually when a believer interacts with
the Holy Spirit according to the pattern of His original outpouring recorded in Acts
chapter two.

God uses His Spirit to erect His plans and purposes in our lives as an alternative to
our natural tendency of exalting ourselves! This is precisely why it has remained a
topic of discussion and even much division within Church ranks for the past 2,000
years! Spiritual things do not make sense to the natural mind according to the Apostle
Paul (1 Corinthians 2:14), yet they must be maintained in a believer's life in order to
continue developing as a Christian.

When you get filled with God's Spirit after accepting Jesus as your Savior, you
should discover a supernatural ability to speak in an unknown tongue. If you do not it
is because your mind is blocking its manifestation through lack of understanding. All
you have to do is keep studying what God says about it until the light comes on in your
heart...then you will find a river of foreign but powerful expression swelling up deep
within you, looking for release through your mouth! It is not unlike when you were a
small child learning to speak in your first language. It was in you to do so but you had
to practice and be trained by those older than yourself until you found your own
natural ability to speak. Then nobody could shut you up! From there it was natural for
you to start walking, exploring your gifts, and learning new skills...exactly what the
devil is afraid you will do spiritually!!

JUNE 17...DAY 168
DON'T GET LOST IN TRANSLATION

"He who speaks in a tongue edifies himself, but he who prophesies edifies the church. I wish you all spoke with tongues, but even more that you prophesied; for he who prophesies is greater than he who speaks with tongues, unless indeed he interprets, that the church may receive edification...for if I pray in a tongue, my spirit prays, but my understanding is unfruitful."
1 Corinthians 14:4-5, 14 NKJV

Praying in tongues IS praying in the Spirit according to our text for today, and it will build you up spiritually. Building others is more important than building yourself, but you can't prophesy for God until you learn to speak by His Spirit. You can't impact someone else's spiritual life until you learn to extend your own!

The ability to speak in tongues and prophesy is a supernatural outcome of the Holy Spirit's leadership in your life. They help you rise beyond your untrained spiritual instincts. These manifest gifts can benefit the church body, and be used to articulate God's heart to individuals.

Notice how our text for today puts both gifts in proper perspective. Prophesy, or the ability to speak under divine inspiration, is the greater of the two gifts because it elucidates God's counsel into language everyone can understand. This is true only IF the person who speaks in tongues does not interpret what is said! Without translation, tongues are still an important mystical way of edifying ourselves spiritually, and the apostle tells us that we should ALL be speaking in this divinely given language. This is the developmental process of the Lord. He first fills you, and then prepares you for service by cultivating your awareness of spiritual things. Once you become skilled using God instincts, at times you will begin to understand what you are praying about in your otherwise unknown language. He then releases a more mature way of relaying that information to others, or restraining and letting you know when not to pray in tongues out loud.

Just like Jesus' first disciples, the Holy Spirit trains us personally and prepares us to be another relay in the spiritual network God is developing for His purposes around the world! Don't buy into the teaching that minimizes God's gifts. Desire to follow the Spirit's lead and use what He gives you responsibly...these are the kinds of gifts you really need to unwrap to prepare for Jesus' return!

JUNE 18...DAY 169
3 KINDS OF SPIRITUAL RESOURCES

"Most assuredly, I say to you, he who believes in Me, the works that I do he will do also; and greater works than these he will do, because I go to My Father...And I will pray the Father and He will give you another Helper, that He may abide with you forever-the Spirit of truth,..."
John 14:12, 16-17a NKJV

The church's mission is to do in our day what Jesus would do if He were personally here on earth! Of course, that is a daunting challenge, and one we are not even sure is possible until after we have read and reread our text for today several times. Before you go any further why not take the time to do just that.

Afterward, it begins to dawn on us that we not only can entertain the idea but that we must somehow accept it as our responsibility. But once we get a revelation of God's true call on our lives as believers, how do we move forward successfully?

Years ago, I read a quote that summed up the answer to that question for me. It came from Charles W. Conn in his book, "A Balanced Church." On page 17 he said, "Since Christ's work consisted of what He was, what He said, and what He did we have a responsibility to be (1) a continuation of His life, (2) an amplification of His message, and (3) an extension of His works." He goes on to detail how Jesus left us in His place with the necessary resources or elements required to function as He did, in conjunction with the Holy Spirit!

These resources are clearly defined for us in the New Testament but Conn's outline has given me a clearer perspective of how they help us stand as "sons" of God or the Body of Christ! Briefly, we can only do this by the working of the Holy Spirit in our lives, both individually and corporately. We continue Jesus' life by walking in the "FRUIT" of the Spirit (Galatians 5:22-23). We amplify Jesus' message through use of the gifts or manifestations of the Holy Spirit (1 Corinthians 12:7-11). And we extend Jesus' works by following the spiritual and practical contributions of people and ministries the Lord has placed in our midst.

As we learn of these things and develop them in the Christian world, we will realize a mighty spiritual dimension of service the devil is hopeless to stop!

JUNE 19...DAY 170
RESOURCES TO GROW BY

"But the fruit of the Spirit is love, joy, peace, longsuffering, kindness, goodness, faithfulness, gentleness, self-control."
Galatians 5:22-23 NKJV

Let's take a closer look at the variety of resources given to us through THE Resource Jesus left to us, the Holy Spirit. Yesterday we took an overview of all the spiritual tools believers have at their disposal. God has given us a full set of gifts to help complete both our personal missions, and more importantly, the corporate work of the Church Jesus started during His life and ministry.

Our scripture today refers to the highest set of resources given in scripture being the "fruit" or essence of God's own nature. These spiritual qualities are most important because they build in us the character necessary for Him to continue living His life through us! True spirituality is something that "grows," which tells us that there are several "conditions" required for a truly productive Christian life.

First, all good vegetation begins with good seed. God's nature is pure perfection in every way. The words He has spoken to us convey that faultlessness to us in seed form (see the parable of the Sower in Matthew 13:1-23).

Second, we must be good, compliant ground or even God's seed will not take root in us; as can be seen in the rejection of Jesus by His own hometown of Nazareth (Luke 4:16-30). Since God has given us His own Spirit we must be responsible to work hard at preparing our hearts and minds to accommodate Him.

Finally, a favorable climate dictates what and where things will grow. It is important that we find the favorable plot God has for us and cultivate relationships with chosen people the Spirit leads us to. There we will find the atmosphere most conducive to growing in the spirit, even though at first that place may not seem to be the most suited to our liking.

Look again at the list of fruit God aims to grow in us. Did you notice how these nine things are qualities everyone wants? God knows how to make us fragrant and inviting to those who need to sense Him. O Taste and see that the Lord is good! (Psalm 34:8). As we learn to walk with His Spirit, our flavor becomes more and more authentic to others. The world can distinguish between home-grown Kingdom Christianity and the store-bought label variety...make sure you take root in God's garden!

JUNE 20...DAY 171
GROWING YOUR SPIRITUAL RESOURCES
#1 NINE KINDS OF LIFE

"I say then: Walk in the Spirit, and you shall not fulfill the lust of the flesh. For the flesh lusts against the Spirit, and the Spirit against the flesh; and these are contrary to one another, so that you do not do the things that you wish. But if you are led by the Spirit, you are not under the law. Now the works of the flesh are evident, which are: adultery, fornication, uncleanness, lewdness, idolatry, sorcery, hatred, contentions, jealousies, outbursts of wrath, selfish ambitions, dissensions, heresies, envy, murders, drunkenness, revelries, and the like; of which I tell you beforehand, just as I also told you in time past, that those who practice such things will not inherit the kingdom of God. But the fruit of the Spirit is love, joy, peace, longsuffering, kindness, goodness, faithfulness, gentleness, self-control. Against such there is no law. And those who are Christ's have crucified the flesh with passions and desires. If we live in the Spirit, let us also walk in the Spirit."
Galatians 5:16-25 NKJV

You will have to fight for the right to access God's resources for your life! There is an involuntary war that goes on within every believer for the control of their soul, and thus the outcomes in their lives. The natural or fleshly part of your nature does not just concede victory to the Spirit once you are saved, it must be overcome and this is what the fruit of God's Spirit is all about.

The nine character qualities you find in our scripture for today are the outgrowth of His influence upon your life. They are also the antidote for the (seventeen listed) sinful tendencies all humans have, which lead to exclusion from God's kingdom. For every impulse you have to act in ways contrary to the standard God sets, His Spirit now gives you an equal and opposite desire. As you choose to follow each of these "leads" you open further spiritual opportunities. You also expand your capacity to produce fruit for others to enjoy along the way. Therefore, the fruit of the Spirit serves the interests of all the important parties in your life: God, others and yourself!

Your old nature tends to serve only you, which is why the Bible repeatedly tells us to put it off. "Putting on the new man" is the biggest resource we have to combat the tide of the end times. . . because it changes us, so we can then water the world!

JUNE 21...DAY 172
GROWING YOUR SPIRITUAL RESOURCES
#2 ONE FOR ALL

" Now the works of the flesh are evident,...But the fruit of the Spirit is love, joy, peace, longsuffering, kindness, goodness, faithfulness, gentleness, self-control. "
Galatians 5:19a, 22-23 NKJV

If you look carefully at the spiritual resources which continue or perpetuate the life of God ("fruit of the Spirit"), you notice an interesting order to the list. "Love" is the first thing mentioned, and I don't believe it is by accident.   This quality is defined in the Greek here as, "affection or benevolence" or, in other words, a heart condition which produces corresponding actions.   Love is one of the words used in scripture to describe the very nature of God, "spirit" is another (see 1 John 4:8 & John 4:24). When you combine these facts, they tell us that what God is producing in us is Himself! He acts in love because He is Love and, in turn, all these other virtues are the natural outgrowth of God's nature being seeded back into the souls of men.

This stands in contrast to the "works" of the flesh, which are externally apparent in society for all to see. They have grown in the heart of mankind because they too have been planted there with the seeds of another spiritual nature.

Satan's diabolic tendencies "work" through our mental and physical faculties because of the rebellion against God in the Garden of Eden that was based on choosing natural ways over spiritual. Christians have been "redeemed" or purchased back in the spirit through the saving work of Christ on the cross.

Now we have a new nature of love with which to stand against our inclination to want to be independent and lawless. God has made a way for us to overcome the "old man" or sin nature with a new set of tendencies that spring from the place in us that is just like Him!

What Satan sought to corrupt, Jesus has resurrected in all those who choose to accept His loving sacrifice. Love has trumped all hands and produced a whole new set of circumstances for the devil to deal with...in the end, this endless God-kind of love will be the adversary's undoing!

JUNE 22...DAY 173
GROWING YOUR SPIRITUAL RESOURCES
#3 REAL LOVE

"But the fruit of the Spirit is love, joy, peace, longsuffering, kindness, goodness, faithfulness, gentleness, self-control."
Galatians 5:22-23 NKJV

The foundational resource of the Holy Spirit is likened in scripture to fruit. Fruit is a word in both the original language of the New Testament and many languages today, which refers to not only a literal food but more importantly an outcome or result. By using this word we are given the impression that when God's Spirit is at work in a believer's life there is a particular productivity that will occur in a specific set of ways.

To me the literal picture is that of a single fruit, like a banana or apple, but with an exotic assortment of tastes. Imagine that picture, and then combine with it the fact that this fruit is very prolific. This is what the writer of Galatians 5 is communicating. The Spirit is going to grow fruit of both quality and quantity in a Christian's life, highly valuable and therefore worthy of one's investment.

The specific facets of the fruit's character are defined for us. These are the areas God is resolute to develop in us, so it is important we look at them close enough to know what kinds of qualities He expects to find in us at Christ's return.   Yesterday, we examined how love is the essential description of this fruit. It is who God is and determines how He acts. Love replaces our impulse to serve first the interests of self. Please notice where the remaining eight distinctions lead us, to a place of "self-control."

It is interesting that Paul uses the same basic outline in defining true love in 1 Corinthians 13:4-8, only with different terminology. God's love in us will begin to develop a taste for these spiritual qualities both within our own hearts and in the example we set before others. When we are sweetly fragrant, resemble His love and taste like the salt of His goodness, we are walking in the fruit of God's Spirit. At that point we go beyond self to a place of being willingly "God-controlled."   In the end these will be the people who cannot be overcome by evil...they overcome evil with the goodness of God!

JUNE 23...DAY 174
GROWING YOUR SPIRITUAL RESOURCES
#4 ENJOY GOD'S TASTE

*"But the fruit of the Spirit is love, joy, peace, longsuffering, kindness,
goodness, faithfulness, gentleness, self-control."*
Galatians 5:22-23 NKJV

*"And Nehemiah...said...This day is holy to the Lord your God; do not mourn
nor weep'...Then he said to them, 'Go your way, eat the fat, drink the sweet,...
Do not sorrow, for the joy of the Lord is your strength.'"*
Nehemiah 8: 9-10 NKJV

How spiritually "tasty" you are as a Christian is largely determined by your taste for the right things! If you walk with God, His Spirit will develop your palate for "Kingdom qualities" and, like a good wine taster you will be able to identify those qualities in yourself and others.

This is important because the end times are noted in scripture for being fraught with seduction and deception. Knowing what is and is not of God's nature acts as a natural protection for us against being mislead in dangerous times. As we will see today, these elements of spiritual fruit are also a secret to drawing our strength and power for living from God in any era.

After "love," the second quality listed is "joy." Nehemiah 8:10 reveals a spiritual connection between joy and strength. As the Israelites of that day were celebrating: 1) their return to Jerusalem, 2) their opportunity to rebuild the city walls, and 3) their reopening of the pages of scripture, their godly leaders instructed them to, "rejoice!" In fact, those people were so moved when the Word of God was publicly read to them for the first time in generations that they wept! This was an understandable response for people who had been taken captive, and experientially understood what it meant to lose their physical and spiritual freedoms. But notice how Nehemiah commands them to enjoy the Lord's favor on this day...because, he says, "the joy of the Lord is your strength."

The Hebrew word, "joy" here in the Old Testament simply means to rejoice, but in our New Testament text it also includes the idea of a "cheerful, calm delight." Just as the people of Nehemiah's day were instructed to eat and drink the best tasting food in honor of the Lord, so we are to live with the overriding assurance and satisfaction that the Holy Spirit has been reserved for us. Each fruit of the Spirit brings its own particular delight. Joy is a must have quality to go far for God. Don't let your Christian experience be a sour one! Delight yourself in the Lord and He will give you the desires of your heart (Psalm 37:4). Enjoy Jesus and you will be a joy to Him!

JUNE 24...DAY 175
GROWING YOUR SPIRITUAL RESOURCES
#5 JOIN THE FLOW

"But the fruit of the Spirit is love, joy, peace, longsuffering, kindness,
goodness, faithfulness, gentleness, self-control."
Galatians 5:22-23 NKJV

"Thus says the Lord, your Redeemer, The Holy One of Israel: 'I am the Lord your
God, Who teaches you to profit, Who leads you by the way you should go. Oh, that
you had heeded My commandments! Then your peace would have been like a river,
and your righteousness like the waves of the sea.'"
Isaiah 48:17-18 NKJV

The next piece of godly "fruit" that will grow in our lives as a result of our yielding to the Holy Spirit is "peace." Jesus mentioned this Himself in John 14:27, just after explaining how the Holy Spirit is purposely given to be every disciple's "Helper."

If you read the context there you will find that the Spirit specifically helps us to remember and keep the Word of God. As we do, the same peace Jesus walked in is promised to us. God's peace is in direct contrast to the uneasy stillness that comes from this world's ungodly operating system. The secret being shown to us here is that the Spirit Himself IS our peace.

The term "Helper" can be translated "Comforter," which is especially fitting. Comfort is the natural feeling that results from being at peace.

The world also offers a conditional kind of peace and comfort for those who swim within the boundaries of its "flow." Its adherents will give you their praise, and its leaders will offer you position if you give your soul over to its hollow cause.

It is interesting that Isaiah described heaven's peace like a "river." This is exactly the picture that is painted by the Greek word used in Galatians. "Eiro" literally means "to join," speaking of the harmonious joining of two separate things into one distinct flow or sound. We can either choose to flow with the world's river and voice, or we can go with the sound of rushing, living water that comes from the heart of God. True peace is what Jesus had, and still has. The result of it was that He was both the heart and the voice of God in this world. That is what Jesus' disciples continue to be as they walk in His name, by His Spirit! The Bible says that this earth itself is groaning as it waits for a greater manifestation of God's sons in the last days (Romans 8:19). It only follows that as Jesus' followers multiply, so then does the peace of God among mankind. This is the cause we stand for and work toward with our lives as Christians!

JUNE 25...DAY 176
GROWING YOUR SPIRITUAL RESOURCES
#6 A DIVINE TWIST

*"But the fruit of the Spirit is love, joy, peace, longsuffering, kindness,
goodness, faithfulness, gentleness, self-control."*
Galatians 5:22-23 NKJV

*"But those who wait on the Lord shall renew their strength;
they shall mount up with wings like eagles, they shall run and not be weary.
They shall walk and not faint."*
Isaiah 40:31 NKJV

"Love suffers long and is kind..."
1 Corinthians 13:4 NKJV

How blessed we are that God has a long emotional fuse. His patience is displayed throughout the Bible when dealing with both the saved and unsaved. Remember how Moses led the Israelites through the wilderness, serving as a mediator between a patient God and impatient people who tried Him at every turn! Hebrews chapter four warns us not to follow after their continually exhibited example of "disobedience". They would not trust that His way was the highest and best route for their intended arrival. This stubbornness ultimately cost them their inheritance (the Promised Land).

Disobedience can have the same effect on us, especially since we are much closer to God in relationship and blessing because of the blood of Jesus. In Hebrews 6:12-15, the Lord reminds us of the faith Abraham displayed, and how by adding patience to it he received the promises God made to him. So, one of the great secrets of successfully dealing with and growing in God is to learn to have a long emotional fuse just like Him.

In fact, all these spiritual qualities are reciprocal. The more you receive and act on them, the more they grow into your character. They are the fruit produced by the new nature God has put into you at your new birth. To be willing to suffer, for a long time if necessary, is to simply act like God!

James 5:7 tells us that He is patiently waiting for the earth to fully produce what He planted into it when He gave His most precious seed, His very own Son! We are told twice, once in verse seven and again in verse eight, to be patient as well and establish in our hearts that we will wait expectantly for the coming of the Lord!

Isaiah teaches us the wisdom of acting in the same way; we become spiritually higher, faster and stronger! The word, "wait" here means to, "bind together by twisting." It also means to collect ourselves and remain expectant, looking forward in our minds with an attitude of fulfillment!

Although it can seem like God's promises sometimes take forever, He is well worth the wait...no matter what your situation is you will be changed for the better if you just rest in patient peace until His promises arrive!

JUNE 26...DAY 177
GROWING YOUR SPIRITUAL RESOURCES
#7 THE BALANCE OF THE FRUIT

"But the fruit of the Spirit is love, joy, peace, longsuffering, kindness, goodness, faithfulness, gentleness, self-control."
Galatians 5:22-23 NKJV

"But love your enemies, do good, and lend, hoping for nothing in return; and your reward will be great, and you will be sons of the Most High. For He is kind to the unthankful and evil."
Luke 6:35 NJKV

When I come to the fifth quality in this list of fruit produced by association with God in the human spirit, I can't help but think of it as the center, or balance for them all. How many times has a kind touch, act or word of a person served to help us either overcome or become?! Like the fictional scene in a famous movie where Jesus, still just a carpenter's helper, gives a drink of water to the man in the lead role, kindness is a small act that "stays with you" and ends up stealing the show!

A subtle but powerful resource, kindness creates entrances for God into places that are otherwise hostile and inaccessible. It is like the wedge that pries the door open for love to enter and then lets in all of its other attributes behind it.

It is hard to refuse the one who has fed you when you were hungry or visited you in prison, or made you feel important when you were feeling the least worthy. Like the face of love, kindness smiles at the unlovely, shows concern for the hurting and frowns on the mistreatment they have received. Or like a baby studies the face of its mother when feeding and learns of her, we look into the face of God and become familiar with His ways. The kindness we find there is what causes us to return.

Notice how the scripture in Luke 6 teaches us to be like God so we can represent His own family as His sons and daughters in this world. The words love, good and kind are used together to express the heart of God toward mankind, despite the negative response of many.

Again, all these nine qualities in Galatians are descriptive of love (as 1 Corinthians 13 clearly shows) and they work together to open a human heart. In the Greek, kindness means to be useful and excellent in demeanor. Its goodness leads to an even higher goodness, and its servant-hood leads to true faith expressed by actions. Its gentle ways lead on to further gentle humility, and its ability to withhold retaliation opens the way for the kind of self control God can exploit.

As verse 23 says, there is no valid law that can bring a charge against these things. When we walk in them we literally walk in the spirit realm. The more we grow in these qualities of God's love the more life we carry, dethroning the spiritual death maker of this world!

JUNE 27...DAY 178
IGNORING THE SPIRIT

"Now concerning spiritual gifts, brethren, I do not want you to be ignorant...But the manifestation of the Spirit is given to each one for the profit of all..."
1 Corinthians 12:1, 7 NKJV

Ignoring the Holy Spirit is a serious Christian concern. As our scriptures have shown, the Holy Spirit is the person who imparts God's nature to us. He is also the well from which all our spiritual resources spring! To turn God's Spirit "off" is to automatically squelch the supernatural amplification of a believer!

Benjamin Franklin said, "Most fools think they are only ignorant." That fits perfectly with what Paul is teaching in this chapter on spiritual "gifts", or more accurately, "manifestations." For Christians to ignore the manner in which God reveals Himself through the Church to the world is to choose foolishness. However, I don't think most believers would plan to remain unwise if they were given all the facts. Let's dig deeper into God's word today to make sure.

Paul advises these Corinthian believers very frankly not to be "ignorant" so they would purpose to be well informed. There are at least three similar but different definitions for the original word used here. "Ignorant" in Paul's mind meant to: 1) Not know 2) Know and not understand and 3) Not want to know.

The final definition is the only one that would be considered "foolish," which means to act without discretion, sound judgment or because of faulty character. The first two are simply the result of being either uninformed or misinformed. The apostle is not working to eliminate foolishness in certain people, but to keep it from spreading to everyone else in this particular church.

According to Proverbs 22:15 and other places, "foolishness is bound in the heart" of every person as a child and only a rod will drive it out! Simple ignorance can be removed by teaching.

Earlier in this same book of the Bible Paul made a clear distinction between these two groups of people. Excerpts from 1 Corinthians 2:6-14 state, "...we speak wisdom among those who are mature...not in words which man's wisdom teaches...the natural man does not receive the things of the Spirit of God for they are foolishness to him; nor can he know them for they are spiritually discerned."

Believers who are only concerned with external things can never know eternal truths! We must be willing to explore the area some have termed as "spiritology" if we really want to know what God has for us. This is what it means to "put on the new man" and to "have the mind of Christ" (Ephesians 4:23-24; 1 Corinthians 2:16). Biblically and spiritually informed viewpoints will be required by both Christians and Christian leadership, if we want to be enlightened throughout darker days!

JUNE 28...DAY 179
GOD WORKS THREE WAYS

"Now about the spiritual gifts (the special endowments of supernatural energy), brethren, I do not want you to be misinformed...Now there are distinctive varieties and distributions of endowments (gifts, extraordinary powers distinguishing certain Christians, due to the power of divine grace operating in their souls by the Holy Spirit) and they vary, but the [Holy] Spirit remains the same. And there are distinctive varieties of service and ministration, but it is the same Lord [Who is served]. And there are distinctive varieties of operation [of working to accomplish things], but it is the same God Who inspires them all in all."
1 Corinthians 12:1, 4-6 AMP

There are three categories of ways in which "God" works together as Father, Son and Holy Spirit to accomplish God's will through the Church. If we know what they are we will be more apt to work with Him rather than to do our own thing and just give it a Christian name!

Because the primary subject of this chapter in the Bible is the Holy Spirit's leading role in how we function as the representation of Christ's body on the earth, Paul lists them in reverse order. First, we find that it is the Holy Spirit who is responsible for distributing a great variety of distinctive personal gifts and abilities among believers. These are the spiritual features we each need, along with the fruit we discussed earlier, to be the people God created us to be before we were ever born. They are also the tools that simultaneously equip us to help others, and to accomplish His will as we play our specific part in the last days of God's great plan for the ages! Tomorrow we will look at them in more detail.

Second in our present list, the Lord Jesus Christ administrates the way we are grouped together for service both in local ministries and around the world. Notice the word "variety" keeps coming to the forefront in this section of scripture. It is a chief key to understanding just how Christianity is meant to work anywhere. Ephesians 4:11 states the various kinds of ministers and ministries the Lord has commissioned to lead the Church. Believers and local churches tend to familiarize themselves with a couple of these, and miss out on serving in the Lord's Kingdom administration. We are designed to not only be a pastoral or evangelistic people but also prophetic and apostolic. Although the teacher holds the key in educating us regarding these facets of the Christian life, he must first realize and understand them himself!

The Holy Spirit is supplying individual requirements. Jesus is building them into a unified Church. God the Father is coordinating all these various tasks to accomplish a Three in One completed picture regarding mankind. As Romans 8:28 tells us, He is causing all things to work together for good, by the Spirit and for those who are called (and managed by the Lord) for His eternal purpose!

JUNE 29...DAY 180
THE HOLY SPIRIT'S MANIFESTO

"But to each one is given the manifestation of the [Holy] Spirit [the evidence, the spiritual illumination of the Spirit] for good and profit. To one is given in and through the[Holy] Spirit [the power to speak] a MESSAGE OF WISDOM, and to another [the power to express] a WORD OF KNOWLEDGE and understanding according to the same [Holy] Spirit; to another [wonder working] FAITH by the same [Holy] Spirit, to another the extraordinary powers of HEALING by the one Spirit; to another the WORKING OF MIRACLES, to another PROPHETIC INSIGHT (the gift of interpreting the divine will and purpose); to another the ability to DISCERN and distinguish [the utterances of true] spirits [and false ones], to another various kinds of [unknown] TONGUES, to another the ability to INTERPRET [such] tongues. All these [gifts, achievements, abilities] are inspired and brought to pass by one and the same [Holy] Spirit, Who apportions to each person individually [exactly] as He chooses."
1 Corinthians 12:7-11 AMP

A "manifesto" is a public declaration of policy used for political or social aims. This twelfth chapter of Second Corinthians is likened to such a document, written from a spiritual platform. Here, we are literally given nine specific ways to expect the Holy Spirit to reveal Himself in the process of helping us solve problems. They are not personal experiences which are subject to different Christian denomination's varying viewpoints instead you can find them all in your Bible!

The first seven are found in the Old Testament and the four Gospels, while the final two are specific to this Church age and can be found with all the others in the New Testament. If you take the time to find out exactly what they each mean and the issues they address, you will immediately comprehend why we should expect to find them working in our lives and churches right now! The only reason they are not in common use is that people haven't read the manifesto...they accept the finding of some lesser documentation, exchanging the supernatural revelation of God's Spirit for the intellectual reasoning of mere human spirits!

In the four Gospels everything the world needs is displayed in the life of Christ. He was anointed to solve every human problem and replace their hurts with hope. In the book of Acts you can find these same qualities displayed, plus the ability to supernaturally communicate with God and man in the language of the Holy Spirit!

God has not changed, and people face the same issues today that they always have. Jesus is the Good News of our redemption! There is wisdom, knowledge and divine discernment for supernatural insight into the real reasons behind the world's despair. Faith, healing and miracles are available to overcome challenges and demonstrate

God's power to alleviate suffering. Prophecy, tongues and their interpretation are for advanced understanding of God's intentions and the ability to communicate them more accurately.

God's priceless gifts bestowed upon you have not been returned to heaven for a rotting earthly refund. You have them inside you put them on display for His glory!

JUNE 30...DAY 181
WHY YOU NEED 5 GUYS IN YOUR CHURCH

"And His gifts were [varied; He Himself appointed and gave men to us] some to be apostles (special messengers), some prophets (inspired preachers and expounders), some evangelists (preachers of the Gospel, traveling missionaries), some pastors (shepherds of His flock) and teachers. His intention was the perfecting and full equipping of the saints (His consecrated people), [that they should do] the work of ministering toward building up Christ's body (the church), [That it might develop] until we all attain oneness in the faith and in the comprehension of the [full and accurate] knowledge of the Son of God, that [we might arrive] at really mature manhood (the completeness of personality which is nothing less than the standard height of Christ's own perfection), the measure of the stature of the fullness of the Christ and the completeness found in Him."
Ephesians 4:11-13 AMP

To be "the man" God has called us to be in the last days, we cannot be afraid to believe the plain truth of scripture! This is exactly what the devil battles most because it is what he is most powerless against (Luke 4:8). Our verses for today remind us of both "who" we are at heart and "how" to remain secure in our spiritual "skin". Extending the kingdom in any era depends on knowing these two things well.

First, the Church is not just the "Body" of Christ, as if it we were more separate than connected to Jesus. Distancing God further from His people than the Bible does is simply a human alternative to the truth of who we really are. The Church is not just an extension of Christ, the Church IS "Christ" (see 1 Corinthians 12:12)! The text literally says we are growing and maturing into His full "age" (see Ephesians 1:22-23). In other words, there is no distinction between the Messianic call on Jesus' life and the extension of that call upon the life of His people! WE ARE NOT JESUS but God's eternal plan, which centers in His person, is now working through those whose lives have forever been changed by Him! This fact changes everything when it comes to defining the nature, identity and job description of the Church.

Second, there is a specific method listed here that the Lord uses to ensure this "perfect" development process continues within the church. The five guys Paul defines here are human "gifts" (verse 8) anointed by Him for different purposes and given to the church as a whole for spiritual vision and physical leadership. The first two are foundational (Apostles, Prophets) while the next three are specialized (Evangelists, Pastors, Teachers). Sadly, we tend to be more aware of the latter because of their abundance and relativity to normal Christian routine. This often comes at the exclusion of the former group, which holds the line of spirituality within the Church and keeps the whole moving in the direction of the Head. Together, they all train God's people to "minister" in the unity of the faith.

Beware of modern ministries who don't talk about or exemplify these truths. If you don't see all five of these guys in and around your local church check for the reasons why. When they work we work and, as Jesus' Body, will naturally reflect His heart and soul. Exactly the kind of "cool-headedness" and "open-heartedness" we will need to face final times!

JULY 1...DAY 182
SURE WAYS TO PLEASE GOD

"So then, those who are in the flesh cannot PLEASE God."
Romans 8:7-8 NKJV

"By faith Enoch was taken away so that he did not see death, and was not found, because God had taken him; for before he was taken he had this testimony, that he PLEASED God. But without faith it is impossible to PLEASE Him, for he who comes to God must believe that He is, and that He is a rewarder of those who diligently seek Him."
Hebrews 11:5-6 NKJV

There are several passages in the Bible which straightforwardly inform us how to be pleasing to God. We will each stand before Him one day and answer for exactly how diligent were our intentions to do so.

Christians most often think in terms of ultimately answering to God for the "works" they have done, according to what Revelation 20:13 tells us about the "Great White Throne" judgment. Romans 14:12 also reveals that every person shall "give account of himself" to God before the "Judgment Seat of Christ." We are going to answer thoroughly to God in the future not only about what we did in this life, but more importantly why we did those things!

As it is stated in the book of Romans to "please" God means to "be agreeable" with Him, and in the book of Hebrews "please" translates "to gratify entirely". So there are at least two levels to pleasing God.

The first is found in turning away from sin and all those things within your human nature that are not in agreement with God's plans for your life. This will begin to re-adjust your motives for doing the things you do.

Secondly, in order to be "well pleasing" to God you must find the place in your heart where faith springs forth. This can only be done by drawing close to God and listening intently to the things He has to say (including both the Bible and those things God speaks to you either directly or through others). It is impossible to come to this higher level of acceptance with the Lord until you begin to "diligently seek Him." Once you do, the intentions of your works will change.

JULY 2...DAY 183
SURE WAYS TO PLEASE GOD #2

"So Jesus added, When you have lifted up the Son of Man [on the cross], you will realize (know, understand) that I am He [for whom you look] and that I do nothing of Myself (of My own accord or on My own authority), but I say [exactly] what My Father has taught Me. And He Who sent Me is ever with Me; My Father has not left Me alone, for I always do what pleases Him." John 8:28-29 AMP

"For the mind that is set on the flesh is hostile to God, for it does not submit to God's law; indeed, it cannot. Those who are in the flesh cannot please God." Romans 8:7-8 ESV

In these verses, both Jesus and Paul gave us the secret to spiritual success. Look closely today and observe it yourself, so that when times get tough for you as a Christian you will remember what is most important before God.

Jesus did only those things which were "PLEASING" in God's sight and Paul taught us to consider our actions in the same way. Talk about the biggest little point in the Bible...this is it! God is all about directing and concentrating our activities to deliver what He wants done. It is so simple, yet we can struggle our entire lives in this aim, even after we have followed Jesus for decades. The reason being our old self-nature still has a mind and will of its own. It struggles against the Holy Spirit within us for control of our lives.

The Bible refers to this as our "flesh" and tells us that it is boldly "hostile" toward God. Jesus was sinless and thus single-minded in His intention to obey the wishes of His Father. This is why temptation was Satan's strategy against Him. The adversary attempted to draw Jesus' focus away from following God's expressed directions. He conducted this appeal in the specific areas of God's personal instructions to Jesus, exactly as he had done with Adam and Eve in the Garden of Eden.

We tend to be double-minded because of our already fallen nature and must keep focused and connected by a straight and unbroken line of obedience, following Jesus' example. We must purpose from our heart to walk in the Spirit. There we find the Lord's power to think and choose and participate in God's will for us over our natural contradictions.

The Bibles says we can pray, sing, walk and live there! Even though this world challenges us with crooked crossroads, we can please God without a stop or diversion, and do amazing things by the mighty influence of His Spirit. Jesus Himself said that He expects believers to do even greater works than He did (John 14:12)!

Remember, you find God first and then as a result you find the power to serve His interests. In dark days, when all can seem lost and many feel forsaken, those who walk the Way of Jesus will never be left alone!

JULY 3...DAY 184
PROMISCUOUS CHRISTIANITY

"No one engaged in warfare entangles himself with the affairs of this life, that he may please him who enlisted him as a soldier."
2 Timothy 2:4 NKJV

"But understand this that in the last days there will come times of difficulty. For people will be lovers of self...lovers of pleasure rather than lovers of God,..."
2 Timothy 3:1-2a, 4b ESV

Here in the Apostle Paul's second letter to Timothy we find two separate but connected verses that touch on the topic of pleasing God. They both deal with "detachment", and show it to be a necessary discipline in the life of a Christian.

First, Paul paints the picture of a soldier to convey the proper mindset for anyone in God's service. He did this on several occasions in the New Testament, leaving me with the impression that authentic Christianity requires non-civilian tactics. A soldier has to willingly detach from many good and lawful things that other citizens enjoy, in order to train and surmount hurdles they are naturally unwilling to scale (for their own and others' protection)!

In our second verse, Paul reverses his approach to the subject and places a picture of the last days before us. Through it we can see and understand the dangers of misplaced affections in the life of a believer, especially in their preparation to one day stand before the Lord. This second verse implies that the "times of difficulty" coming in the end times are created largely due to a heightened level of selfishness found inside the church! Notice, one of the specific things mentioned is becoming "lovers of pleasures rather than lovers of God." Before Jesus returns many, if not most Christians, are going to completely reverse their loyalties, because they have already reversed who they are trying to please!

Like an unfaithful partner who detaches from their spouse emotionally long before actual separation, end time believers are going to be those who have already grown promiscuous in their hearts toward God. Afterwards, it is only a matter of time before they will fall completely away from their first love. Check your watch...that clock seems to be ticking rapidly right now!

JULY 4...DAY 185
GETTING GOD'S TESTIMONY
FOR YOUR CASE

"And when Jesus was baptized, immediately He went up from the water, and behold, the heavens were opened to Him, and He saw the Spirit of God descending like a dove and coming to rest on Him; and behold, a voice from heaven said, 'This is my beloved Son, with Whom I am well pleased.'"
Matthew 3:16-17 ESV

"For we did not follow cleverly devised myths when we made known to you the power and coming of our Lord Jesus Christ, but we were eyewitnesses of His majesty. For when He received honor and glory from God the Father, and the voice was borne to Him by the Majestic Glory, 'This is my beloved Son, with whom I am well pleased,' we ourselves heard this very voice borne from heaven, for we were with him on the holy mountain."
2 Peter 1:16-18 ESV

On several occasions during the life of Jesus, God the Father Himself testified to the authenticity of His ministry. Today, we have two of the most outstanding instances before us to consider. The first is the testimony of Matthew surrounding Jesus' baptism. The second is the eyewitness account of Peter about his experience with

Jesus, (along with James, John, Moses and Elijah) on the Mount of Transfiguration (recorded in Matthew 17:5).

There is much that can be said about the fact that Jesus had clear-cut "out of this world" proof of being the Messiah. Father God spoke audibly about Jesus in the presence of multiple witnesses in each of these cases. As supernatural as it all is, my aim again today is to point out the importance of what the Father said.

Notice how in both places the same phrase is used! God is intent on letting us know the absolute importance of being pleasing to Him. The Greek word for "pleased" in both scriptures translates as "approbation", or to officially approve and sanction someone or something as being well and good. Nothing is more essential than to be found agreeable to God and to be thought as well by Him.

Take the time to find out what recorded testimony in scripture says about Him. It is well worth the rewards. If we will turn our hearts to look at the standard He has set and what it reveals about Who He is, God will give us the grace to become all He wants us to be. Then He will testify to His Father about you!!

JULY 5...DAY 186
PLEASING GOD OR MAN

"For our appeal [in preaching] does not [originate] from delusion or error or impure purpose or motive, nor in fraud or deceit. But just as we have been approved by God to be entrusted with the glad tidings (the Gospel), so we speak not to please men but to please God, Who tests our hearts [expecting them to be approved]. 1 Thessalonians 2:4 AMP

"Finally, then, brothers, we ask and urge you in the Lord Jesus, that as you received from us how you ought to walk and to please God, just as you are doing, that you do so more and more...that each one of you know how to control his own body in holiness and honor, not in the passion of lust like the Gentiles who do not know God;..." 1 Thessalonians 4:1, 4 AMP

Examining these verses will give you a fresh appreciation for the importance of pleasing God.

The pursuit of pleasure is one of the strongest driving forces in our human nature. It is so instinctive that people are often trapped in compromising situations before consciously realizing why. That is not to defer responsibility for our actions, but rather to point out how seductive sin really is.

If "obvious" sins of pleasure can be this challenging, what about the far less apparent offenses? After all, they are potentially much more dangerous in the eternal scheme of things. Here is what I mean. The tendency to please yourself in any area will eventually cause you to act in ways that will bring public shame. That shame also brings the opportunity to recognize your need to repent and get right with God. The sexual sins Paul refers to in our second scripture fall into this category. On the other hand, the failure to please God will tolerate undisciplined thoughts, create room for impure motives, lead to deception and even delusion within a person, long before they ever clearly manifest in their actions.

We need to check and balance ourselves utilizing this understanding of how sin works. The Apostle reminds us here that before we are commissioned to speak for God, our hearts are first tested and tempered by Him. If we desire to please Him we will pass His tests, and our works will be approved by Him. As long as we remain in an immature state of pleasing people first (including ourselves), God's seal of certification will be missing from our spiritual resumes!

So who is the happiest person in your life as a result of who you are and what you say and do? If in the base and core of heart you want to please Jesus, opt to make Him happier than yourself today and each day!

JULY 6...DAY 187
THE SECRET RECIPE FOR
ULTIMATE PLEASURE

"Little children, let us not love with word or with tongue, but in deed and truth. We shall know by this that we are of the truth, and shall assure our heart before Him, in whatever our heart condemns us; for God is greater than our heart, and knows all things. Beloved, if our heart does not condemn us, we have confidence before God; and whatever we ask we receive from Him, because we keep His commandments and do the things that are pleasing in His sight. And this is His commandment that we believe in the name of His Son Jesus Christ, and love one another, just as He commanded us.
1 John 3:21-23 NASB

"If you abide in Me, and My words abide in you, ask whatever you wish, and it shall be done for you. By this is My Father glorified, that you bear much fruit, and so prove to be My disciples...If you keep My commandments, you will abide in My love; just as I have kept My Father's commandments, and abide in His love.

These things I have spoken to you, that My joy may be in you,
and that your joy may be full."
John 15:7-8, 10-11 NASB

Never presume God does not want you to be happy and enjoy the good pleasures of this life. Both Jesus and John plainly tell us the opposite here (also see John 10:10). What can be more enjoyable than asking for whatever you want and getting it?! However, Christians know from experience about praying and asking God for the very things the Bible promises, yet not receiving the expected answer.

The problem is that often our hearts are not confident enough to allow us to believe God's promises, so we settle for the independent pleasures of self-sin instead. The antidote for this condition (of unbelief) is to turn our focus upon the Lord until our affections and loyalties begin to tend toward Him.

Think about it...if we spend enough time with Jesus to let His Words abide in us, our hearts will turn to Him. Then, in turn, this causes us to have an increased openness to love God, act godly and keep His commandments (in our hearts). At this point we find ourselves in the favorable position of abiding in God's love and affection...the natural result being that we are PLEASING to Him and He answers all of our prayers!

So, the secret recipe for full joy is found in these two passages: Time with the Lord + Word in our hearts = love for and obedience to God = God's love working in and through us = answered prayer (fruit) = proof we are His disciples!

In preparation for your ultimate meeting with the Lord just start spending more time meeting with Him now. In the process life will present pleasure and the joy of God!

JULY 7...DAY 188
YOU CAN OBEY GOD

"Wives, be subject to your husbands, as is fitting in the Lord. Husbands, love your wives, and do not be embittered against them. Children, be obedient to your parents in all things, for this is well-pleasing to the Lord. Fathers, do not exasperate your children, that they may not lose heart. Slaves, in all things obey those who are your masters on earth, not with external service, as those who merely please men, but with sincerity of heart, fearing the Lord. Whatever you do, do your work heartily, as for the Lord rather than for men; knowing that from the Lord you will receive the reward

of the inheritance. It is the Lord Christ whom you serve...Masters, grant to your slaves justice and fairness, knowing that you too have a Master in heaven."
Colossians 3:18-24; 4:1 NASB

No one is happier than the person who allows God complete control. It's just that we can never experience the reality of this release until we've already begun to do it! We often haven't many others around to follow, or to serve as examples in this practice.

In every generation Christianity is "the road less travelled". It is important for us to learn the ways God has instructed us to be pleasing to Him, and not follow the crowd of popular opinion. In today's verse we find another biblical key that will help anyone, anywhere. This directive covers the basic personal ladders of life, up or down, either directly or indirectly.

Notice how the command is the same to each kind of person addressed. Paul tells each one, no matter what their circumstances are, to serve the Lord from the heart; this will be demonstrated by their relationships with others on a higher, level, or a lower rung on that ladder.

We all have our own unique perspective from which we view, judge, and form opinions about the things happening to us and around us. So often this freedom of thought can become the very reason we struggle and strive, especially with those above or below us in the "food chain." God teaches us to resist the human tendency to compare ourselves with one another, and instead direct our focus to Him in all things. This keeps God operational in our lives because it puts us in agreement with His perspective.

The Lord's words direct both the children and the slaves in this passage to choose obedience, even though they legally have no choice! The key is to keep serving the Lord in and through your circumstances. This will be vital in the last days when true Christianity will be severely opposed...our heart's just intention is very pleasing to the Lord.

JULY 8...DAY 189
THE POWER OF PLEASING GOD

"When a man's ways are pleasing to the Lord, He makes even his enemies to be at peace with him." Proverbs 16:7 NASB

"For it came about when Solomon was old, his wives turned his heart away after other gods; and his heart was not wholly devoted to the Lord his God, as the heart of David his father had been...So the Lord said to Solomon, 'Because you have done this, and you have not kept My covenant and My statutes, which I have commanded you, I will surely tear the kingdom from you, and will give it to your servant.'" 1 Kings 11:4, 11 NASB

"Then Esau ran to meet him (Jacob) and embraced him, and fell on his neck and kissed him, and they wept." Genesis 33:4 NASB

"And he took great pride in the ways of the Lord...Now the dread of the Lord was on all the kingdoms of the lands which were around Judah, so that they did not make war against Jehoshaphat." 2 Chronicles 17:6, 10 NASB

There is a spiritual connection I want you to make today that will help you for the rest of your natural life. Solomon gives us another standard about the power of pleasing the Lord here in Proverbs that ultimately cost him dearly at the end of his life. If we can connect that "pleasing the Lord" and being "at peace with our enemies" work together, we won't duplicate his mistake.

The truth is, no matter how difficult circumstances can be or how deadly our enemies may become, God manages both when we hand over the control of our lives to Him. Having worked in positions where I have been both the boss and the employee, I know it is easier to be the latter. When you are working for someone else your job description is simplified. You know who you have to please. Since you don't have the ultimate responsibility or pressure of the "bottom line," you are free to do your particular job with singleness of heart and energy. It is the same as a Christian. We are only responsible to please God. He owns the pressure of making things turn out properly in the end.

The only difference is that He is not ordinary boss...He can adjust everything, including our enemies, and the "sky is the not even the limit" when it comes to promotions! Esau and Jehoshaphat both proved this for us. Peace follows pleasing the Lord, and God will subdue our enemies in due time. So, start taking greater pride in your service for the Lord...He won't let you down when you need Him most!

JULY 9...DAY 190
PLEASURE FOR PAIN

"But the Lord was pleased to crush Him, putting Him to grief; If He would render Himself as a guilt offering, He will see His offspring, He will prolong His days, and the good pleasure of the Lord will prosper in His hand.
Isaiah 53:10 NASB

"For you have been called for this purpose, since Christ also suffered for you, leaving you an example for you to follow in His steps,...Therefore, since Christ has suffered in the flesh, arm yourselves also with the same purpose, because he who has suffered in the flesh has ceased from sin, so as to live the rest of the time in the flesh no longer for the lusts of men, but for the will of God."
1 Peter 2:21; 4:1-2 NASB

The event that has most pleased God in human history is the very thing that brought Him the most pain! The offering of His own Son for the guilt of the world was the most costly move He could have made because it meant sacrificing Himself.

There is a great, often overlooked Christian secret to be uncovered from the life and death of Jesus Christ. As Isaiah also said, the Lord's ways and thoughts are much higher than our own (Isaiah 55:8). Which of us would ever think to solve the problem of human sin by exchanging His Pure Life for those affected by the fall? Who could have foreseen the great dividends this exchange has paid, saving all who have accepted its conditions? Even the devil had no idea how much true pleasure, peace and prosperity could come out of pain (1 Corinthians 2:7-8).

You are likely reading this today, however, because God knew! The above scriptures tell us how important it is not only for us to "know," but for us to emulate. The key to lasting success is suffering. Think about it, Jesus willingly gave Himself for this human reclamation project. God's actions lead to divine results. In heavenly terms the costlier the gift, the greater the reward. This is ingenious!

Now, if we can apply ourselves in His service the same way, we will experience parallel results. Since this exchange of Jesus' life for our own cost the Lord so much, He urges us not to take it for granted. So, the most valuable thing you possess is what God now requires in return to complete the exchange for the sacrifice of His Son...YOU! Only His whole heart could have purchased such a great salvation. Only your whole heart will truly satisfy His pain!

JULY 10...DAY 191
THE KIND OF SONG WE NEED TO SING

"It is a trustworthy statement: For if we died with Him, we shall also live with Him; If we endure, we shall also reign with Him; If we deny Him, He also will deny us; If we are faithless, He remains faithful; for He cannot deny Himself."
2 Timothy 2:11-13 NASB

Many Bible commentators believe this portion of scripture was a familiar song among the churches of that day. What makes this particularly meaningful is that it was a time of intense persecution for Christians in the Roman Empire! When the churches gathered in those days, they sang about the "unvarnished" Truth as well as the character and cost necessary to proclaim it!! Some of the most horrific things imaginable were happening to believers everyday as a result of their faith in Jesus Christ. Paul even prefaces this song in verses 8 through 10 by telling us he himself was also suffering on behalf of the people of God through the nature of his message.

What was it about Jesus' story that can cultivate so much negative reaction both inside and outside of the church? Notice verse eight: "Remember that Jesus Christ, of the seed of David, was raised from the dead according to my gospel." Primarily, it is the fact that Jesus overcame death. Divine methods that do not make sense to the human mind and cannot be stopped by demonic forces are what make Christianity so volatile. Even though we endure persecution for His sake, historically we multiply more intensely and rapidly in the midst of such difficulties! Jesus died, and as a result became more powerful and influential after the Cross. As His followers, we have exactly the same effect...the more we lay our lives down the greater life we manifest with which to enlighten other lost men and women! This drives ruling demonic forces manic and effects both the policies of the world rulers they influence, and the mindsets of the cultures they seek to deceive.

Today, we encounter a worse and more dangerous scenario. The church has accepted so much of the world's culture into its ranks disabling the ability to distinguish between godly and ungodly tendencies. Have we have stopped singing the songs of simple plain declarations filled with truth and forgotten the depth and nature of the One for Whom and To Whom we are singing them?! It is time to remind ourselves what it really takes to be overcomers and encourage one another to bravely live out our faith every day. In the end, those who die to themselves will really live and those who endure all things will know what it means to reign...because it is impossible for Him to turn His back on Himself, even when everyone else does!!

JULY 11...DAY 192
THE WRATH OF THE LAMB

"And the kings of the earth, the great men, the rich men, the commanders, the mighty men, every slave and every free man, hid themselves in the caves and in the rocks of the mountains, and said to the mountains and rocks, 'Fall on us and hide us from the face of Him who sits on the throne and from the wrath of the Lamb! For the great day of His wrath has come, and who is able to stand.'"
Revelation 6:15-17 NKJV

Does it strike you as strange that the words, "wrath" and "Lamb" are used in conjunction with one another? Our scripture announces there is a time coming when Jesus' wrath will be poured out upon the people of this world. Even though He is a "Lamb," His "Lion" attribute will be displayed in such a way that those who experience it will immediately realize the "other side" of God!

John the Apostle was shown this approaching future scene. From this revelation we know without a doubt what will surely come to pass. As scary as it is, and as many times as it will have been read in the pages of Bibles all over the world, these same people will find themselves unprepared for a situation they did not anticipate! What's more, because of the language used, I believe many of them will likely be professing Christians!

It is so out of the ordinary for the average believer today to imagine a Jesus who is not exclusively a "lamb." So many churches train parishioners by teaching the "light" side of God to an extreme, in an effort to make Him more acceptable to a society that loves warm and fuzzy and instant gratification. But, have you ever noticed how many times God appears to people in the Bible in ways that are less than placatory or soothing?

He once tried to kill Moses for overlooking the importance of circumcision in his own household. Another time, the Lord appeared as the Angel of God's Armies to Joshua with a drawn sword. On Mount Sinai, He was fierce and dark, while on the Mount of Transfiguration He chastised Peter out of a cloud!

Jesus is the Lamb of God and because of it He is to be feared as well as loved. Just because God is characteristically gentle doesn't mean we should take His good patience for granted!

Today, we are invited to the throne of God (Hebrews 4:16) to look upon the face of Jesus (1 Corinthians 3:18; 4:6)! We are not appointed to experience His wrath (1

Thessalonians 5:9). Be humble before the Lion of the tribe of Judah now and you will never find yourself in opposition to the Lamb later!

JULY 12...DAY 193
THE QUESTION YOU WANT JESUS TO ASK

"...the chief priests and the scribes, together with the elders, confronted Him (Jesus) and spoke to Him, saying, 'Tell us, by what authority are You doing these things? Or who is he who gave You this authority? But He answered and said to them, 'I also will ask you one thing, and answer Me: The baptism of John – was it from heaven or from men?'"
Luke 20:1-4 NKJV

What is the one question Jesus is asking you today? In searching for your answer, you may be shocked to find that His tactics with you might be very similar to the ones He used with these religious leaders in the book of Luke. In classic Jesus fashion, the Lord answered their questions with a question. By doing this He bypassed the logic of their intellect, no matter how clever they may have thought themselves, and appealed straight to the intentions of their hearts!

The Bible tells why this approach is so important and effective. In many ways the religious world of Jesus' time was similar to our own era. According to the Lord Himself, the spiritual leadership of that day was prone to political expediency, or hypocrisy in its normal operational procedures. This attitude lead the nation astray from what God underlined as important in scripture. Instead of valuing the Word of God itself, they had placed more importance on the rules that had grown out of the organizational structures they had built to distribute that Word! Jesus said to these same guys in Matthew 23:24, when we become so blind that we "strain at gnats, yet swallow camels" it is an indicator that our hearts have lost touch with God.

The heart is central to this discussion, being the core part of our being, where spirit and soul come together to amalgamate who we really are. It is where the real "issues of life" emerge according to Proverbs 4:23.

Look at today's text again. The Lord redirected their focus to heavenly things. If they could have "gone there" and sincerely answered His question, He would have answered theirs.

In the end, they were left to only "reason" further among themselves...without the Lord's guidance. Lets check our hearts by God's Word (Hebrews 4:12) so in the end of days we do not miss heaven and hit earth!

JULY 13...DAY 194
AFFECTIONATELY REMEMBERING
THE LORD

"For I received from the Lord Himself that which I passed on to you [it was given to me personally], that the Lord Jesus on the night when He was treacherously delivered up and while His betrayal was in progress took bread. And when He had given thanks, He broke [it] and said, 'Take, eat. This is My body, which is broken for you. Do this to call Me [affectionately] to remembrance.' Similarly when supper was ended, He took the cup also, saying 'This cup is the new covenant [ratified and established] in My blood. Do this, as often as you drink [it], to call Me [affectionately] to remembrance. For very time you eat this bread and drink this cup, you are representing and signifying and proclaiming the fact of the Lord's death until He comes [again].'"
1 Corinthians 11:23-26 AMP

I think it is particularly touching that the instructions how Jesus' "Last Supper" (Luke 22:1-20) with His disciples applies to us, were written by Paul. Although he stands at the top of the list when we think of the original pioneers of the Christian faith and he wrote more of the New Testament than any other single person, he was not one of those who walked and talked with Jesus while He was on earth. Paul was not a secondary Apostle, however, because he did have a personal encounter and intimate relationship with the Lord.

The fact that his experience with Jesus was "after" the resurrection makes it all the more pertinent to you and I today. We can relate to needing time in prayer, worship and the Word of God for our recognition of the Lord's voice to grow and our understanding of spiritual things to mature. When you add everything up you could say that in many ways Paul excelled further than the Apostles who did spend three and a half years with Jesus of Nazareth! That gives us hope and confidence to go as far in the Lord as He will call us into service for Him.

There really aren't any restrictions for the person who comes to "remember" Jesus "affectionately," as the Amplified Bible translates it! What made Paul a special person was that he knew firsthand the love, mercy and forgiveness of God. Then, he learned to operate in the grace (divine power and ability) that works in a believer conducting his ministry assignment.

Take a page out of Paul's testimony today and put your relationship with the Lord above and before your work for Him. If you get to know Jesus affectionately in the beginning...you will be a sublime believer in the end!

JULY 14...DAY 195
LET'S GET IT ON!

"Likewise you younger people, submit yourselves to your elders. Yes, all of you be submissive to one another, and be clothed with humility, for God resists the proud, but gives grace to the humble. Therefore humble yourselves under the mighty hand of God, that He may exalt you in due time, casting all your care upon Him, for He cares for you. Be sober, be vigilant; because your adversary the devil walks about like a roaring lion, seeking whom he may devour. Resist him, steadfast in the faith, knowing that he same sufferings are experienced by your brotherhood in the world."
1 Peter 5:5-9 NKJV

Christians have an unseen adversary working against them who must be identified to be overcome. According to our scripture the devil is responsible, either directly or indirectly, for the sufferings we endure as believers in this world.

In any discussion of last days' preparation, he has to be a topic of discussion since that time period will be the culmination of the struggle between good and evil for the souls of mankind. Therefore, I would like to dedicate some time in this devotional study to exposing exactly who the devil is and how he schemes against us for control of our environment. Let me warn you now. Even though Jesus has defeated Satan decisively on our behalf, this enemy still operates against us just as he did the incarnate Lord, and will test our boundaries. You have authority over the devil, but you will have to be decisive in your resolve to not let anything he may do rattle you. If you expose him you will incur a certain level of adversity from him, but if you stand in the Lord's power you will take ground from him in the long run.

Today's scripture has been placed in our Bibles, not as a suggestion but rather a command. You are responsible to take your stand against the one who withstands you. You must resist the one who will resist you! It is an elementary part of the Christian call, knowing you have a fight on your hands that you cannot run from. Instead you must be strong enough to stand up to him and remain unchanged by extreme pressure.

It is a strange fight. You have been given the victory in advance through Christ Jesus, and all the tools you need of submission, humility, resistance, sobriety, and vigilance as well as God's mighty hand of protection are found in the verses above. So, as they say in the boxing arena, if you are ready to answer the bell for life..."let's get it on!!"

JULY 15...DAY 196
UNMASKING YOUR ENEMY

"Be well balanced (temperate, sober of mind), be vigilant and cautious at all times; your adversary the devil prowls around like a roaring lion seeking someone to seize upon and devour. Withstand him; be firm in faith [against his onset—rooted, established, strong, immovable, and determined], knowing that the same (identical) sufferings are appointed to your brotherhood (the whole body of Christians) throughout the world. And after you have suffered a little while, the God of all grace [Who imparts all blessing and favor], Who has called you to His [own] eternal glory in Christ Jesus, will Himself complete and make you what you ought to be, establish and ground you securely, and strengthen, and settle you."
1 Peter 5:8-10 AMP

As born-again believers, the Lord instructs us to mature in our ability to "discern" spiritual things (1 Corinthians 2:14, Hebrew 5:14). If not we will find ourselves stunted and unable to carry any weight in the spirit realm. The study of Satan is a case in point. Most Christians today do not know much about this dangerous biblical character and as a result do not even recognize him, much less deal with him effectively. Yet, the verses above tell us the devil is our direct enemy and that we are going to have to "withstand" him in a strong, purposeful, patient and determined way!

In light of our potential nearness to the end of the end times, the church needs to start facing this fear of confrontation - courageously! Let's get started by naming some names. The two most common names for this monster are "Satan" and the "devil." "Satan" is a Hebrew word of Chaldean origin, telling us it is as old as civilization. The most literal translation is, "an accuser." It can also be rendered, "an opponent or arch enemy (of good)." "Devil" means, "a traducer" or one who misrepresents, speaks ill of or disparages another.

When you put all this information together you begin to get a pretty precise picture of who we are dealing with and how serious our spiritual position truly is. We are being opposed by an arch-enemy who seeks to accuse, slander us and who is actively arranging for our physical, spiritual, and eternal downfall! He must be resisted and opposed. It is useless to try appeasement. God is allowing our exposure to this devil but has already defeated him for us in the words and actions of Jesus, our Savior. Choose rightly, your strength is in the winning side!

JULY 16...DAY 197
THE CHURCH IN MY HOMETOWN

*"I will bless the Lord, Who has given me counsel;
yes, my heart instructs me in the night seasons."*
Psalm 16:7 AMP

There is a great renovation stirring under the surface of the church right now, which will take God's people beyond the limitations they have unknowingly built around themselves in modern times. This divine reconstruction became clear to me at the end of 2002, when the Lord spoke to me in an extended and perplexing dream. I am sharing some of these experiences with you throughout this study as a way of encouraging you to break free from any restricting religious mindset you may have, and unbind yourself to go forward in the Spirit into these end times.

One of the saddest things I see in the church today is the inability of so many believers to properly balance spiritual things and become a greater voice for God in the world. One extreme is to manufacture spiritual manifestations to the point of misuse, while the other is to simply regulate them out of existence altogether. I trust that you have a heart to "rightly divide" or examine God's Word objectively when you hear it and not go to such extremes.

These are both exciting and dangerous times, where the shakings of God will test every foundation and support of truth in the Christian life. We must be people of substance and study to be equal to them!

What I saw in my dream was a sobering reminder of where we are today...or should I say where we are not!

As I was sleeping, I realized that I was entering my hometown of Kirksville, Missouri and coming into a part of the city where many of the wealthy and more successful people lived. This area is where the homes of the 'who's who' from the medical and educational institutions were located. As I considered those who lived there I suddenly noticed a large, elegant brick church complex that I had never seen before. My mind ran to the surrounding streets and houses, many of which I had been in and around as a child. How weird that I hadn't realized this magnificent church structure had grown there as well. As I found myself almost wishing that I pastored a church like this one, I began to understand that God was talking to me and giving me a symbolic insight into the condition of His church. The following is exactly what has happened to it.

Almost overnight and in our most influential backyards the church has grown up in so many ways and gained a more prominent place in our society than it had twenty or thirty years ago when I was a child. As you will see tomorrow, something wasn't quite right with this "church"...and that "something" is very important for every Christian to identify in these last days!

JULY 17...DAY 198
FIRST IMPRESSIONS

"The prophet who has a dream, let him tell a dream; and he who has My word, let him speak My word faithfully." Jeremiah 23:28-29 NKJV

Yesterday, I began sharing a word I was given in a dream for the Church in this hour. Allow me to continue.

After driving into my hometown and noticing an elaborate church complex I had never seen before, I felt a strange draw to pull into that neighborhood for a closer look.

It is very significant that I grew up in a place called "Kirksville." I realized later that the connection between what God showed me about the end times Church and the subtle meaning of this town's name was no coincidence! "Kirke" or "Circe" was a famous pagan witch/goddess who lured men into her home and used drugs to turn them into pigs as told in Homer's Greek story, the "Odyssey." Her name is believed by many to be the suspicious origin for our English word, "church!" It is said that both famous Christian translators of the reformation, Martin Luther and William Tyndale, refused to use this word because of its demonic inferences. It's not much of a stretch to suspect that today's church has been similarly drugged and turned into something other than the gatherings of believers we see in the Bible!

In my dream, as I came closer to examine the structure of the "church" building, I noticed that it had an external, 'drive-up' area just off the street that was for the quick, convenient payment of tithes and offerings. I immediately thought, "this must be a mainline denominational church of some kind...what an ingenious idea!" At that point a lady I knew to be the pastor's wife began to describe to me and my wife how this was the latest, greatest thing, quite happily explaining its operation to us.

Here again, is the truth. How like the world we have become in our systematic ways of collecting and managing money. Give us another twenty or thirty years and we will have our churches represented on the stock exchange indexes with rolling adjustments for our parishioners to keep daily track of!

Yet, as a pastor having this dream, my first impression was that this was a very interesting concept! Far from "normal" it was tempting to think I could streamline the uncomfortable process of dealing with collections. Although the Bible is clear about God's willingness to provide for His people, I can tell you our overemphasis on such carnal issues is taking us where we don't really want to go spiritually. It is not that we aren't to excel in the area of finance, but rather that it isn't what is truly important.

Modern ministry needs to rethink what faith in God really is and give itself again to things like prayer and the study of the Word. We have seriously institutionalized people when God's goal has always been to deregulate them!

JULY 18...DAY 199
UNNECESSARY TRADITIONS

"And the Pharisees and scribes kept asking [Jesus], Why do Your disciples not order their way of living according to the tradition handed down by the forefathers...But He said to them, excellently and truly...did Isaiah prophesy of you, the pretenders and hypocrites, as it stands written: These people [constantly] honor Me with their lips, but their hearts hold off and are far distant from Me. In vain (fruitlessly and without profit) do they worship Me, ordering and teaching [to be obeyed] as doctrines the commandments of God and cling to the tradition of men [keeping it carefully and faithfully]...Thus you are nullifying and making void and of no effect [the authority of] the Word of God through your tradition, which you [in turn] hand on..." Mark 7:5-13 AMP

In my dream, the scene changed and I found myself inside the church admiring its sanctuary. It was elegant, large and well taken care of. It had many of the amenities that I would expect in this category of professionally manicured building, right down to the beautifully ornate stage with organ pipes on the back wall, a choir section and several steps across its front leading up to the pulpit.

The pastor was on the platform rehearsing the storied history of this church. He conformed to the turn of the 21st century pastoral mold with his business class approach and expensive, conservative attire. What he said clued me in to the specific type of church the Lord was presenting before me. He said that this was a "foursquare" church, referring I believe to the "stable and forthright" foundation on which it had been established (rather than a literal organization). This church had initially been built by a pioneering type of minister who carved it out of nothing years before, who then fell into doctrinal error before having been removed. Another leader was called in to take care of "righting the ship" and had then gone on to take things to even higher levels of numeric growth.

This story was an illustrated general history of ministry in America over the last generation (fifty years or so). The inference clearly was that we have gone down a road that still looks good visually, if somewhat outdated, but doesn't measure up to its previous essential glory. We have settled for the world's seal of approval in place of the authentic spiritual life of Christ that establishes us as God's congregation.

As the conversation turned to the current leadership and more recent history of this local church, I found myself getting bored with the "vision casting" of the pastor and wanting to look further behind all the religious scenes. It isn't particular traditions that have made the church so hollow in our time, tradition in general has stolen its heart!

JULY 19...DAY 200
THE SIGN OF OUR TIME

"I have gone astray like a lost sheep; seek, inquire for, and demand Your servant, for I do not forget Your commandments."
Psalm 119:176 AMP

I next found myself exiting the building. To my amazement I discovered that what I had thought was just one building was actually a complex of three, which occupied all three sides of the intersection of two streets which came together in a 'T' right where this church stood. As I looked across the street to one of the other structures, I suddenly noticed a large sign near the roofline, which spelled out the name of the place. It read, "TAU Tabernacle."

I have learned to never disregard such plainly put dream-state information. TAU is a strange word, but one I was distantly familiar with. When I awoke I remembered it was part of the name of a local fraternity house in my hometown when I was growing up. I knew that it was a Greek letter and probably had a deeper meaning that would help me unravel the significance of my dream. I was right! Not only was it a Greek letter, but more importantly a Hebrew one. In fact, I found it translated in my Bible exactly that way, as a heading for the final section (last 8 verses) of the 119th Psalm. TAU is the 22nd and final letter in the Hebrew alphabet and is used to in that language to paint a picture of something that is symbolic or significant. When you study the history of this letter you will find that it has many facets of meaning to the Hebrew people. It is particularly descriptive of a covenant, the completion of something unfinished and a stamp or impression made into something.

This sign was a "sign" to me that God was showing me some important things about the last days' condition of the Church. As a "mark" or "sign," this letter was always a symbol for a "vehicle of sacrifice." It looks similar to the English letter "t" and represents the stamp of the cross given to God's people far in advance of Jesus' substitution and sacrifice for their sin!

Some have said "Tau," as the final letter in the Hebrew alphabet, represents completion of the Spiritual Cycle and is a sign of Truth and Perfection. It denotes the final spiritual destination for humankind.

I believe the Holy Spirit is going to do a work in God's people similar to what happened to me in this dream. In our spiritual discontentment we see the worldly church falling further into its end-time predicted deception. Even so, a remnant has been stamped by God. Out of the church will emerge THE CHURCH!

JULY 20...DAY 201
RESERVATIONS FOR THE END TIMES

"And with this the predictions of the prophets agree, as it is written, after this I will come back, and will rebuild the house of David, which has fallen: I will rebuild its [very] ruins, and I will set it up again, so that the rest of men may seek the Lord, and all the Gentiles upon whom My name has been invoked, says the Lord, Who has been making these things known from the beginning of the world."
Isaiah 45:21; Jer.12:15; Amos 9:11, 12. Acts 15:15-18 AMP

Instead of being willing to forsake all and follow Jesus, we have forsaken Him without realizing it and are following a form of God with no power! We've built strangely self-serving churches and hung His sign on the outside, just like the Bible said we would (2 Thessalonians 2:3; 1Timothy 4:1; 2 Timothy 3:1-5)! The scary part of it all is that nobody thinks it strange! All appears well to those who are a part of it, and even initially to those like me who were sent to inspect it.

Something inside me loved this place and yet something told me it was all wrong! I realized that the name of this building was the key to God's church. We have to follow who we are, not what we've become! The call of the Church is to be the restored "Tabernacle of David," a rebuilt end-time house of true worship, gathered to the Gospel of Jesus, from among those with pure hearts for God in all the nations of the earth...again, just like the Bible said!

To continue my dream, as I was walking around the "campus," I saw the front doors of the main building being opened. A service was about to begin, so I went back and prepared to go in, when surprisingly one of the ushers spoke to me.

"Mr. Veach we have reserved a seat for you in the back of the auditorium," the older gentleman said with the faintest hint of a wry smile on his face. I was almost relieved, but still a bit perturbed that I was not invited up front into some section for special guests. After all this was "my dream" and they were the ones with the twisted idea of spiritual service. I could see no one was going to get anything right in this wrong place!

I smiled and nodded to the greeter as I entered the building, but found myself not headed for the sanctuary at all. I saw the usual worshipers through the doors of the sanctuary and knew instinctively what was happening in the service. They were worshipping the idea of worship more than the God who deserved their full attention. It no longer interested me.

On a good day this was just another soul driven display of singing, hand shaking and sermonizing. On a bad day, a little lip service and a lot of back scratching. I had more important business...

JULY 21...DAY 202
GO TO THE BASEMENT

Instead of taking my "reserved" seat in the back of the sanctuary in this hollow church's next "event," I decided to pass it altogether! I was compelled to find the basement of this building and see what was down there. When I came to the bottom of the stairs, I realized it was more "concrete" and stable "underground," a much more "livable" environment.

The basement in this church was representative, not of what is missing in the church today, but what has been overlooked in all its "surface" religious activity. It was a fully outfitted, multi-room apartment or house, perfect for visiting guests or ministers. I began to understand that the real "family of God" is a large part of what is waiting to be rediscovered by those who are not satisfied with the condition of compromised Christianity. This underground level was where the real heartbeat of this church should have been. Yet, for all of the 'excitement' going on upstairs, it was strikingly obvious that there was no one downstairs at all! Sitting on those stairs, I realized how special this place was, where the spiritual foundation and real potential of God's people could be appreciated.

At this point I awoke, knowing that what I had just been shown was significant. That last part of my dream was the most substantial because it told me that there still exists something basic in the church that God can excavate. There were a lot of eye-opening negatives in my dream, but this underdeveloped potential is the big positive.

The Lord is combing through the ruins of His tabernacle right now to awaken His "Davids" for the last days! We are going back to the basement vault, back to the underground essence of our nature. His church is coming not as disparate organizations, but as ONE BODY. I am not saying we are going back to some archaic way. God's true believers are going deeper; even as the one dimensional church above ground evaporates into wafer thin shallowness and spiritual anorexia. Back to where His church is store housing the treasure of the knowledge of God Himself, and the reflection of that knowledge in our sincere relationships one to another.

This is the day of escape from the church that we have built for ourselves. Don't assume your perceptions of God are necessarily the reality. Perceptions are gossamer, changing things, just as mine were during this dream. Reality will come increasingly via a new purview. Be in the righteous part of His house when it does, so you can be an integral part of the impression the Lord is about to engrave upon this world.

Instead of allowing church to remain stamped by the societal form, God will be sealing the true church's mark on the world around it.

The consummation of all things is just ahead of us, so let God mark you, your church and your ambitions so you will not only be ready when He comes, but so that you yourself will be a sign to the world that His church has emerged!

JULY 22...DAY 203
SEEING THE WAY

"Pattern yourselves after me [follow my example],
as I imitate Christ (the Messiah)."
1 Corinthians 11:1 AMP

"Therefore be imitators of God [copy Him and follow His example], as well-
beloved children [imitate their father]. And walk in love."
Ephesians 5:1 AMP

When things get blurry, we have two clear paths to follow in the Christian life. We can follow God, and we can follow anyone else in our sights who is following Him!

When a trainee's way becomes uncertain in any field of endeavor, the first instruction is to remember their training. As a disciple of Christ, the things highlighted everyday here in this devotion are principles that will prepare you to have something to fall back on when times get tough.

Since the Lord is our Shepherd who will never leave us on our own, there will never be a time when you can't find Him. Of course it will not always seem that way, which is the point! God is faithful even when we are not, so never panic and think things are so blocked that you cannot move forward. Just get Jesus back into your sights. Remember what He has said and done in your Bible and believe it. He is no respecter of persons, so He will keep His Word to all who exercise faith in Him.

When you are unsure of the road ahead of you just "imitate" or literally "act like" the Lord. Think about the situations He encountered and do the same things Jesus did. If that approach isn't working for you then find someone who it is working for and imitate them! God has and will always have His secret agents to come alongside you, whether in person or through scripture. Simply recall what the Lord has done in other people's lives, whether in the Bible or before you personally, and begin saying, praying, and staying the same way.

Look around to see if there is someone in front of you right now who sees more clearly than you and tailgate them! Like the tail-lights on the car in front of you in a snow storm, they will lead you to safety. God promised us there would always be a way of escape so start looking for it with expectancy...follow the godly patterns you see today and the Holy Spirit will have something to remind you of and guide you with tomorrow!

JULY 23...DAY 204
CLOSE YOUR EYES AND SEE THE WAY

"Now behold two of them were traveling that same day to a village called Emmaus, which was seven miles from Jerusalem. And they talked together of all these things which had happened. So it was, while they conversed and reasoned that Jesus Himself drew near and went with them. But their eyes were restrained, so that they did not know Him...Then their eyes were opened and they knew Him; and He vanished from their sight."
Luke 24:13-16, 31 NKJV

Here is a revealing picture of how Jesus works with anyone who "wants to know" Him. In the midst of the most important series of events in His life and ministry (his death, burial and resurrection), the Lord takes the time to take a seven mile walk with two of His "lower level" followers! Not only were these guys not among the twelve apostles, but consider the fact that Jesus was opening the scriptures to them at the exact same time that Peter was trying to make sense of the empty tomb!

In a seemingly unreasonable display of God's own time management, the Lord appears to two "low priority" disciples while leaving the new leaders of His ministry in the dark! What's more, the topic He addresses is the futility of human reason!! Scriptures like this do us good as Christians because they teach us how important it is to always think outside the box when it comes to understanding spiritual things. Notice how, when Jesus approached these men, he "restrained" their eyes, so they didn't know Him. Often, when God really wants to teach us something, He blinds us to its outward appearance. Why? Because, even when we are directly dealing with the spiritual realm we are so easily distracted by the impulses of our carnal nature that we would be diverted from His deep inner meanings. It is important to make the connection here between "knowing" the Lord and "seeing" Him.

Jesus did not open their eyes until after He was finished revealing what He wanted them to know. Then He promptly vanished from their sight altogether!

The more you get to know the Lord the more you learn to put most reasoning and conversation regarding Him in a secondary position behind the intimacy of knowing Him. If we start there, all of our other knowledge will increase and we will find ourselves naturally excited and motivated to tell others about Jesus. It wasn't until these two "little guys" reported what they had learned that Jesus appeared to the "big guys" (verse 36)!

In the last days, we will need the same firsthand knowledge of God and unity of the brethren to lead us as well!

JULY 24...DAY 205
PASSING "GO" AND COLLECTING YOUR SPIRITUAL REWARD

"Now as he was going out on the road, one came running, knelt before Him, and asked Him, 'Good Teacher, what shall I do that I may inherit eternal life?' And he answered and said unto him, Teacher, all these things have I kept from my youth. Then Jesus looking at him, loved him, and said to him, One thing you lack: Go your way, sell whatever you have and give to the poor, and you will have treasure in heaven; and come, take up the cross, and follow Me. But he was sad at this word, and went away sorrowful, for he had great possessions."
Mark 10:20-22 NKJV

There are several additions here in Mark's account of this story, compared with Luke's version. The "one thing you lack" reference is the same but we see a more personal and intimate view of how the scene unfolded.

These little differences make a big difference when you think about how small the margin can be between a person being "saved" or lost. Let's look at the way this man approached Jesus. Luke merely records that he asked about eternal life, but Mark reminds us about his sense of urgency and honor. He, "came running" and "knelt before" the Lord intent on receiving what he was searching for. Although he ended up choosing not to follow the Lord, this guy wasn't superficial in his approach, he was genuine!

A person can be focused on seeking the godly solution, but still not prepared for the one thing required of him that will cost everything! This "young man" (see Matthew 19:20) learned there was a big gap between his idea of goodness and God's. He was prepared to give everything he thought it would take to be saved, but found that was not good enough. He gave his best...God wanted his all!

Never be surprised to find that God's idea of your best may be more than you think you are ready to give. God never asks more than we are able to do or to give, although it may seem so to us. Surrendering all to Jesus is the heavenly standard for understanding His ways, finding true freedom, and gaining permission to follow the Lord more closely! In the last days, many will not collect their reward because they will have failed to pass "GO" on God's gameboard of spiritual entitlement...they will approach the game correctly, but they will not move forward in the right direction when the world's dice are tossed and the pressure escalates!

JULY 25...DAY 206
LITTLE DIFFERENCES CAN MAKE ALL THE DIFFERENCE

"Now as he was going out on the road, one came running, knelt before Him, and asked Him, 'Good Teacher, what shall I do that I may inherit eternal life?' And he answered and said unto him, Teacher, all these things have I kept from my youth. Then Jesus looking at him, loved him, and said to him, One thing you lack: Go your way, sell whatever you have and give to the poor, and you will have treasure in heaven; and come, take up the cross, and follow Me. But he was sad at this word, and went away sorrowful, for he had great possessions."
Mark 10:20-22 NKJV

Yesterday, we looked at the first significant difference between Mark's and Luke's records of the "rich young ruler's" story. Approaching Jesus (even genuinely) without surrendering your life to Him is like winning the lottery but losing your ticket before cashing it in! Today, let's consider a couple of other subtle distinctions in these two accounts that will be important to our understanding of how to begin a lasting relationship with the Lord.

The next distinction is found in verse 21. Mark records how Jesus, "looking at him, loved him," telling us the young ruler was even closer to his target than he may have realized. Jesus' response to him wasn't meant to prevent him from becoming a disciple it was exactly what was necessary for him to take on his heavenly call! Jesus loved him, just as he loves it when you and I approach him with such sincerity and, open-heartedness. This heart knowledge alone can enable you to overcome all obstacles in your way.

I really knew Jesus loved me when I first met Him. That intimate knowledge has sustained me through many difficult situations over the years. I'm not sure this man looked far enough beyond Jesus' demand to see His underlying desire for the young ruler's reciprocal affection, spiritual communion and for the salvation of his soul.

Finally, Mark points out that this young man's giving of all he had was not meant to be a onetime thing. The all important "one thing" Jesus asked of him would only be the initial lifting of a "cross" he must carry throughout his entire life! He, like us, would have to daily approach God humbly, allow the love of Jesus to lead him to sacrificial obedience; and keep doing both these things over and over!

Commit to memory the negative ending of this man's story, do the opposite so you can have a positive finale with the Lord...these little differences can make all the difference as we prepare to meet the Lord as He makes Himself available, and openly answers all your questions today!

JULY 26...DAY 207
LOVE IS WHAT ITS GOT TO DO WITH

"So when they had eaten breakfast, Jesus said to Simon Peter, 'Simon, son of Jonah, do you love Me more than these?' He said to Him, 'Yes, Lord; You know that I love You.' He said to him, 'Feed My lambs.' He said to him again a second time, 'Simon, son of Jonah, do you love Me?' He said to Him, Yes, Lord; You know that I love You.' He said to him, 'Tend My sheep.' He said to him the third time, 'Simon, son of Jonah, do you love me?' Peter was grieved because He said to him the third time, Do you love Me?' And he said to Him. 'Lord, You know all things; You know that I love You.' Jesus said to him, 'Feed My sheep.'"
John 21:15-17

We have examined this scripture in our February 13-15 devotions, but I want to revisit it from the standpoint of understanding God's love. It is important to realize that we cannot prepare for Christ's return without learning to remain firmly connected to God's heart.

Notice that, possibly because he had denied the Lord three times, Peter was questioned about his love for the Lord three times. I think this was a means of correcting the cause of his weakness. The insights we gain from this exchange will help insulate us against the constant temptations of the same anti-Christian world around us.

The word "love" is used repeatedly in this dialogue. It sounds simple to us but it is actually a little more complex. The Lord started the conversation by using the Greek word, "agapao," meaning a deliberate, unselfish love that chooses to value and esteems another. Peter responds with the word, "phileo," denoting a tender, affectionate, personal, attached, friendly kind of love. Both of these words reference love for the Father, the Son, believers, and by Christ for the apostle John. While they are both legitimate expressions of what we call "love," there is a distinct difference between the two. According to the Greek dictionary of the New Testament in my Bible concordance, they are never used indiscriminately.

Jesus uses "agapao" in his first two questions and "phileo" in verse 17, while Peter uses, "phileo" in his three responses. Adding all the responses together the underlying statement is that God desires to be loved responsibly first and affectionately second.

When we keep our love in that order we remain clear and conscientious about our spiritual priorities and purposeful in our obedience to God. Love is a serious thing...Be tender toward God, but have high regard for God's particular qualities, willfully consider and value Him first - and unlike Peter you will not confuse the two types of love when the pressure is on!

JULY 27...DAY 208
TOUCHING "TRUE" LOVE

"For God so greatly loved and dearly prized the world that He [even] gave up His only begotten (unique) Son, so that whoever believes in (trusts in, clings to, relies on,) Him shall not perish (come to destruction, be lost) but have eternal (everlasting) life. For God did not send the Son into the world in order to judge (to reject, to condemn, to pass sentence on) the world, but that the world might find salvation and be made safe and sound through Him...The [basis of the] judgment (indictment, the test by which men are judged, the ground for the sentence) lies in this: The Light has come into the world, and people have loved the darkness rather than and more than the Light, for their works (deeds) were evil."
John 3:16-17, 19 AMP

Today's passage builds upon yesterday's study regarding the kind of love God prefers. Again, it is the word "agapao" that is used in describing the way God has loved the world. This means He sent Jesus to die for the sins of every human being not merely out of a sense of affection, but the kind of affection that was also well reasoned and selective. God did not send His Son because He was the only one who could appropriately punish the world, but because He was the only one who could reasonably satisfy the degree of affection He felt toward His creation. God loves us with the defined purpose that we would be forever saved to enjoy His own manner of life.

His love makes the ultimate reality possible, when responded to properly! Herein lies the problem; the highest type of love requires our highest form in return. Since we are created in God's image, we too have "agapao" ability. It is what our God nature is seeking to receive and express, even above our deepest human feelings and passions. Oh, how we tend to waste it on all the wrong things, though. When given a choice our human nature, which has been tainted with sin, prefers things contrary to God's nature. We tend to take our "Agapao" affection and spend it on the ordinary or even evil things the world offers us.

The litmus test we must pass is the appraisal of our "true" love. By locating it and giving it back to God, you surround yourself with the Light that drives away darkness...even the end-times gloom!

JULY 28...DAY 209
THE KIND OF LOVE GOD IS

"And we have known and believed the love that God has for us. God is love, and he who abides in love abides in God, and God in him. Love has been perfected among us in this: That we may have boldness in the day of judgment; because as He is, so are we in this world"
1 John 4:16-17 NKJV

Let's take our topic of "love" a step further today. By now you should be beginning to see that love comes in many different packages, even in the Bible! We have been looking at two specific kinds mentioned in the New Testament that teach us to separate our affections and love God with the highest intentions.

"Agapao" is often referred to as the "God-kind" or "highest kind" of love. Although it is very sentimental like our other Greek word, "phileo," it is also purposeful, attaching itself to that which is most worthy of its affection. Here in our text, we are told that God IS this pattern of love personified! If we follow His example and learn to dwell in this specific love, we will be training ourselves to naturally seek and give place to God Himself.

This skill is significant in our study of end-time living because it reveals the secret to staying "right" with God regardless of circumstances. When pressures mount and we are tempted to react to things and people around us, love is always the answer. Talk like God, walk with God, and represent God by choosing to place your affections where they deserve to reside. This will require examining your heart to make sure your love is not reactive, but genuine and responsive before the Lord.

We imagine we love God and man, but often we principally love ourselves! How can we distinguish? Look at the object of your affections. If God is foremost, your love will be in right standing toward others as well as caring for yourself. If self is stand-out, this love will be of no real value to anyone, no matter how passionate and sensitive it seems.

Agapao is not cold. It is just higher than our usual perception of warm. Not dispassionate, but a higher passion. There is a place in God where, because we ask Him to occupy more of ourselves, we notice self less! Selfless. This is the place that makes us look a lot like Him in this world, and at the same time lifts us above its conduct and ways! As we dwell there, we are automatically prepared to meet Him on the day when everything and everyone in this world is judged!

JULY 29...DAY 210
HOW TO EXPERIENCE HEAVEN ON EARTH

"(if I)...have not love, I am nothing...(if I) have not love, it profits me
nothing...Love suffers long and is kind; love does not envy; love does not parade itself,
is not puffed up; does not behave rudely, DOES NOT SEEK ITS OWN, is not provoked,
thinks no evil; does not rejoice in iniquity, but rejoices in the truth;
bears all things, believes all things, hopes all things,
endures all things. Love never fails..."
1 Corinthians 13:2b, 3b, 4-8a NKJV (parenthesis mine)

We have to understand that we can't get out of the spiritual parking lot without the igniting love of God. His expansive love is extremely contrary to fleshly characteristics or everything that we demand ownership over in this world. That is why we are given a complete definition here in the thirteenth chapter of First Corinthians (see verses 4-8).

In verse thirteen, love is called the greatest eternal thing! This being true, we must keep in mind that the enemy will battle us here fiercely! If we can stay in God's love we will surely overcome everything that would stop us from finishing the full circuit of our high call.

If our love does not reflect this list we will fail, short of God's highest and best. How very important then is this chapter?! The flashier expressions of the Spirit like mysterious tongues (verse 1), illuminating prophecies (verse 2), powerful faith (verse 2), popular humanitarian deeds (verse 3), or heroic martyrdom (verse 3) are more appealing and we usually prefer them. We know every one of these things is important and the chapters that sandwich this one are devoted to explaining them. None of them, however, are as important as this central teaching on love. It will prepare you to stand stronger and to go further. You could say this "Agape" form of love, which humans have built into them, is the highest form of spirituality. These other spiritual abilities build the church, but love is the most perfect, completing quality God has given us. Love IS the essence of who the church is and what it carries to the world.

Jesus Himself said the people of this world would recognize us primarily by this supreme spiritual quality (John 13:35), as it is defined here in our text. How over the moon, stars, and sun is it to think that, in love, we have actually been given the greatest part of heaven while still here on earth?!

JULY 30...DAY 211
SIXTEEN "NEW YOU" QUALITIES

"(if I)...have not love, I am nothing...(if I) have not love, it profits me nothing...Love suffers long and is kind; love does not envy; love does not parade itself, is not puffed up; does not behave rudely, does not seek its own, is not provoked, thinks no evil; does not rejoice in iniquity, but rejoices in the truth; bears all things, believes all things, hopes all things, endures all things. Love never fails..."
1 Corinthians 13:2b, 3b, 4-8a NKJV

As we said yesterday, the "God-kind" of love has a clear Biblical definition. Not every scriptural principle is so systematically organized and easy for us to understand. Many truths are veiled in language that requires open-hearted study, comparing scripture with scripture, until wisdom and revelation comes and the Word of God begins to unfold itself.

For example, think how much of your Bible is veiled in the symbolic language of visions and dreams. The topic of love is different. There it is, the greatest of all spiritual qualities candidly explained for us to grasp with our mind and purposefully walk out in our lives.

I believe this is because love is the truest essence of God, the core of our being, how we are created in His image. Since we have all already experienced it to varying degrees in our hearts, the Lord has arranged for us to be able to simply choose to follow Him by imitating His love walk.

Notice there are sixteen qualities listed in the definition found in our text. Eight of them tell us what love does and eight tell us what it does not do. Again, how much more simplistic can it get? First, we respond to God's love at salvation then we follow its lead, which will one day deliver us back to Him face to Face!

You can sum these sixteen things up by saying, "Do what Jesus naturally did and don't do what you are naturally inclined to do." As you replicate Him, your love will increase in every way. Your joy will partner with your kindness, patience, faith, even with your hopes, aspirations, and dreams. Every good, spiritually fruitful quality will develop as you emulate the nature of God in your own lifestyle (see Galatians 5:22-23).

When it comes to end time preparation to meet the Lord, both what we do and what we neglect to do counts. Religiously tedious rules and regulations will not make you a better end-time believer. The simplicity of living out of the new nature God has given you means much more than any legalistic code...love your way through the last days, it's the surest preparation of all!

JULY 31...DAY 212
WHAT REAL SUPERHEROES ARE MADE OF

"Love endures long and is patient and kind; love never is envious nor boils over with jealously, is not boastful or vainglorious, does not display itself haughtily. It is not conceited (arrogant and inflated with pride); it is not rude (unmannerly) and does not act unbecomingly. Love (God's love in us) does not insist on its own rights or its own way, for it is not self-seeking; it is not touchy or fretful or resentful; it takes no account of the evil done to it [it pays no attention to a suffered wrong]. It does not rejoice at injustice and unrighteousness, but rejoices when right and truth prevail. Love bears up under anything and everything that comes, is ever ready to believe the best of every person, its hopes are fadeless under all circumstances, and it endures everything [without weakening]. Love never fails [never fades out or becomes obsolete or comes to an end]." 1 Corinthians 13:4-8 AMP

When you read these verses in the Amplified translation of the Bible, you begin to realize that love is much more than   classification of a verb. It isn't a concept it is a super-human quality that makes a person unstoppable!

Just look at some of the descriptions used of "Agape" love here: "anything and everything," "ever ready," "fadeless," "without weakening," never...becomes obsolete," "never...comes to an end!" Love is Popeye's spinach, while self is Superman's kryptonite. The power of love supersedes the poison of our flesh. It is the antidote to...us!

When our human nature is tempted to be envious and arrogant, the love of God in us is patient and humble. God through His love has written His law on the tablets placed in our hearts, so when we want to partake of sin, God in us instead feasts on truth. We want vengeance but love desires mercy. We pay attention to all the wrong things but love takes into account what is right. When we are ready to fold, love is ready to believe and bear up one more time! We fade and get old, but love never gets outdated. Simply put, love is the answer for everything we can face in this life. It is so potent and powerful that it cannot be realistically challenged by the lower elements of this world.

If we choose love we are unbeatable, regardless of what we may face. Love is the perfect solution for our last days' fears. Walk in it now and you will stride out your salvation then!

AUGUST 1...DAY 213
ITEOTWAWKI

"But Peter, standing up with the eleven, raised his voice and said to them, 'Men of Judea and all who dwell in Jerusalem, let this be known to you, and heed my words. For these men are not drunk as you suppose, since it is only the third hour of the day. But this is what was spoken by the prophet Joel: 'And it shall come to pass in the last days...Before the coming of the great and awesome day of the Lord. And it shall come to pass that whoever calls on the name of the Lord shall be saved...'And with many other words he testified and exhorted them, saying, 'Be saved from this perverse generation.'"
Acts 2:14-17a, 20b-21, 40 NKJV

The meaning of this rather large acronym might be familiar to some: "It's The End of the World as We Know It." It became a popular catch phrase in my generation, usually representing uncertainty about our future in this present age. In recent years I've also noticed some Christian groups using it to refer to the sudden, cataclysmic changes the Bible predicts will occur before Jesus' return. My purpose is to point out that although neither of those ideas can be dismissed by any open-minded reader of the scripture, Peter had something more practical in mind when he made a similar statement here in his first sermon.

In quoting the Old Testament prophet, Joel, he recognized that the term "last days" referred to the multi-faceted period of history that he and his fellow followers of Jesus were entering. Peter had a revelation that this term was indicating a transition period of time between the two comings of Christ that would certainly be volatile and unsure, but also very necessary.

Let's not get lost in the fear factor of the last days, instead focus on the reason and ramification for being a part of it! Comprehend that you are alive and here on earth by God's design during this transition. Begin to let go of your natural need for worldly security. Learn to rest in God's assignment for you to help others attain their security in Jesus Christ.

This is the age of salvation, a time when we who have been saved are commissioned as the Lord's representatives (church) to win the world to His cause. Yes, there will be a great shaking of the earth before He comes again, but we have been empowered to shake the heavenlies now as a result of our being immersed in the Holy Spirit!

The next time you hear this phrase, ITEOTWAWKI, let it motivate you...it is simply a precursor that Jesus is coming again, and a reminder that we still have time to warn others!

AUGUST 2...DAY 214
FORCED BY FRICTION

"You did not choose Me, but I chose you and appointed you that you should go and bear fruit, and that your fruit should remain, that whatever you ask the Father in My name He may give you. These things I command you, that you love one another. If the world hates you, you know that it hated Me before it hated you. If you were of this world, the world would love its own. Yet because you are not of this world,...If they persecuted Me, they will also persecute you, If they kept My word, they will keep yours also." John 15:16-19a, 20b NKJV

Christianity is fraught with friction! Its very nature incurs opposition, which indicates that Christians will face adversity just for choosing to believe. Even if you've been saved for a short period of time, you must have already experienced this truth.

Listening to Jesus and looking at the lives of His followers (Acts of the Apostles) also attest to this fact. Adversity is a major reason why many opt not to follow God and why many followers choose not to finish their race.

Today, I want to empower you with God's Word to both follow and finish! You can take control of your life and be productive in Jesus' name. This encompasses putting on His nature, approaching the Father, and using the authority Jesus has delegated to us to confront adversity.

Scriptures like those quoted above and guys like me are here to tell, teach, and train you to take root, grow and take your position in an end-times force that the devil will have to reckon with when his wide web of deception enmeshes its insidious control of the world around you! My job is to help you handle yourself and your circumstances then by prescribing the way of the Lord to you in every way I can now.

Shake off your past hurts, defeats and failures and learn to put on Christ's strength and purpose. Use the grace He has purchased by exercising faith in Him, like Paul did even in the midst of friction. Let the troubles you face be the motivators you need to rise up and be ready for your future.

The last days' distractions, deceptions and temptations are no match for believers who know their God...no matter how challenging the world may become!

AUGUST 3...DAY 215
WORLD-CHANGERS

"Let this mind be in you which was also in Christ Jesus, Who, being in the form of God, did not consider it robbery to be equal with God (literally, something to be held onto to be equal), but made Himself of no reputation, taking the form of a bondservant, and coming in the likeness of men. And being found in appearance as a man, He humbled Himself and became obedient to the point of death, even the death of the cross. Therefore God also has highly exalted Him and given Him a name which is above every name, that at the name of Jesus every knee should bow, of those in heaven, and of those on earth, and of those under the earth, and that every tongue should confess that Jesus Christ is Lord, to the glory of God the Father."
Philippians 2:5-11 NKJV

Jesus' "name" has the highest authority in the universe attached to it. As you read through the New Testament book of Acts, it becomes quickly clear how powerful His name can be in the life of one who knows how to apply it.

Peter healed the lame man in Acts 3:6 in that name. In verse sixteen he explains that the man was miraculously made well by "His (Jesus) name, through faith in His name." In the chapter before Peter had announced to a crowd of Jews that God had made Jesus both, "Lord and Christ" and that they must "repent and be immersed into

His name." Three thousand men responded to Peter's first sermon! Again, it was not the man, Peter, but the name of Jesus working with the faith of the man.

Paul's accomplishments are even greater than Peter's. He healed the lame (14:9), cast a demonic spirit out of a fortune-teller (16:18), performed signs and wonders (14:3), blinded a sorcerer for a season (13:11), worked "unusual" miracles (19:11), persuaded hardened antagonists and shook whole pagan cities and regions with the Gospel (19:1-20)...all because Jesus chose him to "bear My name before Gentiles, kings and the children of Israel."

Now back to our text. Jesus obtained the authority attached to His name by the "mindset" He maintained. It is defined for us here as humble; putting aside His glory and subsequently laying down His life for us! For that reason God has highly exalted Him and empowered Him to rule over all things! Finally, we are told to let this same mentality operate in us...if we learn to put faith in what God has done and follow in Jesus' footsteps we too will be world-changers!

AUGUST 4...DAY 216
A 3-D MAN

*"So the men marveled, saying, 'Who can this be, that even
the winds and the sea obey Him?'"
Matthew 8:26-27 NKJV*

*"And many hearing Him were astonished, saying, 'Where did this Man get these
things? And what wisdom is this which is given to Him,
that such mighty works are performed by His hands!"
Mark 7:1-2 NKJV*

*"And they were astonished at His teaching, for His word was with authority."
Luke 4:31-32 NKJV*

As yesterday's scriptural text indicated, Jesus' authority reaches into three different dimensions. Philippians 2:10 says that every "knee" has to bow or yield itself to His "name' (character, authority), whether they be in 1) heaven, 2) earth or 3) under the earth (referring to the realm that is infernal and thus "below" this earthly sphere, the place of departed souls and rogue spirits).

This was obviously true to anyone who followed Jesus' life and ministry. Every kind of being, condition, circumstance or possibility yielded before His presence and obeyed His commands...except where He crossed the freedom of choice God has granted mankind. There acceptance and faith was required, which is why Jesus often conversed with those He ministered to.

Notice that wherever the Lord was present, God's power was available. In our three scriptures for today, twice that authority changed the reality. Only once did it fail to create an open, supernatural door of assistance, when the hard-hearted, natively familiar people in Nazareth chose not to believe (Mark 6).

In the last days, storms will rage, people's hearts will grow cold, and evil spirits will seduce men into openly opposing Jesus, even in His own church. However, there will also be a people who not only believe in His Name, but live under its authority and exert it to dictate the same outcomes Jesus did. Like Him, these believers will be well known in heaven, hell and on the earth for their bravery...may you be one of them!

AUGUST 5...DAY 217
GETTING YOUR GROAN ON

"Therefore, when Jesus saw her weeping, and the Jews who came with her weeping, He groaned in the spirit and was troubled...Jesus wept...Then Jesus, again groaning in Himself, came to the tomb...(He) said, 'Take away the stone'...And Jesus lifted up His eyes and said, 'Father, I thank You that You have heard Me...Now when He had said these things, He cried with a loud voice, 'Lazarus, come forth!' And he who had died came out bound hand and foot with grave clothes, and his face was wrapped with a cloth. Jesus said to them, 'Loose him, and let him go.'"
John 11:33, 35, 38-39a, 41b, 43-44 NKJV

In every situation Jesus was recognized to be an exceptional person. The words from His mouth carried weight. In fact, the only times Jesus' supernatural uniqueness was questioned were when He either a) chose not to say anything, as in the case of his interview with Herod (Luke 23:6-12), or b) when what He said was contradictory to those with ulterior motives (i.e. John 9:24).

Even in His own hometown, where they didn't receive His ministry as a result of their personal familiarity with Him, His authority was acknowledged! Take note today of the words, "groaned," and "troubled" in our text. Their meanings tell us much about how Jesus used His authority to move heaven, earth and hell! These were things He "said" when dealing with issues. This emphasizes to us how He used His words to take authority in difficult, opposing or challenging situations.

"Groaned," according to my Greek concordance, paints the picture of "snorting with indignation" and "going after something in a straightforward manner." "Troubled" is defined as, "to stir or agitate." In both cases, Jesus was moved to speak and act from deep within. This is similar to times in the four Gospels when the Lord was "moved with compassion" and healed people (Mark 1:41; Matthew 9:36; 14:14). It means he was motivated from the mercy which literally seems to come from one's spleen or bowels.

It is not by mistake that John recorded Jesus groaning in His "spirit." This is the origin of His carried authority and, when used in accordance with God's purpose for His life, it carried tremendous power.

Those of us who minister "in His name" must also carry a spiritual authority that causes our words to change the environment if we expect to face the end times Head on!

AUGUST 6...DAY 218
LEARNING TO CARRY MORE WEIGHT

"And Jesus rebuked the demon, and it came out of him; and the child was cured from that very hour." Matthew 17:18 NKJV

"So He stood over her and rebuked the fever, and it left her. And immediately she arose and served them." Luke 4:39 NKJV

"When the sun was setting, all those who had any that were sick with various diseases brought them to him; and He laid His hands on every one of them and healed them. And demons also came out of many, crying out and saying, 'You are the Christ, the Son of God!' And He, rebuking them, did not allow them to speak, for they knew that He was the Christ." Luke 4:40-41 NKJV

"Rebuked" in these New Testament passages and others, means to "tax upon or exert pressure." That was the secret of Jesus' spiritual success. The pressures He faced retreated under the force of His overcoming authority, because they were unequal to Him. He carried more spiritual weight!

We must remember this as we live and minister as believers. Since the Lord has called us to "overcome," it only makes sense that the power He has given us in His name is greater than anything we will face. When telling us to "test the spirits" of those who speak for the Lord in order to discern false Christians and prophets, the apostle John tells us in no uncertain terms, "...He who is in you is greater he who is in the world."

Think about it, Jesus overcame sickness and demonic oppression (both inside and outside the religious circles of His day) on a regular basis. I have found at least eighteen cases in the four Gospels where He "took authority" directly over these twin afflictions of mankind in its fallen state. We have been trained religiously to "pray" about such things but we find Jesus "speaking to" and exerting pressure upon them to relent.

This is not to demean prayer or to say that the Lord did not pray. He just did most of His praying BEFORE He encountered the problems He faced! This is what Jesus explained to His disciples when they could not cast the evil spirit from the epileptic boy in Matthew 17:18. Their failure to fast and pray in advance of using the authority He had given them was the reason for their failure.

Some sicknesses are caused by spirits. When a disciple is confronted with such unexpected cases he must give extraordinary space and place to the Lord, not just echo His words! This makes the difference in most of our shortcomings as well as in the arena of spiritual authority. Learning to seek Him until you find the way to overcome those unexpected things is how we expand our ability to carry more weight and exert more pressure in the spirit.

AUGUST 7...DAY 219
GOD'S DRIVING SCHOOL

"Therefore, if you have been raised with Christ, keep focusing on the things that are above, where Christ is seated at the right hand of God. Keep your minds on things that are above, not on things that are on the earth...And whatever you do, in word or deed, do everything in the name of the Lord Jesus, giving thanks to God the Father through him." Colossians 3:1-2, 17 ISV

Although the results of using the name of Jesus are sometimes quite spectacular, the reality of living by His authority is very practical. I want you to especially notice the combination of verses in our text today. In the last one, we are told to approach everything that we say or do, "in the name of Jesus." This means living our life from Jesus' spiritually authoritative, "seated" position, while purposing to carry out all that His life (and death) has "stood" for!

By pointing out two key personal qualities, you could say that the first two verses tell us how to receive the Lord's personal recommendation. First, we must be truly saved in order to know the things that are "above." Then, we must maintain our focus on the heavenly things we know. Our salvation hinges on the fact of truly having given ourselves to Him in an initial act of "death to self." Only from this position can one be spiritually, "raised with Christ," overruling in the process the dominance of our old nature. Having then received the power to become sons of God, we can access His power continuously, by faith, to carry out our Christian life and service.

In short, Jesus' name must cover everything in our lives. By using His nature to overcome ourselves, we then find the authority to overcome the world!

One last point - It is much easier to remain focused on the spiritual realities God has purchased for us if we capture a thankful attitude. Appreciation is an automatic connector with others. God requires it before He will trust us very far with His Son's authority.

It's like the car a father purchases for his teenager. Before letting his child drive it on his own, a good dad makes the youngster drive with him first, until he learns how to operate the vehicle in a way that is approved by the higher authority. We are authorized to drive the Christian Church, but only in the name of Jesus...and that is the only way our words and deeds will genuinely steer a lost, last days world!

AUGUST 8...DAY 220
LETTING JESUS EMERGE IN OUR LIVES

"Set your mind on things above, not on things on the earth. For you died, and your life is hidden with Christ in God. When Christ who is our life appears, then you also will appear with Him in glory. Therefore PUT TO DEATH your members...PUT OFF all these:...since you have PUT OFF the old man with his deeds, and have PUT ON the new man who is renewed in knowledge according to the image of Him who created him,...as the elect of God, holy and beloved, PUT ON...above all these things, PUT ON love,...AND LET the peace of God rule in your hearts, to which also you were called in one body; AND BE thankful. LET the word of Christ dwell in you richly in all wisdom, teaching and admonishing one another in psalms and hymns and spiritual songs, singing with grace in your hearts to the Lord."
Colossians 3:2-16 NKJV

Today, I have filled in some of the blanks between the text verses I gave you yesterday. Please focus your mind on what you just read in addition to what you learned yesterday. Joining both will lead you to the next level in the God-given authority reserved for your use; in "the name of Jesus."

Notice how I have placed key words in capital letters throughout the verses, which do not appear that way in your Bible. This is to emphasize the qualifications and responsibility we have to carry such power, even though it has been freely given to us through the atoning sacrifice of Christ.

These verses teach us plainly that what God grants in heaven, we must clothes ourselves with here on earth. These verses today teach you exactly how to do that. They "boil down" to simple but contrary choices, both positive and negative, that can be made with our minds and wills, as we yield to the Lord.

In Christ, we will naturally be able to put off the right kinds of things by putting Christ on in our thinking, allowing the "new man" He has created within us to emerge! Once we get familiar with this process, we just keep "letting" Christ's tendencies have access through our thoughts, feelings and choices. If we do this within the context of His body, or the "church," we will find even more power to be effective and bring change along the way.

The secret is letting the love, peace, and honor of God find its way into your heart by immersing yourself into a lifestyle of reading, studying, and acting out His Word. This is how last days battles will be won...by the Lord Himself living authoritatively through a bold, spiritually responsible people righteously using His Name!

AUGUST 9...DAY 221
GO COMMANDO

"Most assuredly, I say to you, he who believes in Me, the works that I do he will do also; and greater works than these he will do, because I go to My Father. And whatever you ask in My name, that I will do, that the Father may be glorified in the Son. If you ask anything in My name, I will do it."
John 14:12-14 NKJV

"Therefore you now have sorrow; but I will see you again and your heart will rejoice, and your joy no one will take from you. And in that day you will ask Me nothing. Most assuredly, I say to you, whatever you ask the Father in my name He will give you. Until now you have asked nothing in My Name. Ask, and you will receive, that your joy may be full."
John 16:22-24 NKJV

Two important aspects of our spiritual authority are revealed in these passages from John's Gospel. However, if you don't read between the written lines of your Bible, you probably won't see them.

Although the word, "ask" is used repeatedly in both places, the context is a little different, which changes the focus of its meaning. In the fourteenth chapter, Jesus is teaching His disciples about using His authority to do the kinds of works that He did. In the sixteenth chapter, He is discussing the need to learn the ways of the Holy Spirit in building a personal relationship with the Father who issues all authority.

Let's look at the first case today. Since Jesus would be with the Father during the new day that was dawning as a result of His resurrection, everything would now run through His "name" just as godly authority was invested in His person while He walked the earth. As they learned to "ask" that God assist them, Jesus would see to it personally that even greater things would happen for them! This means you and I, as we follow in their footsteps, have access to the same "commanding" power Jesus did. We can rebuke sin, sickness and disease just as He did, because the authority carried in His name has not changed.

There are now many more of us carrying out what the Lord started, guaranteeing at least a "greater" quantity of works being done! The devil isn't going to stop trying to destroy the human race. His strategy for world domination is going to intensify. Christians must become "commandos"; specially trained soldiers in Jesus' name, part of a spiritual military force more than able to effectuate dangerous raids against the enemy's camp, and to make him stop - wherever they go in the last days!

AUGUST 10...DAY 222
CONNECTED POWER

"Most assuredly, I say to you, he who believes in Me, the works that I do he will do also; and greater works than these he will do, because I go to My Father. And whatever you ask in My name, that I will do, that the Father may be glorified in the Son. If you ask anything in My name, I will do it."
John 14:12-14 NKJV

"Therefore you now have sorrow; but I will see you again and your heart will rejoice, and your joy no one will take from you. And in that day you will ask Me nothing. Most assuredly, I say to you, whatever you ask the Father in my name He will give you. Until now you have asked nothing in My name. Ask, and you will receive, that your joy may be full.
John 16:22-24 NKJV

Yesterday we highlighted the similarities found in these two portions of scripture, while pointing out that there were also important subtle differences. Notice again, how the use of Jesus' name for the believer is connected to "asking" in both places. Let's look today at a second, hidden facet of spiritual authority.

In John 16:23-24 we find the word "ask" being used four distinct times by Jesus, to go along with the other two times we examined yesterday in John 14:12-14. In every instance but one the Greek word "aiteo" is used, which means to request, require, beg and call for something. Distinguishing the various shades of meaning for this word I discovered that it can, 1) be bold, especially when you know what is within your rights and privileges and 2) it always issues from a position of submission and compliance.

On the one hand, Jesus is teaching us to expect God to do the things He did without doubting, and on the other hand, He is reminding us that such boldness must come from a faithful and tender heart toward our heavenly Father.

Yesterday, we revealed the "commando" in every Christian. Today I want you to see the place of enjoyment and divine satisfaction reserved for you. Because God is our Father, He delights in answering our prayers. Jesus knew what it was like to know God as His own Father and to discuss things with Him in a place of personal intimacy. As a result of this relationship, when the Lord went and walked those things out, He conducted Himself with great boldness. In spiritual authority, "commandos" have to stay "connected." When they do, heaven will come to earth to carry out their requests!

AUGUST 11...DAY 223
IN THAT DAY

"And in that day you will ask Me nothing. Most assuredly, I say to you, whatever
you ask the Father in my name He will give you.
Until now you have asked nothing in My name. Ask,
and you will receive, that your joy may be full.
John 16:22-24 NKJV

Because of its importance with respect to last days' living, let's take one more day to look at Jesus' comments on the subject of "asking" God. It was noted yesterday that each time this word is used in our two texts it is the same Greek word, "aiteo." This word can mean to be both bold and broken at the same time...except for the first time it is used in verse 23 or John chapter 16.

This scripture is where Jesus said, "And in that day you will ask Me nothing." The word for "ask" here is completely different in the Greek language. As opposed to "aiteo" in all the other verses, this time it is "eratao" describing one who "asks on the same level as another." This differentiation is interesting because it defines a "changing of the guard" that Jesus was initiating. Up to that time, His disciples interacted with the Lord from a very familiar distance as they followed His leadership. In every instance where the Bible records Jesus asking something of the Father God this same word is used (John 14:16; 16:26; 17:9, 15, 20). The Lord's followers were then not only familiar with Jesus personally, but also with His approach of equality within the Trinity or Godhead (names describing the unity of the three personalities in the Biblical concept of God...Father, Son and Holy Spirit). This is why Jesus gives the disciples specific instructions on how to approach God after His own death and resurrection.

IN THAT DAY they would also ask, but not as Kings asked other Kings (Luke 14:32), or as the Pharisees had asked questions of Jesus (Luke 7:36). It would be their responsibility to stay humbly subservient and connected to God through the name of Jesus, not on their own merit. From that place they could then boldly demonstrate the same kind of commanding power Jesus displayed! For example, notice how the early church used their private prayer gatherings to enhance their active obedience in public (Acts 4:29).

Today, in the "Church Age,' we carry the same tremendous potential for explosive power. It will only manifest through us, however, as we learn to rely completely on the Father because of what Jesus has already done!

AUGUST 12...DAY 224
CONTRASTING JESUS' NAME WITH YOUR NATURE

"Now therefore, it is already an utter failure for you that you go to law against one another. Why do you not rather accept wrong? Why do you not rather let yourselves be cheated? No, you yourselves do wrong and cheat, and you do these things to your brethren! Do you not know that the unrighteous will not inherit the kingdom of God? Do not be deceived. Neither fornicators, nor idolaters, nor adulterers, nor homosexuals, nor sodomites, nor thieves, nor covetous, nor drunkards, nor revilers, nor extortioners will inherit the Kingdom of God. And such were some of you. BUT you were washed, BUT you were sanctified, BUT you were justified in the name of the Lord Jesus and by the Spirit of God. All things are lawful for me, but all things are not helpful. All things are lawful for me, but I will not be brought under the power of any."
1 Corinthians 6:7-12 NKJV

Talk about contrast! This portion of scripture certainly paints a picture that leaves no area for doubt as to the depths of sin and the heights of salvation! What's more, it depicts the comparison between a life lived through the power of Jesus' name with one lived veiled and stumbling by a believer's own identity.

With this letter the apostle Paul is confronting the Corinthian church on many fronts. The scripture poses a question we must ask ourselves in this moment of time as well. Do we truly desire to remain faithful until the second coming of the Lord?

I've learned as I have aged that correction is often necessary, even in my more successful stretches of life and ministry for the Lord. Accountability keeps me from straying very far. If I miss God in small things, I'm grateful for His correction. It could save my life if ever faced with the enemy's "perfect storm" against me!

Although, some of the most immoral sins are listed here, Paul targets the root causes of all sin. The fact that these believers were willing to take each other to court proved they were capable of anything; except selfless love of God and man. If they would cheat a brother by refusing to be wronged if necessary, they would also cheat sexually, religiously, with property, with their bellies, their tongues...anything!

It isn't the big things we have to be most careful of, it's the little things that can be more easily rationalized and endorsed by other sinful believers. In contrast, notice how I have capitalized the word, "but." It is one of the biggest little words in the Bible, and in this context it will save us from ourselves. Tomorrow I will tell you why...

AUGUST 13...DAY 225
JESUS, THE DIFFERENCE MAKER

"Do not be deceived. Neither fornicators, nor idolaters, nor adulterers, not homosexuals, nor sodomites, nor thieves, nor covetous, nor drunkards, nor revilers, nor extortioners will inherit the Kingdom of God. And such were some of you. BUT you were washed, BUT you were sanctified, BUT you were justified in the name of the Lord Jesus and by the Spirit of God. All things are lawful for me, but all things are not helpful. All things are lawful for me, but I will not be brought under the power of any." 1 Corinthians 6:7-12 NKJV

Yesterday, we looked at our tendency to sin in ways we would never have imagined when we gave our lives to Jesus.

Paul's letter to the Corinthians, which is situated right in the middle of your New Testament and mine, warns us about this being true - so read the handwriting on the walls of the page and, "DO NOT BE DECEIVED!"

If you allow yourself to cheat your brother out of his money or position you are a perfect candidate for finding yourself sleeping with someone who is not your spouse! Believe me it has happened to more esteemed believers than either you or me!

The fact is that most of us have done some of these ten listed sins and some of us have done them all..."BUT!!" I have capitalized these three words so you will remember to capitalize the three words they are associated within our text. Three particular things have been done for us because of what Jesus accomplished on our behalf. Once we believe on and accept His name we must choose to receive these new realities and walk them out by the power of the Holy Spirit, Whom He has given to us for this purpose. Notice first of all, that regardless of our past we have been "WASHED." This means by the blood of Jesus, even the worst of us have been made totally pure in the eyes of God!

Second, we have been, "SANCTIFIED" or set apart as His personal property. The Lord has separated us to His service no matter what anyone else may think, and He reserves the right to keep working on us as we maintain our relationship with Him.

Finally, we have been, "JUSTIFIED." We already (past tense) have been accepted, preserved and also released from all legal guilt and liability for our past! We were great sinners and that potential still lies latent in our old nature...BUT Jesus is a Great Savior, and His nature working in us more than compensates for our weaknesses, both past and present!

AUGUST 14...DAY 226
HARDCORE CHRISTIANITY

"For I determined not to know anything among you except Jesus Christ and Him crucified...that your faith should not be in the wisdom of men but in the power of God. However, we speak wisdom among those who are mature, yet not the wisdom of this age, nor of the rulers of this age, who are coming to nothing."
1 Corinthians 2:2, 5-6 NKJV

In order to get a better idea of the attitude we should possess as believers to live our lives to the fullest, let's look at Jesus' greatest follower. The apostle Paul wrote thirteen of the books that make up the New Testament. He traveled tirelessly around the Mediterranean world of his day spreading the Gospel, training disciples and establishing churches in some of the most pagan cities of the Roman Empire.

For his efforts, this man received ceaseless persecution and intense opposition (2 Corinthians 11:23-28). The devil personally saw to it that his journey was anything but easy (2 Corinthians 12:7)! Maybe the most impressive part of his core curriculum vitae is the fact that Paul had left a position of power and prestige among the Jewish religious establishment in order to follow Jesus and His misunderstood new faith, which most thought of as only a strange cult (Philippians 3:4-8)!

Keep all this in mind as you read our text for today. You will find not even the slightest hint of regret from Paul. On the contrary, Paul is reveling in the wisdom and power of the truth he has found. This passage recounts how he initially approached ministering in the city of Corinth. Notice his determination was to put all else aside, making sure Jesus was everything in his life in preparation for taking new territory.

Paul found that this produced unusual results (which can be read about throughout the book of Acts). It caused others to respond to the Christian message, regardless of how steeped in sin or how bound they were in the strongholds of an ungodly culture. Wisdom and power worked through Paul to convince some of the hardest kinds of unbelievers that Jesus was the Son of God, Savior of the world and Source of spiritual life!

One last very important thing, Paul's mindset toward Satan was firm. He tells us that the devil's grip on the age we live in is according to the New English Bible, "declining." The phrase, "coming to nothing" literally means, to "render idle, inactive, unemployed and inoperative." It also means, to "deprive of force, influence and power."

We have to live in the fullness of the truth that Jesus' victory at Calvary's cross was complete...when we do, we will complete our race and help others get started!

AUGUST 15...DAY 227
REVERSE PRAYER!

"Now...He was hungry. And seeing from afar a fig tree having leaves, He went to see if perhaps He would find something on it. When He came to it, He found nothing but leaves, for it was not the season for figs. In response Jesus said to it, 'Let no one eat fruit from you ever again.' And His disciples heard it...Now in the morning, as they passed by, they saw the fig tree dried up from the roots. And Peter, remembering, said to Him, 'Rabbi, look! The fig tree which You cursed has withered away.' So Jesus answered and said to them, 'Have faith in God.'"
Mark 11:12-14, 20-22 NKJV

This passage cannot be overlooked when it comes to discussing the power of Jesus' name. It records the authority He carried and shows how it was released through His words, but this time in a very unusual way.

We have already viewed several examples citing the "usual" targets of Jesus' authority; sin, sickness and demonic spirits. This time, however, He speaks to a tree!

And, whereas in most cases the Lord used the weight of His walk with God to bless the people affected by those different conditions, here He "curses" a nonhuman object!

This fig tree was not producing the fruit for which it was intended, no matter if it was in season or out. The Lord had no use for it. Just as fruitless are those who are dried up from the separations of sin, certain sicknesses and demonic spirits. Like this fig tree many are kept back from their original purpose in God.

Praise the Lord for His mercies upon us, but here Jesus was taking the importance in the Father's eyes of being and doing what you are created and put on earth for to its ultimate end.

These kinds of Bible verses can seem so bizarre that we are tempted to simply read past them with little or no understanding of their intended meaning. God will often use symbolism to reveal His heart and mind and teach us what is not obvious until we "look" at them meditatively.

Although He "cursed" something He did so, in part, to increase our "faith!" God is all powerful. His words have cause and effect, because He is the cause, the source of all creation. It's like the old admonition that of a parent, "I brought you into this world, and I can take you out of it!"

This fig tree illustration is so odd because the word, "curse" means, "to doom something to destruction." When I studied its etymology I discovered that a curse is basically reverse prayer. It is praying something downward rather than to lift it up to receive God's blessing!

If you study the entire New Testament you will find Jesus and his disciples telling us never to curse people, even our enemies. Yet God pronounces curses on people and things. So what is the point?

Well, primarily that we don't decide what or who should receive blessing or judgment on our own. When God pronounces a word it is always to officially articulate a Kingdom purpose, regardless of whether we understand it.

As we will see tomorrow, Jesus spoke to this tree rendering it a symbolic representation of the spiritual condition in the nation at that time. His curse was really an alternative kind of prayer because it was expressly what God had directed Him speak out. Obedience is not only, "having faith IN God," but as this phrase can be translated, "having the faith OF God." This is what we are going to need as the Lord's return draws closer…not faith that gets us what we want, but faith that gets done what God wants!

AUGUST 16...DAY 228
THE CAUSE OF THE CURSE

"So they came to Jerusalem. Then Jesus went into the temple and began to drive out those who bought and sold in the temple and overturned the tables of the money changers and the seats of those who sold doves. And He would not allow anyone to carry wares through the temple. Then He taught, saying to them, 'Is it not written, My house shall be called a house of prayer for all nations?' But you have made it a den of thieves.' And the scribes and chief priests heard it and sought how they might destroy Him; for they feared Him, because all the people were astonished at His teaching. When evening had come, He went out of the city."
Mark 11:15-19 NKJV

Today, I want to fill in the blanks from yesterday's story of Jesus cursing the fig tree. Interestingly enough, "cursing" has its place alongside "blessing" when it comes to the ways God-given authority can be used. This may sound harsh if you only consider the times the Bible warns us not to use curses, so you must consider the entire subject if you want to get a proper idea of our boundaries when using the name of Jesus.

Yesterday, we saw the Lord curse or "doom" a fig tree but I only gave you a partial scriptural picture of the pertinent circumstances. Today, let's look at the "rest of the story" by examining what He did between the time that He spoke to the fig tree and the point when Peter noticed it was outwardly dead.

During that day Jesus purposely went into the temple and forcefully reorganized those who occupied that space. He also spent time teaching them to conduct the business of God's house according to the instructions God had given, and rebuking them for producing an atmosphere of sin in the very hub from which all of the nation's righteous attitude and activity were meant to flow.

The nation of Israel had become like that fig tree, especially its religious leadership at that time! Jesus had literally come from the presence of God to see if He might find fruit on this "tree" but when He found nothing God could bless, He instead delivered the curse in its place!

Remember, curses are the opposite of blessings. It seems in scripture they are frequently found in the absence of the blessings intended for faithfulness; often at the time when God comes to inspect His fields and orchards (see Cain, Genesis 4:11)! As is usually the case, those who deserved to be cursed proved it by their response to God's judgment. Instead of repenting when there is no other way out, they harden in their opposition to Him!

If you look closely you will see that there is clearly a time for cursing, "The curse of the Lord is on the house of the wicked, But He blesses the dwelling of the righteous," Proverbs 3:33. This statement applies to when one lives consistently on the wrong side of God's expectations!

AUGUST 17…DAY 229
WHAT FIG TREES HAVE TO DO WITH MOUNTAINS

"For assuredly, I say to you, whoever says to this mountain, 'Be removed and be cast into the sea, and does not doubt in his heart, but believes that those things he says will be done, he will have whatever he says." Mark 11:23 NKJV

When Peter marveled at the fact that the fig tree Jesus cursed had "dried up from the roots" in only one day's time, Jesus gave a surprising response. "Have faith in God" alludes to God's dominion and our need to be able to do the same things Jesus did, in Christ. "This mountain," indicates that formidable challenges will also array themselves against us, attempting to prevent us from succeeding.

The immediate mountain Jesus referred to was the hypocritical condition of Israel that God had sent Him to confront. He removed it quite forcefully by pronouncing a symbolic curse on the tree and then promptly laying God's axe to the "roots" of its problem in the temple at Jerusalem. He then laid down His very life on the cross of a tree that produced eternal fruit to seal both the judgment of rogue satanic forces and the terms of deliverance for mankind.

When you look below the surface you find the Bible is teaching us to deal with the spirit realm first before we face and confront problematic issues, just as Jesus did! While the fig tree represents a nonproductive living condition upon which responsible action must be taken by God, the mountain represents the weight of our responsibilities in comparison with the seemingly insignificant actions we can take! Jesus did not first deal with people or problems. Instead He addressed the spiritual forces at work behind the scenes.

We must do the same, trusting God above all else, in every situation we face and using the name of Jesus to enforce God's plans when Satan's opposition seems larger than ourselves. This is a big, big deal! We must learn to speak to our mountains in prayer, like Jesus spoke to His responsibilities. If we believe and receive that our answers are found in the Throne Room of God first, every mountain and fig tree we face will also testify of the authority we carry with God!

The Lord will not let His people remain fruitless indefinitely, and we cannot allow obstacles to linger in our path that will disable us from completing the assignment He sets before us!

So then, Jesus' fig tree and our mountains are two sides of the same spiritual coin. We apply His curse to the spiritual side of our problems to move forward responsibly in the blessing and strength of His salvation, so others can escape the final judgment! When we realize that we can follow Jesus, no matter what, we will find the power to speak to every object God has called us to remove…this is the authority we carry in Jesus' name!

AUGUST 18…DAY 230
STAYING IN THE BOUNDARIES OF PRAYER

"Therefore I say to you, whatever things you ask when you pray, believe that you receive them, and you will have them." And whenever you stand praying, if you have anything against anyone, forgive him that your Father in heaven may also forgive you your trespasses. But if you do not forgive, neither will your Father in heaven forgive your trespasses." Mark 11:24-26 NKJV

Prayer has boundaries that are both "positive" and "negative." On one hand, we can pray to set things "up" in the blessings of God, as Jesus did for the better part of His ministry. This was seen in His continuous preaching, teaching, healing and delivering of those who were oppressed of the devil (Acts 10:38). According to Matthew 28, Mark 16 and Luke 24, our commission is to do the very same things as we go into the entire world, making disciples "in His name."

On the other hand, we can also pray to bring things "down" at times by pronouncing a "curse" as the Lord directs. This gets a little tricky because it is not our "standard operating procedure," as they say in the military. Nevertheless, there are clear references to such actions in scripture. For example, Peter spoke a curse over both Ananias and his wife, Sapphira (Acts 5:1-11) for yielding to Satan and lying to the Holy Ghost. Paul also cursed Elymas the sorcerer in Acts 13:8-12 for interfering with the work of the Gospel as a "son of the devil!"

In the first case, death was the result while in the second God's hand applied blindness for "a time." We are authorized to carry tremendous power with our words but our hearts are the key. Notice our text says we have to "believe" in prayer that we receive the answers before we even ask them! Verse 23 says we can move mountains only if we "believe in our hearts" the things we say. Then the last two verses demand that we maintain a forgiving heart attitude toward other people in order to be forgiven by God!

When you sum all this up you realize that we can do nothing of ourselves (John 15:5), God has to be the author of our beliefs, words and actions. James 3:9 says it is inconsistent for a believer to conduct his business, blessing God and cursing men indiscriminately. We must be responsible with the power invested in us or we will find that it does not work at all. We must keep our hearts right before God in these last days so that our mouths can say the things He is speaking, for the right purposes. Bless and do not curse as a normal course of life and ministry. If you stay positively connected to the Lord, He will lead you to appropriately deal with the negative situations that come your way, according to His own higher purposes.

AUGUST 19...DAY 231
DON'T PLAY DUMB

"Then Jesus came again to Jerusalem. And as He was walking in the temple, the chief priests, the scribes, and the elders came to Him. And they said to Him, 'By what authority are You doing these things?' But Jesus answered and said to them, 'I also will ask you one question; then answer Me, and I will tell you by what authority I do these things. The baptism of John - was it from heaven or from men? Answer Me.' And they reasoned among themselves, saying, 'If we say, 'From heaven,' He will say, 'Why then did you not believe him?' But if we say, 'From men' - they feared the people, for all counted John to have been a prophet indeed. So they answered and said to Jesus. 'We do not know.' And Jesus answered and said to them, 'Neither will I tell you by what authority I do these things.'" Mark 11:27-33 NKJV

You can't pretend to be stupid with God! If you are playing religious games for your own benefit, like so much of our modern organizational Christianity, Jesus won't even answer your questions.

This second visit to the temple by the Lord shows the true nature of God and the full extent of His authority. After declaring the fate of that crooked generation, sweeping the temple of the culprits in charge and instructing his disciples how to exercise godly power, Jesus returns to the temple just to "walk" around! What a show of strength and mercy working together to accomplish the perfect will of God. I love how Jesus didn't just drive out the demonic, more importantly He inserted the divine! Notice how He Himself was the answer to their question.

On the first day, after cleaning up the cave-like environment those imposter pastors had established inside what was meant to be a "prayer house," the Lord immediately "moved in" and taught them how things should be. On the next day Jesus returned, as if to ensure things kept moving in the right direction.

Wherever He went, the authority of God was present. How interesting that the religious leaders He encountered on this return visit questioned that very truth! The influence of God was preventing them from operating as usual "their" way, so the devil, through them, sought to diminish Jesus' authority.

However, as long as the Lord was there these guys still had an opportunity to embrace Him and His influence by coming clean in their own hearts about Who He was, What He carried and where it came from! Like so many "authorities" today, they weren't as interested in God, as they were in their vested and retained power...the kind they could possess and control! But, as this story teaches us, God is singularly interested in giving His authority to those who are willing to acknowledge it, walk with Him, and yield everything under His control!

AUGUST 20...DAY 232
THE SPIRITUAL CLEANER

"Now there was a long war between the house of Saul and the house of David. But David grew stronger and stronger, and the house of Saul grew weaker and weaker." 2 Samuel 3:1 NKJV

I sometimes jokingly refer to myself as a spiritual "cleaner." Similar to Jesus' cleansing of the temple or David's takeover of Israel, God has often put me in situations or positions which required helping to restore His people and reestablish His places. Sometimes it seems like you fight an uphill battle in this "lost art" of godly intervention and occupation, but it is always an adventure, and in the end God has His way!

I once accepted an invitation to become the pastor of a church with big potential in a small community. From the outside everything looked so inviting, but immediately after taking the position, my wife and I discovered major internal problems lurking behind the scenes. To make a long, long story shorter than it probably should be, let's just say that "breeches" in authority had caused spiritual doors to open for satanic activity in that congregation, which began to manifest inside the building itself!

For example, parishioners were literally afraid to use the restrooms in our church and, as a result, I noticed that many visitors would never to return to our services! Their fear wasn't based on the long distance or the dark hallway one had to enter upon arrival, but rather the fact that the hair on the back of their neck would literally "stand up" when anyone went there!

I soon found that organizational restructuring didn't really do much in this kind of situation, and bible school hadn't exactly instructed us in how to rectify such a situation! In the end, I learned it was simple trench warfare. Exercising my authority as the man God, called to be in charge of that territory, against the invisible forces that were at work there, eventually changed the environment. I kept going back into that dark hallway, turning off all the lights (for a "faith effect") and commanding Satan to leave in the name of Jesus, even though I felt scared and powerless myself!

Authority has effect as you embrace it and use it. Spiritual authority is the highest kind of authority there is which means we have to be responsible but very bold in its use. We are heading down the dark corridors of the end times...stand your ground and practice walking in the Lord's presence now so you will know how to carry yourself and change your world then.

AUGUST 21...DAY 233
PROVISION VS. THE PROMISE 1

"And the king and his men went to Jerusalem against the Jebusites, the inhabitants of the land, who spoke to David, saying, 'You shall not come in here; but the blind and the lame will repel you,' thinking, 'David cannot come in here.' Nevertheless David took the stronghold of Zion (the particularly fortified area the Jebusites lived in)...Then David dwelt in the stronghold, and called it the City of David. And David built all around...So David went on and became great, and the Lord God of Hosts was with him." 2 Samuel 5:6-10 NKJV

It is a spiritual verity that those who carry God's authority will have to overcome repeated challenges to the validity of their calling in order to fully inherit the Kingdom of God in their lives. Here is David at age thirty-six, finally being asked to be king of all Israel, after years of struggling through every kind of resistance to the promise God had spoken over his life as a boy!

Although the prophet Samuel had anointed him to replace Saul, it had been anything but easy. David became accustomed to the life of faith required for the long-term task he came to realize he had been given. In the process he also learned that God provides for His own while they are being molded and groomed into God's higher call for them. God's provision is great, but you must always remember it is the means to a greater end. The Promise is the goal for our lives. Like David, we each have a Jerusalem in our future. To obtain it, we will have to acquire the disposition that repeatedly embraces the Lord's provision built into us.

I love how David didn't hesitate when going after the most prized possession the Israelites had never taken. It was truly a match made in heaven…he needed them and they needed him. He marched straight up to the Jebusite stronghold in Jerusalem in the face of their ridicule and took the inheritance.

If you look closely you will find that this tribe of people had been entrenched in what was meant to be the capital of Israel! They had a long history of resistance, but so did David! He not only threw them out, he literally moved into their fortress and there set up both God's house and his house...from then on, it became known by the Lord's name (Zion) and David's (City of David)!!

AUGUST 22…DAY 234
PROVISION VS. PROMISE 2

"And the Lord spoke to Moses, saying, 'Send men to spy out the land of Canaan, which I am giving to the children of Israel; from each tribe of their fathers you shall send, every one a leader among them'…And they returned from spying out the land after forty days…Then they told him (Moses), and said: 'We went to the land where you sent us. It truly flows with milk and honey, and this is its fruit. Nevertheless the people who dwell in the land are strong; the cities are fortified and very large; moreover we saw the descendants of Anak (giants) there.
Numbers 13:1-2, 25, 27-28 NKJV

A good friend of mine named Robert Miles once said, "Provision is nice, but to inherit the promise usually means you have to kick someone's butt out of your territory!" We can see the truth of this statement very clearly from the story of the twelve spies that the Lord had Moses send into the "Promised Land!" Although God promised He was "giving" the Israelites land that was "choice real estate," it was occupied by five other major tribal groups they would have to kick out!

Our New Testament assignment is the same, in the name of Jesus. He was God's promise and He has defeated our primary enemy, but we still have to enforce the victory and move into our possession by displacing each "alternative persuasion" to His Word for our lives. Notice, the very first fight arena in this battle is within our hearts and minds.

Ten of Israel's spies brought back an evil report of unbelief (verse 32) because they compared themselves, apart from God's power, with those five opposing cultures. These are the same five giants that try to keep you small! Remember satanic opposition always looks bigger than it really is. The imposing presence of the people he puts in our way usually defeat us before we ever get the chance to discover the "David" inside us!

That first generation of Israelites was never able to see past the life of "provision" they had become accustomed to in the wilderness. It wasn't until the next generation, under leaders with a "God persuaded spirit" (Numbers 14:6-9, 24), that they began to focus on the "Promise of the land." That is when God sent them in to take it! Tomorrow we'll begin to find out what our enemy "says" to keep us in the wilderness of provision, afraid to take our promise!

AUGUST 23...DAY 235
PROVISION VS. PROMISE 3
Dealing with the Predominant Persuasions in your Life

"'The Amalekites dwell in the land of the South; the Hittites, the Jebusites, and the Amorites dwell in the mountains; and the Canaanites dwell by the sea and along the banks of the Jordan.' But Caleb quieted the people before Moses and said, 'Let us go up at once and take possession, for we are well able to overcome it.' But the men who had gone up with him said, 'We are not able to go up against the people, for they are stronger than we.'"
Numbers 13:1-2, 25, 27-28 NKJV

The giants in the "Promised Land" were imposing impostors, already occupying God's intended chosen land well ahead of His schedule! In order to deal with Satan's scheme, God told the Israelites to "possess" their land and displace the squatters.

In studying this portion of scripture, I began to see what that would entail. Each of the names listed has a specific meaning which correlates with a persuasion that is not in line with the kind of faith God requires of His people. In order for us to inherit the promises of God we will have to use the greatest name, "Jesus" to eradicate all these other names from our thinking and believing. Let's look at each one very closely.

Being descents of Esau, "Amalekites" spoke with total disrespect regarding the things of God. Esau had sold his birthright to the inheritance of this land for a bowl of soup.

The Bible says many Christians are like him, professing a desire to follow God but in reality serving their own belly (self)! They had become like the indigenous people of that "world," even taking on the physical characteristics of those they had intermarried! Instead of welcoming their cousins back into the land, the Amalekites prevented and blocked their path causing God to curse them to utter destruction. God warned Moses to write their destined destruction in a book, and Moses warned the Israelites not to forget to finish them off when the time came (Exodus 17:14, Deuteronomy 25:17-19)! Because they did not follow God's command and utterly destroy these enemies (1 Samuel 15), there is trouble in the land of Israel to this day!

Disrespect is a giant oppressor. Expel it from your life in the name of Jesus...it is a threat to your promise!

AUGUST 24...DAY 236
PROVISION VS. PROMISE 4
Dealing with the Predominant Persuasions in your Life

"Then they told him (Moses), and said:...'The Amalekites dwell in the land of the South; the Hittites, the Jebusites, and the Amorites dwell in the mountains; and the Canaanites dwell by the sea and along the banks of the Jordan.'
Numbers 13:1-2, 25, 27-28 NKJV

"Therefore God also has highly exalted Him and given Him a name which is above every name, that at the name of Jesus every knee should bow, of those in heaven, and of those on earth, and of those under the earth, and that every tongue should confess that Jesus Christ is Lord, to the glory of God the Father."
Philippians 2:9-11 NKJV

Let's continue our word study of the "names" of those persuasive giants the children of Israel encountered when God sent them to spy out the "Promised Land." They are important because they represent popular persuasions found in the church in these last days, which we too must overcome. The good news is that we have already been given the name of "JESUS," with which to crush each of them in advance!

This second tribal name, "Hittites" means, "terror," or, "to be broken down, dismayed and shattered." Satan uses fear above all other tactics to impede us from believing for God's best. Many Christians today are like these Israelites, not wishing to deal thoroughly with the things that most terrify them.

When confronted with the prospect of having to deal with terrorists, often we would rather remain wanderers in the less comfortable past place God has provided for us (even though we usually complain the entire time we dwell there)! God knew the criminals that lived in that land needed to be dealt with, which is why He commissioned His own people, commanding them not to fear or be discouraged (Exodus 23:23; Deuteronomy 1:21).

Interestingly, Abraham was already buried in his "purchased" plot in the Hittites land (Genesis 25:10), proving God had laid claim to it generations earlier. Although fear is a very persuasive composite in life, we have not been given a "spirit of fear" (I Timothy 1:7). Like Caleb, we have a different, victorious Spirit...so, let's keep taking the ground promised to us until Jesus comes!

AUGUST 25...DAY 237
PROVISION VS. PROMISE 5
Dealing with the Predominant Persuasions in your Life

"Then they told him (Moses), and said:...'The Amalekites dwell in the land of the South; the Hittites, the Jebusites, and the Amorites dwell in the mountains; and the Canaanites dwell by the sea and along the banks of the Jordan.'
Numbers 13:1-2, 25, 27-28 NKJV

"Therefore God also has highly exalted Him and given Him a name which is above every name, that at the name of Jesus every knee should bow, of those in heaven, and of those on earth, and of those under the earth, and that every tongue should confess that Jesus Christ is Lord, to the glory of God the Father."
Philippians 2:9-11 NKJV

We have already discussed how David finally dealt with the Jebusites as he ascended the throne of Israel as a replacement for the disobedient king, Saul. It is interesting to note that both of these men dealt directly with two of the different cultures or "names" the children of Israel were distracted by in their initial approach to the "Promised Land." In fact, because they speculated about these "giants" and were "persuaded" to doubt God the original generation of Israelites was not allowed to even enter! Later, when each of these two kings had second chances to change the mindset of Israel, one failed while the other succeeded.

Saul respected the disrespectful Amalekites by failing to utterly destroy King Agag and all of his people. In disobedience, he became like them and disrespected God. To see how costly this was, one has only to look at the story of Esther where Haman, the "Agagite" nearly destroyed the Jews!

David, on the other hand, had a heart after God and swiftly displaced the trespassing Jebusites. Their name originally meant: "to trample down or pollute." They had done this for hundreds of years without punishment in the most prominent place in the Promised Land. Their very presence was a discouraging failure to the nation...one that David eliminated in preparation for her greatest years!

If we want God's best, we will have to deal with His worst enemies as well. Disrespect and discouragement go hand in hand. Let your heart be a David and not a Saul...when you carry honor and hope, the faith to take your promise is within your grasp.

AUGUST 26...DAY 238
PROVISION VS. PROMISE 6
Dealing with the Predominant Persuasions in your Life

"Then they told him (Moses), and said:... 'The Amalekites dwell in the land of the South; the Hittites, the Jebusites, and the Amorites dwell in the mountains; and the Canaanites dwell by the sea and along the banks of the Jordan.'
Numbers 13:1-2, 25, 27-28 NKJV

"Therefore God also has highly exalted Him and given Him a name which is above every name, that at the name of Jesus every knee should bow, of those in heaven, and of those on earth, and of those under the earth, and that every tongue should confess that Jesus Christ is Lord, to the glory of God the Father."
Philippians 2:9-11 NKJV

Today let's look at the last two cultures that caused ten of the twelve Israelite spies to bring back an evil report to their brothers and wander needlessly in the wilderness for an extra forty years. Close inspection can help us get beyond a similar lifestyle of only knowing God's provision, into the fullness of experiencing His promise.

First, the "Amorites" name literally means, "to say, command or answer." They were known as, "the mountaineers" or those who held a high place of publicity. Their persona was intimidators. The presumption was that they were better than you, inferred by just looking at them or listening to their words! The mouths of these guys spoke condemnation to all those who would try to ascend to a higher place at their expense.

Then there were the "Canaanites," or the merchants of the land. Of all the giants in the land of Canaan, these were at the top of the "food-chain." They were the high tech, commercial people the land was largely named after. Their culture reflected the ways and means of the broader world around them. The Canaanites had iron-equipped armies while the Israelites were a shepherding society with a background of slavery! When the spies looked at them they saw David against Goliath long before it happened and without the faith needed to win that battle! Beyond their military superiority, they possessed all the trappings and temptations of the world of their time. These were wealthy worldly travelers with a bent for sexual perversion. Their lifestyle tempted the children of God to return to Egypt and let God's promise turn into a compromise!!

All of these "ites" represented "barriers" to the plan God had in mind for Israel. Only as God's Word became their thoughts and persuasion would it become possible to overthrow them.

Nothing has changed...except we have greater authority in a superior name under which we march toward the promise!

AUGUST 27...DAY 239
PROVISION VS. PROMISE 7
The Speed of Promise

"Therefore, since a promise remains of entering His rest, let us fear lest any of you seem to have come short of it. For indeed the Gospel was preached to us as well as to them; but the word which they heard did not profit them, not being mixed with faith in those who heard it...there remains therefore a rest for the people of God. For he who has entered His rest has himself also ceased from his works as God did from His. Let us therefore be diligent to enter that rest, lest anyone fall according to the same example of disobedience." Hebrews 4: 1-2, 9-11 NKJV

The best thing about the promise God gave the Israelites is that it is still available! Although they did not fully embrace the "rest" God planned for them to inherit, the same spiritual ground remains open for us to enter into today, through Jesus Christ. He IS and always has been the essence of God's PROMISE!

This may seem strange at first glance. It makes sense when you consider that time is not linear or absolute, we only experience it that way from our limited three-dimensional perspective. According to Einstein's theory of relativity, time is subject to the velocity of the observer. This means time is a physical property that God is not subject to. He is beyond and outside of it as it has been recorded for thousands of years in Isaiah 57:15. Therefore, God can easily see the end from the beginning in all things from His perspective in eternity, while we see events unfolding in a chronological order over the sequence of many years.

This is why Peter reminds us (2 Peter 3:8) of Moses' words in Psalm 90:4, "But beloved, do not forget this one thing, that with the Lord one day is as a thousand years, and a thousand years as one day." Then in verse nine he says, "The Lord is not slack concerning His promise, as some count slackness, but is longsuffering toward us, not willing that any should perish but that all should come to repentance."

So, the "history" of the promise is: 1) Before Jesus stepped out of eternity into time and, 2) After Jesus stepped out of time back into eternity. Either way, He is the answer for humanity...the Promise of God who, when entered into, amounts to more than mere provision.

The Israelites only saw the finite, time-limited side of this equation, but today we can focus from the speed of God's spiritual perspective and realize that what they missed is still available to us, only in its fuller, supra-chronological understanding!

Think "fourth-dimensionally." God says He is willing to save you...be willing to mix your faith into His equation and trust Him.

AUGUST 28...DAY 240
PROVISION VS. PROMISE 8
Know the Way

"Grace and peace be multiplied to you in the knowledge of God and of Jesus our Lord, as His divine power has given to us all things that pertain to life and godliness, through the knowledge of Him who called us by glory and virtue, by which have been given to us exceedingly great and precious promises, that through these you may be partakers of the divine nature, having escaped the corruption that is in the world through lust." 2 Peter 1:3-4 NKJV

Not only is Jesus our end-time "Promise" but throughout history God has given His people many "promises" inclusive to His life. This is what fathers do and, according to Jesus, God is a good One! In Matthew 7:11 He says, "If you then, being evil, know how to give good gifts to your children, how much more will your Father who is in heaven give good things to those who ask Him!" This is a classic Biblical example of how God first assures us of our right to approach Him, then "promises" results for following His guidelines.

It is important to know that you can "A.S.K." (acronym for Ask, Seek, Knock) God, but it is more important when you also know that He will "give, reveal and open" answers to you! This is just one example of the many promises God has distributed throughout His Word for us to find. There are many more the Lord will personally make directly to you as you build your relationship with Him.

Here in our text for today, Peter declares that all God's promises originate in one's knowledge (the Greek means "intimate" knowledge) of Him. The suggestion is that the closer we get to Him the more grace, peace, power, life, godliness, glory and courage and love will manifest in our lives; which are all segments of His nature. In this way we partake or literally share in and grow in the very nature of God Himself! This then is "the way" of escape for us out of this crooked and fallen world.

The further we travel towards the end of days, the closer we need to retrace our origins. In the early days of the Church they did not view their Christianity as merely a religious persuasion...they knew it as THE WAY (Acts 19:9; 24:2)! To act on this belief, we need to intimately know God and His promises.

AUGUST 29...DAY 241
THE ONE

"Christ has redeemed us from the curse of the law, having become a curse for us (for it is written, 'Cursed is everyone who hangs on a tree'), that the blessings of Abraham might come upon the Gentiles in Christ Jesus, that we might receive the promise of the Spirit through faith...Now to Abraham and his Seed were the promises made. He does not say, 'And to seeds,' as of many, but as of one, 'And to your Seed,' who is Christ." Galatians 3:13-14, 16 NKJV

Recently a friend jokingly said to me, "Abraham was the first missionary!"

When we talk about either "the Promise" or "the promises," every blessing God intended for the world post Eden has its roots in Abraham's willingness to obey the call. This is important for us in our understanding of the overall purpose of Jesus coming to the earth. God originally spoke of the promised "Seed" in the Garden of Eden to Eve. This would be "the One" who would come through her descendants, because they had fallen, to stand in opposition to that sin which the devil had planted among mankind by deceiving Eve and Adam (Genesis 3:15).

Notice the promise was reiterated later to one single individual, Abraham (Genesis 22:18). This is why Paul highlights it this way to the Galatian believers in our text for today. Jesus Christ, God's own "Son," came in the flesh, as the Promise that had been kept alive in the genes of His own ancestors, until the time came for His appearing. After the flood, where God preserved that Seed through the saving of Noah's household, men began to populate the earth and quickly fall away from God because of the impulsive sin nature in them.

Abraham was then chosen by God from the lineage of Noah, as a pagan man from a family living in the region of modern day Iraq and Syria. He was given the promise of a particular blessing..."all the nations of the earth" were to be specially favored by the Lord because of his obedience! Abraham was to be the father of many nations (Genesis

17:4-5) with one specific nation carrying that Promise through his son, Isaac who would inherit the land of the Cannanites.

When we fast forward to Jesus' first coming we find that everything God had promised mankind is now contained and centered in Him. As a result, everything He promised is simply an extension of and fuller expression of the promises made to those forebears, particularly Abraham, whose faith ensured His coming, and now stands sure until He comes again!

As we believe, we are blessed with faithful Abraham...walking in the richness of God's promises, but more importantly, walking with the ONE who blesses and keeps His Word!

AUGUST 30...DAY 242
THE ULTIMATE PROMISE

"Christ has redeemed us from the curse of the law, having become a curse for us (for it is written, 'Cursed is everyone who hangs on a tree'), that the blessings of Abraham might come upon the Gentiles in Christ Jesus, that we might receive the promise of the Spirit through faith."
Galatians 3:13-14 NKJV

What is the primary blessing Jesus promised to those who follow Him, obey His teachings and wait for His return?

We have already looked at the fact that the real promise God has given us is Himself. The singular "Seed" of Abraham is Christ according to verse sixteen, but the blessing that comes upon all the Gentiles goes one step further. The "Messiah" or "Christ "was the promised Prince of Israel (Daniel 9:25-26; John 1:41; 4:25) but they failed to receive Him in the "day of their visitation" (Luke 19:44). Foreknowing their unresponsiveness, God promised that Abraham's descendant would expansively become a blessing to all nations.

Through the prophet Joel, He also promised that the Holy Spirit would literally be poured out on all flesh in the last days. This is why Peter could say on the day of Pentecost to the thousands who responded to his first sermon, "Repent, and let every one of you be baptized in the name of Jesus Christ for the remission of sins; AND you shall receive the gift of the Holy Spirit. For the promise is to you and to your children, and to all who are afar off, as many as the Lord our God will call."

The Holy Spirit is the Promise of God for our day, the last days! Throughout history every member of the "Godhead" or "Trinity" (names meaning the unity of the Father, Son and Holy Spirit) has been directly involved in our salvation. Jesus introduced us to God as Father and then gave us the Spirit by which He ministered, in order that we might do the same works and even greater works than He. How much more unrestrained is the true blessing of God's presence in our lives than any particular blessing we can receive by our association with Him?! And all because Jesus was willing to become a "curse" in our place!

Think about this....embracing this truth is why the early church was so explosive and why the last church will be even more so!

AUGUST 31...DAY 243
TWO GAMES NOT TO PLAY WITH GOD

"And they (Joshua and Caleb) spoke to all the congregation of the children of Israel, saying 'The land we passed through to spy out is an exceedingly good land...Only do not rebel against the LORD, nor fear the people of the land, for they are our bread; their protection has departed from them, and the LORD is with us. Do not fear them.' And the congregation said to stone them with stones."
Numbers 14:7, 9-10a NKJV

"And they (the congregation) rose early in the morning and went up to the top of the mountain, saying 'Here we are, and we will go up to the place which the LORD has promised, for we have sinned!' And Moses said, 'Now why do you transgress the command of the LORD? For this will not succeed. Do not go up, lest you be defeated by your enemies, for the LORD is not among you...But they presumed to go up to the mountaintop...Then the Amalekites and the Canaanites who dwelt in the mountain came down and attacked them, and drove them back..."
Numbers 14:40-42, 44-45 NKJV

God's promises can be a blessing or a curse depending on how one handles them! We can learn from our text for today that there are two deadly games any believer must not play with God.

First when these Israelites had the promise of entering the land God was giving them, they did not act accordingly. Afterwards they acted presumptuously, as if the promise was still valid after God had withdrawn the offer!

The last days are not just a catchphrase intended to scare people into getting their lives right with God, any more than the Promised Land was just an illusion to the Israelites on the other side of the Jordan River!

I am pointing out things that will help you deal with what the Bible warns are grim days ahead of us with serious implications. The only way we can hope to be ready to meet the Lord at His coming is to not take our Christian faith for granted! That means learning from the examples of others, both positive and negative. The Israelites stand as a warning sign for all of us to understand that God is good but we can miss His blessings. What they did is a reverse lesson for us not to do, even though it is easier for us to imitate. They had Moses to follow, a great man of God. We have the Son of God and His Spirit in us...the Promise in advance!

SEPTEMBER 1...DAY 244
THE PRINCIPLE OF INVERSION

"And He said to me, 'My grace is sufficient for you, for My strength is made perfect in weakness.' Therefore most gladly I will rather boast in my infirmities, that the power of Christ may rest upon me. Therefore I take pleasure in infirmities, in reproaches, in needs, in persecutions, in distresses, for Christ's sake. For when I am weak, then I am strong." 2 Corinthians 12:9-10 NKJV

There is a very important truth outlined here and found throughout scripture, which I call the "Principle of Inversion." In my dictionary inversion is defined as both, "the act of turning upside down or inside out" and "the reversal of a normal order, position or relation." According to the book of Acts in your Bible, that is exactly what Paul and other early Christian disciples did within the Roman Empire! In fact, Acts 17:6 records a frenzied mob accusing them before the rulers of the city of Thessalonica saying, "These who have turned the world upside down have come here too." Even the Emperor, Nero was said to have conveniently blamed the Christians for his own malicious burning of Rome because they were already seen as those who had created such a turnaround of what had been normal in the world of that time!

It is quite amazing if you stop and think how such a fringe group of largely unorganized common citizens, with a new religious viewpoint really did build this radical reputation in such a short period of time!

So what was the secret of the early church? The inverted lifestyle Paul discovered. They could turn people and places upside down and inside out because their lives were the reverse of the normal order of things. Christ became stronger in them as they learned to lean on Him in their weaknesses. The stronger He became inside their hearts the more evident was His power outside/through them; literally inside out. The more they were persecuted as a people the stronger they became! Using "strong-arm" tactics to eliminate them was like pouring gas on a fire!

Historically this has always been true when dealing with Christians who are sincere in their faith. What has been true in the past will be just as absolute in the future...so learn to lean on and look to Jesus then you truly will be a strong end time believer and Kingdom builder!

SEPTEMBER 2...DAY 245
THE DIRTY FIGHT

"And lest I should be exalted above measure by the abundance of revelations, a thorn in the flesh was given to me, a messenger of Satan to buffet me, lest I be exalted above measure. Concerning this thing I pleaded with the Lord three times that it might depart from me. And He said to me, 'My grace is sufficient for you, for My strength is made perfect in weakness.' Therefore most gladly I will rather boast in my infirmities, that the power of Christ may rest upon me. Therefore I take pleasure in infirmities, in reproaches, in needs, in persecutions, in distresses, for Christ's sake. For when I am weak, then I am strong." 2 Corinthians 12:9-10 NKJV

Paul accepted the fact that if he was going to be used by God, he was going to receive trouble as well. The particular kind of trouble he experienced for receiving such a high level of supernatural visions and revelations was especially painful and difficult. Notice the word, "buffet" is used to describe what a literal "messenger of Satan" did to him, pricking and annoying his flesh in order to soften his approach to the Gospel. This is a serious deterrent to less committed Christians, until we realize that lessons like this one are what made Paul the soldier he was!

"Buffet" means to hit with the fist. One commentator says it specifically describes the act of a man boxing another in the ear. Ouch! If you've ever been hit like that you know how painful and dangerous it can be. Dirty fighters often use this tactic to disable their victim because it causes loss of orientation due to the breaking of the eardrum! Paul describes his plight as a dirty fight with the devil for the souls of people all across the pagan Roman world! Even his repeated pleas to the Lord for relief did not get him out of this fight, but it did get him something far better. Jesus gave Paul His own personal secret for spiritual success. He said that grace works best when we are at our worst.

"Grace" is a sweet sounding religious word with a much more rugged definition. It means "God's favorable action on our behalf." Really it is another way of saying, the "power of God working for you!" Yes, the power of God goes into operation when we stop trusting in ourselves and start trusting in the Lord. Unfortunately, this often happens on a greater scale when we feel the pressure and have nowhere else to turn.

Paul learned, through this one experience, to use the "principle of inversion" in every circumstance he faced. Leaning into our difficulties was and is the sure way to have that power "rest upon" us for success in every assignment we are called to carry out.

SEPTEMBER 3...DAY 246
WHY THE END TIMES WILL BE THE CHURCH'S BEST TIME

"Therefore we wanted to come to you-even I, Paul, time and again-but Satan hindered us...Therefore, when we could no longer endure it, we thought it good to be left in Athens alone, and sent Timothy, our brother and minister of God, and our fellow laborer in the gospel of Christ, to establish you and encourage you concerning your faith, that no one should be shaken by these afflictions; for you yourselves know that we are appointed to this. For, in fact, we told you before when we were with you that we would suffer tribulation, just as it happened, and you know. For this reason, when I could no longer endure it, I sent to know your faith, lest by some means the tempter had tempted, and our labor might be in vain."
1 Thessalonians 2:18; 3:1-5

Jesus taught the apostle Paul the secret of using opposition to his advantage. Any competitive person knows this to be a smart psychological tactic, but it can be taken to another level spiritually.

As Christians, we compete not with flesh and blood but with Satan, a spiritual adversary (Ephesians 6:12) who has hosts of wicked forces at his command. That is the bad news. The good news is Jesus is our champion, which is what the "Gospel" message is all about! He not only defeated the devil on the spiritual battlefield, he also showed us how to compete with him on every level. You can see here that Paul was "hindered" by Satan but could not be outmaneuvered! This word paints the picture of a traveler whose progress is being impeded because an enemy has broken the road, burned the bridges or breached difficult objects sharply in his way.

The devil formulated a strategy against believers in the church at Thessalonica tempting and shaking their faith through the afflictions he directed at Paul and his apostolic company of ministers. Even though he prevented them from traveling back to check up on a church that needed their attention, how does Paul respond? By once again, "inverting" the situation! He is weakened, so he depends on the Lord to help him find another way. Since he can't go, he decides to send Timothy in his place to be the "brother," "minister," and "fellow" apostle they needed. Paul also openly informs and reminds them, through Timothy, of the demonic strategy he had warned them he must endure. He refused to quit trusting in Jesus' victory on the cross. Paul continued to work on that basis, regardless of the hardships he faced.

With this same approach, we can take advantage of every seeming disadvantage we face. Now you know why the end times will be the best times for the church!

SEPTEMBER 4...DAY 247
TURN THE TABLE ON THE DEVIL

"As they were coming home, when David returned from killing the Philistine,...the women responded as they laughed and frolicked, saying, 'Saul has slain his thousands, and David his ten thousands. And Saul [jealously] eyed David from that day forward. The next day an evil spirit from God came mightily upon Saul, and he raved [madly] in his house, while David played [the lyre] with his hand, as at other times; and there was a javelin in Saul's hand. And Saul cast the javelin, for he thought, I will pin David to the wall. And David evaded him twice. Saul was afraid of David, because the Lord was with him but he departed from Saul." 1 Samuel 18:6-12 AMP

If you read the very next chapter of First Samuel (19:8-10), you will find this same scene being played out again in almost exactly the same way! In this Old Testament scripture, we have another example of my biblical, "Principle of Inversion."

God has always taught believers to turn the tables on their enemy, the devil, and David did it masterfully. King Saul on the other hand, allowed the table to be overturned upon him. He was someone who couldn't detach from his own interests. He had every spiritual advantage, but lost his job to a man after God's own heart, David (16:13-14)!

From the nanosecond he received this evil spirit Saul's life barreled progressively downhill while David's success in God crested. Because the anointing of God's Spirit was upon him, David was inspired to challenge and kill Goliath. Afterward he defeated the Philistines again and again. Every move he made worked because his heart touched something in God!

David also unwittingly touched the core of Satan's strategy against the entire nation of Israel, because David possessed spiritual authority. In victory after victory, David struck at the center point of the residual fear that Satan had employed since the day the ten spies (Numbers 13) had prevented Israel from taking the "Promised Land."

As Saul subtly became the devil's tactic against Israel, David was revealed as God's reverse tactic, planned and punctuated in advance for Israel's deliverance! This same war stratagem often works against the church today, although it seems few believers discern the true cause of their fear and concerns, or exemplify the heart to overcome the actual opponent. It was David's refusal to "touch God's anointed" which disallowed the devil to touch him or destroy Israel! He used his disadvantages to give God the advantage and showed us the kind of heart that God loves to empower and bless!

We will have to present the same type of unnatural character if we intend to turn the tables on the devil in these last days.

SEPTEMBER 5...DAY 248
KEEP YOUR EYE ON THE BACK DOOR

"Then the angel said to her...And behold, you will conceive in your womb and bring forth a Son, and shall call His name JESUS. He will be great and will be called the Son of the Highest; and the Lord God will give Him the throne of His father David. And He will reign over the house of Jacob forever, and of His kingdom there will be no end.' Then Mary said to the angel, 'How can this be, since I do not know a man?' And the angel answered and said to her, 'The Holy Spirit will come upon you, and the power of the Highest will overshadow you; therefore, also, that Holy One who is to be born will be called the Son of God.'"
Luke 1:30-35 NKJV

"And she brought forth her firstborn Son, and wrapped Him in swaddling clothes, and laid Him in a manger, because there was no room for them in the inn."
Luke 2:7 NKJV

What we have here is the greatest example of the "Principle of Inversion" in the history of the world! It is the heart of the Gospel message. God Himself was not only willing to become a man, but He did it with such humility that even the most humbled by this life would be able locate and discover Him. Jesus didn't only go to the cross at the end of His life He picked it up and carried it from the very beginning!

Let the irony of the text for today make a lasting impression on your Christian and worldview. How could God lower Himself to the point of being born in a manger? Why would this be beneficial to His cause of world reconciliation to God?

To our way of thinking, God should forcefully impose Himself as the Highest, the Greatest, and the rightful Heir to the Kingdom. His mindset couldn't be more different! Instead, God's Son enters the world He is destined to save through the "back" door. Mary is an unknown and her fiancé doesn't even have enough money or influence to get them into the cheapest room at the worst motel in Bethlehem! God is born in the barn!!

To most modern Christians this would be madness, which is why we need to think twice about how to discern and live our lives in anticipation of His return!

SEPTEMBER 6...DAY 249
TWO KINDS OF INVERSION

"And they came to John and said to him, 'Rabbi, He who was with you beyond the Jordan, to whom you have testified - behold, He is baptizing, and all are coming to Him!' John answered and said, 'A man can receive nothing unless it has been given to him from heaven. You yourselves bear me witness that I said, 'I am not the Christ, but, I have been sent before Him.' He who has the bride is the bridegroom; but the friend of the bridegroom, who stands and hears him, rejoices greatly because of the bridegroom's voice. Therefore this joy of mine is fulfilled. He must increase, but I must decrease. He who comes from above is above all; he who is of the earth is earthly and speaks of the earth." John 3:26-31 NKJV

Throughout scripture we come across people who practiced the "principle of inversion" in order to more fully follow God. Looking at good godly examples, like John the Baptist, will help us do the same. He said here it was necessary for him to "decrease" when the time came for Jesus to "increase."

Unfortunately today's preachers often isolate verses such as this one (verse 30) and quote it in such a philosophical way that they turn important spiritual truths into poetic language for which believers can no find no practical application! If you will look behind the curtain of mere religion you will find a clear distinction between those who live the truth and those who only quote it! There are two practices of "inversion." First, there are the spiritual ones, who invert their choices to match God's will so they can live out the principles they believe in. Then there are the religious ones who invert the words of the truly spiritual so they can make a living out of principles and beliefs.

Guys like John the Baptist were required to give up standing, what we might call our ministry; even as God was giving all of this anointing and 'ministry' to John's successor...for real and forever! The wisdom John displayed was from above, not some kind of intellectual foolishness which does more to inflate the ego of teachers than it does to increase the understanding of students. When a Christian leader can rejoice in the exaltation of another while it results in his own retirement, and do it at the peak of his own success, you have found one qualified not only to talk about God but one who knows Him well. This is a martyr more than a minister...the end times will require us to know the difference!

SEPTEMBER 7...DAY 250
LESS IS MORE, MORE OR LESS

*"But I make known to you, brethren that the gospel which was
preached by me is not according to man. For I neither received it from man, nor
was I taught it, but it came through the revelation of Jesus Christ...But from those who
seemed to be something - whatever they were, it makes no difference to me; God shows
personal favoritism to no man - for those who seemed to be something added nothing
to me. But on the contrary, when they saw that the gospel for the uncircumcised had
been committed to me, as the gospel for the circumcised was to Peter...and when
James and Cephas and John, who seemed to be pillars, perceived the grace that had
been given to me, they gave me and Barnabas the right hand of fellowship..."
Galatians 1:11-12; 2:6-9 NKJV*

Paul is another example of one who learned the value of decrease when it comes to serving the Lord. In between our verses for today, the Bible says he spent three years in obscurity, retiring to Arabia and seeking God after his supernatural Damascus conversion. It was during this time that Paul received a direct download of the good news (literal meaning of "Gospel") from the Lord Himself. This would have been contrary to the methodologies which had made him one of the up and coming "who's who" in the Jewish leadership of his day! Again, we find the "principle of inversion" working in someone God has called to be an important piece of the heavenly puzzle He is piecing together throughout scripture.

Paul's training history doesn't stop there. He then served in Christian ministry in obscurity for another fourteen years before stepping into that "apostolic" level on which he came to be recognized!

Not only did the Lord call Paul in an unusual manner, He also used him that way! Contrary to the development of the rest of the church in those early days, his ministry was fashioned almost completely outside the touch of the Lord's own disciples. These verses tell us why. God called him to reach the Gentile world in particular, while Peter, James and John were assigned to target the Jews. It took them a while to figure out that God was using them all in ways that sometimes seemed in opposition to one another. Less (self) is more (God) every time in the Lord's Kingdom. Regardless of who we think we are or what we believe we are called to do the more humble and dependent upon God we become, the more Jesus is going to accomplish His will in and through our lives...sometimes in ways that are quite different from how we contemplated things would or should turn out!

SEPTEMBER 8...DAY 251
THE SENTENCE OF DEATH

"For we do not want you to be ignorant, brethren, of our trouble which came to us in Asia: that we were burdened beyond measure, above strength, so that we despaired even of life. Yes, we had the sentence of death in ourselves, that we should not trust in ourselves but in God Who raises the dead, Who delivered us from so great a death, and does deliver us; in Whom we trust that He will still deliver us, you also helping together in prayer for us, that thanks may be given by many persons on our behalf for the gift granted to us through many."
2 Corinthians 1:8-11 NKJV

When I was young and serving in my first ministry assignment I had several defining spiritual experiences that have helped me stay steady and focused on the right things to this day.

I remember dreaming one night that I was in a smaller church where there were problems going on behind the scenes. After being shown some of these things, it came time for me to step to the front of the congregation and deliver the message in a particular service there. When I got behind the pulpit, to my surprise I found that I had nothing to say! Uncomfortably, I was scanning across the crowd trying to collect my thoughts when I noticed a familiar face to my right at the end of the front row. Of all people, it was one of the kindest elderly ladies I knew. She was my real life pastor's mother, sitting right there in my dream in another church, and she had a message for me!

"Try Second Corinthians 1:10," came out of her mouth. It was a short and simple solution to what I would consider a major problem for any preacher, especially me! Looking back I can see how God used this early experience to focus my purpose. Regardless of what kinds of problematic situations I have faced in local church ministry, and there have been many, I have always been able to go back to the tenth verse of our text for today and recollect my thoughts.

God has called me to embrace the "sentence of death" and focus on His delivering power. Like Paul, I have seen Him deliver me in the past. I have come to depend on the fact that I am in need of His deliverance today. I know that I will surely need God's deliverance tomorrow and He will come through as long as I live for Him and not for myself.

We learn from Christ's example that God authorizes what He resurrects from a state of weakness and death. As you "seed" your life into His purpose and presence, spiritual power springs forth to accomplish His will and impact many others in the process. Whatever the Lord has called you to do, always remember to choose death in advance knowing that He specializes in raising the dead!

SEPTEMBER 9...DAY 252
DOUBLE TROUBLE

"For we do not want you to be ignorant, brethren, of our trouble which came to us in Asia: that we were burdened beyond measure, above strength, so that we despaired even of life. Yes, we had the sentence of death in ourselves, that we should not trust in ourselves but in God who raises the dead, Who delivered us from so great a death, and does deliver us; in Whom we trust that He will still deliver us, you also helping together in prayer for us, that thanks may be given by many persons on our behalf for the gift granted to us through many."
2 Corinthians 1:8-11 NKJV

Paul had great trouble in Asia because of his great success in ministry there. During his "first missionary journey" (you can find this outlined in the map section in the back of many Bibles), along with Barnabas, he was persecuted in nearly every town they entered.

They were able to gather almost the entire city to hear the Word in Antioch, and were expelled for it. In Iconium, they gathered a great multitude, performing signs and wonders and narrowly escaped being stoned. In Lystra, the people thought they were Greek gods when they witnessed the healing of a local cripple who had never walked. After refusing their worship, Paul was eventually stoned and left for dead, until the believers there prayed and raised him up! In Derbe there was no recorded preaching or miracles and interestingly no recorded persecution!

Everything horrific that happened to Paul was a direct response to the good that was being accomplished through his life and ministry in each of these places. Satan used every possible tactic to prevent the explosive spread of the Gospel, because Paul had learned to walk in the "principle of inversion"!

In our day, Christians are often trained to see difficulty as a negative, but in that day they understood it as a necessary risk they were willing to take in order to let God's Spirit move throughout His Church! When we truly turn our lives over to the Lord we will need His delivering power. This is why Paul emphasizes the need to accept a spiritual death sentence in advance...so the measure, strength and life of God can be delivered to us when we need it most.

Notice that Paul did not intend to do this work alone. He was laying his life down on the front lines of ministry, expecting others to do the same behind the scenes in prayer. When we work courageously as a team, we equalize the trouble we get from our adversary and maximize the trouble we create for him!

SEPTEMBER 10...DAY 253
EXTRA DEGREES OF SEPARATION

"Yes, we had the sentence of death in ourselves, that we should not trust in ourselves but in God who raises the dead, Who delivered us from so great a death, and does deliver us; in whom we trust that He will still deliver us, you also helping together in prayer for us, that thanks may be given by many persons on our behalf for the gift granted to us through many."
2 Corinthians 1:9-11 NKJV

"Now in the church that was at Antioch there were certain prophets and teachers: Barnabas, Simeon who was called Niger, Lucius of Cyrene, Manaen who had been brought up with Herod the tetrarch, and Saul. As they ministered to the Lord and fasted, the Holy Spirit said, 'Now separate to Me Barnabas and Saul for the work to which I have called them.' Then, having fasted and prayed and laid hands on them, they sent them away."
Acts 13:1-3 NKJV

You can see by reading our scripture for today that ministers and lay believers are meant to work together to reach the world for Christ. Churches are the primary result of that combined effort. These are gathering places where God assembles believers and trains up ministers so they can work together to further create opportunities of collective service and thanksgiving to God. He then uses those opportunities to keep touching more cities and nations as the overall Church keeps growing and its circle of influence continues expanding!

In 2005, I was working as an overseer of several churches in North and South America within a larger church planting organization. Imagine how surprised I was when one morning, as I sat quietly on my living room sofa, the Lord spoke to me and said, "Nobody in the Bible ever 'planted' a church." After thinking about it and combing through the chapters of the book of Acts I realized the accuracy of God' statement, we don't deliberately plant churches! They are the natural outgrowth of the activities of those ministers who are sent by the Holy Spirit, and those who believe and attach themselves to their (Gospel) message. Today, these lines have been so "blurred" in the church world that most Christians can't tell whether their churches are man-made or God-made.

Jesus is certainly building His church regardless of whether we understand His ways or not but, because of our ignorance, the outline does not always conform to our way of thinking! It really comes down to just how much we trust in ourselves versus how separated to God and His purposes we really are.

I was tied to my way of doing things for God until He reminded me of His way...living in the last days is going to require these extra degrees of separation!

SEPTEMBER 11...DAY 254
NEVER FORGET

"But when you hear of wars and commotions, do not be terrified; for these things must come to pass first, but the end will not come immediately. Then He said to them, 'Nation will rise against nation, and kingdom against kingdom. And there will be great earthquakes in various places, and famines and pestilences; and there will be fearful sights and great signs from heaven.'"
Luke 21:9-11, NKJV

In the United States, September 11th, 2001 was a transition point. Before that time, scriptures like our text for today were usually viewed as happening somewhere else and hopefully in some other time. Afterward, however, many Americans lost much of the spiritual childishness that created such a foolish worldview in the first place...at least for awhile!

It just so happens that I was in New York City yesterday (September 10th, 2009, at the time of this writing). As I looked around, there were certainly some reminders of the "fearful sights" seen eight years prior, but I saw very little sense of urgency about the condition of the city or nation's soul.

In Herald Square my associates and I were interviewing people on camera, asking one question. "Do you know that you are going to heaven when you die?" The majority of Christians I met responded that they knew but were not initially very persuasive with either their words or body language. Most non-believers said they hoped so, but didn't think it was a critical question!

These are pretty average results, the standard answers you will get anywhere in this nation. How shocking when you consider we were asking a question that goes to the heart of the area that should be the least indifferent!

Do you remember where you were on 9/11? For every American it should be one of many signs reminding us that Jesus is coming. We must never forget to be responsible enough to stay alert and to teach those around us to do the same. I will never forget how my wife and I were conducting an early morning prayer gathering in our home in Colorado, when a dear spiritual lady suddenly began to prophesy loudly. "This will be a day that people will not forget!" I just took it to be a nice encouragement until we turned the television to discover what happened in New York less than an hour after hearing this prophesy!

For us, "never forget" is not a catch phrase...it was a word from God! We live in a day of alertness so don't become complacent. The Lord wants us to look at these kinds of signs as indicators of the times. Refuse to be terrified but resolve to be about His business so you will remain ready to meet Him when He comes!

SEPT 12...DAY 255
GOING FROM BETTER TO BEST

"Now in the church that was in Antioch there were certain prophets and teachers: Barnabas, Simeon who was called Niger, Lucius of Cyrene, Manaen who had been brought up with Herod the tetrarch, and Saul. As they ministered to the Lord and fasted, the Holy Spirit said, 'Now separate to Me Barnabas and Saul for the work to which I have called them.' Then, having fasted and prayed and laid hands on them, they sent them away." Acts 13:1-3 NKJV

I love how this scripture speaks in such a matter of fact way about how simply the church in Antioch went about ministry. In stark contrast to the modern complexities one has to wade through in order to find the heart of the Christian religion, this church was streamlined! Notice how that, although men were in stated positions of leadership, the Holy Spirit was in charge issuing vision and direction.

Chronologically, this was somewhere around seventeen years after Jesus' resurrection and the birth of the church on the day of Pentecost. Yet, here we find a church still operating under the same basic procedures modeled for them in the beginning! It is refreshing to see the Holy Spirit continuing to be the dominant factor in Antioch, just as He had been in the life of Jesus and in the ministry His disciples carried out in His name.

We tend to complicate everything by pushing Who and what is unseen into the background and exalting the positions of those and that which we can see with our natural eyes.

To prove my point I did a quick internet search to find out just how many Protestant denominations there are in the United States. The first answer I found was, "seriously, only God knows" followed by, a more helpful "hundreds" at my second request. I didn't see a need to go any further!

In Antioch, they had one church in one city with leaders who ministered to the Lord before they counseled among themselves or preached to the congregation. Without any mention of a pastor as we know it, these prophets and teachers obeyed the Lord's simple instructions, putting it at the top of their goals and strategies list. They didn't eat until they heard from God, and then didn't eat again until they had done what He said!

In this most efficient manner the Bible records the launching of a new "work" into the Gentile world. Barnabas and Saul became the next wave of apostles, sent to expand the Church to its next level. Antioch teaches us how to go from better to best. The Church should always embrace the new...as long as it is God's idea and not our own.

SEPT 13...DAY 256
BELIEVE AND BE BAPTIZED

"And it happened... that Paul... came to Ephesus. And finding some disciples he said to them, 'Did you receive the Holy Spirit when you believed?' So they said to him, 'We have not so much as heard whether there is a Holy Spirit.' And He said to them, 'Into what then were you baptized?' So they said, 'Into John's baptism.' Then Paul said, 'John indeed baptized with a baptism of repentance, saying to the people that they should believe on Him who would come after him, that is, on Christ Jesus.' When they heard this, they were baptized in the name of the Lord Jesus.' And when Paul had laid hands on them, the Holy Spirit came upon them, and they spoke with tongues and prophesied." Acts 19:1-6 NKJV

This chapter is among my favorite in the Bible. God has been showing me central spiritual truths as I have read and reread it for over a quarter of a century! Let me share one with you.

As we have been learning, things happen when people get baptized in the name of Jesus! An authority comes upon our lives as we are immersed into His nature and the legalities of the weight that it carries. Paul went all over the Roman world of his time preaching the Gospel and establishing works in many largely pagan cities such as Ephesus. Because of the power of God's Word and with the authority upon his life for ministry he was able to take this handful of men and turn them into a stupendous supernatural voice within such a dark place!

Through his own relationship with the Lord he was enlightened to follow the Holy Spirit's directions. Also Paul was willing to proclaim the full message of the Gospel and work diligently with those who meagerly believed. Today, we have too many educated ministers who lead people into a shallow faith.

Incredibly, these twelve disciples were given the exact same experience the original disciples had received on the day of Pentecost in Acts chapter two! What was the key? It was in getting them to believe sufficiently to be "baptized." This means they didn't lightly accept the Gospel of Christ, they fully embraced it. This was the baptism of the Holy Spirit, not water baptism; however, water baptism is a perfect picture of our responsibility in spiritual things.

As you will see tomorrow, a little bit of the real thing goes a long way when you are "immersed" in it! Once they "dove in" with their faith, Paul dove in with them, imparting freely the gift Jesus promised all who will believe enough to repent and be baptized (Acts 2:38-39).

In these last days, if we will fully embrace the name of Jesus, the Holy Spirit will also fully empower and equip us to meet the challenges of dark times ahead!

SEPTEMBER 14...DAY 257
YOUR PART, GOD'S PART

"And he (Paul) went into the synagogue and spoke boldly for three months, reasoning and persuading concerning the things of the kingdom of God. But when some were hardened and did not believe, but spoke evil of the Way before the multitude, he departed from them and withdrew the disciples, reasoning daily in the school of Tyrannus. And this continued for two years, so that all who dwelt in Asia heard the word of the Lord Jesus, both Jews and Greeks. Now God worked unusual miracles by the hands of aul, so that even handkerchiefs or aprons were brought from his body to the sick, and diseases left them and the evil spirits went out of them."
Acts 19:8-12 NKJV

The apostle Paul used the authority of Jesus' name masterfully. After going into Ephesus and finding twelve disciples who had only heard about water baptism or the message of repentance carried by John the Baptist, he did exactly what Jesus commanded us to do. He preached salvation in Christ. He then imparted the Holy Spirit out of his own experience and personal relationship in the Lord, and empowered them for Kingdom service. Finally, he continued to reason with those who were open, and he diligently taught the serious believers.

This is what is often called the "Great Commission" given by Jesus to His followers in Matthew 28 and Mark 16. Today, I'd ask you to notice two very simple but very important aspects of ministering the Gospel, especially in light of the lateness of this hour in human history.

Firstly, Paul did his part and secondly, the Lord did His! Mark 16:17 promises, "attesting signs" will follow the carrying out of this great commission, one of which is physical healing. Verse 20 then, follows up by saying, "...while the Lord kept working with them and confirming the message by the attesting signs and miracles that closely accompanied [it]. Amen (so be it)."

This is normal Gospel activity! We do our part and the Lord does His immersing us via the person of the Holy Spirit. Paul refused to relent in his ministerial duties over an extended period of time, thus the "unusual" and extraordinary level of miracles we read about here. This activity points to "Jesus-like" authority! Paul was doing things that had not been heard of and those things were whatever signs the Holy Spirit deemed necessary to establish the work of God in Ephesus.

What an amazing thing it is to watch the Lord work His authority in another man! You are authorized to take Jesus to your community as well. Step up a level and do your part...I guarantee you God will do His.

SEPTEMBER 15...DAY 258
THE RIGHT SIDE OF JESUS NAME

"Then some of the itinerant Jewish exorcists took it upon themselves to call the name of the Lord Jesus over those who had evil spirits, saying, 'We exorcise you by the Jesus whom Paul preaches.' Also there were seven sons of Sceva, a Jewish chief priest, who did so. And the evil spirit answered and said, 'Jesus I know, and Paul I know; but who are you?' Then the man in whom the evil spirit was leaped on them, overpowered them, and prevailed against them, so that they fled out of that house naked and wounded. This became known both to all Jews and Greeks dwelling in Ephesus; and fear fell on them all, and the name of the Lord was magnified...So the word of the Lord grew mightily and prevailed."
Acts 19:13-17, 20 NKJV

The name of Jesus is contagious! When God is moving in a powerful way, all kinds of characters will try to get in on the action. It can also be dangerous because the power His Name contains can be turned against anyone who uses it without authorization.

This is exactly what happened in Ephesus with Paul. Not only did God use him to perform unusual things (verse 11) as a means of getting a pagan community's attention, He also used the ignorance of some other unusual people to reinforce the power of His word! These sons of Sceva were Jewish exorcists. They were involved in dealing with people oppressed by evil spirits. Many exorcists like these fellows were roaming spiritual merchants looking for those they could manipulate for gain. Maybe they even carried a level of governmental authority, being sons of a Jewish chief priest, and were able to bring a level of relief to some.

When they came in contact with the name of Jesus they found a higher and (they thought) much more effective way to work their trade. We deal with this same dilemma in the world of religion today. Depending on where you live and what kind of culture you've been raised in, the reality of the spiritual dimension may or may not be obvious to you. People in third world countries and underprivileged inner city environments are much more accustomed to dealing with the influences of evil.

Whether you're aware of it or not, demons are very real and God will use their presence to further His purposes as each situation allows.

Paul used the name of Jesus authoritatively and powerful things happened. Pretenders tried to do the same for their own purposes, and God exposed them to the power of the evil spirits they were trying to expose! Be careful how you approach Jesus and His power...it's better to be open and naked before God than to be exposed by the devil!

SEPTEMBER 16...DAY 259
LEARN HOW TO WIN

"Do you not know that in a race all the runners compete, but [only] one receives the prize? So run [your race] that you may lay hold [of the prize] and make it yours. Now every athlete who goes into training conducts himself temperately and restricts himself in all things. They do it to win a wreath that will soon wither, but we [do it to receive a crown of eternal blessedness] that cannot wither. Therefore I do not run uncertainly (without definite aim). I do not box like one beating the air and striking without an adversary. But [like a boxer] I buffet my body [handle it roughly,

discipline it by hardships] and subdue it, for fear that after proclaiming to others the Gospel and things pertaining to it, I myself should become unfit [not stand the test, be unapproved and rejected as a counterfeit].
1 Corinthians 9:24-27 AMP

In Acts 26:19 the Apostle Paul testified before the King of Judea that he had not been "disobedient to the heavenly vision" Jesus called him to accomplish. This divine call had not only allowed Paul to experience many miraculous things and accomplish many incredible tasks, it had also caused him much trouble. He was rehearsing his testimony to King Agrippa in a courtroom setting, acting as his own defense attorney because he had been persecuted by the Jews and imprisoned by the Romans!

There is indeed a high cost involved in following God's purpose for your life. Our text for today emphasizes this but also teaches us the value of "paying the price." Notice Paul, uses the illustration of a sprinter in verse 24 to highlight the fact that he had a definite vision which carried a reward. Also by using the boxing analogy, he specifically mentions in verse 26 that he had an adversary! Anyone who has a vision will experience adversity, especially when that image is God-given. (Paul tells us this even more plainly in 1 Timothy 3:12).

In between these two verses, Paul gives us the secret to winning the prize, which makes our race worth enduring. In verse 25, he says we must train ourselves properly so we will run with certainty against our opponent! The language becomes even more direct in verse 27 where we are told what this means.

Handling our bodies roughly and disciplining them by hardships is what prepares us to gain more speed and throw quality punches! You can't take it easy during practice and expect to win your race. We have to run and we have to fight.

A little bit of suffering in the flesh everyday will cause us to overcome in the last days!

SEPTEMBER 17...DAY 260
THREE THINGS TO ENSURE GOD'S BLESSING

"He who is faithful in what is least is faithful also in much; and he who is unjust in what is least is unjust also in much. Therefore if you have not been faithful in the unrighteous mammon, who will commit to your trust the true riches? And if you have not been faithful in what is another man's, who will give you what is your own? No servant can serve two masters; for either he will hate the one and love the other, or

else he will be loyal to the one and despise the other. You cannot serve God and mammon." Luke 16:10-13 NKJV

There is a definite parallel between the way we handle earthly riches and the way we receive heavenly riches. Notice Jesus refers here to something called, "mammon". This is defined in my Bible concordance as "wealth personified," or "greed deified!" It is an ancient Chaldean word, which some have speculated was actually once the name of a demonic "god" worshipped in Babylonian times! In New Testament times the word had been handed down through the Aramaic language where it meant, "that which is to be trusted." It was similar to the Hebrew word, "amen" and, according to Rick Renner (Sparkling Gems from the Greek page, 436) it had simply come to represent "worldliness."

The Lord tells us 1) we must be faithful in this worldly mammon and 2) we cannot serve it and God at the same time. The true personality behind money in this world system is the devil. When we begin to "love" money we get entangled at the very root of the evil he uses to systematically control this world (1 Timothy 6:10). If you have lived very long you know that money makes you its slave. Since both God and money require our time, our talents and our energy, we cannot effectively serve them both as Christians.

The good news here is that Jesus gave us the secret to using money in our service to God! If we do three simple things we are actually able to transfer our trust from what we possess to the One who has caused us to possess all things. If you will make it your aim to be faithful in three areas; little things, natural things and, another man's things, God will receive the glory in your life, instead of your bank account and bless you with much to call your own...in both this life and the one that Jesus will be bringing with Him at His return!

SEPTEMBER 18...DAY 261
THREE POSITIONS OF PREPARATION

"I, John, both your brother and companion in the tribulation and Kingdom and patience of Jesus Christ, was on the island that is called Patmos for the Word of God and for the testimony of Jesus Christ. I was in the Spirit on the Lord's Day and I heard behind me a loud voice, as of a trumpet, saying, 'I am the Alpha and the Omega, the First and the Last,' and, 'What you see, write in a book and send it to the seven churches which are in Asia: to Ephesus, to Smyrna, to Pergamum, to Thyatira, to Sardis, to Philadelphia, and to Laodicea.'"
Revelation 1:9-11 NKJV

The last book in the Bible is known as "The Revelation of Jesus Christ." It is the record of the Apostle John's supernatural experience, which outlines the end times. Today I want you to notice the circumstances surrounding this vision.

You will find that John was in three key positions anyone preparing for the return of the Jesus Christ should imitate.

First, he was experiencing the tribulation that comes as a result of testifying faithfully to the truth of God's Word. Imprisoned on an island off the coast of modern day Turkey, John was in a Roman penal colony, most likely forced to do hard labor in the granite mines located there. The name of this place, "Patmos," interestingly enough, means "my killing!" Yet, even in the midst of such a physically demanding situation, he was able to remain patient and focused on the Lord!

Second, John is not just found praying there, but rather he was specifically in "the Spirit" of prayer. This means he had pushed passed the limitations of the natural body and mind, taken hold of the Holy Spirit's leading and crossed over into a place of the conscious awareness of God. This is what you find described by Jude (verse 20) and Paul (1 Corinthians 14) as necessary for a believer in building a supernatural lifestyle. John wasn't just religious he was truly spiritual in that he was willing to do in secret what he preached in public!

Finally, this apostle serves as a great example for us as last day believers by being found in a position of a faithful messenger. Jesus could assign the work of God's Kingdom to him knowing he would carry it out, even from prison! So, the first revelation for us from "The Revelation" illustrates how to live in a constant state of readiness to meet Jesus!

SEPTEMBER 19...DAY 262
SEVEN TRAITS FOR ALL TIME

"I was in the Spirit on the Lord's Day and I heard behind me a loud voice, as of a trumpet, saying, 'I am Alpha and the Omega, the First and the Last,' and, 'What you see, write in a book and send it to the seven churches which are in Asia: to Ephesus, to Smyrna, to Pergamum, to Thyatira, to Sardis, to Philadelphia, and to Laodicea.'"
Revelation 1:9-11 NKJV

These seven cities are listed exactly as they were arranged along a Roman postal route of that time. I believe this is symbolic of the "route" God's people would take with His message until Jesus returned. They were also located within a region which linked different parts of the then known world. Therefore, the message Jesus gave them must be vital and common to the cross-section of cultures around the world throughout time. In short, these seven messages contain truths that can never be lost among the church where you live or the church at large! They are a checklist of things to know, both good and bad, about corporate Christian behavior.

There is much valuable teaching here, but I want you to notice seven traits I found in these short letters. These are in general the characteristics that believers will need to cultivate in order to overcome the seven different conditions the church will go through en route to Jesus' return!

The Ephesus letter teaches us to value LOVE for God above everything, recapture it when necessary and refuse to allow petty divisions. Smyrna is a call to COURAGE. It commands churches to refuse the fear of persecution, to recognize the danger of false religious spirits and to remain faithful. Pergamum teaches the importance of protecting true FAITH and dealing with those who peddle false doctrines and deception amid serious satanic influences. Thyatira tells us to work hard and FINISH what we start by diligently dealing with those who open doors to seducing spirits among God's people. Sardis is a call to spiritual AWARENESS. We have to wake up, watch our condition and work with what we've got. Philadelphia was the picture of a church that carried AUTHORITY as a result of their obedience, and was under the protection of God. Laodicea teaches us to remain PASSIONATE about keeping Jesus at the center of our lifestyles, or else!

Taken together, this list will keep us prepared to meet the Lord.

SEPTEMBER 20...DAY 263
CHECK THE CHURCH LIST
Ephesus...Hardhearted Church

"I was in the Spirit on the Lord's Day and I heard behind me a loud voice, as of a trumpet, saying, 'I am Alpha and the Omega, the First and the Last,' and, 'What you see, write in a book and send it to the seven churches which are in Asia: to Ephesus, to Smyrna, to Pergamum, to Thyatira, to Sardis, to Philadelphia, and to Laodicea.'"
Revelation 1:9-11 NKJV

The first three chapters of "The Revelation" give us another perspective of what church life should look like. It is so easy to become comfortable with what we have known in the past, but here we are forced to ask ourselves what should a church be all about from Jesus' point of view? Notice, there is no specific model given as the only true and right one, although two of the seven are not chastised for any wrong behavior. Instead we are given a glimpse of various kinds of real corporate Christian situations from several different vantage points, both positive and negative. With each one we can learn something about how to behave ourselves appropriately in the House of God, which Paul says, is the very pillar and ground of the truth (1 Timothy 3:15) in the world today! So, let's simply go through this list of cities where some of the earliest local versions of "The Church" were found and see if we can recognize what God is looking for in our churches today.

Each of these churches were noted by the Lord as having a distinguishing feature, from which many Bible commentators have used to label them throughout history. For example, the Ephesian church is known as the "LOVELESS" church because Jesus criticized the lack of heart fervency found in the congregation there.

I think any person who has attended more than a few different churches can relate to that in this era! In fact, Jesus noted in Matthew 24:12, that the end times will be marked by the love of many growing cold due to rampant lawlessness. Paul reiterates this in 2 Thessalonians 2:3, telling us it will create a falling away of God's people which will open the way for the Anti-Christ to appear!

Now you can see how important these messages to the churches really are! If we find our churches wanting in even one area as important as love, and they refuse to repent, it can put us at risk of losing the whole thing (see Revelation 2:5)! We should be able to see that a church without love isn't really a church at all. Because we forget to examine God's checklists, we often settle for something less than authentic Christianity!

SEPTEMBER 21...DAY 264
A REAL, GOOD CHURCH
Smyrna...Persecuted Church

"I was in the Spirit on the Lord's Day and I heard behind me a loud voice, as of a trumpet, saying, 'I am Alpha and the Omega, the First and the Last,' and, 'What you see, write in a book and send it to the seven churches which are in Asia: to Ephesus, to Smyrna, to Pergamum, to Thyatira, to Sardis, to Philadelphia, and to Laodicea...He who has an ear, let him hear what the Spirit says to the churches'"
Revelation 1:9-11; 3:22 NKJV

Smyrna is the second city mentioned by Jesus on the first century Roman mail route which received the greatest end-time message of all time! It is said to have been a great city of commerce, wealthy and beautiful, but the church there was noted by Jesus for its courage under heavy persecution. What a contrast of environments!

The world around these believers was prospering while they struggled to make ends meet as a result of the stand they had taken for Him. This sounds very similar to the scenario in which the Lord describes His own second coming in Luke 17:22-30. Using both Noah and Lot as examples, Jesus warned His disciples not to build their lives exclusively within the rhythm and commerce of the world system. Even as things around these two men continued to prosper and develop according to the "normal" course of life, God prepared them and their families to escape an otherwise unforeseen destruction! Likewise, the Lord didn't chastise the Christians in Smyrna for any wrongdoing because they were also faithfully holding forth the word of God in the midst of their community.

As important as love is to a fallen church like the one in Ephesus, so the willingness to endure persecution is to a church that is faithful. For those who have a hard time understanding tribulation, Jesus gives us a few insights into what made this congregation such a target. First, there was the slander they faced from the always envious religious who's who...who weren't really who they pretended to be! Second, this was a direct result of being on the real "slanderer's" (literal meaning of "devil") hit list for a specific period of time. Finally, the Lord was personally demanding their faithfulness in this test be carried out until "death" if necessary!

The church in Smyrna is often overlooked, maybe because it was such a hard case to understand. Christianity can be ironic in that it doesn't seem right to us that good people should be allowed to suffer. At the end of the day, however, Jesus often trusts the most dependable with the most important jobs!

SEPTEMBER 22...DAY 265
THE NATURE OF COMPROMISE
Pergamum...Compromising Church

"I was in the Spirit on the Lord's Day and I heard behind me a loud voice, as of a trumpet, saying, 'I am Alpha and the Omega, the First and the Last,' and, 'What you see, write in a book and send it to the seven churches which are in Asia: to Ephesus, to Smyrna, to Pergamum, to Thyatira, to Sardis, to Philadelphia, and to Laodicea'...'He who has an ear, let him hear what the Spirit says to the churches'"
Revelation 1:9-11; 3:22 NKJV

Jesus called out the church in Pergamum for its compromising tendencies. This should cause believers who live closer to the end times to sit up and take notice!

What is so lethal about compromise is the implication of its definition; "to settle by mutual concession." True mutual concession involves the mixture of opposing points of view, which is good as long as it doesn't require one party to depart from what is true and right. When this happens, the nature of the compromise gives way to its secondary definition; "to bring into disrepute or danger through indiscretion or folly".

As with every group of people gathering around a single purpose, the church in Pergamum obviously made many good working compromises. Jesus praised them for keeping the faith in the midst of the worst circumstances of all these churches. They lived in a city the Lord Himself notes as being the center of satanic activity in the region and as a result they had the first martyr for Christ!

Unfortunately, however, Jesus also had a "few" things against them, which were serious enough to warrant His own direct attack on members of the church if the leadership did not deal with them! Their compromises had gone too far, allowing wrong doctrine or erroneous teachings to become a cause of stumbling to the congregation. Normally, any serious believer would know that idolatry, immorality, and class distinctions are not compatible with the teachings of Jesus or His disciples.

When the devil introduces sin little by little, through the process of compromise, naiveté can become all out indiscretion in any church. We have more than enough similar cases in our day to understand how easily this can happen! The only way to avoid this mistake is to "hold fast to Jesus' name" refusing to "deny His faith" (Revelation 2:13).

Although Satan has been defeated spiritually, he remains a formidable foe. As a genius tactician our wiles are no match for his, if we give him place. The secret is that Jesus, his conqueror, is the One we must fear displeasing!

SEPTEMBER 23...DAY 266
HOW FAR DOWN CAN A CHURCH GO?
Thyatira...Corrupt Church

"I was in the Spirit on the Lord's Day and I heard behind me a loud voice, as of a trumpet, saying, 'I am Alpha and the Omega, the First and the Last,' and, 'What you see, write in a book and send it to the seven churches which are in Asia: to Ephesus, to Smyrna, to Pergamum, to Thyatira, to Sardis, to Philadelphia, and to Laodicea...He who has an ear, let him hear what the Spirit says to the churches'"
Revelation 1:9-11; 3:22 NKJV

Again, we are looking at the distinguishing features of the seven handpicked churches Jesus chose to address this final word concerning the end times. As we come to the middle three you will notice a surprising downward spiral which seems to serve as a warning to us of how a little sin inside our churches can get a lot worse before it gets better!

Remember these messages were specific to each congregation in those cities at that time, but they serve as one big warning for the church at large until Jesus returns. Yesterday, we keyed on the compromise found in Pergamum. Church politics often serve as a substitute for seeking God's will and a breeding ground for the two faces of scriptural sin, rebellion (not doing what God wants) and presumption (doing what God does not want). From that platform a church can soon find itself mired in shocking levels of corruption. Then, before anyone realizes it, that body stalls spiritually lifeless. This is exactly the condition of the next two churches!

Thyatira was the next city on our postal route, and it would have been the first stop headed back south after traveling north from Ephesus, through Smyrna to Pergamum. If you look at a Bible map of the region you will see it is almost as if the Lord painted us a pictographic simile. Once the point of compromise is reached it can be a slippery downward slope!

This next church is known as the "Corrupt Church" by many because it compromised its compromise! If the church in Pergamum was affected by living so close to a satanic atmosphere, Thyatira was responsible for letting one of his servants usurp control of the church! Jesus called the suspicious woman in question, Jezebel as a way of communicating the level of wicked spiritual manipulation she exercised within this congregation. This entity took the entire church into "the depths of Satan" (Revelation 2:24) and Jesus came with fire in His eyes to deal with the situation! Think about it today, Satanism inside a local church?! Tomorrow we take it a step further...

SEPTEMBER 24...DAY 267
FOLLOW THE RIGHT SIGNS
Sardis...Dead Church

"I was in the Spirit on the Lord's Day and I heard behind me a loud voice, as of a trumpet, saying, 'I am Alpha and the Omega, the First and the Last,' and, 'What you see, write in a book and send it to the seven churches which are in Asia: to Ephesus, to Smyrna, to Pergamum, to Thyatira, to Sardis, to Philadelphia, and to Laodicea...He who has an ear, let him hear what the Spirit says to the churches'"
Revelation 1:9-11; 3:22 NKJV

In my opinion the scariest condition among the seven churches in the book of Revelation was found in the city of Sardis. Remember the negative progression of the overall message I pointed out to you yesterday, which started in Pergamum (where

Jesus said the "seat of Satan" was located in this region), and got worse in Thyatira (where Jesus said they knew the "depths of Satan").

Pergamum crossed the threshold into doctrinal error then Thyatira descended to further level by embracing an erroneous leader. This is important when examining the distinctive climate found in Sardis. Whenever we believe wrong teaching or the teacher himself, we are still primarily dealing with an issue of ignorance that can be resolved if the eyes of our heart continue to remain fixed on Jesus. He will enlighten the mind of one whose ear is inclined toward Him, giving grace to those who choose to hear the Truth above all else.

However, when we begin to closely follow a person teaching error, we subject ourselves to the influence of the spirit behind their words and actions. The Thyatirans had given authority in their church to one who masqueraded as a prophet but through the use of insight that came from evil spirits, rather than the Holy Spirit. Jesus reminded them that He is the One "who searches the minds and hearts," knowing the real condition of not only the church, but each individual. He then promised the power to rule the nations to those who were guiltless, if they dealt with the guilty properly!

It is crucial to confront sin in our churches. If we do not, our enemy will see to it that the wrong people rule over us even in the church that Jesus has built!

Sardis stands as a signpost on the road leading to a Christian ministry "Dead End". Because of their compromise and corruption they had no doubt failed to overcome, they were left only "alive" in name. For them, "Wrong Way" was written for the entire church age to read where it should have said, "One Way!"

SEPTEMBER 25...DAY 268
THE KEYS TO CHURCH SUCCESS
Philadelphia...Faithful Church

*"I was in the Spirit on the Lord's Day and I heard behind me a loud voice, as of a trumpet, saying, 'I am Alpha and the Omega, the First and the Last,' and, 'What you see, write in a book and send it to the seven churches which are in Asia: to Ephesus, to Smyrna, to Pergamum, to Thyatira, to Sardis, to Philadelphia, and to Laodicea...He who has an ear, let him hear what the Spirit says to the churches'"
Revelation 1:9-11; 3:22 NKJV*

Both the second, and the second to last churches mentioned on Jesus' list were the ones without fault. They almost serve as rest stops along the way for the reader as John delivers the Lord's stern warning to the end time Church at large. As we read through them, Philadelphia, like Smyrna stands out as a place that had the same trials and troubles as all the other churches, yet without yielding to the same temptations. So, what was it about them that caused the Lord to express such a favorable opinion of these congregations?

We've already seen how the church in Smyrna modeled a willingness to endure persecution to the end. This selfless loyalty is the first thing to note about a church that pleases the Lord. In Philadelphia we find further qualities that specifically cause Jesus to use the "keys" of authority He had earned to help them overcome. He promised to set an "open door" before them and to "keep (them) from the hour of trial which shall come upon the whole world, to test those who dwell on the earth." Twice it is stated that the Philadelphians had "kept" the things Jesus had said to them. Once He says they have kept "His word, and have not denied His name." Then He reiterates that they have kept His "command to persevere."

We miss a major truth about Christianity when we fail to remember how so much of the New Testament is written to groups of believers. As congregations, these believers were holding on to God's Word and obeying His commands together. Primarily that is what Jesus is praising them for.

Of course, no group of individuals can do anything together they are not willing to practice separately, but we seem to be easily tempted to presume that our personal obedience will somehow automatically translate into corporate faithfulness. Maybe the most important thing written to this church was their need to keep holding fast to these things Jesus praised them for because He was coming quickly (Revelation 3:11)!

Make sure your church resembles Philadelphia and Smyrna, and not the others. These are the keys to being ready...Surely He is coming sooner now than He was then!

SEPTEMBER 26...DAY 269
HALF-HEARTED CHURCH, WHOLE-HEARTED PROMISE
Laodicea...Lukewarm Church

"I was in the Spirit on the Lord's Day and I heard behind me a loud voice, as of a trumpet, saying, 'I am Alpha and the Omega, the First and the Last,' and, 'What you see, write in a book and send it to the seven churches which are in Asia: to Ephesus, to Smyrna, to Pergamum, to Thyatira, to Sardis, to Philadelphia, and to Laodicea...He who has an ear, let him hear what the Spirit says to the churches'"
Revelation 1:9-11; 3:22 NKJV

There is one final city of believers to examine on Jesus' complete list of end time church conditions. This one has become the most famous. It is at the end of the list and its distinguishing features are so common to our modern experience. Because some Bible commentators hold that these churches represent seven successive eras of church history (Dispensational Interpretation), Laodicea stands out as exhibiting the likely conditions the world can look for in the Church just prior to Jesus' return. This is the church nobody wants to be in, especially at the end times, but everybody has probably attended at one time or another!

The Laodicean church was criticized by the Lord for being tepid or indifferent. Their attitude toward spiritual things was half-hearted and neutral when it should have been passionate and enthusiastic. Revelation 3:19 is one verse that says it all; "As many as I love, I rebuke and chasten. Therefore, be zealous and repent." This tells us that God was angry enough to confront and discipline them openly for their sin even when most onlookers would have probably considered them "blessed," being a wealthy church in a prosperous city! More importantly, God loved them and His chastening was based on His belief that they could be ignited once again!

We recognize them in the civilized world of our day. We easily slip into the comfort of our surroundings until our inner temperature is affected by the conditions of the environment around us. We aren't refreshingly cool or soothingly warm, just blasé!

The distinguishing Laodicean feature was that they were indistinguishable!! We too have believed our own opinions of ourselves, at the expense of the Holy Spirit's wisdom and revelation.

This is an hour to purchase directly from God the insight, equipment and outlook we need to stay where we need to be in these last days. As we do, we will sit with Christ in heavenly places (Ephesians 2:6) now, and reign with Him on His throne forever (Revelation 3:21)! Let the Laodicean church be a reminder to you that the best promises are reserved for those who overcome the most!

SEPTEMBER 27...DAY 270
JESUS KNOWS RIGHT WHERE YOU'RE AT

"I know you works, your labor, your patience, and that you cannot bear those who are evil. And you have tested those who say they are apostles and are not, and have found them liars; and you have persevered and have patience, and have labored for My name's sake and have not become weary."
Revelation 2:2 NKJV

"Be watchful, and strengthen the things which remain, that are ready to die, for I have not found your works perfect before God."
Revelation 3:2 NKJV

One unmistakable thing all seven of Revelation's churches have in common is this phrase, "I know your works." Since this portion of scripture contains such an important end time message for the entire Church age, its most repeated statement stands out to me as being extremely important!

A person's "works" are the result of what they first think and then act out in belief. They are the outward manifestations of our inward condition, the end of a series of events which have led us to the point of putting our choices into practice.

Bible teacher Nancy Missler describes this process as the "chain reaction" of our souls in her book, "Be Ye Transformed." She writes "our thoughts stir up our emotions; our emotions then influence our desires; and our desires produce our actions."

I would add that our works, being our repeated actions over time, define who we really are. Jesus wasn't judging these congregations of believers based on any single series of events but rather by their cumulative corporate habitual activity. We know from reading chapter two, verse 21, how merciful the Lord is. He told the church in Thyatira that He had given the sexually immoral, false prophetess in their leadership, "TIME TO REPENT," but she had not. He then was about to execute certain justice. Jesus then goes on to say, "…and ALL THE CHURCHES shall know that I am He who searches the minds and hearts. And I will give to each of you according to your works."

It is very possible that the closer we get to the Lord's return, the more focused the Lord's inspection is going to become in our lives and churches. It certainly seems to have been that way in the beginning stages of the church age when they were closer to His first coming (see Acts 5:1-11)! We should be as concerned about what we are doing as these churches when they read the messages Jesus sent to them. Accountability is not something to fear but rather something that allows you to face reality. Come to terms with the fact that Jesus knows exactly where you're at today...so you'll be working and ready to meet him on His terms when He comes on that day!

SEPTEMBER 28...DAY 271
THIS IS HOW WE OVERCOME

"And he who overcomes, and keeps My works until the end,
to him I will give power over the nations..." Revelation 2:10 NKJV

"Stand fast therefore in the liberty by which Christ has made us free, and do not be entangled again with a yoke of bondage...For in Christ Jesus neither circumcision nor uncircumcision avails anything, but faith working through love."
Galatians 5:1, 6 NKJV

You need to know about another common phrase Jesus used in addressing all seven of the churches in the Bible's final book if you are serious about being ready for the last days. In reading the first three chapters of "The Revelation," you will notice that a personal closing promise is made to each church, in which the words, "He who overcomes" or a similar variation is found (See 2:7, 11, 17, 26; 3:5, 12, 21).

The original language of the New Testament basically defines "over comers" as those Christians who are able to subdue the impulse to turn back under all circumstances and thereby gain the victory over any adversity. In this context, these are conquering believers because they have remained "faithful" to the Lord and specifically to His directives for their church.

Let's compare the wording Jesus used in his closing statements to Thyatira and those in Smyrna. Combined they make my point for today. To the former He says, "...Be faithful until death" (Revelation 2:10), followed by a promise to give them the crown of life. To the latter, Jesus promises power to rule the nations for those, "who overcome, and keep My works until the end" (Revelation 2:26).

In the last days it is very important for us to understand the need to remain completely "faithful." This means being so true to what we believe that we actively obey the One in Whom is our faith! Overcoming everything the devil puts in our path to keep us from accomplishing God's will in our lives demands that we work out our faith until the very end. Instead of merely confessing the virtues of Christianity, believers must show the world what it is. What is the key? Jesus said the world would recognize who we are (His disciples and ambassadors) by our love.

Doing what the Word of God teaches is easier said than done...but when we pursue the process with God's love as our compass we will navigate our way through this life, faithfully overcoming all odds and showing others Jesus all the way!

SEPTEMBER 29...DAY 272
LIGHTS, CAMERA, ACTION!

"...and I know the blasphemy of those who say they are Jews and are not, but are a synagogue of Satan."
Revelation 2:9 NKJV

"My little children, let us not love in word or in tongue, but in deed and in truth. And by this we know that we are of the truth, and shall assure our hearts before Him."
1 John 3:18-19 NKJV

"What does it profit, my brethren, if someone says he has faith but does not have works? Can faith save him?...But do you want to know, O foolish man, that faith without works is dead? Was not Abraham our father justified by works when offered Isaac his son on the altar? Do you see that faith was working together with his works, and by works faith was made perfect?"
James 2:14, 17-22 NKJV

Jesus' words to the seven churches in the book of Revelation teaches us that deception can happen just as effortlessly in churches where things are harsh as they can where things are undemanding. Therefore, regardless of what city we live in or the condition of our local church, it is important to guard against false religious extremes. The devil specializes in setting them up anywhere he is allowed as roadblocks to prevent true believers from walking in their God-given victory and inheriting their God-given promises.

One very subtle traditional error is this tendency, addressed in our texts, of thinking we can earn our way into God's favor either by just believing or by just doing. Truth demands that our words and deeds must match. God's word takes it to another level...His Word and our actions must align in order to walk in THE Truth! This is one of the simplest yet profound realities in all of scripture and one we cannot afford to overlook if we are interested in our churches making it through the events described in the Bible that are scheduled to take place between now and Jesus' return.

So, two spiritual qualities, "faith" and "works," have to cooperate in your life if you want to stay out of the dark. In fact, they each depend on the other in order to be an authentic representation of their own individual definitions. In other words, faith works or it is not really faith, and works have to be done by faith or they aren't worth doing! Anything less is a recipe for eventual deception.

Now you know why Jesus was so straightforward with the churches of Revelation, saying what He said loving them above and beyond mere regard for their feelings. The kind of faith they had begun to model was leading them into direct conflict with God rather than into His blessing! If they listened, believed and acted they could change their outcome. We know some of them did not...It is our opportunity now, will we?!

SEPTEMBER 30...DAY 273
EMBRACE THE WORD UNTIL IT HURTS

"...These things says the First and the Last, Who was dead, and came to life..."
Revelation 2:8 NKJV

"Therefore lay aside all filthiness and overflow of wickedness, and receive with meekness the implanted word, which is able to save your souls. But be doers of the word, and not hearers only, deceiving yourselves. For if anyone is a hearer of the word and not a doer, he is like a man observing his natural face in a mirror; for he observes himself, goes away, and immediately forgets what kind of man he was. But he who looks into the perfect law of liberty and continues in it, and is not a forgetful hearer but a doer of the work, this one will be blessed in what he does."
James 1:21-25 NKJV

Jesus presented Himself differently to each of the churches we have been researching in the book of Revelation. In doing so you can see He reminds them of His personal approach to their situation and His ultimate authority over their affairs. These two things enable us to understand how far the Lord will go to create an intervening scenario to save us from deception.

Jesus confronts us with His word in order to push us back to a place of embracing the Word that God has planted within our nature at salvation. It contains the power to save our "souls," which is the transformation process whereby we are continuously changed into His likeness step by step over the course of our lives.

It is the same for our churches. Our corporate mentality has to be renewed, especially when we are weighed in His balances and found wanting! These particular congregations were in danger of losing their privilege of having a local church. The Lord presented Himself to the Ephesians as the One who held their leadership in His hand, while actively walking around in their midst examining their condition! The word these people were given was sharp and cutting just as Hebrews 4:12 describes it, yet it was the Word of God nevertheless, able to save them from destruction.

Do we really see that holding God's Word without walking and working it out can turn our blessing into a curse and create complete deception?! Never forget that self-betrayal leads to self-deception...the more we know what to do but refuse to act, the further expelled from the truth we find ourselves. This is a time to be sifted and analyzed thoroughly by the Lord...before it's too late to change our ways!

OCTOBER 1...DAY 274
ACT OUT YOUR PRAYER

In the earliest days of the church everything was effectuated as a result of prayer. Today, however, we have discontinued following the original manual on world impact, actually reversing the order of operation prescribed there for believers! It is embarrassingly simple to understand why the modern Church is so often accused of being lifeless and powerless. Back then, Christians prayed first and then acted afterward on the received divine guidance that becomes available through prayer. They knew the wisdom of keeping things simple, and streamlined in their pursuit of God. This is why throughout the book of "Acts" you see many of the "gifts" of Holy Spirit being manifested "following" times of intense prayer. Miracles are simply further expressions of the same Spirit you have connected with while "moving toward" God.

During prayer this morning at my local church, I began to think through specific places in this New Testament history book of early Christian exploits. In Acts 1:13 those 120 faithful first disciples prayed in one accord. Their results are seen in Acts chapter two! Believers were spectacularly filled with the Holy Spirit and empowered to reach the first three thousand converts.

It is interesting to me that Peter did not invite them to pray, but simply told everyone to repent and be baptized into Christ. Afterward, as they gathered with each other around the apostles, they were taught the Word of God and learned how to pray (Acts 2:42). The results of that are found in verse 43, where it is recorded that, "a sense of awe came upon every soul, and many wonders and signs were performed through the apostles' hands."

In the third chapter of Acts, Peter and John are seen going to the Temple, at the "hour of PRAYER!" Consequently, a man born lame was publicly healed, Peter and John were arrested and imprisoned for ministering in the name of Jesus and, thousands more people were saved! When the two apostles reported how God had miraculously set them free in spite of the Jewish religious leadership's opposition, a powerful prayer meeting broke out that produced even more fruit!

Great power came upon the apostles as they witnessed to others, and great grace came upon the entire church until there was nothing lacking among them (Acts 4:23-35). Of course there were negative repercussions. Two believers died for lying to the Holy Spirit in the midst of manifestations of God's glory! But that only led to more signs and wonders...to the point that the crowds brought sick people into the streets so Peter's "shadow" (the tangible glory of God around his life) could touch them, and they were healed! Oh, and by the way, the apostles were imprisoned again...BUT God sent an angel to supernaturally release them! (Acts 5:1-42) The recorded history goes on and on.

The early church acted out their prayers. They let God shake them first then they shook the world around them!

OCTOBER 2...DAY 275
WARNING: PRAYER IS DANGEROUS!

Because I've recently been praying more, the subject of prayer has been on my heart. So, let's continue looking at how the earliest Christian structure used prayer to move so simply yet so powerfully into the world of its day.

When we come to Acts Chapter Six, we find the apostles abutting their first major, and potentially divisive, problem. You will notice in verse one that the problem itself was caused by the abundance of answers to their prayer! Because the "disciples were greatly increasing" it created an inflated opportunity for strife between the people groups who benefited from the increase! Churches can often get stuck in these kinds of issues, and begin putting too much emphasis on the problem. They forget to consult with He Who answered their original prayer.

I like how the apostles simply refused to trade prayer for planning! Instead, they increased the influence of prayer by continuing to give themselves to it and by having the most prayerful men under their oversight appointed to handle the problems! The result of this brilliant decision was that even more disciples were multiplied into the church as the Gospel kept spreading unhindered.

Stephen was actually released in this process into a higher level of his own anointing! He became so "full of grace and power" that he "worked great wonders and signs" even among the people he was assigned to manage tables for!! Those who tried to stop him were "unable to resist the wisdom and spirit by which he spoke," to the point that his face began to shine before them all as had Jesus' when he was "transfigured" (Matthew 17:2).

There should really be a warning placed at the beginning of the book of "Acts" that says, "Do not hang around the apostles of Jesus or try what they do in your own home or town...unless you want similar results!" Guys like Stephen are the reason. By investing himself as a part of the building spiritual momentum that all their prayer had produced, he not only became the next great preacher in Acts seven but he became a martyred one in verse 60! His life was a heavenly flare for all to follow, having full knowledge of both the benefits and costs of getting closer to God!

Finally, notice this godly man's last act...he kneeled down and prayed loudly for those who killed him! That is the pinnacle and extent to which we must take prayer!

OCTOBER 3...DAY 276
PUTTING THE PRAYER BACK IN CHURCH PLANNING

Many things the early did church initially were done completely differently the next time God led them. Reading the book of "Acts" clearly confirms this.

Today we take all the fun out of the Christian experience by not staying spontaneous. "Pre-planning" is good but "prayer-planning" is better! New Testament leadership was designed to work best when it follows first and plans second, which is why prayer is so momentous. It keeps us "upside down" enough in our heads to stay "right-side up" in our hearts!

Pastors wish to eliminate the unknown and their congregations would like to stay too comfortable to pray seriously in the modern church world. Yet, if we want to break free of these barriers, we must boldly return prayer to its rightful position in the church.

By the time you get to Acts Chapter Eight you find that the earliest church isn't tempted to "think through" its next strategy even under severe duress. It is obvious that prayer creates a spiritual momentum that, while liberating on the positive side, can also be very dangerous! Since Stephen had just been killed for his faith and resultant miracles in the chapter before, and because it had created a huge wave of persecution for the church, we could understand if the apostles had backed off a bit...but they did not!

Even though Saul was raised up by Satan to lead the assault to eliminate all those who prayed in the name of Jesus from Jerusalem, Stephen's death only caused followers like Philip to take the Lord's message everywhere else they went! It is as if Stephen's last prayer passed a torch to this next guy on the "strife management team" (Acts 6:3-5), and the next thing you know Philip is doing the same miraculous things in Samaria! And the results continued...the city received an immersion in "great joy" (verse 8) and the local sorcerer (Simon) was "ferreted out" into the open!

In verse fifteen, the apostles back at Jerusalem send the Peter and John prayer team (Acts 3:1) down to Samaria where they pray for all the newly saved people to receive the Holy Ghost (Acts 2:4). When Simon (the sorcerer) finds out he can't buy the gift, he asks for prayer himself! Philip gets direction from an angel about witnessing to an Ethiopian official in Gaza, then gets "translated" bodily to Azotus! He finally ends up in

Caesarea, where a man named Cornelius lives who prays a lot… interesting…more on that tomorrow.

OCTOBER 4…DAY 277
KEEPING YOUR CLIMATE "PRAYER-CONTROLLED"

I've been meditating on prayer in the New Testament book of Acts. I believe considered contemplation of these examples will lead us to greater success (Joshua 1:8) in our prayer lives, and might even help to re-institute a spirit of prayer within the Church at large today!

In this book of the Bible Jesus' apostles kept everyone praying and, as a result, the Gospel kept advancing! The two things are vitally connected for believers and churches anytime, anywhere. Acts 9 is sandwiched between Philip's evangelistic campaign in Samaria in chapter 8 and the account of Peter and Cornelius in chapter 10. Saul's conversion from "religious terrorist" to "prayer partner" by divine visitation is recorded right in the middle! After praying in verse 11, Paul was healed, filled with the Spirit, brought into fellowship with the disciples and is found preaching Christ by verse 20!

The Church was truly birthed in a spontaneously fast-morphing, supernatural environment! How did it maintain what Christians today so desperately long for? Simply through a controlled climate of prayer! Remember how Philip was led miraculously to Caesarea when last seen in Acts 8:40? The importance of that little footnote becomes clear when you pick up Peter's story in Acts 10.

After healing a paralyzed man in Lydda, and raising a woman named Tabitha from the dead in Joppa, both through prayer in Acts 9, he ends up on the coast of Judea, just south of Caesarea as well! Notice how praying in the Spirit puts these men in touch with the will of God, Who is constantly causing all things to work together for the good of those who love Him and are called according to His purpose (Romans 8:26-28)!

Even though the Jewish-based Church at this time doesn't realize it, God is about to release the Gospel into the Gentile world. The key to His plan is a devout man named Cornelius living in this particular city that has recently been subtly targeted by the Holy Spirit! Acts 10:2 defines his devotion with three statements. Cornelius: 1) Feared God; 2) Gave much to the poor and; 3) PRAYED to God always! It should be no surprise that he had a vision in which an angel entered his home, telling him that God has remembered him because his PRAYERS and gifts have risen up as a "sacrifice" before Him. Truly God will move heaven and earth to get to one man who is praying and paying a price to find Him.

Everything the Jews had received in Christ, the rest of the world was given as a result of the prayers of the Church in that season, the prayers of Cornelius that day and the prayers of Peter the next day! This should teach us to expect the impossible...and pray accordingly!

OCTOBER 5...DAY 278
PRAYER-SECUTION

In Acts 10 Cornelius prayed in one city, Peter prayed in another and, through a series of divinely arranged circumstances, when they met in a house in Caesarea the first family of non-Jewish believers started speaking in tongues! Prayer changed Christian doctrine before anyone was even called "Christian" and before anyone knew believers didn't have to be Hebrew! The Gospel kept expanding through persecution beginning with Stephen's martyrdom in Acts 7. But the supernatural results were caused by the "prayer-secution" of the Church upon the leadership of dark forces in the spirit realm! One kept them moving forward in the lord while the other kept them trusting in Him!

The word "persecution" as used in Acts 11:19 means, "a pressing" or "pressure." It describes the tribulation, suffering and distress believers often experience as a result of living and ministering for God (2 Timothy 3:12, Mark 10:30, Hebrews 11:25). "Persecution" is the pressure Satan applies to believers for obeying God and interfering with the destiny of those souls under his influence in this world system. It is also the word Jesus used in Acts 9:4-5 when interrogating Saul after knocking him to the ground in his famous "Damascus road" experience. That caught my attention and it should catch yours!

If a person in Satan's service can persecute Jesus directly by harassing and killing those in His "Body" or Church, then believers can persecute Satan by meditating on God's Word, praying in the Spirit, standing in faith, not relying on the flesh and preaching the Gospel boldly. Prayer inflicts a kind of pressure Paul later mentioned in 2 Corinthians 10:3-5, which assists us in waging a spiritual warfare that "pulls down strongholds," "casts down high (minded) things," and brings "mindsets into a captive obedience to Christ!" He went so far as to reveal in 2 Corinthians 12:10 how, in prayer, he had learned to lean entirely on God's grace and come to use all persecutions to his own advantage. Even though they can weaken us physically at times, they provide an avenue to increased spiritual strength by causing us to rely more on the Lord!

This "prayer surge" the early Church experienced created two key scenarios in Acts chapter 11 that we need to remember today. First, it caused the more religious minded Jewish believers to take their own limits and restrictions off of God. Second, it freed the Gospel to go into places they might not have imagined even if they had been more open! The church at Antioch (Syria) was birthed by mere unknown men of God who were scattered by the persecution further than anyone else...it later became the new Apostolic sending center for the next wave of Gospel soldiers and their subsequent "prayer-secution" that would turn the whole world upside down (Acts 13:1-5)!

OCTOBER 6...DAY 279
ENTER THE ARENA OF PRAYER

How does a church in Syria effectuate the death in Jerusalem of an original Apostle? Because of the weight prayer carries in the spirit realm. It is not hard to begin to understand the seriousness of spiritual warfare when you look closely at Acts chapters 11 and 12. A strategic church is established in a far away country because of the work of those men who walked with Jesus in Judea. This church will send out Paul as a new kind of apostle, who will write the majority of the New Testament during his travels and reach millions of people not only throughout the Roman world but down through the rest of world history!!

If you were the devil what would you do? Maybe seek to take out one of the Church generals of that day. It must have been shocking when James, the first of Jesus' disciples to be killed, was cut down with a sword by the orders of evil king Herod. As difficult as it sometimes is for us to accept, such is the cost of a warfare that goes on beyond humanity's perception. Herod finds out firsthand just how dangerous it is to touch God's anointed even before the chapter is over!

We are truly involved in something far more impacting than traditional religion or exciting motivational preachers. What will cost you the most is the only real protection you have! Prayer will stir up spiritual adversity. If you don't think so then try it, especially as a group project for an extended period of time and get back to me. You will witness amazing things, both light and dark, but once you enter the arena of prayer you must be prepared to remain committed to the Lord. The church in Acts did not relent, because they were on a God-driven mission, not conducting individual ministries!

Peter's story is told in between the deaths of James and Herod. He was imprisoned during this Christian leadership purge, but something blocked Herod's hand and no doubt ensured his demise. Acts 12:5 says, "...but fervent prayer for him was persistently made to God by the church."

You have to love the fact that the church was praying so passionately for their chief leader that, after an angel miraculously released him from prison and Peter found his way to the prayer meeting, the girl who answered the door freaked out and all those praying didn't believe he was really outside! After the same angel (it seems) killed Herod, the results were familiar. "But the word of God grew and multiplied!"

That is exactly what we desire and seek today, but are we willing to enter the arena of prayer? I say we pray first, and ask questions later!

OCTOBER 7...DAY 280
PRAYER SHIFTS

Prayer is the original "internet" for Christian connectivity. Long before modern technology God designed a way for us to "log in" to His network and search for the information we need to improve our lives, help others, exchange ideas and change the world! With the explosion of natural technology there has never been a more opportune time for believers to put the supernatural technology of prayer to work for them both at home and abroad. Churches today need to be local expressions of a global faith and global expressions of local faith at the same time!

Most believers desire a "community" church; the worldwide church is becoming one unified community right now in preparation for the end times. This requires a shift in thinking that is hard for many churches to accept because of the depth of tradition that exists in our concepts of organized Christianity. Surprisingly, this mentality is nothing new...it started all the way back in Acts chapter 13! The time was approximately A.D. 46, only a few years after some unnamed believers had traveled to Antioch as a result of the persecution that arose after the death of Stephen (Acts 11:19-30), and established a work there by the hand of God that eventually became a church. Acts 13:1-4 records how prayer created a shift in the way "Church" was done, even while still in the earliest days of its existence! Whereas the original "main" church in Jerusalem with all its famous leadership had concentrated on reaching the Judean culture, this church full of nobody's seemed more willing to target everybody! Since prophets were the leading officials noted in this church, and they were limited as to the influence of the bigger named guys, there would have been a premium put on prayer. This was a choice environment for the "perfect storm" God had churning in the spirit realm for the rest of the Roman Empire!

Notice how God can get us to do the craziest things in prayer. The Holy Spirit got them to separate their two best leaders for an assignment that probably seemed too big for their breeches. A new wave of apostles would be sent into the next front of world evangelism. God took the most loving guy and the scariest one with the biggest mouth! What a perfect combination?! By the time you finish reading Acts, you go from the pagan world to an outpost in Syria...in one generation! What was the primary secret of their success? The kind of abandoned, surrendered PRAYER that can shift the thinking of any church willing to try it!

OCTOBER 8...DAY 281
PRAYER TELLS THE WHOLE THE STORY

The prayer of the Antioch church leaders in Acts 13 led to a major shift in the mission and strategy of "the Church." It is interesting to me that, although the Jerusalem-based Apostles also began to reach out with the Gospel beyond their previous boundaries, the main story of the book of Acts past this point revolves around Paul's ministry. The remainder of the snapshots of prayer and power are found within the context of the places he and his various companions traveled, up until just before his death.

Paul was obviously the Lord's replacement for Judas, having been supernaturally given the completed Gospel message for the Gentiles and then sent to them. The whole story is a result of prayer! First, the years (at least fourteen, Galatians 1:15-2:2) of prayer and study he spent with the Lord unlocked a "mystery" that the Hebrew nation had never fully understood. The salvation of the Gentiles was revealed to this former Jewish religious zealot, written through his letters to the churches he pioneered and later compiled in a New Testament for us to grasp! Next, when you look at the rest of "Acts" you can't help but think how important the prayers of Stephen were at his death. He prayed that those responsible would be forgiven and God answered by confronting Saul (Hebrew name of Paul, which is a Greek variation in pronunciation) and opening these things to him.

Then, remember how Jesus had prayed in John 17. In His famous last prayer for His disciples, He asked that besides themselves God would keep and separate to Himself all others who would believe through their word (verse 15-21). This, along with Jesus' words in John 10:16 imply that there were other "sheep" in other "flocks" in many other places...including the Gentile world.

Finally, as Paul goes about the Mediterranean world of his time working for the Lord, his own prayers, beginning with his experience on the road to Damascus factor into the emphasis on God spreading of the Gospel to the 'western' world first. He prayed and ordained the first elders in those first churches he and Barnabas established in Asia Minor (Acts 14:23). He prayed with the council in Jerusalem to decide how to deal with Gentile/Jewish relations in Acts 15 when they received a leading from the Holy Spirit that would set the stage for people to freely come to Jesus all over the world!

Paul and Silas prayed and sang to the Lord in the famous Philippian jail in Acts 16:25. The jail was shaken, their shackles were unfastened and the jailer's entire house was miraculously saved! It goes on and on chapter after chapter, although it is more implied as you go further into the history book of the early church. Everywhere Paul went, prayer was offered and Gods' power was available to more and more people...and we are the rest of his story!

OCTOBER 9...DAY 282
YOU CAN'T OUTGUESS GOD

"Indeed, I myself thought I must do many things contrary to the name of Jesus of Nazareth. This I also did in Jerusalem, and many of the saints I shut up in prison, having received authority from the chief priests; and when they were put to death, I cast my vote against them. And I punished them often in every synagogue and compelled them to blaspheme; and being exceedingly enraged against them, I persecuted them even to foreign cities. While thus occupied, as I journeyed to Damascus with authority and commission from the chief priests,...along the road I saw a light from heaven, brighter than the sun, shining around me and those who journeyed with me. And when we all had fallen to the ground, I heard a voice speaking to me and saying in the Hebrew language, 'Saul, Saul, why are you persecuting Me? It is hard for you to kick against the goads.' So I said, 'Who are You, Lord?' And He said, 'I am Jesus, whom you are persecuting...'"
Acts 26:9-15 NKJV

Don't ever think God can't save and use someone you think of as a lost cause. I am convinced that is partially why the Apostle Paul was used so prominently in the establishing of the early church. He was such a complete "rule breaker" that he even changed his own name to emphasize the life-changing power he encountered in the name of Jesus! Here we see how the Lord took someone who was authorized by the religious establishment of his day and, after breaking him down, authorized him to build the very thing he had sought to destroy!

Interestingly enough, this very passage of scripture is the transcript of Paul's rehearsing his own testimony before King Agrippa (Roman ruler of the land of Palestine). Talk about a statement on the power of authority! Jesus brought this man before the highest authorities of his day, just as He promised He would. Again, this is a picture of Paul in action, taking hold of his promise, as opposed to just settling comfortably in waiting for God's provision.

When you read Acts 9:15 you find out that the Lord promised to use him specifically as a "chosen vessel" to "bear My name before the Gentiles, kings, and the children of Israel."

Paul's passionate personality, once for persecution of the church, was not about to accept anything short of fully finishing Jesus' instructions to now build it around the world.

When we are fully exposed to the Light of God, we will want to bear His name and the authority it carries ourselves. Anything less will not finish the task that we are assigned in these last days…it is unworthy of Who He is!

OCTOBER 10…DAY 283
THE LONGEST DAY

"Then Joshua spoke to the Lord in the day when the Lord delivered up the Amorites before the children of Israel, and he said in the sight of Israel: 'Sun, stand still over Gibeon; and Moon, in the Valley of Aijalon.' So the sun stood still, and the moon stopped, till the people had revenge upon their enemies. Is this not written in the Book of Jasher? So the sun stood still in the midst of heaven, and did not hasten to go down for about a whole day. And there has been no day like that, before it or after it that the Lord heeded the voice of a man; for the Lord fought for Israel."
Joshua 10:12-14 NKJV

It is fitting that Joshua was the man who commanded the "sun" to stand still since he was a direct type of God's "Son." Not only do Joshua and Jesus share the same name in Hebrew (Y'howshua), but you will remember that Jesus commanded a storm to cease in similar fashion in Mark 4:37. The forerunner and the One foretold both used the power of light in overcoming ungodly dark forces. In commanding the day to be extended, Joshua used the power of light to thoroughly overcome the evil Amorites God had directed the Israelites to fight against.

Jesus, being the "Light of the world" (John 8:12), did exactly the same. He illuminated God's people and dispelled every dark force arrayed against mankind, while engaged in His mission of living out God's commands and destroying all the works of the devil (Acts 10:38)!

Joshua proved that a truly godly man has tremendous influence with God. The Lord "heeded" this man's voice on a level that crosses the highest physical boundaries of what is humanly possible! In doing so, he not only led the way for Israel to accomplish incredible things and possess the Promised Land, he prepared the way for a

Greater Man to be received as the Promise Himself! When Joshua spoke God empowered his words, when Jesus spoke He imparted the power of God's Word to other men!

Christians carry tremendous power with God and man as a result of the "name" of Jesus. Today, we are like Joshua...we extend the Light of God and cause mountains to move for the furtherance of His will. Joshua was a foreshadowing of Jesus, we are His afterglow. Jesus presides in the middle, forever causing the darkness to be pushed back at the word of those who are called according to the purposes of God.

OCTOBER 11...DAY 284
RIGHT PLACE, RIGHT TIME

"After the death of Moses the servant of the Lord, the Lord said to Joshua son of Nun, Moses' minister, 'Moses My servant is dead. So now arise [take his place], go over this Jordan, you and all this people, into the land which I am giving to them, the Israelites. Every place upon which the sole of your foot shall tread, that have I given to you, as I promised Moses."
Joshua 1:1-3 AMP

Joshua is a good Bible character to learn from regarding preparing to be used by the Lord. Being a direct type of Christ his example foreshadows the life of Jesus, teaching us how to be the kind of servant God molds into a leader.

The end times will demand action from us just as it required more from these people than the generation before them had been willing to give! As Joshua readied them to enter into God's chosen land in preparation for the Messiah's first coming, we have been sent into the whole world to prepare it for the second coming! This one man's leadership was a big reason why they succeeded where their parents had failed, so let's look closely at his life and discern how to equip ourselves to finish our collective course effectively.

Notice that Joshua was waiting for his time. Although his life reveals a personal promise he put the Promise of God, given through the man of God, above himself. Moses was the "servant of the Lord," Joshua was the servant of Moses! Imitating Moses' approach to God by attending to Moses is what put him in position to take his place as leader of Israel when God called!

Joshua embraced God's timing. Everybody in our day wants God to bless them. God isn't characteristically inclined to promote and use someone until proving that person's worth. Joshua had a right spirit (courage and faithfulness, Numbers 14), but he also had the right work ethic to qualify for spiritual leadership in God's eyes. The death of Moses signaled the end of the Lord's judgment on an unbelieving era, and the sudden coming of a new set of opportunities for the new Israel. Joshua was ready because he worked while he waited.

Notice how verse one defines Joshua as the son of "Nun." There is something special here to understand about the bigger picture. "Nun" means to "re-sprout." It is a word used to indicate "perpetuity." Joshua was not only in the right place at the right time…he was the right man for the long range! God had placed him there for the greater good of the people. His willing participation in that divine plan caused him to receive tremendous authority, just like Moses!

We are to take the same approach, serving Jesus without ego or complaint in obedience and faith, meditating on His Word day and night, leading others to Him as we await His return…because we are the Hand-chosen appointed and anointed sons of God!

OCTOBER 12…DAY 285
DIFFERENT LEADERS, SAME COMMISSION

"Every place upon which the sole of your foot shall tread, that have I given to you, as I promised Moses. From the wilderness and this Lebanon to the great river Euphrates-all the land of the Hittites [Canaan]-and to the Great [Mediterranean] Sea on the west shall be your territory. No man shall be able to stand before you all the days of your life. As I was with Moses, so I will be with you;
I will not fail you or forsake you."
Joshua 1:3-5 AMP

That last verse should sound very familiar. They are Jesus' last words to His disciples as He commissioned them in the New Testament. After telling them to take His authority and go into all nations making more disciples in Matthew 28:20, He says, "…and lo, I am with you always, even to the end of the age."

This verse in Joshua is God commissioning Moses' servant to take his place of leadership just before his leader's death, while Jesus in Matthew is commissioning His disciples to take His place just after His resurrection! There are many subtle ironies like this in scripture, all of which carry significance for the believer. Just as Joshua was selected to lead the Israelites into the Promised Land, we have been chosen to guide a great campaign to bring the "Promise" (Jesus, the Messiah and subsequently His gift of the Holy Spirit) of Israel to the rest of the world! Notice how similar these commissions really are.

First, Joshua was told that where he was about to go was already his. Whatever ground he placed his feet upon he would possess. Jesus promises us miraculous signs as we deliver His Word (Mark 16:15-20), as evidenced in the book of Acts through the experiences of the early church.

Second, Joshua is given boundaries on which to focus his vision delineating God's appointed territory for Israel. Jesus repeatedly defined the scope of our mission to the entire world! It is a big job, yet it is specific. We must reach every nationality before the end will come according to Jesus Himself in Matthew 24:14.

Third, no man would be able to stop Joshua as he led Israel into its conquest. Jesus tells us throughout the New Testament that nothing man can do to us will stop the work of the Gospel because Satan is already defeated. We possess the power in Jesus' name to resist him, bind him and cast out his evil associates wherever we encounter them.

Finally, Jesus said He would not leave us spiritually "orphaned" (John 14:18). God will no more abandon us in our end-time stand than He did Joshua at the death of Moses. As He was with Moses so He was with Joshua...and so He is with us! Tomorrow we will see that we have to have the courage to believe it.

OCTOBER 13...DAY 286
FACING GOD FIRST

"Be strong and of good courage, for to this people you shall divide as an inheritance the land which I swore to their fathers to give them. Only be very strong and very courageous, that you may observe to do according to all the law which Moses My servant commanded you; do not turn from it to the right hand or to the left, that you may prosper wherever you go...Have I not commanded you? Be strong and of good courage; do not be afraid, nor dismayed, for the Lord God is with you wherever you go." Joshua 1:5-7, 9 AMP

In Deuteronomy 31 Moses charged Joshua three times to "be strong and of good courage." Here in our text for today, we see God doing the same thing after the death of Moses. I have often preached on how God had to tell Joshua three times to be brave, but in fact it was six! That makes it more than a little important in our study of what qualified him to be Moses' successor as the leader of God's people.

Until that time there had never been a prophet like Moses. God "knew him face to face" (Deuteronomy 24:10), so imagine what it must have been like to try and fill his shoes?! It would have taken many qualities, but the greatest of them was obviously strength and courage. These terms are very similar in Hebrew, one seeming to mean "strong enough to be brave" and the other, "brave enough to remain strong!" Notice how in each instance where God uses this phrase a different aspect of these important qualities is outlined.

First, God tells Joshua these qualities will be necessary for leading God's own people into their own inheritance! Since God was going to cause the Israelites to defeat all the people in the Promised Land, they were going to be a "stronger" force to deal with and it would necessitate an even stronger leader to supervise them. It took more bold determination for Joshua to get the people of God to take their land, than it did to get their enemies out!

Second, it requires strength and courage to carry out what a godly predecessor like Moses had established! Joshua had not only to mimic a strong leader, but he had to genuinely be one. This meant enfolding the Word of God into his own heart, so God's favor would be evident for all to see.

Third, valor is compulsory for anyone to continue walking with God! It is one thing to start and another to finish. Trusting that God is within reach at all times is something that takes supreme bravery, especially when we find ourselves in the most difficult places. When our emotions tell us to run, God's virtue will hold us steady under pressure and crisis. Lasting in the last days will mean boldly facing these same challenges...if we have learned to gaze at the face of God first, we will succeed.

OCTOBER 14...DAY 287
THE MAN OF GOD'S BRAVEST ACT

"Only be very strong and very courageous, that you may observe to do according to all the law which Moses My servant commanded you; do not turn from it to the right hand or to the left, that you may prosper wherever you go. This Book of the Law shall depart from your mouth, but you shall meditate in it day and night, that you may observe to do according to all that is written in it. For then you will make your way prosperous, and then you will have good success."
Joshua 1:7-8 AMP

Yesterday, we examined the supreme importance of displaying strong godly leadership. Today, I want to remind you of the most important arena in which any believer will need to use this quality.

Notice that here in verse seven the Lord adds the term "very" to His command to be strong and courageous. He was emphasizing the need for more than the usual amount of bravery in handling the instruction manual Moses had given him. This was going to take the majority of Joshua's focus, a man who would be leading armies into battle and strategizing the entire set up of claiming the Promised Land.

I think what God was saying is that focused strength and courage was the ONLY way Joshua was going to be able to lead as God required. In the same way, meditating on and practicing the Word of God IS our job as Christians. Without it, we will not know God's will, or have a source for developing faith and trust in Him. Even more importantly, we won't be able to obey it!

"Observing to do" the things God has written down for us demands a vehement, diligent, total dedication (Hebrew meanings for the word "very"). The Word of God is an extremely powerful weapon (see Hebrews 4:12), which yields extreme rewards, for those willing to invest themselves to the extreme.

Nothing Joshua would face in the land of Canaan could take more of his focus than "meditating" on the Law of Moses day and night!! If he accepted the invitation to take the lead he would have to do it on God's terms. To meditate here means to "murmur" or "muse." It is the picture of one who ponders, deep in thought and whispers what his mind imagines. In doing this a person begins to see what they should do, creating an avenue to act on what they have already begun to believe. God promised Joshua twice that he would "make" his own way prosperous by his "observing to do" what the Law instructed. If we look deep enough into the Word of God we will end up doing the same as well. When we act...like spiritual leaders...we will also prosper and succeed, no matter what we may be facing!

OCT 15...DAY 288
ADVANCE VICTORY!

"So it was, when all the kings of the Amorites who were on the west side of the Jordan, and all the kings of the Canaanites who were by the sea, heard that the Lord had dried up the waters of the Jordan from before the children of Israel until we had crossed over, that their heart melted; and there was not spirit in them and there was no spirit in them any longer because of the children of Israel. At that time the LORD said to Joshua, make flint knives for yourselves and circumcise the sons of Israel again the second time...And it came to pass, when Joshua was by Jericho, that he lifted up his eyes and looked, and behold, a Man stood opposite him with His sword drawn in His hand." Joshua 5:1-2, 13 NKJV

By looking at the Israelites' entry into the land of Canaan we learn the importance of following God's specific instructions. The Levite priests merely "dipped their feet" into the Jordan river, while carrying the Ark of Covenant (presence of God) in obedience to what Joshua commanded, and the waters stood up so the whole nation could cross over on dry ground (Joshua 3:15). God then began to initiate a whole new series of events designed to help His people take the land.

Notice three particular things the Lord did as a reminder of how He will work with you. I believe we can expect similar scenarios to unfold as we follow Jesus toward the promise of His return. Let's look at them in reverse.

The final thing mentioned in this chapter is Joshua's supernatural encounter with a commanding angel sent to reinforce God's battle plans. This "commander" followed Joshua's obedience to a new "command" to circumcise or separate the Israelites fully into God's service. Both of these things were preceded by the Lord preparing in advance the way for victory! He supernaturally put the fear of Israel into the hearts of their enemies.

The Lord has always planned far ahead of our obedience. Until we give Him an absolute reason to change course, God works on our behalf as if we are going to obey and receive His heavenly assistance! I love the fact that He actually uses the miracles He performs on our behalf to exalt us in the eyes of our enemies!

With this Israelite generation, just like with the previous one, God had promised the land would be cleared by a joint effort between Him and them. First they would have to listen, then believe enough to walk out His promise battle by battle until they conquered every adversary He had already declared defeated!

As you take your first steps toward your promise, listen, obey and act in faith because God's promises are true for you.

OCTOBER 16...DAY 289
WHAT ARE YOU TEACHING OTHERS?

"Train up a child in the way he should go,
and when he is old he will not depart from it."
Proverbs 22:6 NKJV

Whether or not we are the generation that lives to see Jesus Christ's return, we should make sure that we have taken the time to "pass on" the faith. This includes preparing others to know Him and to be always ready to meet Him.

The primary place for this "training" is in our homes with our own children. An understanding of this Proverbs 22:6 is central to taking the responsibility the Lord has entrusted to us. I like the Webster's definition: "the act or process of drawing, alluring, educating, and forming by practice." Many dads and moms don't realize they are preparing their kids for their Christian responsibilities, just by parenting!

We form or mould our children, often carelessly, through a process of imitation; repeatedly drawing them toward the things we say and do. You've no doubt heard the old saying, "the apple doesn't fall far from the tree." That describes the automatic training that goes on in families everywhere by simple association. Whatever we are or seem to be in the eyes of those who admire us gets passed on to one degree or another.

If you have children the training process happens every day, either purposefully or unknowingly. If you're not a parent this scripture is still important for you in the role of an aunt, uncle, cousin or friend. Also through friendships or work related situations, we are all surrounded by so many young impressionable people in society! There may never have been a time like the present where such a general shortage of good, willing biological or spiritual "fathers" and "mothers" exists, to help both children and those with child-like problems.

Those of us who have been trained up in the Lord might as well make our maturity count for those around us who are spiritually less mature, in either age or experience. Settle this fact that somewhere within your sphere of influence, there are children who are looking to your example...they need your help to go the right way in their lives and to be ready to meet Jesus when He comes.

OCTOBER 17...DAY 290
USING THE THROTTLE

"Train up a child in the way he should go,
and when he is old he will not depart from it."
Proverbs 22:6 NKJV

Our children are living out what God has entrusted us to properly put in place. They are born to learn and they thrive on training. Notice, according to this scripture, it is our job to prepare them for their path in life. Again, the word "training" is important.

In the Hebrew language of Proverbs the word training means, "to narrow or throttle." It is talking about imparting discipline by narrowing the options a child has to choose from. This design is exactly opposite to what many "children's experts" teach today, often advocating wider approaches to training to allow exposure to a mind boggling array of options.

Freedom is a truly a wonderful thing, even for a child, but experience teaches us that it is even better when a foundation of discipline is put in place first. This is what Solomon's wisdom is passing on here in the Bible. Parents don't always have multiple lifestyle options at their disposal, what they have to give is themselves. However, any of us can open future horizons to our kids if we use what we have to train them properly today. We do that by imparting our discipline to them. We must mold them in the ways of God, Who holds all their options, by teaching them to restrain themselves according to godly guidelines. Show your children how to read the Bible and pray. Be a follower of Jesus in front of them. Create a living example of how an ordinary but sincere person approaches God in humility and confidence. Let them see you waiting on the Lord patiently, trusting Him until the answer comes.

If you know God, He will reveal your child's gifts, and you will receive the wisdom you need to help them go forward in His plans. You won't be afraid to restrain the carnal tendencies in them to allow for the release of God's Spirit of liberty!

Throttling is the best thing you can ever do for your child. It will teach them to throttle themselves and by doing so, accelerate their favor with God and man. In the end, it will call to them from within and keep them ready for Jesus' return!

OCTOBER 18...DAY 291
GENERAL AND SPECIAL TRAINING

"Train up a child in the way he should go,
and when he is old he will not depart from it."
Proverbs 22:6 NKJV

Yesterday we talked about how our kids need discipline. Today let's examine two different aspects of it.

A favorite Bible teacher of mine once said, "Anything living seeks to thrive" (paraphrase, Watchman Nee). We probably don't need a preacher to tell us that, but it is always good when God sends someone to remind us of the important things we so easily forget.

Children exude life, and it is important for us to remember that they have a natural need to thrive. Our scripture reminds us to "train" them "in the way" they should go.

In other words, our training needs to be both generalized and specialized so they can succeed in life according to God's standards.

Generally, all kids need the spiritual and moral foundation Christians are given in the Bible upon which to build a godly lifestyle. Specifically, your child needs the one on one attention and treatment only you can give them! It is vitally important for every father or mother to know both the Bible and their child. Once they do it becomes much easier to find the best "way" to lead as a parent.

The word "way" here means a literal "road." It refers to both one's course in life and his mode of action. This tells me that it is our job to get our kids into the appropriate shape for the proper journey.

Let's go back to the word "train" for a moment. In reviewing its various definitions again, I noticed that my Webster's dictionary used the example of how a gardener forms a young tree to a wall, molding and shaping it until it begins to grow in the desired direction. That is how God expects us to work with our children, knowing first what is within their capability and then taking the right kinds of measures to initiate and monitor their own growth process. The love we have for who they are should compel us as believers to train our children in the "nurture and admonition" of the Lord (see Ephesians 6:4). If we do, they won't turn and go in another direction even when we are long gone!

OCTOBER 19...DAY 292
USING YOUR ROD WISELY

"He who sows iniquity will reap sorrow, and the rod of his anger will
fail...Foolishness is bound up in the heart of a child;
the rod of correction will drive it far from him."
Proverbs 22:8, 15 NKJV

Notice that the word "rod" is used twice in this chapter. It is an interesting Hebrew word referring to a literal stick, which could be used for several different purposes. According to my research an Old Testament rod could be used for punishing, writing, fighting, ruling or walking. If you think about it that means it represented correction, instruction, power, authority and leverage, in the hand of the one using it. It could represent action taken either for you or against you, as was Aaron's rod in the hand of Moses. As an instrument of God's control, that particular rod was an indicator of either blessing or cursing based on how people reacted to the presence of its owner!

Here in our scripture for today, we see this word used in connection with discipline. In the first instance, an evil man is pictured misusing his rod. He wields it in anger and fails or "comes to nothing." Meanwhile, a good father, using his rod to discipline and train his son in verse fifteen, drives failure away. One multifaceted instrument, two radically different results!

The point Solomon is making is that a rod is much more than a ruler's staff or parent's paddle, it includes everything found in the meaning of authority. Used properly, a father's authority, directed wisely in the punishment of his child, actually drives the fleshly forces of failure within their human nature far from them. Used improperly, as an extension of an ungodly ruler's uncontrolled temperament, this seemingly "successful" man eventually ends up being corrected himself!

We have a responsibility to use our authority as parents and leaders, but be careful how you use it! The man who does so foolishly invites foolishness, while the man who uses it wisely releases foolishness from his family!

The "rod" includes corporal punishment but is much more than that. It is a very important aspect of raising successful children. Remember, you should only punish your children out of your true love for them and with the discretion of a wise man. If you do, it will drive evil away from your home...if not it will most likely drive your child far from you!

OCTOBER 20...DAY 293
GETTING YOUR KIDS UNDER CONTROL

"A good name is to be chosen rather than great riches,
loving favor rather than silver and gold."
Proverbs 22:1 NKJV

Children today are out of control! Nowhere is the lack of discipline more evident than in churches. To Christian parents everywhere let me just say, "Train your children!"

My wife, Bobbi, and I have been married for over twenty-five years and have raised four daughters of our own. We also took in one of our girl's friends when she was in junior high school and count her as our daughter as well. All but the youngest are now serving God in various capacities as responsible young women. We are far from "authorities" on child-raising, but we have learned a few things about parenting along the way that might help others. So today, I would like to share from my experience a couple of scriptural pointers on training godly children.

First of all, don't lose heart if you struggle to discipline your children properly. It's not all your fault and it is not that big of a deal to turn your situation around. Successive generations of deteriorating values in the American family have created a scenario where so many parents were never disciplined properly as children themselves.

This was true in my case to a degree. Not being raised in a serious Christian home, and without a father, I had to learn how to raise my own children on the fly. Thankfully, my wife was more fortunate in some ways and helped me grow and change along the way. Take help wherever God sends it, but realize you probably need a lot of it!

Second, begin to learn how God thinks by reading the Bible and then apply His values to your family's lifestyle. Our verse for today is a good place to start along with the entire twenty-second chapter of Proverbs. In this book of wise sayings, this chapter seems to be especially geared toward wisdom for raising children. If your kids can see you sincerely working at being a better person they will naturally become that way themselves.

I once read a study that showed how many money addicts are the children of parents who were too busy to respond to their simple need for attention. Therefore, they never stop trying to obtain withheld applause and human attention that only money seems to bring! We can teach our kids many valuable things by simply loving God enough to choose His ways over the things this world has to offer...as a result they will spend their lives seeking to do the same!

OCTOBER 21...DAY 294
INVEST IN YOUR VALUES

"A good name is to be chosen rather than great riches,
loving favor rather than silver and gold."
Proverbs 22:1 NKJV

As we mentioned yesterday, Proverbs chapter twenty-two seems to be especially written as a guide to raising successful godly children. I say this because it contains two specific verses which deal directly with that subject, among a progression of verses that lead us to understand what kind of adult ends up at the highest levels in life. This is a good place in scripture to structure our own lives in the process of building top notch kids!

I have noticed fifteen specific qualities listed here, scattered throughout these twenty nine verses that will help you build your family in God. Again, this is an important end-time subject. If not for all the determined parents throughout Christian history, most of us wouldn't be here preparing for Jesus' return. This is really a study in the grooming of great men and women of God!

Our children are "somebodies" in the making, who need us to be "somebodies" in God they can follow! They need us to show them the way by embracing God's Word so much that we practice it and teach them how to do the same! We already mentioned how verse one starts this list by teaching the ultimate lesson on right and wrong VALUES.

Any true man of God will choose "favor" over "silver" when it comes to deciding what he will live for. This man's conscience will lead him to build godly character reserves before cash reserves. A godly man knows it is more important to stay in a position that God will favor so his true enemy will have nothing in him to work with. Blessings follow the righteous and even though they are not always as readily available as opportunities to make fast money through compromising means, they are worth waiting on because they last longer. Our kids need to see that we will delay our own gratification in order to ensure our devotion to the Lord.

Love is the most valuable currency that exists in His economy, it purchases a good name for us when we invest it in God and trust Him to take care of our gold! As verse three teaches, this attitude keeps us in touch with everyone around us as well. Since the Lord doesn't categorize human beings by how much they possess, we can't afford to either...unless we want to be sorely disappointed with the results of parenting and the amount of our reward when He returns!

OCTOBER 22...DAY 295
GOD'S ROCK AND YOUR HARD PLACE

"Now the Lord spoke to Moses saying: 'Speak to the children of Israel, that they turn and camp before Pihahiroth, between Migdo and the sea, opposite Baal Zephon; you shall camp before it by the sea.' For Pharaoh will say of the children of Israel, 'They are bewildered by the land; the wilderness has closed them in.' Then will I harden Pharaoh's heart, so that he will pursue them; and I will gain honor over Pharaoh and over all his army, that the Egyptians may know that I am the Lord.' And they did so...And Moses said unto the people, 'Do not be afraid. Stand still, and see the salvation of the LORD, which he will accomplish for you today.'"
Exodus 14:1-4, 13a NKJV

What Moses tells the Israelites in these verses is what God raises up men to tell people in every age. "Stand still, and see," is something I believe He is telling the

Church now! We must be willing to go in the direction the Lord instructs us to go, even when it makes no sense and stay firmly fixed in the places He calls us to, even when there seems to be no way out. In that position, we will always see Him move on our behalf.

One important thing we learn here is that God's plan is never for us to fulfill the call. Whether His purpose is individual or corporate in scope, and it is always both on some level, the Lord's plan is to fulfill the call Himself via the Holy Spirit working through us! He expects us to have enough faith to first follow and then to confidently watch what He does both for us and through us.

This is exactly what was going on as Moses led the Israelites out of Egypt. He was carrying out a plan that was beyond anyone's understanding at that time. The purpose was to liberate Israel but also to reveal Himself to the world, through Pharaoh's complete destruction! In order to play their part, God's people had to do a couple of unusual things. Initially they had to follow Moses to the edge of a wilderness. Their freedom was tricky! It meant they had to willingly move toward ground that was not very inviting. It took courage to go against all their emotions. Then, once they arrived at the entrance of the area where they were to escape, God rerouted them into open straights between a gorge and the Red Sea. They would feel like "sitting ducks" right in front of an area named after the demonic idol, "Baal Zephon," or the destructive "Lord of the North!"

God was going to deal with every spiritual and physical obstruction of the Church of that time...but it required them to be in the right place at the right time!

OCTOBER 23...DAY 296
STAND STILL SO YOU CAN GO FORWARD

"For Pharaoh will say of the children of Israel, 'They are bewildered by the land; the wilderness has closed them in'...And Moses said unto the people, 'Do not be afraid. Stand still, and see the salvation of the LORD, which He will accomplish for you today. For the Egyptians whom you see today, you shall see again no more for ever. The LORD will fight for you, and you shall hold your peace.' And the LORD said to Moses, 'Why do you cry to me? Tell the children of Israel to go forward.'"
Exodus 14:3-4, 13-15 NKJV

The most severe battles in my life had one thing in common; it seemed there was nothing I could do! I remember, for example, the day my wife told me she didn't love me anymore. Everything in me wanted to say, "I am going to fight back, this is not fair, don't talk to me like that, how can you say that!? Don't you value anything I've done for you? Let's create a ledger right now, with my name on one side and your name on the other, and let's find out who has been the better spouse in this relationship, after nearly thirteen years of marriage, anyway!"

In fact, I said all of those things and more, but it was like talking to a brick wall. My words and former "husband" persuasions were totally ineffective. As a result of my selfishness and the help of demonic forces that work to break up godly marriages, Bobbi had reached a place of seeming complete emotional numbness without my realizing it. It was textbook. I was the classic foolish husband who had driven his wife to misery and didn't see the train wreck coming. Even the counselor we went to see as a last resort said it would take at least ten years to resolve! I was hurt and angry but the Lord kept speaking to me and working with me through the crisis I had helped to create. "No," He said, "you are not going to do any of the things you feel. I've helped bring you up to this place for your own deliverance...and I will bring you over to the other side and get all the glory in your marriage! Rocky, you don't want to hear this right now, but stand still and remain at rest. If you fight the battle you will lose your wife, but if you let me fight for you, you will both be delivered and gain more than you ever had before."

We ended up winning that battle quickly and we have never had to fight it again! The faith we needed to go forward was found by first following God out of the place we had been! This is what Israel learned under Moses...the place God has promised, comes by the way He directs!

OCTOBER 24...DAY 297
THE ONE THING

"Now a certain ruler asked Him, saying, 'Good Teacher, what shall I do to inherit eternal life?' So Jesus said to him, 'Why do you call Me good? No one is good but One, that is God. You know the commandments: Do not commit adultery, Do not murder, Do not steal, Do not bear false witness, Honor your father and your mother.' And he said, 'All these things I have kept from my youth.' So when Jesus heard these things, He said to him, 'You still lack one thing. Sell all that you have and distribute to the poor, and you will have treasure in heaven; and come follow Me.' But when he heard this, he became very sorrowful, for he was very rich...So He said to them, 'Assuredly, I say to you, there is no one who has left house or parents or brothers or wife or children, for the sake of the kingdom of God, who shall not receive many times more in this present time and in the age to come in eternal life.'"
Luke 18:18-30 NKJV

This passage is often looked upon as a lesson for the wealthy about the dangers of trusting in their riches. Although that idea is certainly contained in the point Jesus made, there is something much more important here for us to see. The "one thing" principle is something that everybody has to learn, whether they have money in their pocket or not. It really is the "only thing" that matters for a believer, but it is also the "hardest thing" we will ever choose to do. Without it, like this ruler who approached Jesus full of self-confidence, we will find ourselves prevented from following Jesus any further or receiving eternal life!

Notice how the Lord redefined this man's idea of "good." Goodness isn't something easily found in ourselves, or in one another. It is the quality of God alone defined by the commandments He gave us to reveal the heavenly standard.

Jesus went down the checklist of commandments with him to spiritually "locate" him. Although He had kept each of the five specifically mentioned he had not understood the spirit of these things. Jesus uncovered the fact that this guy thought he was in good standing with God because of his own merits. If that were true he would not have left feeling sorry for himself that day.

He wasn't far from God. However, he just needed the "one thing" that we all need. What was it? EVERYTHING! We must succeed where this man failed and be willing to lay it all down for the ultimate prize...eternity! If we do, we will enjoy all the benefits of doing so right now in this life. Since the end times are not going to be easy, let's choose to build a sincere relationship with God that will stand the test of time!

OCTOBER 25...DAY 298
BE A MAN, BOY!

"But you, O man of God, FLEE these things and PURSUE righteousness, godliness, faith, love, patience, gentleness. FIGHT the good fight of faith, lay hold on eternal life, to which you were also called...that you KEEP this commandment without spot, blameless until our Lord Jesus Christ's appearing, which He will manifest in His own time,...COMMAND those who are rich in this present age not to be haughty,...O Timothy, GUARD what was committed to your trust,..."
1 Timothy 6:11-12a, 14-15a, 17a, 20a NKJV

You will notice a six-point charge for men of God given by the Apostle Paul to Timothy in this passage of scripture. In fact, this entire chapter of the Bible is a guideline for being effective in the Lord's service, particularly as a man, while staying prepared for His return.

It is important for us, as modern believers, to realize the distinction between "success" and "effectiveness." Today, so many believers are drunk with religion and don't even know it! We must beware of substituting what we do well for what God wants done. They are not always the same. God's idea of success is that we not flinch as His followers when the pressures mount BECAUSE He has assigned us things that do not lead to bigger bank accounts and better reputations!

The above list was given to help a leading young man in ministry know how to be a MAN of God before trying to build a successful ministry. Paul was helping Timothy from becoming misguided in his own calling, which in turn, would allow him to remain a safe Christian guide for others. It shows us that God is always more about the making of the man than the doing of the work. If the man is godly the work he does is usually God's work, whether it looks like it to the world or not!

One of the best prophetic words I have ever heard was given by a seasoned minister to a younger man being groomed for ministry. As the young man lay on the ground, the older preacher nudged him on the shoulder with his foot and simply said, "Be a man, boy!"

These six things will help any Christian leader answer that same call and, in doing so, build a solid foundation to stand on at Jesus return!

OCTOBER 26...DAY 299
BRINGING THE CHRISTIAN BACKGROUND TO THE FOREFRONT

"But you, O man of God, FLEE these things and PURSUE righteousness, godliness, faith, love, patience, gentleness. FIGHT the good fight of faith, lay hold on eternal life, to which you were also called...that you KEEP this commandment without spot, blameless until our Lord Jesus Christ's appearing, which He will manifest in His own time,...COMMAND those who are rich in this present age not to be haughty,...O Timothy, GUARD what was committed to your trust,..."
1 Timothy 6:11-12a, 14-15a, 17a, 20a NKJV

Let's discuss the six things that will make a man of God out of any minister. As I said yesterday, any honest believer alive today knows the religious world needs this desperately! Something has to be done quickly to "de-feminize" Christianity or we are in danger of losing several generations! This is not to suggest at all that God does not use godly women as leaders. An honest look at the Bible and the reality of history says that He does. It's just that ever since the Garden of Eden men have been the born leaders of the human race. Even when a women is called into ministry it is usually most effective when a strong godly man is somewhere at the forefront of the background!

Churches today are so "feminine" with regard to the atmosphere they build and the strategies they implement that many men are scared away before taking a second look. The fact that the Gospel message has been so diluted is a direct reflection of this condition within the church world.

Thank God for the godly mothers and strong female examples among us. They have taught us much about how to be sensitive to the Holy Spirit, attentive to the Word, and diligent about the things of God. Many precious women have helped to nurture and shape my own spiritual life over the years, but it is the real, godly men who have pushed me the furthest. Because I am a man, I have needed some serious men who knew God to teach me the things Paul taught Timothy here.

Notice that these six things fall into three easy categories for us guys to remember. First, there are things to run away from and things to run toward. Second, there is a time to fight and a time to keep spotless. Finally, there is a time to transmit what you have learned to others and a time to guard what has been committed to you.

Every man of God has to know WHAT he needs to do WHEN it needs to be done. As we do, the church takes on a more balanced, appealing overall look...and everyone begins to function on their highest level!

OCTOBER 27...DAY 300
AVOID THE SLIPPERY SLOPE

"But you, O man of God, FLEE these things and PURSUE righteousness, godliness, faith, love, patience, gentleness.
1 Timothy 6:11 NKJV

"If anyone teaches otherwise and does not consent to wholesome words, even the words of our Lord Jesus Christ, and to the doctrine which accords with godliness, he is proud, knowing nothing..."
1 Timothy 6:3-4a NKJV

If you examine this second scripture after looking at Paul's charge in the first, you will begin to understand his reasoning for starting his six point admonition to Timothy with the command to "flee" certain things. There is a "slippery slope" believers, ministers and churches must avoid, which is meant to trick them into pursuing the wrong things!

I want you to notice the great lengths the apostle goes to in making sure we are familiar with this process. In the first ten verses of the chapter, leading up to our text on the importance of being a true man of God in verse eleven, we are given a list of things that go wrong when Christians are afraid to commit. As you read on, you find the central issue to be one of complacency versus contentment.

If a godly leader is content, or satisfied separate from and regardless of outward conditions, he or she will be able to follow the call of God bravely. If not, this person will go deeper into deception at the rate by which they continue to act contrary to their conscience and betray themselves.

The word content is found twice, once in verse 6 and again in verse 8. Taken together, the literal meaning of these words suggests a kind of spiritual self-satisfaction that raises a barrier of confidence around God's man, causing him to be competent in his undertakings. Now you know why Satan works so hard inside local churches and ministries to create atmospheres of discontent!

Today, we see discontentment everywhere, and before Jesus returns it is going to lead many to forsake Him altogether. If you look closely, you will see how this downhill slide begins with a refusal to suffer properly in verses one and two then progresses quickly into much more obvious and open forms of sin. Because the wrong is not resisted in the beginning, it is not recognized in its latter stages.

The devil traps God's people into a process of running into the very things they should be running from! As you know, this is not going to get better before Jesus returns, it's going to get a lot worse...see the signs in scripture and catch early what to pursue and what to run from so discontentment and other sin doesn't slide into to you or your church!

OCTOBER 28...DAY 301
RECIPE FOR SPIRITUAL DISASTER

"But you, O man of God, FLEE these things and PURSUE righteousness, godliness, faith, love, patience, gentleness.
1 Timothy 6:11 NKJV

"But if anyone teaches otherwise and does not consent to wholesome words...he is proud, knowing nothing...from such withdraw yourself."
1 Timothy 6:3-4a, 5b NKJV

If you look closely at this chapter in your Bible you'll realize that you have a guide in your hand outlining Satan's most basic strategy for world domination! I know it may sound a little over-hyped, but it is so important to understand that he really does intend to do this by first targeting you and your church!! Today let me give you an overview of the subtle process that starts with our pride in verse one, and progresses to the very root of all evil by verse ten.

Paul uses a situation in Timothy's church (Ephesus), to describe how the difference between godly and ungodly behavior among believers hinges on their attitude toward being wronged. It would seem normal and right for us to think that if we were Christian slaves, as some of them were, we should be allowed to demand our freedom, especially when our masters are also saved! However, this is completely opposite of the position outlined! For the sake of the Gospel message itself, Paul says it was their "duty" to honor and serve them all the more!! This is exactly why Jesus demanded that His followers carry their crosses to the death if necessary, just as He did (Mark 8:34-38).

When we won't accept inconvenient truths, we open ourselves and our churches to shocking levels of pride and arrogance. From there, through lack of responsibility, we can easily become argumentative and literally, "misemployed" (wrangling) in activities that create the wrong atmosphere among other believers. It then becomes easy in this suspicious, controlling environment of strife and jealousy, to find fault in areas where it doesn't really exist, opening ourselves to all kinds of deception and corruption.

Believe it or not, churches and people can sink to such a low place of constant desire for all the wrong things that they end up overwhelmed by temptations and drowned in morbid pleasures! Their extreme discontent and pursuit of outward comforts leads them in their obsessive state into a fixation on wrong values. Christians can become so consumed with external conditions that they begin to run after money at the expense of and eventually in the place of God and His will! The worst thing of all is that they eventually think they are right, when in reality they have actually wandered far from the true faith!

In the end, misguided believers find themselves at the mercy of evil itself, full of deep mental and spiritual wounds. Only God knows if such people can even be brought back into a right state...but now you know exactly what to avoid...at all costs, for all time!

OCTOBER 29...DAY 302
RUN FOR GOD, RUN FROM RICHES

"Useless wranglings of men of corrupt minds and destitute of the truth, who suppose that godliness is a means of gain. From such withdraw yourself. Now godliness with contentment is great gain...But those who desire to be rich fall into temptation and a snare, and into many foolish and harmful lusts which drown men in destruction and perdition. For the love of money is a root of all kinds of evil, for which some have strayed from the faith in their greediness and pierced themselves through with many sorrows. But you, O man of God, FLEE these things and PURSUE righteousness, godliness, faith, love, patience, gentleness."
1 Timothy 6:5-11 NKJV

There is currently a very high "misemployment" rate in the Church! Remember, I explained yesterday how this is the literal definition for the word "wrangling" in this biblical passage.

The devil doesn't seem to have much trouble seeing to it that once believers start down the road of self-deception they end up "supposing" all the wrong things. Money is a topic we avoid because of scriptures like these, or we just completely avoid these scriptures!

In discussing this "recipe for spiritual disaster," it is not wise to discount the pivotal role riches play in keeping God's people moving in the right direction. Notice here the main ingredient in the devil's false Christian concoction is the assumption that being spiritually successful means being also financially furnished. To that notion, the apostle Paul simply says to stay away from people that live as if God serves their purposes. If we don't, our misplaced carnal desires will lead us to spiritual ruin.

Don't forget that rich people have an extremely difficult time getting into God's kingdom according to Jesus (Luke 18:24). That rich ruler who approached Him illustrates a believer who is indeed applying God's Word to his life, yet trips up solely on the subject of his finances. It's all about where our heart is ...do we desire to be rich or do we desire God? Do we love God or love what we can get out of working for him?

This confusion can happen to anyone, whether they have money or just dream of having it. It can also work in reverse, in the heart of someone who has an unhealthy fixation on not having money! "Loving" anything about money is dangerous! It is the basic element upon which this world system operates.

Let's learn to treat money as the concrete on our sidewalk, just an optional alternative to walking in the dust! We are reliant upon God and moving forward with or without it. When money means nothing to us, God will have open avenues into our hearts. We will offer Him untangled branches from which to produce rich blessings extended from Him to His people!

OCTOBER 30...DAY 303
COMMAND THE RICH

"Command those who are rich in this present age not to be haughty, nor to trust in uncertain riches but in the living God, who gives us richly all things to enjoy. Let them do good, that they be rich in good works, ready to give, willing to share, storing up for themselves a good foundation for the time to come, that they may lay hold on eternal life."
1 Timothy 6:17-19 NKJV

Poverty is not a good thing, but wealth is not the best thing! Balance is key when it comes to understanding the place of money in the life of a man or woman of God. Notice that Paul did not tell Timothy to command all the rich people in the church to give away their money like the rich ruler who came to Jesus. As in most things, finances are a case by case thing with God. It is between us and God what we do with them just as it was with Ananias and Sapphira in Acts 5. Once we commit ourselves to the Lord, however, our belongings become God's along with everything else we think we own!

The command here is that we not allow riches to cause us to be conceited or to divert our faith away from the Lord. We all know that money can do both of those things to the best of believers, including ourselves! So, what is the key? Simply to stay focused on being rich toward God regardless of financial conditions. This means using our possessions to do things that ensure we don't get the wrong attitudes toward God's church.

These are listed for us as: 1. Doing good or seeking to always be a benefit, working for God, 2. Staying personally active in His service and, 3. Sharing what we have with others, especially those who have less than us.

In commanding rich believers to follow these guidelines we teach them to be just as right with and useful to God as anyone in His house. Both rich and not have the same set of responsibilities, it is just sometimes easier for those less wealthy to remember what things are important to the Lord because they do not have the temptations of their money to distract them.

One of history's richest men of God, Solomon, may have said it best in Proverbs 30:8-9, "Remove far from me falsehood and lies; give me neither poverty nor riches;

feed me with the food that is needful for me, lest I be full and deny You and say, Who is the Lord? Or lest I be poor and steal, and so profane the name of my God."

Christianity works best when wealth and poverty remain in their proper places...under the authority of the Lord and far below our affection for him! When they are, we will likely have very little trouble overcoming either issue and staying prepared to meet the Lord!

OCTOBER 31...DAY 304
THE RECIPE FOR SPIRITUAL DEVELOPMENT

"But you, O man of God, FLEE these things and PURSUE righteousness, godliness, faith, love, patience, gentleness."
1 Timothy 6:11 NKJV

Now that you know how to personally avoid contributing to the coming end time disaster, let's look at the things God specifically instructs us to pursue.

Did you notice the similarity of the six things listed with other lists in the New Testament? Doing so will help you formulate an understanding of exactly which biblical qualities will pay the greatest dividends for you as a Christian if you focus on practicing them. This is not to say that any other qualities in scripture are less important. However, when you see something clearly repeated in God's Word the points He's making should stand out.

Remember how the Lord called to Samuel three times as a little boy before Eli the priest understood that it was God (1 Samuel 3). Then, the fourth time, God used his name twice, saying, "Samuel, Samuel," to get his full attention. This signifies something very important to us just as it did in that situation. The Word of the Lord had grown rare in those days because of corruption in Eli's household, and it is not much different in our day as we quickly approach the last of days. Samuel was God's answer to that age, but he had to be able to hear God clearly in order to follow His instructions and develop spiritually.

Today, we must know what the recipe is for true spiritual development and thank God it is not hidden. These same qualities, plus a couple of others, are also known as the "Fruit of the spirit," in Galatians 5:22-23. They teach us how to practice walking in the presence of God so we can learn to live from our inner man and overcome the flesh.

These two lists are then shaken together and partially used again in Peter's "fail-safe" list of spiritual success (2 Peter 1:4-10). As you take the time to examine these portions of scripture the importance of these qualities become increasingly clear.

Here are the six things and their general definitions: 1. Righteousness means doing the right things from the heart. 2. Godliness is turning to and leaning on God continually. 3. Faith means to believe the things the Lord says in His word so much that one practices them. 4. Love is a responsible decision to act like God feels about people and things. 5. Patience means to delay our gratification, willing to endure whatever is necessary to see God's will be done. 6. Meekness is that humble flexibility that allows one to be molded and used by God.

Any believer or Christian leader who allows the Holy Spirit to work these things through their spirits will grow and be prepared in these end times!

NOVEMBER 1...DAY 305
WATCH WHAT YOU'RE FOLLOWING

"But you, O man of God, FLEE these things and PURSUE righteousness, godliness, faith, love, patience, gentleness."
1 Timothy 6:11 NKJV

"You ran well. Who hindered you from obeying the truth?...For you, brethren, have been called to liberty; only do not use liberty as an opportunity for the flesh, but through love serve one another...I say then: Walk in the Spirit, and you shall not fulfill the lust of the flesh."
Galatians 5:7, 13, 16 NKJV

One great fact about true spiritual things is that when you follow them they create new realities for you. After spending ten verses instructing us what to run from as Christians, notice Paul simply states six things in this one verse for us to run to!

It may seem a little out of balance at first glance, almost as if we need to be more concerned about what not to do than what to do. I don't believe that is the case. It's just that sliding downhill is easier than climbing uphill. Because believers possess God's Promise, we have to accept the pressure of carrying it responsibly. This means being so familiar with Who we follow that we easily recognize the error of what is contrary to His nature in and around us. When we don't follow well we get entangled with wrong thinking, which leads to incorrect perceptions that cause us to stumble in false realities.

What took Paul ten verses to straighten out, should have been obvious to the people Timothy was overseeing in Ephesus. They had lost proper control of the conduct and teaching in their church because of their ignorance in recognizing the fruit or (in this case the lack of it) that God produces in His followers.

Galatians chapter five gives us an alternative list of these same qualities, calling them the fruit of the Spirit. Many Bible commentators believe the "S" in "Spirit" should not be capitalized because it refers not to God's fruit but that of the human spirit. After all, Jesus Himself told us in John 15:5 that He is the Vine and we are the "branches." He went on to say that "much fruit" is developed through our lives as we "abide" or spend time with Him.

The secret to doing that is found in the word "walking" back in Galatians 5:16. This word means to literally "walk all around in" or "explore" the spiritual realities found in a continual relationship with God. Following God in this way has a positive effect on our human desires and inclinations that are naturally contrary to Him.

Running from sin is important but running to God is more important because Jesus is the only one who has the solution for it! The difference in the two kinds of believers described by Paul is simply a matter of following...one follows the right things to right end and, another who follows the wrong things to the wrong end!

NOVEMBER 2...DAY 306
LEARN HOW TO FIGHT

"FIGHT the good fight of faith, lay hold on eternal life, to which you were also
called and have confessed a good confession in
the presence of many witnesses."
1 Timothy 6:12 NKJV

I was a pretty good high school wrestler and also had my share of fights growing up. I want to teach people how to fight, but first let's establish why it is an important skill to cultivate today.

Christians must remember what they are fighting with and the arena they are fighting in if we are going to become legitimate end-time contenders for the faith! This may come as a surprise to some of you, and don't let it scare you away from finishing this article, but we are fighting with the devil!

Ephesians 6:12 tells us explicitly that a believer is in a "wrestling" match with demonic forces, whether he, she or their pastor knows it or not! Unseen enemies of

God at the highest levels are willfully standing against us, demanding a response that is only going to get more intense as time goes on. So often, however, Christians and churches are unwilling to respond because true men of God have not taken the lead in showing them how to deal with the spirit of aggression. Beyond the knowledge of what we are fighting, there is a defined battleground arena ordered by God.

Our scripture specifically calls it a fight of "faith" for a reason. Satan is working to steal our courage and trust in the promises of the Lord. The terminology sounds "metaphoric" to the modern religious mindset. Faith has almost become a more "soft-sounding" malleable word as it is used in the Christian vocabulary of today, making those who have lost its meaning no match for our real opponent!

Ephesians chapter six pictures the successful believer as outfitted in God's own armor, but notice how verse sixteen highlights what he is holding as the most important piece of his spiritual equipment. "Above all, taking the shield of FAITH with which you will be able to quench all the fiery darts of the wicked one."

Because Jesus has already defeated Satan, our fight is primarily one of resistance. Faith is how we hold the ground that has been taken. It is the arena or ring in which we have to tenaciously make our stand to win the fight God has singled out for us. No matter what, we cannot be moved by contrary circumstances or situations. Instead, we have to become proficient at making contrary choices of faith in the face of those things! If we do, God's Word will become a powerful weapon in our own mouths to advance the cause of Christ regardless of our circumstances!

We may take a few shots along the way but they only make us tougher and more certain of the authority God has given us through Christ to win the "world" championship vs. the foe!

NOVEMBER 3...DAY 307
WINNING A FIGHT

"FIGHT the good fight of faith, lay hold on eternal life, to which you were also called and have confessed a good confession in the presence of many witnesses."
1 Timothy 6:12 NKJV

"Therefore I run thus: not with uncertainty. thus I fight: not as one who beats the air. But I discipline my body and bring it into subjection, lest, when I have preached to others, I myself should become disqualified."
1 Corinthians 9:26-27 NKJV

"I have fought the good fight, I have finished the race, I have kept the faith. "
2 Timothy 4:7 NKJV

By the time I was eleven I developed a reputation among my classmates as one of the "toughest kids in school." This was purely a result of my having the "perfect combination" of a tough-sounding name, living on the rough side of town and being born with a big mouth! The only contradiction was that I had never really been in a fight!

This title served my interests well for a few years, until one day during the sixth grade another kid called my bluff. After accepting his challenge to meet after school at a certain place, on a certain day, he and I fought before a circle of our peers in a local park for what seemed like a couple of hours.

To be honest we both did well, fighting to a virtual draw UNTIL something unforeseen happened. Although I was not losing, I also was not winning and, at some point in the fight I suddenly realized that I was outnumbered in the cheering section. Unexpectedly, I cracked mentally and started crying and running for home! It was the worst experience of my life, and it changed everything.

The next morning at school I had several challengers to my tainted "tough guy" title! In fact, I fought the best fight of my life that very next day out of the sheer anger of being humiliated the day before! Now, I don't recommend physical fighting unless it just has to be done, but I did learn a lot about hand to hand combat that will help you in the spiritual arena.

Here are three quick lessons for you if you want to stand strong in the Lord and build your reputation as an overcomer in Christ. First, always answer the bell! Talking a good fight doesn't make you a match for the devil, boldly using Jesus' name does! Second, keep your head in the game. Once you take a couple of blows you get an entirely different perspective of what fighting is all about. It requires your full focus and attention or you will crack like I did! Third, finish what you start. Prizes are given for finishers in the kingdom of God just like in the sporting world. Learn to earn your reputation as a formidable faith fighter, expecting the enemy to call every bluff in preparation for Jesus' return!

NOVEMBER 4...DAY 308
EXCLAMATION POINTS
#1 KEEP

"I urge you in the sight of God who gives life to all things, and before Christ Jesus who witnessed the good confession before Pontius Pilate, that you KEEP this commandment without spot, blameless until our Lord Jesus Christ's appearing, which He will manifest in His own time, He who is the blessed and only Potentate, the King of kings and Lord of lords, who alone has immortality, dwelling in unapproachable light, whom no man has seen or can see, to whom be honor and everlasting power. Amen."
1 Timothy 6:13-16 NKJV

Here the word "keep" literally means "to attend carefully to" or "take care of" something. In the context of this verse, the apostle Paul is reiterating the absolute necessity of his previous charge for Timothy to "Flee, Follow and Fight," given in verses 11-12! In our modern, fast paced world, this scripture should teach us to not travel past the things we learn too quickly, especially when they are important spiritual mandates handed down by greater men before us who have walked closely with the Lord.

This is the first of three exclamation points found in the last portion of this chapter. It presents a three-fold charge, to be taken as a "commandment" from a superior officer, not just encouragement from a spiritual father! The tone is set this way for us, so that we don't make the mistake of taking what is said too lightly. Because Paul was a loving father in the spiritual sense he took liberties in bluntly ordering his son, Timothy, to handle himself and church issues in a way that was safe for them and best for the Kingdom of God in the face of high-level spiritual pressure. This meant remaining consistent with Jesus' courageous stand of faith before Pilate when confronted with the deadliest of circumstances.

Not only is he being told to identify spiritual issues, but more importantly he is being required to do so aggressively on every front, as a watchman on the wall. "Fight," in this case meant waging spiritual battle on three fields: 1) Confronting the lies; 2) Preserving the truth; 3) Standing in the position of faith.

Remember how James 4:7 tells us to "resist the devil" and then promises, "he will flee from you." Peter also, using similar language in 1 Peter 5:9, says to, "...resist (the devil) steadfast in the faith..."

Believers today have become resistant to all the wrong things, by being too self-absorbed and thus creating hardness in their hearts! We best represent the Lord by following His example and taking His words as our direct commands (John 15:9-17).

When we do, which means walking in love above all things, He promises us His friendship and fruitfulness! Keep Jesus in the highest place as you approach the last days...this is where He dwells and where you will be kept safe in all your ways!

NOVEMBER 5...DAY 309
EXCLAMATION POINTS
#2 COMMAND

"COMMAND those who are rich in this present age not to be haughty, nor trust in uncertain riches but in the living God, who gives us richly all things to enjoy. Let them do good, that they be rich in good works, ready to give, willing to share, storing up for themselves a good foundation for the time to come, that they may lay hold on eternal life."
1 Timothy 6:17-19 NKJV

The apostle Paul punctuated his comments to the younger apostle, Timothy, with some exclamation points. In fact, the New King James Version of the Bible literally puts an exclamation point right after Timothy's name in the twentieth verse of this chapter!

To "exclaim" refers to a "strong, sudden cry," which depicts the emphasis with which Paul highlights the importance of his statements regarding "fleeing, following and fighting," found in verses ten and eleven. Yesterday we examined the value of taking godly commands and turning them into crucial acts of obedience to God. This is a big key to developing into a legitimate "man of God. Today let's take it one step further by noting what else this level of maturity will require from us.

Immediately in verse seventeen we find the verb form of the noun Paul pointed to in verse fourteen. In three quick verses of scripture, we learn that once you can take a "commandment," you are going to have to give a command!" In particular Timothy is told to "charge" or "transmit" a clear message to those under his oversight who are rich in this world's goods. This verbal conveyance was crucial in that environment to diffuse the arguments and the ungodly doctrine circulating in that church.

Their error centered around the discontentment we discussed previously, which had lead to an overemphasis on the topic of gain. Paul knew the root of all evil was the love of money (verse 10), so he directed Timothy to attack the source of the problem that was luring believers into carnality, deception and harm. By telling those who had money to handle it properly before God, an example would be set for those who were tempted to lust after it! Notice that God did not direct the rich Christians in Ephesus to give all their money away. He only clarified how to successfully transfer its usefulness into the kingdom of God.

The secret for them was to: 1) not be arrogant with money, 2) not trust in money but in God, 3) do good with their money and, 4) share their money with others in need. In doing this they would kill two birds with one stone...they would eliminate the hypothesis Satan was using to destroy their church, and create a foundation for God to continue blessing them and their church eternally!

NOVEMBER 6...DAY 310
EXCLAMATION POINTS
#3 GUARD

"O Timothy! GUARD what was committed to your trust, avoiding the profane and idle babblings and contradictions of what is falsely called knowledge - by professing it some have strayed concerning the faith, Grace be with you. Amen."
1 Timothy 6:20-21 NKJV

God has committed things into all of our hands, whether we are believers or unbelievers. He has also scheduled a date in the future when we will all give a direct account to Him for those gifts (see Acts 24:15, 2 Corinthians 5:10 & Revelation 20:11).

This is the focus of this final "exclamation point" Paul uses to emphasize his charge to Timothy in this chapter. It is as if the older "man of God" puts all his strength into these last two verses by using his son in the faith's name one last time. Then notice the next word, "GUARD," is another command to protect the life of the church under his care. It means to "isolate and protect," specifically pointing to the need to acknowledge something and to avoid something. In exercising his full responsibility, Timothy will hold the standard of godliness and sound Christian thinking high enough that the grace of God will have continued access into both his life and ministry.

Many Christians today no longer seem to realize that they have an adversary bent on bringing adversity into their lives. Satan is not concerned with who we are but in stealing what has been committed to our trust! This is why the Lord reminds us, through Paul's letter to Timothy, of our need to "isolate and protect" what God has entrusted us with. The picture is that of a bodyguard, one who trails another, watching his every move, and through surveillance, scrutinizing any abnormal movements of those around the one he's guarding...even to his own detriment!

In the same manner we are to value the things God has truly put under our supervision more than our own sense of well-being. This is an appropriate response to the attacks we face.

First, we must ACKNOWLEDGE the fact that we are COMMITTED. Many believers stray and fall away because they do not realize the implications of God's commitment to them. Holding the truth demands living up to it, even in the most difficult of choices, which requires trusting ourselves into the hands of God.

Second, AVOID the tendency to let spiritual things become COMMON, especially as a result of the over-driven ambitions and self-servicing contradictions of babbling intellectuals in the church. Always remember that the knowledge of God is more important than knowledge about Him. One unifies while the other divides, one builds faith while the other tears it down. A true "man of God" learns to both guard what he has been given and to be on guard against those who would take what is not their own.

Last days men will have an exclamation point after their name...in the Book of Life!

NOVEMBER 7...DAY 311
HOW A MAN OF GOD LEARNS

"Yea, and all that will live godly in Christ Jesus shall suffer persecution. But evil men and impostors will grow worse and worse, deceiving and being deceived. But you must continue in the things which you have learned and been assured of, knowing from whom you have learned them, and that from childhood you have know the Holy Scriptures, which are able to make you wise for salvation through faith which is in Christ Jesus. All Scripture is given by inspiration of God, and is profitable for doctrine, for reproof, for correction, for instruction in righteousness, that the man of God may be complete, thoroughly equipped for every good work."
2 Timothy 3:16-17 NKJV

In our passage for today notice the emphasis on learning in the making of a "man of God." Beyond our commitment to carrying our crosses (doing the right things) and dealing with whatever comes our way (particularly the wrong things), we believers must make learning God's Word the ultimate importance.

A godly education comes in many forms. First, Paul tells Timothy to "continue" in the things he has already learned. This is a definitive element towards building a disciples' foundation. It is human nature to move on to the next new interest before establishing ourselves in the knowledge we have already gained. Spiritually, we will never become "complete" until we get God's information into our hearts. This is where wisdom and understanding properly process all knowledge.

Next, learning involves the person we learn from. Be careful whom you choose for a mentor. Fortunately, Timothy had a godly parent and grandparent, the apostle Paul and other genuine, reliable guides from which to learn the intricacies of manhood in Christianity. When you have good mentors the challenge is to truly get to know THEM! This means getting more than information…it also involves impartation, or the ability to receive something of the quality, character and ability of the person who instructs you. Great leaders usually come from other great leaders, not just from the universities or other institutions of learning.

Finally, the most important source of knowledge for a Christian leader is the Bible itself. The "Holy Scriptures," simply refer to the written Word of God. What some of the greatest men and women of God throughout history have spoken and exemplified has been written down for us and combined into one book! Despite the fact that it has been written by many different authors over a period of thousands of years, it contains a unity of message that can only be supernatural in nature. No other book in history, religious or otherwise can compare because God inspired this one Himself! Tomorrow, we will look at why it is the best leadership book as well.

NOVEMBER 8…DAY 312
WHAT YOUR BIBLE WILL DO FOR YOU

"Yea, and all that will live godly in Christ Jesus shall suffer persecution. But evil men and impostors will grow worse and worse, deceiving and being deceived. But you must continue in the things which you have learned and been assured of, knowing from whom you have learned them, and that from childhood you have know the Holy Scriptures, which are able to make you wise for salvation through faith which is in Christ Jesus. All Scripture is given by inspiration of God, and is profitable for doctrine, for reproof, for correction, for instruction in righteousness, that the man of God may be complete, thoroughly equipped for every good work."
2 Timothy 3:16-17 NKJV

As we discussed yesterday, the emphasis in our text is on the various ways that God communicates His Word with us. God Himself speaks to us as we keep our hearts open to Him, other people who carry heavenly qualities can speak to us for God, and most importantly the Bible forever speaks on His behalf.

Today, let's look at exactly what your Bible can do to increase your spiritual life and leadership ability. First, please notice that Paul calls the scriptures, "Holy." We have to know how "special" or "separate from what is common" God's Word really is. He personally inspired spiritual men and women to learn many of the most important things that He wants people to know, and then directed the writing of that information. The proofs of the Bible's heavenly authorship are many, but maybe none are more evident than simply examining its authors' lives...they spent their time being separated through prayer, and proving the Word through study and firsthand experience!

This leads us to a second point; the Bible is not only provable, it is also profitable. The principles of the Bible work and serve as more than just a general instructional manual with which to merely advance ourselves or teach others. All true men of God learn quickly how well God's holy Word can size them up and teach them what they specifically need to learn. As with those who wrote the Bible, it proves itself to those who venture into its pages with an open heart to its genuine author. It will persuade you, convict you, correct you and teach you the nature of what is good and right. From there we learn to look for what is truly God in all things and not to be deceived by things that only look good.

The Bible does not always teach you exactly what to do, but it does teach you how to think from a properly framed spiritual perspective. In this way God completes and equips us to do what He calls forward for each "man of God". The Bible trains you to know Him and yourself well enough to properly introduce Him to those who don't...especially as it gets harder and harder to be sure!

NOVEMBER 9...DAY 313
THE WOMAN TO FIND AND THE WIFE
TO FOLLOW

"Who can find a virtuous wife? For her worth is far above rubies.
The heart of her husband safely trusts in her; so he will have no lack of gain. She
does him good and not evil all the days of her life."
Proverbs 31:8-12 NKJV

Just as we have discussed the subject of being a "man of God" with a view toward Christian leadership in general, now I want to mention the virtues of a godly woman for the same purpose. My hope is that by looking at leading spiritual qualities through the eyes of both genders, everyone will be able to recognize godly leadership as they see it developing in themselves and others.

Our subject today is either the description of Solomon, or another king, who had a divine revelation. If it was Solomon as some suppose, then according to his history with women it seems he may never have found his own version of this wife! Yet because of his great wisdom, he certainly knew what to look for and passed those qualifications on to us. Also the author is said to be passing along the wisdom given to him by his mother (verse 1); so it is actually written from the perspective of both a woman who knew women, and the man who learned to follow a godly mother!

Anyone with a good mother knows first-hand that women are made in the image of God, just like men. Remember too that in heaven there is neither male nor female. You can receive what the Lord sends your way, in either package! When it comes to leadership in the kingdom of God, we should be smart enough to choose godly over ungodly regardless of gender differences. One only has to consult the Bible to find that God used women like Deborah to lead His own people and blessed others like the Queen of Sheba, who recognized His authority in Solomon.

This is a good combination to remember when seeking to find the Lord's direction in any area. He will use whom He chooses for His own purposes, at His own times, whether we understand and accept it or not! Don't get hung up on outward distinctions at the expense of your spiritual discernment and well-being. Although Adam was the leader in the Garden, Eve showed instant leadership ability when it came to the first case of difficult decision-making. Although she chose wrongly, it was because of her error in communication, not lack of skill!

In Proverbs 31, we see another kind of woman who leads valiantly because of a higher understanding of God's overall plan. If you are a man, don't be afraid to follow this kind of godly woman when necessary and please don't fail to find her in a wife if you still have a choice…for the sake of the Christian Church everywhere!

NOVEMBER 10…DAY 314
SUPERWOMAN

"Who can find a virtuous wife? For her worth is far above rubies.
The heart of her husband safely trusts in her; so he will have no lack of gain.
She does him good and not evil all the days of her life."
Proverbs 31:10-12 NKJV

Beginning in verse ten, there are twenty-two verses in this chapter which form an alphabetic acrostic. That means each letter of the Hebrew alphabet is used to begin a verse in describing attributes that make a woman "virtuous" in the eyes of the Lord. This is similar to the way Psalm chapter 119 is outlined, except that there each letter serves as a poetic title for an eight-verse combination of thoughts. This kind of noticeable highlight, arranged in a way for us to more easily remember, should compel us to look more deeply into what is written expecting to find God's nuggets of insight!

Hebrew is a language that blends both eastern and western concepts and is designed to contain multiple layers of meaning. Not only do words often have both phonic and pictographic values, but each letter in a word also has its own meaning, which can further enhance its overall meaning! For that reason this particular topic should be recognized as holding a very special place in scripture.

It is interesting that God's emphasis on women is expressed much like a woman; veiled, yet strong and deep. Women have a prominent place in God's economy and should be studied far beyond what we are able to discuss here. But then again, any real man knows that women are special in their makeup without reading it in Hebrew! The kind of woman described in these verses, who knows how to conduct her life according to God's purposes, is very special indeed...to God, men, and other women!

"Virtuous" here could be translated as a "wife of valor," in the sense of exhibiting all forms of excellence. Her "worth" is immediately compared in value to the level of precious jewels, telling us she is in demand as a result of the developed sense of maturity her superior finish reveals. In fact, "rubies" or "pearls," (depending on which facet of meaning you take from the Hebrew word used) are far below the time-processed "mother lode" God is describing. She can simultaneously hold her husband's heart and help cause him to prosper, while treating him better than other men's wives, maybe especially when he doesn't deserve it...and doing it all for a lifetime!

King David look out, when God creates a woman after His own heart, she just may be the real power behind the kingdom!! The most amazing thing I have seen about God shining through the life of a true godly woman is her ability to truly reflect and give God all the glory...a true picture of Christ's bride (church) at His coming!

NOVEMBER 11...DAY 315
A WOMAN WITH A HIGHER PURPOSE

"Who can find a virtuous wife?...She seeks wool and flax, and willingly works with her hands. She is like the merchant ships, she brings her food from afar. She also rises while it is yet night, and provides food for her household, and a portion for her maidservants."
Proverbs 31:10a, 13-15 NKJV

Although the church is sometimes likened to a man in scripture (Ephesians 4:13), it is more directly pictured as a woman; the bride in preparation for Christ, her groom, awaiting His return (Ephesians 5:22-33).

When we scrutinize the virtuous wife in our text, it is important for us to remain aware of the weighty spiritual symbolism behind the practical description of this woman of God. Everything that makes a great female leader in everyday life also serves to outline how the Church is to effectively minister to and for the Lord! Each group of verses examined in this chapter are clues about how to become a better member of God's kingdom, and a better leader in it.

Today, our woman of God is pictured as a lady who is willing to care for her household by working with what she has at her disposal. Beyond that, she doesn't just wish for the finer things of life for her family, she "seeks" out those things she needs and finds ways to acquire them even though others can't always figure out how! Her attitude is one of faith and determination. By getting up early she goes to bed satisfied...because her entire family and staff are taken care of and thus everything in her household functions at high levels of efficiency. Her willingness to go the extra mile is contagious, causing a reciprocal effect and creating a climate of care and cooperation. She makes everything and everyone around her better!

Of course this attitude will work for anyone who employs it, but it seems to be a special quality that women have inherently received from God at creation. Watching my wife handle pregnancy, give birth to a child and be immediately willing to do it again, is proof of what I am saying here! My wife's sacrificial courage did something that automatically made me more willing to do whatever necessary to take care of them! This also portrays the ability the Church has to build itself and change things around it. The perfect illustration of this is found in Ephesians 4:16: "...according to the effective working by which every part does its share, causing growth of the body for the edifying of itself in love."

Like this virtuous woman, the Body of Christ (Church) has an uncanny ability to create its own momentum by pulling all of its resources together in order to fulfill a higher purpose...an especially important picture of the work of prayer that is so necessary for us in preparation for the return of the Lord.

NOVEMBER 12...DAY 316
A WOMAN OF SOME MEANS

"Who can find a virtuous wife?...She considers a field and buys it; from her profits she plants a vineyard. She girds herself with strength, and strengthens her arms. She perceives that her merchandise is good, and her lamp does not go out by night."
Proverbs 31:10a, 16-18 NKJV

When I read this particular section of scripture describing the entrepreneurial nature of a godly wife, it reminds me of several other outstanding passages in the Bible. As I have said before, there are many layers of meaning within the terminology of God's word. I believe this woman represents more than just the model female or exemplary "helpmate" for a godly man. She is also a picture of the people of God as a whole, and therefore her depiction contains many principles from which we gain an idea of how believers should collectively conduct their business in this world.

According to His own words in Luke 19:13, a courageous church must "occupy" until Jesus comes by trading with and using the resources it has particularly been given. Notice, this woman buys a field, after weighing its value, and adds it to her overall portfolio.

This is exactly what the Lord was talking about in the "parable of the pounds," where He instructed his servants to "buy and sell" for the purpose of increasing His investment in them while He is away on a distant (heavenly) journey. Here our virtuous woman has the wisdom to use what she has, not only to care for her family, but also to create long-term wealth as an opportunity arose. By purchasing the field she is able to plant a vineyard, producing grapes which in turn will create a source of income.

This reminds me of Jesus' words in Matthew 13:44 where He likens the kingdom of God to a treasure hidden in a field. The person who discovers it is willing to sell everything he has to buy the entire field because the treasure itself is worth far more than the ground it is buried in! God's Spirit has been hidden inside His people as a result of what Jesus has done for us on the cross. It is our responsibility to use the resources of the Spirit to further the expansion of God's kingdom. Jesus is coming back one day to fully restore God's kingdom on this earth and it is our job to sell ourselves out, so we can fully buy into the part of that which has been buried inside us as the Church. The "virtuous woman," like the chosen last days remnant of God's people, doesn't let her lamp get low on oil because she knows the true value of the "goods" she has acquired!

NOVEMBER 13...DAY 317
THE ALL-AROUND GIRL

"Who can find a virtuous wife?...She perceives that her merchandise is good, and her lamp does not go out by night. She stretches out her hands to the distaff, and her hand holds the spindle. She extends her hand to the poor, yes, she reaches out her hands to the needy. She is not afraid of snow for her household, for her household is clothed with scarlet. She makes tapestry for herself; her clothing is of fine linen and purple. Her husband is known in the gates, when he sits among the elders of the land. She makes linen garments and sells them, and supplies sashes for the merchants."
Proverbs 31:10a, 18-24 NKJV

Notice again today that God's "illustrated lady" is strong, sharp and able to get things done! Her high quality goods allow her to acquire enough oil to keep her lamp burning through the night. This reminds me of Jesus' parable of the ten virgins in Matthew 25:1-13. Only half of them were able to keep their lamps burning in anticipation of the Hebrew bridegroom's customary late night bridal call. We are warned by this story to keep our vessels (hearts) filled with oil so we can watch in anticipation of Jesus' return. This woman uses her time wisely, keeping late hours not only to work hard, weaving clothing for her family and/or business, but also to watch over them in prayer (Matthew 26:41; Luke 21:36).

A godly woman is a resourceful person who has success in mind for her family and the entire kingdom of God. The Church thinks the same way, using any and every godly means to take care of its own responsibilities so it can also reach out by faith in God to touch others for the sake of its Master! Notice also that this woman is not afraid, she is prepared!

The term 'scarlet' referred to something that was double dipped in dye to achieve a thoroughly crimson color, but it also was used to describe clothes that were doubly lined. She wasn't concerned about the cold because she had made clothes for her family to wear on every occasion. I like this fearless picture of God's end-time Church. She prepares herself to be the Bride of Christ and is unapologetic for looking the part. Her family is warm, stylish and well known! So much so, that her husband is famous and elevated in his own position! She also has what other's want and is therefore able to sell her goods, and further, to supply merchants! She is the kind of mature woman the world really has to respect...the kind the Lord is in reality coming back for!

Rocky Veach

NOVEMBER 14...DAY 318
THE LEADING LADY

"Who can find a virtuous wife?...Strength and honor are her clothing; she shall rejoice in time to come. She opens her mouth with wisdom, and on her tongue is the law of kindness. She watches over the ways of her household, and does not eat the bread of idleness. Her children rise up and call her blessed; her husband also, and he praises her: Many daughters have done well, but you excel them all. "Who can find a virtuous wife?...Charm is deceitful and beauty is passing, but a woman who fears the LORD, she shall be praised. Give her of the fruit of her hands, and let her own works praise her in the gates."
Proverbs 31:10a, 25-31 NKJV

There has always been much debate within the Church as to whether women should be allowed the authority to lead. One thing you can't debate is the fact that anyone can lead by example! I tend to think that most women have too much "sense" to want to be a leader according to traditional definitions anyway. It requires giving up her position of strength; which would usually mean less overt influence. Does this "virtuous woman" of Proverbs seem to be anything less than a highly successful and influential person to you?! She exactly represents my point. I think she is an interesting illustration of the spotless Bride of Christ precisely because she is leading strongly from the shadows of her husband, just as we are to do "following" Jesus. She doesn't need a titled position to affect things around her, what quality of character she possesses does that quite naturally! Her strength and honor bring the rejoicing of victory into her future. In this way she reminds me of the armor of God found in Ephesians 6:13-18, which enables a believer to stand strong in the Lord. When she opens her mouth, genuine wisdom and kindness come forth, ensuring that goodness will return. Because she watches over her family, no time wasted, they all bless and praise her. The end result is her reputation for excellence and virtue...her name comes from the way in which she has consistently carried herself, not only before men but especially before God.

The Church's success is found in turning away from what non-virtuous women choose to do, charming and deceiving their way to the favor and control they seek. Instead of being enamored with our own beauty we must learn to fear the Lord. It is our humility and sincere preference of Him that wins us respect, and causes us to reap even the natural benefits of our spiritual efforts.

I love how the last phrase teaches us the goodness of God's nature...give your all for Him and the things He values, and He will give it all back plus some! Be a virtuous woman, wife and Christian...we will need every bit of His favor in the last days!

308

NOVEMBER 15...DAY 319
SUPPORT YOUR FAITH IN PRAYER

"Watch therefore, and pray always that you may be counted worthy to escape all these things that will come to pass and to stand before the Son of Man."
Luke 21:36 NKJV

"And the Lord said, 'Simon, Simon! Indeed, Satan has asked for you, that he may sift you as wheat. But I have prayed for you that your faith should not fail; and when you have returned to Me strengthen your brethren.' But he said to Him, 'Lord, I am ready to go with You, both to prison and to death.' Then He said, 'I tell you, Peter the rooster shall not crow this day before you will deny three times that you know Me.'"
Luke 22:31-34 NKJV

"Watch and pray, lest you enter into temptation. The spirit indeed is willing, but the flesh is weak."
Matthew 26:41 NKJV

As Christians our faith should be extremely important to us. It is a highly valuable spiritual substance, being both the thing that can move our mountains and the thing we can't do without if we wish to be pleasing God (Mark 11:23; Hebrews 11:1-6).

The Bible warns us that in the last days many believers will fall away from the faith, and many people will literally die for fear of the things that will come upon the earth (Luke 22:26; 2 Thessalonians 2:3)! This is why our scriptural texts for today are so important. Since faith is something that can be measured, gained or lost, Jesus teaches us how to protect our faith in critical situations. We will need to be "watchful" in prayer in order not to fail in either the way Peter initially did or worse!

Notice three important aspects of staying alert in prayer. 1) It can cause a person's faith to not "fail." 2) It can keep us from "entering into" temptations. 3) It can help make a way of "escape" in tribulations and cause us to "stand."

You can clearly see all these aspects of prayer working in Peter's example. Because Jesus "stood in the gap" or interceded before God on behalf of Peter, he eventually escaped Satan's clutches; even though he first fell to the pressure of saving himself, and sinned by denying the Lord! Peter could have listened to his Master, and prayed himself with Jesus in the garden of Gethsemane. Prayer will play a critical role in aiding any Christian to stand faithfully in the last days. Yet, in the modern Church world we have slipped in our understanding of how key prayer is every day!

The only way to be "ready" is to get ready now. Don't continue sleeping like Peter and his fellow disciples when Jesus invited them to pray with Him. Instead, let's make our stand with Jesus day after day in the preparatory school of prayer...in anticipation of His greatest Day!

NOVEMBER 16...DAY 320
GET A RELATIONAL CHECK-UP

"Be subject to one another out of reverence for Christ (the Messiah, the Anointed One)... Wives be subject (be submissive and adapt yourselves) to your husbands as a service to the Lord...Husbands, love your wives, as Christ loved the church and gave Himself up for her...This mystery is very great, but I speak concerning [the relation of] Christ and the church."
Ephesians 5:21, 32 AMP

"For if a man does not know how to rule his own household, how is he to take care of the church of God...that you may know how people ought to conduct themselves in the household of God, which is the church of the living God, the pillar and stay (prop and support) of the Truth. And great and important and weighty, we confess, is the hidden truth (the mystic secret) of godliness."
1 Timothy 3:5, 15, 16 AMP

The Church is built upon relationships, which is why Satan works so hard to destroy them! When believers and ministers lose their testimony because of relational issues, the world loses much of its visible distinction between darkness and light. Today, this problem demands your recognition and response, or the spiritual disease of apathy can grow around your life and affect you as well. Deciding to love one another, on purpose, with God's help and according to His standards, is the secret to fighting for the very heart of the Christian faith. History proves that a healthy church always leads to an expansion of the saved world!

Let's look at a general biblical order of fellowship which is outlined for us in the above scriptures. Following it will help us improve our relationships on every level. First, we must allow our souls to become "tied" to God, through personal communion with Him. This keeps us from improperly relating to others and building co-dependent tendencies with people in the flesh. Through Bible-based reflection and decision-making, both our conscious and subconscious minds become transformed into thinking and acting like God, rather than being subtly conformed to the general thought processes of a world in conflict with Him.

Most Christians today do not ask themselves the right questions. Is what or how you are thinking in line with the mind of Christ or the mind behind the system in which you live?! The next level of relationship is built within our families. The marriage bond in particular is described in the Bible as the real measure of authenticity for the believers. This is where that mysterious heavenly connection with the Lord is to be specifically lived out as an earthly picture before the culture around us. This secret link between marriage and Christianity cannot be overlooked or taken as mere symbolism. It is the real "litmus-test" of what you really believe! Third, after family, comes our fellowship with the true Christian community. If we are healthy in the first two areas, the church becomes a place of freedom, fulfillment and fruition. If not, believers lapse into mere traditional church methodologies, which carry little true spiritual expression. Finally, there are those friendships we have outside the kingdom of heaven. It seems today we have nearly arrived to the point of no return! So many believers are tired of pretending to be something they were never meant to be, and unbelievers are tired of the religious nonsense Christians have expected them to adhere to! I welcome the day that boils everything down to what is simply true and false. When interacting with others, that is what all genuine souls seek in one another.

You can see how our scoring in this last level depends on the first three for an influence that will enable us to reflect the life, light and love of God to lost humanity. Now is a good time to check your relational health. Make sure you are in the right condition to handle your preparations for Jesus return!

NOVEMBER 17...DAY 321
QUALIFIED TO SERVE GOD

"Be subject to one another out of reverence for Christ (the Messiah, the Anointed One)... Wives be subject (be submissive and adapt yourselves) to your husbands as a service to the Lord...Husbands, love your wives, as Christ loved the church and gave Himself up for her...This mystery is very great, but I speak concerning [the relation of] Christ and the church."
Ephesians 5:21, 32 AMP

If we can successfully follow the teachings and example of Christ in our marriages, then we can also advance them in society. Marriage is quite literally a physical illustration to the world of the ultimate spiritual relationship Jesus died to make possible with humanity. It is referred to in this passage as a very mysterious and awesome principle, which demands the Church's attention, for the sake of its surrounding social order.

During the twenty-eight years of my "born-again" life, the primary assault being waged against the church has been in this area. It has become so common to hear of pastors and ministers who have lost their ministries because of marital problems that nobody is surprised today, even when it affects someone close to them! The latest statistics I have looked at report that 53% of the marriages in our nation end in divorce. That's the good news! Christians divorce each other at a rate of 54%! How can sinners understand Jesus while His saints remain such a pathetic representation of commitment to His instructions? Call me old fashioned, but I can't go for that. My wife and I have been married for over twenty-seven years. We have had good times and bad, with a near miss separation right in the middle. But for the grace of God, we or any other couple reading this article, could have experienced a tragic ending to our marriage and the loss of 'ministry destiny' that goes along with it.

According to 1 Timothy 3:2 & 11, marriage is one major 'proving ground' that qualifies believers to stand as servants and overseers in what God is doing in the earth. We are going to be tested there and graded before we are given fuller measures of heavenly blessing with regard to our anointing and influence. Therefore, the goal must be to persevere and grow in the area of our marital relationships.

The Holy Spirit is calling us to accountability on this subject today and warning us to take responsible action. It is time to rise up out of our mentality of convenience and take a little spiritual inventory, one person at a time, one couple at a time, one house at a time and one church at a time! Listen to the prophetic warning that is being sounded about the dangers of losing the last remnants of what we call "American family" values. Believers must reinforce their faithfulness to both God and each other...BEFORE the coming separation of wheat and tares!

NOVEMBER 18...DAY 322
THE COLD, HARD FACTS

"And because lawlessness will abound, the love of many will grow cold. But he who endures to the end shall be saved."
Matthew 24:12-13 NKJV

What can happen when we fail to keep our faith and relationships tied together in Christ is more than obvious in the church world of today. How many times have we heard the following story rehashed since the late 1980's? A local pastor along with his wife and family complete their training, either under another ministry or in a Bible school, and launch out into a city to start a new church. After many years of hard work, an unforeseen learning curve and then positive growth, this couple begins to feel satisfied with their level of success but unsatisfied with each other. The marriage has often subtly been on 'autopilot' for much of that time because of all the other seemingly more pressing needs. While the wife begins to move further into the ministry background and more involved with her children or other interests, the pastor, in a "King David - Bath-Sheba" moment relaxes his guard for a season, secretly wondering what life could be like with someone else. By allowing his unchecked thoughts to become distractions, his eyes begin to secretly wander until the ever-present "Bath-Sheba" is found in some department of ministry just outside his direct oversight, yet under his control. Distraction becomes curiosity, which becomes obsession and we all know what happens next! It isn't long before the man of God and the pretty young piano player with such potential, have jetted off to yet another city for a poor replay of the first twenty years of this man's ministry! The shocking announcement is made on a Sunday morning by the dazed associate pastors to the grief stricken church membership. The man's wife and children are severely damaged and the board of elders still has no idea how they didn't even realize that anything was wrong. Sound familiar?

This next true-life story didn't! When a friend told me, it took me into a whole new dimension of awareness of just how embarrassingly passive and spiritually retarded whole sections of the modern church world really are! One Sunday morning, in a large church somewhere in the Bible belt region of America, a pastor suddenly announced that he would be divorcing his wife and remarrying. With that, from the side of the stage, a woman appeared holding a baby, and was introduced as the pastor's fiancé along with their newborn child! He then closed the announcements for that morning by stating that anyone having a problem with his new arrangement could find another church to attend if they wished...but that he will be back in the pulpit the following week to conduct services as usual. The story ends with a full church that next Sunday!

Beware of becoming either the blind who lead or those who follow blind guides...the culvert is closer than ever as we near Jesus' return!!

NOVEMBER 19...DAY 323
3 LEVELS OF MARRIAGE

"...as being heirs together of the grace of life, that your prayers may not be hindered."
1 Peter 3:7 NKJV

In his book "The Distinctively Christian Marriage," Dr. Paul Olson lists three basic models of marriage, which can be inferred from scripture.

Using the illustration of mountain climbing as a description of the marriage relationship, he pictures these as plateaus or peaks along the way. From a distance we see the great snow capped peak representing the perfect marriage, but along the climb we hit these different levels of experience, which change our perspective of the goal and challenge our resolve to continue moving upward.

The first level of marriage is the "ME-CENTERED" category. Most marriages never progress past this plateau. Even Christian couples often decide that it is simply too much work to keep climbing past selfishness and personal gratification. The result of camping out at this level is often settling for a hopeless future of unhappiness and disappointment or worse, divorce. The secret to overcoming a "level one," "Me-Centered" marriage is to surrender our personal marital demands and abandon our use of controlling methods to get what we want. Selfishness destroys your intimacy with your spouse, and directly contradicts the biblical model of marriage.

At "level two" the category is referred to as "WE-CENTERED." In an interesting twist of events, many couples get trapped on this plateau not realizing that they haven't arrived at the peak. Because it is higher than the selfish level, partners who live in this model of marriage are easily deceived into thinking that they have "arrived." In reality, what they have done is simply settled for a common, ordinary, and average marriage. Everything serves the "couple" and their interests.   Family is given high priority, and personal desires have given way to the higher ideal of revolving around those with whom we are vitally connected. The problem is that real communication and problem solving are never totally achieved. The couple has only settled into a place of "joint-satisfaction," which still falls far short of God's model and plan for intimate relationships.

Finally, at "level three" we can achieve a distinctively Christian, "GOD-CENTERED" marriage relationship. At this point, three particular things begin to happen. First, our marriages become a living parable to the world of Jesus' powerful relationship with His Bride, the church. Second, our children begin to participate in this parable, living in and around the virtues of a godly environment on a daily basis. Thirdly, both partners experience this living parable and find an unending source of fulfillment flowing from the Holy Spirit through the relationship with their mate. Christianity has a breathtaking view from this perspective. Here we discover an endless array of peaks and levels of enjoyment for us to continue to pursue and explore.   We can also look back and appreciate what we have come through, and use our experiences to help others who are climbing behind us.

NOVEMBER 20...324
SINGLE, SINCERE AND SIMPLE

"Oh, that you would bear with me in a little folly-and indeed you do bear with me. For I am jealous for you with godly jealousy. For I have betrothed you to one husband, that I may present you as a chaste virgin to Christ. But I fear, lest somehow, as the serpent deceived Eve by his craftiness, so your minds may be corrupted from the simplicity that is in Christ. For if he who comes preaches another Jesus whom we have not preached, or if you receive a different spirit which you have not received, or a different gospel which you have not accepted-you may well put up with it!...For you put up with fools gladly...for you put up with it if one brings you into bondage, if one devours you, if one takes from you, if one exalts himself, if one strikes you on the face." 2 Corinthians 11:1-4, 19-20 NKJV

Hidden in this passage on the dangers of deception in a local church is the key to remaining free from its subtle influences. Paul uses the word, "simplicity" to describe the normal condition of a believer's mind who is in proper relationship with Christ.

The Greek word, "haplotes" has various shades of meaning, which help us to gauge our thinking. To be "simple" in this sense does not mean to be intellectually slow or retarded in emotion but rather to exercise, "singleness, sincerity and generosity." In fact, these exact ideas are conveyed in different places in the New Testament, as this same word is translated in alternative ways. For example, Romans 12:8 tells us to "give with liberality;" while 2 Corinthians 1:12 says to, "conduct ourselves in the world in simplicity and godly sincerity," both using "haplotes."

At the same time, Colossians 3:22 uses it in commanding us to honor and obey those in authority over us, "not with eye service as men pleasers, but in singleness of heart, fearing God." Simplicity literally means the "virtue of one who is free from pretence and hypocrisy." It describes the condition of a believer who's selfless; open-heartedness manifests itself in their generosity.

To the apostle Paul, this spiritual quality was a vital and advanced Christian disposition. It is an attitude we assume when we "put on" Christ and the new spiritual life we receive as a result of our intimate relationship with Him (Ephesians 4:22-24; Colossians 3:10). It was also a protection from other harmful forces and ideologies which creep into churches.

So, just remember this in your preparation for Jesus' return - if simplicity protected believers then from a spirit around people and things that acted and sounded like Jesus but wasn't...it will keep you from accepting dirty, cheap and hollow imitations of Him on that day!

NOVEMBER 21…DAY 325
KEEP IT SIMPLE STUPID

"Oh, that you would bear with me in a little folly-and indeed you do bear with me. For I am jealous for you with godly jealousy. For I have betrothed you to one husband, that I may present you as a chaste virgin to Christ. But I fear, lest somehow, as the serpent deceived Eve by his craftiness, so your minds may be corrupted from the simplicity that is in Christ. For if he who comes preaches another Jesus whom we have not preached, or if you receive a different spirit which you have not received, or a different gospel which you have not accepted-you may well put up with it!...For you put up with fools gladly...for you put up with it if one brings you into bondage, if one devours you, if one takes from you, if one exalts himself, if one strikes you on the face." 2 Corinthians 11:1-4, 19-20 NKJV

I was recently conducting a series of church meetings. One morning, just as I awoke, the Lord said to me, "Keep it simple, stupid." I remembered the phrase as a quote given in a motivational speech somewhere but this was a personal word intended to help me assist this particular group of people. I immediately remembered the above scripture and thought about the ramifications of leading a simplistic spiritual life. As we have discussed before, this term refers not to one who is stupid, but to a spiritually open and mentally uninhibited or sincere attitude before God. In opposition to a carnal, self-seeking mindset which readily serves its own interests, simplicity is a position of dependency on God in all things. God reminded me to remind His people that Christians are to remain in this state, not as a matter of helpless irresponsibility but rather out of a need for the constant transformation that comes as a result of leaning their entire personalities upon Him and His Word.

Today, I want you to notice how important the spiritual attitude of "simplicity" is, by highlighting what the Bible says it will protect us from. First of all, it will keep you clean and ready to meet the Lord as a legitimate member of His Bride, the Church. Second, simplicity will keep you from falling into error as a result of the personal deceptions our crafty enemy concocts to corrupt our thinking, even within our local churches! Third, it will keep you sharp with regard to knowing Jesus and recognizing the spirit and accuracy of His words. Finally, simplicity is the remedy for discerning foolishness in ministry and drawing the line in fellowship with questionable people.

The world thinks our faith is too elementary and religion makes it too complex. The Bible states that God calls us to simplify life in order to accurately follow Him. Keep your mind on Jesus. He will get you ready to meet Him when He comes. It's as simple as that!

NOVEMBER 22...DAY 326
BRAID YOUR VISION

"The eye is the lamp of the body. So if your eye is sound, your entire body will be full of light. But if your eye is unsound, your whole body will be full of darkness. If then the very light in you [your conscience] is darkened, how dense is that darkness!"
Matthew 6:19-25 AMP

The same Greek word for "simplicity" found in 2 Corinthians 11:3 we've discussed the past couple of days, is used here in our text for today as well. "Haplous" translated "sound" in verse twenty-two is actually a root from which the previous word "haplotes" is derived. It speaks of something that has been "intertwined or braided together" so that multiple pieces become a single entity. In this state, a thing is seen as being whole in a practical sense, or healthy and clear in a figurative sense.

Catholic bishop, Francois Fenelon said in his book, "The Seeking Heart" (page 156), "Simplicity is hard to define...it is better to practice it than to know how to define it." As much as I agree with that, I also believe there is something really important to be gleaned by looking deeper into the definition of Christian simplicity. By doing so, our conscience can become an unclouded and safe guide that will allow the light of God to illuminate the way for us (welcoming the Holy Spirit's leading) until Jesus returns.

Notice in our text for today how the word "sound" is used in contrast to the word "unsound." The latter is literally used of Satan as THE evil one in Matthew 13:19 and implies the hurtfulness that results from the influence of his guilty, calamitous and malicious ways! By this connection alone we can see that Jesus is defining simplicity as His own divine nature, which is available to all those who intertwine themselves with the Holy Spirit in His Words.

Romans 16:19 tells us, "to be wise in what is good and simple concerning evil." In taking this spiritually simplistic approach, Paul promises in the next verse that, "the God of peace" will take up our cause "crushing Satan" under our feet. In short order our cause will become His cause and the grace of our Lord Jesus will become ours!

I believe the depiction is of the Hebrew betrothal process. After taking four cups of wine throughout the process of covenanting to marry, the couple then crushes the wine glass under their feet at the end of the wedding celebration. This is symbolic of the fact that their relationship is exclusive and no others will be allowed between them. So it is with us after we believe. We, as the Bride of Christ, "simply" walk out the transformational process of our covenant with God, and then HE takes up our cause to crush every evil influence under OUR feet! Our authority works together with and under His until our Christian experience is one of total peace and grace.

NOVEMBER 23…DAY 327
HIGH DEFINITION SIMPLICITY

"Do not gather and heap up and store up for yourselves treasures on earth,…But gather and heap up and store for yourselves treasures in heaven,…for where your treasure is, there will your heart be also. The eye is the lamp of the body. So if your eye is sound, your entire body will be full of light. But if your eye is unsound, your whole body will be full of darkness. If then the very light in you [your conscience] is darkened, how dense is that darkness! No one can serve two masters; for either he will hate the one and love the other, or he will stand by and be devoted to the one and despise and be against the other. You cannot serve God and mammon (deceitful riches, money, possessions, or whatever is trusted in). Therefore I tell you, stop being perpetually uneasy (anxious and worried) about your life…"
Matthew 6:19-25 AMP

There are several similar words used in the New Testament, which are somewhat interchangeable within the Christian idea of "simplicity." Each lends different shades of meaning to the overall concept and thus gives us fuller understanding. Let's look at four of them today.

First our word from yesterday, "haplous," which is translated "sound" in verse twenty-two, literally means to "braid together." Then second, please notice three of its Greek synonyms, "akakos," "adolos," and "akeraios."

"Akakos" is translated as "simple" in Romans 16:18 and "harmless" in Hebrews 7:26. In 1 Peter 2:22 you will find, "adolos" translated as "sincere." And "akeraios" is the word "harmless" both in Matthew 10:16 and Philippians 2:15 and also, "simple" in Romans 16:19.

In researching the definition of this first word "haplous," I found a very interesting paragraph in "Strong's Exhaustive Concordance of the Bible," which sums them all up and makes this whole principle begin to stand out as if in "high definition." On page 34 of the "Greek Dictionary of the New Testament," under number 573 in the center column, it says this: "This word (haplous) means 'simple, single' and is used in a moral sense in Matthew 6:22 and Luke 11:34, said of the eye; 'singleness' of purpose keeps us from the snare of having a double treasure and consequently a divided heart. As the akakos has no harmfulness in him, and the adolos no guile, so the akeraios no foreign mixture, and the haplous no folds within which to hide something."

It may all sound like "Greek" to you now, but if you think through what the Bible is teaching us here about the essence of Jesus Christ's nature within us, it will begin to clear things up and help you see how to braid the loose ends of your Christianity together and simplify your life!

NOVEMBER 24...DAY 328
3 ENEMIES OF GOD'S WORD
#1 TRADITIONS

"For the word of God is living and powerful, and sharper than any two-edged sword, piercing even to the division of soul and spirit, and of joints and marrow, and is a discerner of the thoughts and intents of the heart."
Hebrews 4:12 NKJV

"Then I turned to see the voice that spoke with me. And having turned I saw...One like the Son of Man...out of His mouth went a sharp two-edged sword,..."
Revelation 1:12-16 NKJV

Jesus Christ is defined for us as the living Word of God whose speech is a powerful spiritual weapon! In preparation to meet the Lord, every Christian needs to protect their relationship both with Him and their Bible in order to make sure God's sword is working for them, not against them!

Let's start by looking at three things to avoid, each of which will directly affect the way He works in your life: 1) Traditions, 2) Worldliness and, 3) Fawning. Today, we'll take on enemy number one, the "traditions of men."

According to Mark 7:8, attaching a religious and legalistic mindset to God's commandments for our own comfort and control render what God says to us ineffective. By adding increased significance to the ways they went about obeying God, the Pharisees were actually changing the meaning of His Word. We must beware of the little controlling religious leaders in us all if we want to remain spiritually sharp.

Jesus caught the religious world of His day by surprise and He will probably return to a similar set of circumstances among many of those who say they believe. So, what is the key to avoiding the pitfall of man-made traditions as a Christian? Jesus backed up His words on this occasion by using the written Word as his reference. Quoting Isaiah's prophecy of a coming religious hypocrisy, the Lord pointed out that saying one thing and doing another is the crux of this error. Attempting to worship God while not keeping their hearts engaged lead them to substitute their own teachings for God's commands in the instruction of His people. We humans are very natural at betraying ourselves, or saying but not doing, without even recognizing it! That is what this is, except on the higher level of leadership. Once we assume a position in God's Church and start religiously saying things without doing them, other people become deceived by our hypocrisy.

This makes me immediately think of a similar time in the future. The stage has been set for the Church to expect an end time turning away of believers from the faith. Both Jesus and Paul prophesied this (Luke 18:8, 2 Thessalonians 2:3), but how many will remember to keep their own hearts attached to their mouths so their acts will be in line with God's Word in that day?! The sharper God's Word is in your life, the more ready you and all who listen to you will be!

NOVEMBER 25...DAY 329
3 ENEMIES OF GOD'S WORD
#2 MISPLACED LOVE

"For the word of God is living and powerful, and sharper than any two-edged sword, piercing even to the division of soul and spirit, and of joints and marrow, and is a discerner of the thoughts and intents of the heart."
Hebrews 4:12 NKJV

"Then I turned to see the voice that spoke with me. And having turned I saw...One like the Son of Man...out of His mouth went a sharp two-edged sword,..."
Revelation 1:12-16 NKJV

After the "traditions of men," a second enemy to the sword of the Lord is the "love of the world."

In order to stay spiritually sharp a man must deal with the religious tendencies to dull down the truth of God's Word. Then he must address the temptations of the organized system which operates the human network outside of God's authority. Finally, a man will have to deal with his own desires concerning other people.

Today, let's deal with this second problem of worldliness. James, the physical brother of Jesus, says quite bluntly that whoever wants to be a "friend of the world makes himself an enemy of God" (James 4:4, 1 John, 2:16). The church today conforms more to the world than it does to its own traditions! I recently heard of one church that had perfected the 17 minute service. Talk about minimizing the spirituality...and they advertised it! This is today's fast food religion. It's the drive through method, have the Gospel your way, and hold the Jesus! We think we can produce a more consumer friendly version of the church by the world's design and don't even realize it!! This is a result of living too much of our lives by the standard and pace that the world system dictates. The buzz of its energy pulsates around us in nearly everything we do, television, internet, multiple forms of entertainment that set the stage for how we think and feel. Our appetites are whet with the sights, sounds and scent of everything and everyone else but what God is saying and doing! I want a church where Jesus is on display. I do not care if I stay there seventeen minutes or seventy straight days, as long as the LORD can again become the leader of our lifestyles.

When I was a young minister the Lord showed gave me a dream. I saw the Lord behind the pulpit and He said, "Live more godly, stop doing sports, and I will send the angels for you." What was he telling me? Start doing more of the things He loves most, stop doing the things that I love the most, so He can release His promises upon my life and ministry. I have been working on that ever since and might be still at it until Jesus comes. The purpose is to get my heart beyond myself.

The Word is the guide to what is "godly," the truest way to prepare ourselves for His return.

NOVEMBER 26…DAY 330
3 ENEMIES OF GOD'S WORD
#3 FEAR OF MAN

"For the word of God is living and powerful, and sharper than any two-edged sword, piercing even to the division of soul and spirit, and of joints and marrow, and is a discerner of the thoughts and intents of the heart."
Hebrews 4:12 NKJV

"Then I turned to see the voice that spoke with me. And having turned I saw…One like the Son of Man,…out of His mouth went a sharp two-edged sword,…"
Revelation 1:12-16 NKJV

The third thing that will dull down the sword of the Lord and make it ineffective in your life is the fear of man. In First Chronicles 21 we learn how dangerous it can be for a man of God to please himself or others before the LORD. Satan was able to make a stand against Israel by tempting David to take a census of the nation. In attempting to show his "manpower," David tempted God and received His wrath! We cannot fear what people are going to think about us or try to impress them with our cleverness!

In both Ephesians 6:6 and Colossians 3:22 the apostle Paul tells us to serve our authorities with sincerity of heart, "not with eye service, as MENPLEASERS," but in the fear of the LORD, as if we are serving Christ directly. This phrase refers to the act of positioning ourselves to look good in the sight of men, so we can court their favor.

The devil specializes in putting decoys around us and impostors above us to feed our need to be seen!

Over the years, I have noticed how he often easily sends them into local congregations to disseminate spiritual disinformation in order to trick us into sabotaging ourselves. By tempting church leadership to either do things God has not instructed, or to disobey the things he has, Satan seeks to create situations where the Church gets caught up in a systematic process of counting its blessings, rather than just counting on the Lord! Then the Lord Himself will oppose the pride of those who should have remained humbly favored.

I remember how once, as a young minister who didn't know any better, I was being interviewed for a "position" in a large church by two suspiciously arrogant elders. After displaying their power to appoint and dismiss personnel in that ministry, they finally asked me if I was ready for their questions. Realizing it was a set-up, I simply asked them if they were ready for mine?! I didn't get that position, but I also didn't get in the adverse position of opposing God, as they later did! In the eternally long run, it only matters what God thinks of you. So fear God and be serious about His Word, and it will remain sharp in your life. Anything less is risky!

NOVEMBER 27…DAY 331
THE PERFECT COMBINATION

"Behold, I send you out as sheep in the midst of wolves. Therefore be wise as serpents and harmless as doves. But beware of men, for they will deliver you up…But when they deliver you up, do not worry about how or what you should speak. For it will be given to you in that hour what you should speak; for it is not you who speak, but the Spirit of your Father who speaks in you."
Matthew 10:16-20 NKJV

The follower of Christ has a challenging assignment. Look at the specialized skills it requires. Like anything else in life, we will perform better if we know both what we are supposed to be doing and how we are supposed to go about it. Jesus did not leave the foundational approach to Christianity to our imagination. You can see in our text that He summed up His "call" for the twelve disciples after first empowering them for service, and then outlining their standard operating procedures. They were specifically authorized to deal with demons and diseases as they delivered Jesus' message for the kingdom of heaven. Their approach consisted of going to a specific people group, finding key people, and bringing the peace of God where they found fitting places.

According to verses seven and eight, they were called to be preachers, healers, cleansers, miracle workers, exorcists and givers. Where they were received they brought the blessing of the Lord Himself, but where they were rejected they released judgment by merely having been there! Jesus' synopsis in verse sixteen is that they were being given an assignment equivalent to sending sheep into the midst of wolves! Talk about a motivating halftime speech!! What an odd thing to say...unless you wanted to ensure that your "Christian team" took on the right attitude to help it complete the heavenly game plan! Because they had a serious spiritual opponent, Jesus emphasized their need to approach their job from the viewpoint of both God and the devil! This is why, after talking about sheep and wolves, He then uses serpents and doves to reinforce His point. In order to combat the adversity that malicious predators like wolves present, a sincere, trusting sheep in the Lord's service needs to rely on more than his own simplistic instincts.

Using the serpent, Jesus exposes the real enemy and teaches us how to outsmart the wolves in his service. Believers must remember at all times that they are not battling with flesh and blood, but with a spiritual snake (Ephesians 6:12)! Learning to think like a serpent, without becoming one, is what helped the early church stay focused on the purposes of God while overrunning the empire of psychotic Roman dictators. Their "perfect combination" of cunning wisdom and simple obedience kept them from either taking unnecessary risks or running from unavoidable ones! Stay ready and stay full of the Spirit to finish the race.

NOVEMBER 28...DAY 332
WORTHY TO RECEIVE?

"...for a worker is worthy of his food. Now whatever city or town you enter, inquire who in it is worthy, and stay there till you go out...if the household is worthy, let your peace come upon it. But if it is not worthy, let your peace return to you. And whoever will not receive you nor hear your words, when you depart from that house or city, shake off the dust from your feet."
Matthew 10:10-14 NKJV

It seems obvious by reading this chapter that both the Gospel message and its messenger are more effective where they are more readily received.

One distinction that must be made between this commissioning of the disciples and the one given after Jesus' resurrection is that they are sent to two different groups of people. Whereas at the "Great Commission" (Matthew 28:16-20; Mark 16:14-18) Jesus' disciples were sent to the "world" at large, here in Matthew ten they were sent specifically to the "lost sheep of the house of Israel" (verse 6). You will notice that in this context the world's standing with God is reckoned by their initial choice to either "believe" or "not believe" (Mark 16:16). However to God's people who are already supposed to believe, the litmus test is whether or not they "receive" (Matthew 10:14) who and what He sends to them.

This is a difference that is highlighted again and again throughout this chapter by the repeated use of the word, "worthy." This word "worthy" simply means "weighty, deserving or suitable" in the Greek language of the New Testament, with an emphasis on the value of a person or thing. Knowing this fact gives us a basis upon which to build healthy believers and churches now in the end of the Christian age.

It seems we are in a very similar setting with many lost sheep, as were the Israelites in Jesus' day. We need to know how to recover them, as well as continuing to reach the rest of the lost world.

The first thing to understand about God's concept of worthiness is that those who do believe in, receive and follow Jesus are accepted and valued by their developing level of association with Him. His disciples were reminded that they should reliantly trust God's provision before they were sent. Whomever they were sent to, on the other hand, were to be valued by the disciples according to whether or not they displayed a believing attitude by receiving them! Based on this value system Jesus' messengers decided where to stay, how long to stay there, and when to leave.

The Lord is using this same method when looking at the Church who has lost its first love, in our day. In order to receive Jesus properly in the last day, we need to become great retriever-receiver-believers today!

NOVEMBER 29…DAY 333
THE SACRIFICE WORTHY OF OUR KING

"...for a worker is WORTHY of his food. Now whatever city or town you enter, inquire who in it is WORTHY, and stay there till you go out...if the household is WORTHY, let your peace come upon it. But if it is not WORTHY, let your peace return to you...He who loves father or mother more than Me is not WORTHY of Me. And he who loves son or daughter more than Me is not WORTHY of Me. And he who does not take his cross and follow after Me is not WORTHY of Me. He who finds his life will lose it, and he who loses his life for My sake will find it."
Matthew 10:10-14, 37-39 NKJV

As I pointed out yesterday, Jesus' repeated use of a word should emphasize its importance to us. It should catch our attention when in this chapter we find the word "worthy" seven times! Each time it is the Greek word, "axios," meaning something that is valuable or "right on the ground of fitness." One of the criminals crucified with Jesus uses this same word in describing that he and his fellow offender were receiving their "due reward," whereas Jesus had done nothing wrong. It paints the picture of someone who is in a posture, ready to accept the consequences of their actions; either for having done something right or having done something wrong.

Coming back to our text, we see that Jesus is talking about the lost sheep of God's people having to choose between having a negative or positive reaction to the Gospel message He was sending to them through His disciples. Notice, they were being put in a position to "receive" something one way or the other. Because we live in a similar age as we draw near to Jesus' return, we are facing a similar set of circumstances. The advantage we have is that we can know ahead of time what is required of us. This means when the messengers of Jesus show up in your town or city you will be rewarded according to your acceptance or rejection of them! It is kind of like a pop quiz, neutrality is not an option! Knowing how to "receive" is key. Again, the Greek word means to "take with the hand," "grant access to" or "learn," with an emphasis on "having something offered to one."

What a privileged opportunity it truly is to have the Lord send someone to us with a message from Himself! This is why the end of Matthew ten adds an extra definition of this kind of "worthiness." In God's mind it means putting Him above the dearest things we cling to in this life! If we really want to be worthy of Jesus at His return, like Abraham we have to be willing to sacrifice all our family on the altar...starting with ourselves!

NOVEMBER 30...DAY 334
ADDITION BY SUBTRACTION

"Do not think that I came to bring peace on earth. I did not come to bring peace but a sword. For I have come to set a man against his father, a daughter against her mother, and a daughter-in-law against her mother-in-law; and a man's enemies will be those of his own household. He who loves father or mother more than Me is not WORTHY of Me. And he who loves son or daughter more than Me is not WORTHY of Me. And he who does not take his cross and follow after Me is not WORTHY of Me. He who finds his life will lose it, and he who loses his life for My sake will find it."
Matthew 10:34-39 NKJV

In the Jewish culture when a person turns from the Hebrew faith their family often excommunicates them, treating them as if they do not exist any longer even though they remain bodily alive! This being true, Jesus' words in this passage of scripture are not nearly as difficult for us to understand. A literal process of judgment was occurring to the nation of Israel at this time that they were largely unaware of. Their response to His presence and message, as their Messiah, was critical. When the Lord begins to move in our midst they, like us, were actually being used in many ways to determine their own fate!

Mark 4:24 informs us in the way God measures things, especially when it comes to listening to what He has to say. According to the scripture, Jesus said "...the same measure you use, it will be measured to you..."

It appears that the same rule used in that culture to deal with the issue of worthiness in the family unit was to be the one used to determine among them who would be fit for His family! Jesus was demanding the same level of adherence to Him from them!

In using the word "earth" in verse 34, which is better translated "land," He was referring to what He really came to do in Israel. Adam Clarke's Bible Commentary explains that they thought the Messiah would accumulate all temporal prosperity in the land of Judea at His coming. In reality, what all religious but unspiritual people have a hard time with is that Jesus was not bringing their idea of peace at all! He was bringing the sword of His Word, THE Truth, to expose, sift, analyze and judge the very purposes of their hearts (Hebrews 4:12 Amplified Bible)!

This was a time when it was critical to receive Him, His message and His messengers, because they had already been released in their land. The last days will produce a similar set of circumstances (Matthew 24:12), so we must be ready to make the kinds of choices that only some of them made...choices to add to our lives by subtracting from it, for Jesus' sake!

DECEMBER 1...DAY 335
YOU CAN'T OUTGUESS GOD

"Indeed, I myself thought I must do many things contrary to the name of Jesus of Nazareth. This I also did in Jerusalem, and many of the saints I shut up in prison, having received authority from the chief priests; and when they were put to death, I cast my vote against them. And I punished them often in every synagogue and compelled them to blaspheme; and being exceedingly enraged against them, I persecuted them even to foreign cities. While thus occupied, as I journeyed to Damascus with authority and commission from the chief priests, . . . along the road I saw a light from heaven, brighter than the sun, shining around me and those who journeyed with me. And when we all had fallen to the ground, I heard a voice

speaking to me and saying in the Hebrew language, 'Saul, Saul, why are you persecuting Me? It is hard for you to kick against the goads.' So I said, 'Who are You, Lord? And He said, I am Jesus, whom you are persecuting…"
Acts 26:9-15 NKJV

Don't ever think God can't save and use someone you think of as a lost cause. I'm convinced that's partially why the Apostle Paul was used so prominently in establishing the early church. He was such a complete "rule breaker" that he even changed his own name to emphasize the life-changing power he encountered in the name of Jesus!

Here we see how the Lord took someone who was authorized by the religious establishment of his day and, after breaking him down, authorized him to build the very thing he had sought to destroy! Interestingly enough, this very passage of scripture is the transcript of Paul's rehearsing his own testimony before King Agrippa (Roman ruler of the land of Palestine). Talk about a statement on the power of authority! Jesus brought Paul before the highest authorities of his day, just as He promised He would.

This is a picture of Paul in action taking his promise, as opposed to just settling for God's provision. If you read Acts 9:15 you find out that the Lord promised to use him specifically as a "chosen vessel" to, "bear My name before the Gentiles, kings, and the children of Israel." Passion personified Paul having the kind of personality that had persecuted the church so ardently, was not about to accept anything short of fully finishing Jesus' instructions to now build it around the world.

When we are fully exposed to the Light of God, we will want to bear His name and the authority it carries. Anything less will not finish the task assigned to us in these last days…it is unworthy of Who He is!

DECEMBER 2…DAY 336
THE REAL THING

"For we are His workmanship, created in Christ Jesus for good work…"
Ephesians 2:10a NKJV

When I was a kid Coca-Cola was being challenged for its title as "the real thing" in the soda-pop world. Coke has become one of the biggest companies in the world, but there was a time when Pepsi was doing really well in the "taste tests." Under pressure Coke even changed its time-tested formula at one point, coming out with something called "New Coke." What a mistake it was when the "real thing" decided that the "real thing" wasn't good enough because they were seriously being challenged! After nearly discontinuing its main product, the company realized that people merely preferred

Pepsi in small doses but they didn't like it as much in larger doses. Even though Pepsi was defeating Coke in taste tests, it was not actually outselling it in the marketplace. When it came to drinking a whole soda, people wanted the "real thing" after all.

It reminds me of something a prominent television figure said recently. He related how as an aspiring actor he found himself with an offer in front of him to do a reality show instead of an acting role. Less than thrilled, he remembered an old drama teacher saying to him years earlier, "don't focus on HOW you are doing, you need to focus on WHAT you are doing." He realized his problem had been in always focusing on how he felt about what he was doing, which only sabotaged his ability to concentrate on doing what he did in whatever arena was available!

This is the same problem Coca-Cola had and the equivalent predicament we have in the Church today. In thinking so much about how we are doing, we end up losing touch with what the Lord wants us to do. In thinking too much about how other people think we're doing we overfeed our sense of self-awareness and destroy our ability to just relax and be who we are. The real key to success as a believer is achieving God consciousness. For a Christian "what" helps keep us focused on Jesus and removes the pressure to fulfill our own expectations.

The Church today has a hard enough job to do without adding the pressure of trying to do God's job! We have to reach people who aren't asking to be reached, so we have to make sure we're not a cheap substitute! Our best approach is to remain focused on WHO we are doing Christianity for...WHO we are doing it with...WHO's really doing it through us! He is the only one who really knows how the Church should operate, and how to direct us at any given time. If it is just us doing it, it's only a taste test...the world needs JESUS, He's the REAL THING!

DECEMBER 3...DAY 337
SHOULDA, WOULDA, COULDA!

"For therein is the righteousness of God revealed from faith to faith: as it is written, the just shall LIVE by faith."
Romans 1:17 NKJV

"For we WALK by faith, not by sight"
2 Corinthians 5:7 NKJV

"Not for that we have dominion over your faith, but are helpers of your joy: for by faith ye STAND."
2 Corinthians 1:24 NKJV

Notice the Bible says to, LIVE by faith, WALK by faith and STAND by faith."

I began to see a connection between these words early in my Christian life while attending Bible school. Later, while reading Watchman Nee's book, "Sit, Walk, Stand," I learned how Paul's letter to the Ephesians suggests a simple progression for the spiritual development of believers and churches. It is our spiritually "seated" (1:20; 2:6) position in Christ that enables us to "walk" (4:1) out His calling on this earth and successfully make our "stand" (6:10) against the forces of darkness. How fitting that a book, often hailed by biblical scholars as the greatest epistle because it lays out the great truths of "the faith," simultaneously teaches us to live and move from a position of "faith?!"

My point today is to remind you again that there is a right way to do Christianity and a wrong way. Not that we know everything or are faultless. In fact we all know very little and make many mistakes, but we can learn to trust the Lord more and more. That means acting like His word is true even we don't feel like living for Him, walking with His promises or standing firm in the name of Jesus! We can have problems and go through difficulties and help each other face challenges, but at the end of the day we've got to be the people that stand up and say, "But I am trusting God in everything...the God Who has all the answers and will do what He has promised!"

I want to encourage you to choose not to live with regrets. Let's not be people who have to keep turning around and saying, "I could have…if I would have…done what I should have." "Shoulda, Woulda, Coulda" is for those who choose not to exercise the courage to do what the Lord prescribes along the way. When we have to say those words we are really admitting that we could have stood strong in the Lord, if we had only walked more worthy of our calling, by doing what we should in living our lives each day for Him! The right way to build our Christian lives and churches is to reverse the regrets ahead of time by trusting God and looking to Him in everything, both big and small. When you read the parables of Jesus you find these to be the people who will be ready to meet Him at his coming!

DECEMBER 4...DAY 338
LIVING FOR THE LONG RUN
SHOULDA, WOULDA, COULDA! PT 2

"For therein is the righteousness of God revealed from faith to faith:
as it is written, the just shall LIVE by faith."
Romans 1:17 NKJV

"For we WALK by faith, not by sight"
2 Corinthians 5:7 NKJV

"Not for that we have dominion over your faith,
but are helpers of your joy: for by faith ye STAND."
2 Corinthians 1:24 NKJV

Live by faith, walk by faith, stand by faith. This is the natural progression of the Christian life. To live enables you to walk. To walk successfully before the Lord enables you to stand. You can not walk successfully unless you are firmly planted, unless you're resting and seated in those heavenly places that Ephesians 2:6 talks about. When you approach life from the perspective of belief in spiritual realities, you create an avenue for God's life to work through you. What you then do for other people becomes more effective. Once Jesus becomes your lifestyle, then anytime the enemy comes against you, you will find that you will be able to stand against his strategies for either your own demise or that of others around you.

The reason a lot of people aren't standing firm today and the Church seems so weak is because they have learned to speak "Christian" in the place of living it! Just take note of how many people are out doing what they want to do on any given Sunday morning instead of going to church. As a preacher, I notice this every time I travel to a service. Many are quick to mention what this says about the true condition of today's world but it tells us a lot more about ourselves. The outward condition of the world usually reflects the inward condition of the majority of God's children. It is the Church's responsibility to live by faith, yet many of us are out living just like the world, believing what they believe, participating in what they do and lowering the standard of who we really are! I often wonder just how many believers I pass on my way to church on a Sunday are people who no longer focus on the Lord because somewhere along the way they stopped "resting" in the Truth of what He has said.

There is a kind of person who rests and sits so firmly in the Lord, possessing so much spiritual essence that they have an overflow to give wherever they walk, of both life and strength. Anytime they encounter a need, they have an answer. Anytime the enemy comes against them they naturally begin to make a stand. Think of those first disciples and the way the Church originally took root. It didn't always look like they were successful, it didn't always look like they were going to overcome, but in the long run - and that is what Christianity is all about - you see that they always overcame…and had no regrets!

DECEMBER 5...DAY 339
AGAINST THE ODDS

"And there was a famine in the land, beside the first famine that was in the days of Abraham. And Isaac went unto Abimelech king of the Philistines unto Gerar. And the LORD appeared unto him, and said, Go not down into Egypt; dwell in the land which I shall tell thee of: Sojourn in this land, and I will be with thee, and will bless thee; for unto thee, and unto thy seed, I will give all these countries, and I will perform the oath which I swore unto Abraham thy father;..."
Genesis 26:1-3 KJV

The account of Isaac's obstacles in the 26th chapter of Genesis teaches us how to live for the Lord, even in the face of contrary circumstances. Again, if you live for the Lord, you'll walk for the Lord, if you walk for the Lord you'll stand for the Lord and there won't be any regrets in your life. You won't get to the end of your Christian life and say, "You know I sure could have done that if I would have done this, and I should have done that so I could have done something else." Shoulda, Woulda, Coulda...DON'T!

"Do not go down to the land of Egypt" is a phrase to remember. It would have been easy for Isaac to follow in Abraham's footsteps and gone straight to the "well-watered world of regrets" (Genesis 12) but God literally appeared to him to make it clear that he must stand and trust Him right where he was. As it turned out, Isaac still made some of his father's mistakes, just not this one.

We need to learn that God doesn't care about famine, and He doesn't care about distresses. God doesn't really even care about whether we would prefer not to be in distressing situations. He cares about you and me by promising to be with us in every situation...so we will stand our ground on the land He has given us!

In other words, God said to Isaac, "Have your life and your lifestyle in this land and watch what I do. I am going to do exactly what I spoke to your father Abraham that I would do." He was telling Isaac, "Just relax man, it's okay.

God could have gone on to say, "there was a famine before, there is a famine now, but you are going to have a descendent named Joseph, who will save the world from an even bigger famine later! I am going to be with you and with your people in all of them and I am going to bless you!"

Abimelech's name meant, "my father is king." His land, "Gerar," was God's lodging place for Isaac during this time because it spoke of His provision as a father, in the face of the circumstances and against all odds...exactly what we will need in the last days!

DECEMBER 6...DAY 340
THE WIFE PRINCIPLE

"And Isaac dwelt in Gerar: And the men of the place asked him of his wife; and he said, She is my sister...because she was fair to look upon. And it came to pass, when he had been there a long time, that Abimelech king of the Philistines looked out at a window, and saw, and, behold, Isaac was sporting with Rebekah his wife...and said, Behold, of a surety she is thy wife; and how saidst thou, She is my sister? And Isaac said unto him, Because I said, Lest I die for her. And Abimelech said, what is this thou hast done unto us? One of the people might lightly have lain with thy wife, and thou shouldest have brought guiltiness upon us. And Abimelech charged all his people, saying, He that toucheth this man or his wife shall surely be put to death."
Genesis 26:4-11 KJV

Over the years people have often thought that my wife and I were siblings. When you like somebody and you spend time with them, after awhile you can even start to look like them. I can imagine that if I was in the situation Isaac was in here I might also be tempted to say Bobbi was my sister, but I would rather keep her as my wife!

Isn't it funny how we can become so easily sidetracked by pressures and forget the most important things God has given us? Like Rebekah with Isaac, it is the people around us that are the true jewels in life. We forget their importance in our haste to protect our own interests.

Today, so many believers try desperately to have an individual Christianity, forgetting they have this same "wife" principle to protect! It is easy to remain separate as merely the brothers and sisters in Christ that we are, but only together can we become the Bride of Christ, walking out the full heavenly call God has given us. We cannot feign a false unity while finding ways through our own difficulties! God has so clearly demonstrated to us His willingness to fulfill the "family" promise.

By staying in the land that God had provided Isaac was actually at rest in the "recession." Abimelech was the Lord's provision and protection for them in a difficult season. He recognized Rebekah was Isaac's wife because he was laughing and playing with her, like only husbands and wives can do in the midst of such uncertainties!

Our "marriage" is also in trouble as Christians today, not because Jesus has forsaken us but because we have pretended to be something we're not! We have become so used to only being spiritual siblings that we have forgotten to enjoy being the Bride. This point is so important that God caused the least likely of characters to represent his own interests where Isaac and Rebekah were concerned...even making a law that no one could touch their marriage!!

DECEMBER 7...DAY 341
LIVIN' LARGE

"Then Isaac sowed in that land, and received in the same year a hundredfold: and the LORD blessed him. And the man waxed great, and went forward, and grew until he became very great: For he had possession of flocks, and possession of herds, and great store of servants: and the Philistines envied him... And Abimelech said unto Isaac, Go from us; for thou art much mightier than we...And he went up from thence to Beersheba. And the LORD appeared unto him the same night, and said, I am the God of Abraham thy father: fear not, for I am with thee, and will bless thee, and multiply thy seed for my servant Abraham's sake."
Genesis 26:12-16, 23-24 KJV

It is important to remember that back in verse three of this same chapter, God reminded Isaac of the "oath" He had given to Abraham. Then, you can begin to understand the abundance of blessings Isaac experienced even in the midst of a famine! Because God had already sworn to bless him as an heir to the covenant He had with his father, Isaac only needed to follow Abraham's faith and trust in the heavenly promise. Instead, when pressure came he started to follow his dad's signature weakness of trying to continually help God keep His word.

Always remember, faith is all about listening to God...it begins when we hear what He is saying and it grows as we act on what we understand to be His will. We, like Isaac, can try to do it our way but we will end up frustrated and risk endangering those with whom we should be jointly participating in God's promises! When we learn that God is the one "doing it" according to His own plans, we stop trying to achieve our anticipated outcome and leave it in His hands. This is how Isaac learned to trust God for himself.

Christianity is depicted in this story. Isaac illustrates Christ, the son and heir to the Father's promise. We as the church are "in Him," as was Jacob. Each successive generation has free access to the blessing of the original oath yet each must still be personally involved in the process of knowing God and exercising faith regarding what He has promised.

However, God's ultimate promise was greater than any symbolism. It was literally Christ Himself, the "seed," who would come through Abraham's family to save the world and multiply his faith in every nation! Isaac, in dealing with his mistakes by going back to the original place (Beersheba) where Abraham had dealt with his crisis of faith, set the stage to receive all God had for him as an heir to that promise. He quickly became a "great" and "mighty" man of riches and resources.

We are heirs to the same promise in Christ...let's believe that we will increase when things around us decrease, because we have chosen to die to our own ideas and live for the Lord's!

DECEMBER 8...DAY 342
TWO KINDS OF CHRISTIANS

"And He (Jesus) said, 'There was a certain man who had two sons; and the younger of them said to his father, Father, give me the part of the property that falls [to me]. And he divided the estate between them.'"
Luke 15:11-12 AMP

One of Jesus' greatest stories is this parable of the "prodigal son." Two sons are specifically mentioned, but it was only given this title by translators as a description of the younger son's character. The word, "prodigal" simply refers to one who spends money extravagantly or without necessity. The younger son was impulsive in asking for his inheritance prematurely, and then wasting it in loose and reckless living. There was also the older son who remained "faithful," and the parable in reality is equally about him.

If you read on in your Bible from our text today, you will find the first several verses are about the younger son's mistake, but the last several are about the older son's response. In between you see the heart of the father in his attitude toward both sons.

There are several levels to the symbolism in this parable. The father obviously represents God, but what about the sons? On an immediate cultural level, Jesus was speaking about the Gentiles to the Hebrews. But on a spiritual level, He is distinguishing between the lost and the found, the non-religious and the religious. There are some surprising twists to be learned here, but above all the point is, locating the true heart of the Father God in His children. Notice first that when the Prodigal son came back his father didn't even mention the money he had lost on him. You know why? God's not ultimately worried about money. He is concerned about the condition of our hearts and the bottom line of our salvation. When he saw his son coming back he said, "There's my son, now he has truly learned something. He sees life differently now; he's not the way he once was. Serve up the very, very best that we have." Why? Because God's best is always reserved for the homecoming...our realization of where home really is!!

Secondly, notice how Christians often react too much like the older brother at the moment when rejoicing is in order. "He is going to have to pay for that," was the religious mindset of the Pharisees and scribes, but they were far from God's perspective. The older brother represents the believer who has never physically left the fathers house…but has been missing in action for quite some time, spiritually! He thought he had never left, but his heart spoke volumes about where he had really been all along! We need to check our hearts today to make sure they can rejoice when God rejoices…if not we won't be ready when either our little brother comes home or when our big brother, Jesus returns!

DECEMBER 9…DAY 343
CELEBRATE GOOD TIMES

"Now the tax collectors and [notorious and especially wicked] sinners were all coming near to [Jesus] to listen to Him. And the Pharisees and the scribes kept muttering and indignantly complaining, saying this man accepts and receives and welcomes [preeminently wicked] sinners and eats with them. And he told them this parable…" Luke 15:1-3 AMP

Jesus actually shared three parables in a row in this chapter of the Bible. The first one is about lost SHEEP (verses 4-7), the second about SILVER coins (verses 8-10) and the third about two SONS of one father (verses 11-32). The thing they all have in common is that they speak to the issue of "rejoicing." The first two parables highlight the response of people who have found something of material value that had been lost, and compare it with the joy found in heaven over one sinner who repents. The final parable is that of the "prodigal son,' which illustrates the Father God's true delight in finding his lost sons.

All three teach us to us to echo the emotions of heaven, not the tendencies of those who have lost touch with it. Jesus is reminding us that our natural response to "recovery" is JOY! Yet churches today are often so dead in feeling and joyous sound because they have lost this missing ingredient of true spiritual life.

It makes sense when you consider that this chapter was spoken in response to religious leaders who "murmured" at the sight of many "wicked" sinners' willingness to listen to Jesus' words!

Take note of the different times words of joy are found here. It will help you know where joy comes from and how to harness it as a Christian. The closer we come to Jesus' return the more important it will be to "count it all joy" because we will be faced with increased "temptations" (see James 1:2).

In verses 5, 6, 7, 9 and 10, the words "rejoice" or "joy" are found five times. The Greek words used are from the same root, which simply defines a person's response when they are well…it shows in their happy emotions. Then in verses 24, 29 and 32 the words, "make merry," "music," "dancing" and "glad" are repeatedly found. These are similar expressions describing what happens when someone rejoices. They act on the outside like they feel on the inside!

In the third parable the only person who grumbled like the religious leaders was the older son who was envious of his brother's recovery. To him, it was more enjoyable to further the loss of his own brother than to join the party his father threw when he found him!

Verse twenty, on the other hand, tells us WHY God likes to throw such parties. His "compassion" teaches us that a heart that feels the right things celebrates the right things!

DECEMBER 10…DAY 344
THE ONE GOD GOES AFTER

"What man of you, if he has a hundred sheep and should lose one of them, does not leave the ninety-nine in the wilderness (desert) and go after the one that is lost until he finds it? And when he has found it, he lays it on his [own] shoulders, rejoicing. And when he gets home, he summons together [his] friends and [his] neighbors, saying to them, 'Rejoice with me, because I have found my sheep which was lost.' Thus, I tell you, there will be more joy in heaven over one [especially] wicked person who repents (changes his mind, abhorring his errors and misdeeds, and determines to enter upon a better course of life) than over ninety-nine righteous persons who have no need of repentance."
Luke 15:4-7 AMP

I know a guy who lost his watch on a whitewater rafting expedition, and found it a year later in exactly the same place in that river! Imagine his thrill in finding something so hopelessly lost. Sometimes, even a thing of lesser value seems so much greater when it is found after such a long and difficult searching process. This is what Jesus is trying to get us to see. We will willingly abandon everything else in life to search for one of our own sheep when they go missing, but we do not apply the same urgency to finding God's sheep. Notice how this earthly attitude is just the opposite of what goes on in heaven.

Remember the context in which these things were written. Jesus was talking to the who's who of the "church world" in His time. Today, the church is often so sanitary that we lose perspective in the same insanity! Everything can seem so religiously acceptable that we can easily forget we have lost anything. "Our" sheep seem to be gathered into many perfect little flocks, but we have forgotten that God has a different master list of who belongs to Him. Notice how the Lord uses the term "hundred" in scripture to represent a "full measure." He starts this parable presenting the "desert" as a hostile place we are happy and willing to go to in search of something "we" have lost. When we find it we happily take complete responsibility and ownership, putting it on our shoulders to return again through what we would otherwise consider to be "impossible" conditions on our way home! We then throw a party so "we" can fully enjoy "our" good fortune and share "our" struggles surrounded by the comfort of "our" friends.

Jesus doesn't reject our processes; He just reverses the reasoning behind it. The fact that we care so much about our own interests is what distresses God most! He sent His Son to this earthly wilderness to search for every last person lost in the wickedness of sin...when we realize He commenced this same rejoicing with our return to the Father, we truly find what we have lost!

DECEMBER 11...DAY 345
HIGH STANDARD SPIRITUAL LIVING

"Or what woman, having ten [silver] drachmas [each one equal to a day's wages], if she loses one coin, does not light a lamp and sweep the house and look carefully and diligently until she summons her [women] friends and neighbors, saying, Rejoice with me, for I have found the silver coin which I had lost. Even so, I tell you, there is joy among and in the presence of the angels of God over one [especially] wicked person who repents (changes his mind for the better, heartily amending his ways, with abhorrence of his past sins)."
Luke 15:8-10 AMP

Silver is valuable, but it does not compare with the worth of gold. This parable continues Jesus' lesson to the murmuring religious leaders of Israel who couldn't estimate the proper value of the spiritual "precious metals" around them! Remember how they complained in verse two of this chapter because He "received" and ate with the "sinners" who came to hear Him speak? This tells us much about why Jesus spoke to them, first in terms of sheep, then here in terms of money, and later about a father's sons. These were areas ministers in the Lord's service should be familiar with; being pastorally watchful, practically responsible and paternally concerned about His affairs. Jesus knew they weren't, as a whole, so He spoke to them about things that would challenge them, in language that required deeper thought, interest and action on their part.

This woman represents God's people, picturing them again as so diligent with regard to the things that are good, yet less than best. I read somewhere that silver is the last impurity that is removed from gold in the purifying process. When viewed this way, one can see how God sees so much of our earthly religious activity. Much of it is good. It often helps the poor, holds a moral standard in society and even leads many to the Lord, but it is still silver…a mere days' wages compared to God's eternal gold that can be found in the broken heart of ANY repentant human being! This is what Jesus was after in "receiving" those that religion had thrown away. He was reversing their rejection and giving them the access to God that many of the leaders of Israel had lost.

Make sure you don't get caught up in what I call, "spiritual day to day living." Working some system for God without serving His true interests is like living paycheck to paycheck. It will eventually catch up with you! Have an eternal savings plan instead. Spend your time on earth searching for God's golden, but more hidden, treasures…you will be a lot happier in this life and your rewards at Jesus' return will be enough to survive forever!

DECEMBER 12…DAY 346
YOU ARE THE CAST AND CREW!

"Now you [collectively] are the Christ's body, and [individually]
you are members of it, each part severally and distinct
[each with his own place and function]."
1 Corinthians 12:27 AMP

"Rather, let our lives lovingly express truth [in all things, speaking truly, dealing truly, living truly]. Enfolded in love, let us grow up in every way and in all things into Him Who is the Head, [even] Christ (the Messiah, the Anointed One.) For because of Him the whole body (the church in all its various parts), closely joined and firmly knit together by the joints and ligaments with which it is supplied, when each part [with power adapted to its need] is working properly [in all its functions], grows to full maturity, building itself up in love."
Ephesians 4:15-16 AMP

The church is not an "illustration." What many Christians think of as church is not taken from a literal belief of scripture, but more from the symbolism it often uses to get God's points across! Mix this fact with our own tastes, notions and experiences and our churches can become mere "illusions" of the real thing. It doesn't take much discernment to see how we have packaged popular cultural ideals in ways that appeal to the parts of Christianity that interests us most…and have called God's people something they are not!

In the New Testament, the apostle Paul specifically calls believers collectively the "BODY" of Christ. Again, these things are written in symbolic language so God can enlighten us about reality!

In other words the "church" is a real systemic network that connects in unison, to serve the interests of its head. First Corinthians 12:14-27 mentions that there really are people and groups, from God's perspective, who are the "hands," "eyes," "feet," "ears" and "noses" of His operation. It is something you become individually aware of and then get corporately involved in. It's not a Hollywood picture! Today, believers everywhere are accustomed to treating their service of Jesus much like catching the latest flick at their local cinema. As long as the same basic top movie selections are playing in their city that are also available ad nauseam everywhere else, they feel satisfied that they have played their part by being involved in the current spiritual scene. We have allowed the entire concept of church to become a franchise people can buy into, which guarantees to interest large segments of the population! Because Christians think of "church" as only a picture where most of the motion and sound come from the projection room, they fail to understand that they themselves are the production!

So, make sure you see yourself as a cooperative member of the cast and crew on God's stage, playing out your role in the Kingdom of Heaven's earthly Gospel presentation. Ready...forget the camera...action!!

DECEMBER 13...DAY 347
CHURCH OR CIRCUS?

"...and on this rock I will build My church, and the gates of Hades shall not prevail against it."
Matthew 16:18 NKJV

"Now God worked unusual miracles by the hands of Paul...And many who had believed came confessing and telling their deeds. Also, many of those who had practiced magic brought their books together and burned them in the sight of all...So the word of the Lord grew mightily and prevailed...Now when they heard this, they were full of wrath and cried out, saying, 'Great is Diana of the Ephesians!' So the whole city was filled with confusion, and rushed into the theatre with one accord..."
Acts 19:11, 18-20, 23, 28-29 NKJV

The word "church" is not exactly found in your Bible...at least not the way you might think. Why then is it printed on the signs of Christian houses of worship all over the world? Most people would say it is only a matter of semantics, others find it a little suspicious, and some think it is very questionable. I think all three responses have some validity. Consider this question for yourself as we examine "church."

The Greek transliteration of the word church in Matthew 16:18 is "ekklessia," which describes a people who are "called out together into a public forum." The Hebrew translation uses the word, "kehilot," found in the Old Testament when describing the Israelites as God's "congregation," or "chosen people," under Moses' leadership.

The problem is that the English word "church" most likely has its roots in the German word "Kirke," which in turn comes from the Babylonian word "Circe." "Circe" was a Babylonian moon goddess whose members met for religious purposes standing in a "circle." Her name was known to all readers of Homer's Greek "Odyssey" in the ancient world, where she is portrayed as a seducing witch, who lures unsuspecting men into her house, sits them upon benches, poisons the food she offers them and, through her subtle craftiness, traps them by turning them into pigs!

Interestingly enough, "she" CAN be found in your Bible! By alternative names this same suspicious spirit seems to have been worshipped as a moon goddess in different cultures around the world. In Egypt there was "Isis," "Kali" in India, "Kannon" in Japan, "Coatlicue" in Mexico. All of these likely come from "Semiramis," the original mother goddess of Nimrod's Babylon (Genesis 10:8-9). "In Ephesus she was named "Diana" or "Artemis," whose followers rioted as a response to the revival Paul experienced here in our text from Acts chapter nineteen! Notice the people there, "rushed into the theatre" in a demonically inspired economic panic! This was because the theatre was the local public forum, where assemblies of this nature normally took place.

The true congregation of the Lord isn't bound by a locality or a forum. God has called it out of the falsely religious and worldly "circus," to be His peculiar assembly and a light to both saved and those yet to believe!

DECEMBER 14...DAY 348
ALL GODS ARE NOT EQUAL

"And the Lord said to Joshua, See, I have given Jericho, its king and mighty men of valor, into your hands. You shall march around the enclosure, all the men of war going around the city once. This you shall do for six days. And seven priests shall bear before the ark seven trumpets of rams' horns; and on the seventh day you shall march around the enclosure seven times, and the priests shall blow the trumpets. When they make a long blast with the ram's horn and you hear the sound of the trumpet, all the people shall shout with a great shout; and the wall of the enclosure

shall fall down in its place and the people shall go up [over it], every man straight before him." Joshua 6:3-5 AMP

All the pagan "moon" goddesses we looked at yesterday seem to have their origin in "Semiramis," the original mother goddess of Nimrod's Babylon. It is said she claimed an "immaculate conception" after her husband's death and declared the "son" a miracle reincarnation of him!

This was just another one of Satan's strategies to create religious confusion in the world before God would introduce His promised Son, Jesus. Guess what the favorite object of worship was here in the "moon city" (Hebrew meaning of Jericho) Joshua was commanded to destroy? They would have worshiped one of these false deities. Some say there was an ancient Arab moon goddess named, "Allah "! This should get the attention of believer today! When you think about how Muslim pilgrims worship around the famous "black stone" in the center of Mecca, you see why God orchestrated this elaborate ceremony of seven circuits around Jericho during seven days. God was taking complete control of not only the city but also of the demonic ruling principalities of all Canaan! He was totally disgracing the moon goddess worship that centered there, mocking every aspect of their rituals prior to the physical destruction of the city.

First, God had Joshua place twelve stones as an altar to Him, in their most sacred nearby place, "Gilgal," where they had traditionally put seven stones around a fire in worshiping the seven phases of the moon. Then he marched them around the city once a day for six days to make the point David Flynn, highlights in his book, "Temple at the Center of Time" (pages 118-119). He comments that, when you multiply six by 360 degrees, and then multiply it again by pi, you get the exact circumference of the moon in miles! He goes on to mention how the seven laps they did around Jericho on the seventh day, when put through the same equation, equals exactly the circumference of the earth!! Does Islam purposefully obscure this hidden meaning behind its famous crescent moon by saying "Allah" is the same as the God of Israel? But God proved to everyone in the universe though Joshua, whose own name meant, "Yahweh is salvation," that all (gods)/Gods are not equal!

DECEMBER 15...DAY 349
CHANGING OF THE GUARD

"But Peter, standing up with the eleven, raised his voice and said to them, 'Men of Judea and all who dwell in Jerusalem, let this be known to you, and heed my words'...Now when they heard this, they were cut to the heart, and said to Peter and the rest of the apostles, 'Men and brethren, what shall we do?'"
Acts 2:14, 37 NKJV

There are times when you just can't say something better than it has already been said. When it comes to appealing to the church to check itself in preparation for Jesus' return, twentieth century preacher, A.W. Tozer was my kind of spokesman. In the following two quotes he says so well what our text for today illustrates; the necessity for both preachers and the religious people they often address to maintain an awareness of the Lord's leadership in their interaction with Him.

"A generation of Christians reared among push buttons and automatic machines is impatient of slower and less direct methods of reaching their goals. We have been trying to apply machine-age methods to our relations with God. We read our chapter, have our short devotions, and rush away, hoping to make up for our deep inward bankruptcy by attending another gospel meeting or listening to another thrilling story told by a religious adventurer lately returned from afar. The tragic results of this spirit are all about us. Shallow lives, hollow religious philosophies, the preponderance of the element of fun in gospel meetings, the glorification of men, trust in religious externalities, quasi-religious fellowships, salesmanship methods, the mistaking of dynamic personality for the power of the Spirit; these and such as these are the symptoms of an evil disease, a deep and serious malady of the soul." – A.W. Tozer

"If Christianity is to receive a rejuvenation it must be by other means than any now being used...there must appear a new type of preacher, the proper ruler of the Synagogue type will never do. Neither will the priestly type man who carries out his duties, takes his pay, asks no questions nor the smooth talking pastoral type who knows how to make the Christian religion acceptable to everyone. These things will never do. All of these have been tried and found wanting. Another kind of religious leader must arise among us, he must be of the old prophet type, a man who has seen visions of God and has heard a voice from the throne of God. When he comes and I pray God that there will be not one but many, he will stand in flat contradiction to everything our smirking smooth civilization holds dear. He will contradict, denounce and protest in the name of God and will earn the hatred and the opposition of a large segment of Christendom." – A.W. Tozer

DECEMBER 16...DAY 350
TWO EDGES, ONE SWORD

"Now see that I, even I, am He, and there is no God besides Me; I kill and I make alive; I wound and I heal; nor is there any who can deliver from My hand. For I raise my hand to heaven and say, 'As I live forever, if I whet My glittering sword, and my hand takes hold on judgment, I will render vengeance to My enemies, and repay those who hate Me." Deuteronomy 32:38 NKJV

"For the word of God is living and powerful, and sharper than any two-edged sword, piercing even to the division of soul and spirit, and of joints and marrow, and is a discerner of the thoughts and intents of the heart. And there is no creature hidden from His sight, but all things are naked and open to the eyes of Him to whom we must give account." Hebrews 4:11-13 NKJV

In July of 1999 I saw the Lord standing just off the northeastern coast of our country, in a little prayer "mini-vision". I watched Him reach over and take out the sword that was sheathed on his left thigh then point it out westward over our country. It seemed to me that He was going to begin judging some things in the church, and in this country.

In the Old Testament the Lord is pictured at times as a heavenly messenger with a sword, but in the New Testament He IS the sword, the very Word of God made flesh! He is both judgment and salvation to God's people and the world, accountability and blessing.

There is no getting around Jesus, you must through Him to get to heaven. What many people don't know is that you also have to let Him go through you to really be blessed! We need to be the kind of people that say, "God, cut me down to nothing, slice me with both edges, I want the Word to penetrate my life."

God's sword is two-edged, dangerous and beneficial at one and the same time. Its primary function is for the fulfilling of His purposes. Those who embrace His Word are then empowered to wield it. Jesus seeks permission from the church to let His Word have its full effect upon its members. When Peter stood up and preached that first sermon, the Bible says his listeners were "cut to the heart" (Acts 2:37). Why? Because he spoke the Word of God, he preached the Word of truth, the Gospel of Jesus Christ. He may have not known much at that time, but by speaking what he did know, it pierced them to their very core convincing them of their dangerous position in relation to God. In these last days we need to submit ourselves willingly to the point of His sword, so the Lord can employ us in convincing ways and we can truly be blessed!

DECEMBER 17...DAY 351
A POSTER-CHILD FOR JESUS

"So, for my part, I am willing and eagerly ready to preach the Gospel to you also who are in Rome. For I am not ashamed of the Gospel (good news) of Christ, for it is God's power working unto salvation [for deliverance from eternal death] to everyone who believes with a personal trust and a confident surrender and firm reliance,...For in the Gospel a righteousness which God ascribes is revealed, both springing from faith and leading to faith [disclosed through the way of faith that arouses to more faith]. As it is written, 'The man who through faith is just and upright shall live and shall live by faith.'" [Hab. 2:4] Romans 1:15-17 AMP

I want to show you just how powerful God's Word is. Because it is a sword in the Holy Spirit's hands with two razor-sharp edges, it can cut through anything in a person's life, and find a way to get a response from their heart.

When I was a teenager I went with my mother to a department store in my hometown of Kirksville, Missouri. As she shopped I began looking through the poster rack, flipping through all the rock group covers, celebrity photos and graphic art of the day. In the midst of all this, my eye was drawn to this strangely interesting black poster with all these colorful words written on it. The name, "JESUS" was in the very center. I later realized all the words were references to the different names of God found throughout the Bible. Even though my mom didn't have extra money to burn as a single parent, she bought me that poster. I was probably about fourteen years old and nowhere close to being saved. I did not regularly attend church, but through the guise of a cool poster God smuggled His Word into my home and had me hang it on the wall at the foot of my bed, positioned directly in my constant view. It was there until the day I moved out of my house - but on that day I was saved!

That is the inherent power of the Word of God I am talking about! The sword of the Lord was working on me and working in me...and I did not even know it! When I got up it was there, when I went to bed it was there, and sooner or later, it CHANGED my life. It was analyzing, sifting, judging, speaking and dealing with me. I do not remember an exact date, but somewhere along the line, I started believing the good news I had been reading...and finally, about four or five years later when God sent somebody to preach the full gospel to me, I accepted Jesus! Nothing is more essential for end time people than seeing believers full of the Word hanging around them!

DECEMBER 18...DAY 352
UNSTOPPABLE

"Now I do not want you to be unaware, brethren, that I often planned to come to you (but was hindered until now), that I might have some fruit among you also, just as among the other Gentiles. I am a debtor both to Greeks and to barbarians, both to wise and to unwise. So, as much as is in me, I am ready to preach the gospel to you who are in Rome also. For I am not ashamed of the gospel of Christ, for it is the power of God to salvation for everyone who believes, for the Jew first and also for the Greek. For in it the righteousness of God is revealed from faith to faith; as it is written, 'The just shall live by faith.' For the wrath of God is revealed from heaven against all ungodliness and unrighteousness of men, who suppress the truth in unrighteousness..." Romans 1:13-18 NKJV

Paul's "readiness" is infectious as you read this first chapter of Romans. I love how he addresses the church in the city that was the center of the known world of his time. He lets them know that the only reason he hadn't been there yet is because he had been "hindered" up until this point. This word means to "cut into" and is a picture of impeding a person's progress by breaking up the road they travel on or by placing obstacles sharply in their path.

In 1 Thessalonians 2:18, Paul uses the same word when telling another church how "Satan" had temporarily interfered with his itinerary to stop him from spreading the Gospel further into a region steeped in the darkness of pagan ritual. A man of action, the apostle was not shy about letting people know that he was in a battle for territory wherever he went and that the devil was a factor in the way things played out. This is what made him so confident! He knew there was true power in the message of Jesus Christ and, armed with it, he would ultimately overcome any impediments he faced. It was true in every other city, and I can just see Paul itching to turn loose what he carried in Rome!

He had been a man on a mission to reach the Gentiles since the Holy Spirit separated him and Barnabas to that specific "apostolic" work in Acts 13:1-4. This is how we get the titles to many of the different books of the New Testament. They were literal places Paul went with the good news of what God had done for the world through Christ to save, deliver and heal them. It proved able to reach all kinds of people in any culture; elite or common, "white collar" or "blue collar," intellectuals or unlearned. Any real preacher knows the message he preaches is unstoppable...regardless of how dark it gets or how narrow the road may seem!

DECEMBER 19...DAY 353
THE DIVINE ANTIDOTE

"So, as much as is in me, I am ready to preach the gospel to you who are in Rome also. For I am not ashamed of the gospel of Christ, for it is the power of God to salvation for everyone who believes, for the Jew first and also for the Greek. For in it the righteousness of God is revealed from faith to faith; as it is written, 'The just shall live by faith.' For the wrath of God is revealed from heaven against all ungodliness and unrighteousness of men, who suppress the truth in unrighteousness, because what many be known of God is manifest in them for God has shown it to them."
Romans 1:13-19 NKJV

The apostle Paul was "ever-ready" to preach the Gospel because he knew its power. By the time he wrote to these Roman believers his point had been proven repeatedly. We know from the history of the Book of Acts that the churches in the cities of Thessalonica, Corinth, Ephesus, Philippi, Colosse, as well as those located in the region of Galatia, were reached before Paul made it to Rome. It is most likely that Paul had written to at least three of them before he wrote this letter to the church in Rome.

Notice today how the scripture here gives us the secret to Paul's urgency. He kept himself in a constant state of readiness to be able to carry and deliver God's Word because he knew what it "revealed." It disclosed or unveiled "righteousness" or right-standing with God, progressively, as people responded to it in faith believing it to be God's message to them personally. This means they received the revelation that there was forgiveness, healing, salvation, deliverance and blessing for them in Jesus Christ!

This is in sharp contrast to what Paul goes on to point out in chapters one and two of this same Bible book. Verse eighteen tells us that the wrath of God had already been "revealed" vividly in this world, as a result of the willing sinfulness of mankind who have been made aware of the truth and existence of God. Because people had not looked at creation or listened to their conscience in order to find the proof of His almighty power, they were under His judgment, both Gentile and Jew!

The "good news" is that the Gospel is the antidote to that judgment, the anti-venom for the bite of that old serpent, Satan, upon the soul of mankind. It is the thing that will not only bring us out from under God's just punishment, but even greater, it brings us directly under the influence of His blessing!!

DECEMBER 20...DAY 354
THE SWORD OF THE LORD AND YOU!

"Then the children of Israel did evil in the sight of the Lord. So the Lord delivered them into the hand of Midian for seven years, and the hand of Midian prevailed against Israel. And the angel of the Lord appeared to him (Gideon), and said to him, 'The Lord is with you, you mighty man of valor!'...So Gideon and the hundred men who were with him...blew the trumpets and broke the pitchers that were in their hands...and they cried, 'The sword of the Lord and of Gideon!'"...and the Lord set every man's sword against his companion throughout the whole camp; (of Gideon's enemies)." Judges 6:12; 7:19-20 NKJV

The story of Gideon seems to be a general and subtle preview of the end times. Like Israel, the Christian religious world will be in the dangerous position of hardheartedness and unbelief. Yet within her, waiting for the right moment to be awakened, will be a remnant that will respond to the leadership of those who have heard from God and received His strength.

Someone smarter than I am observed this about modern Christianity, "Religion today is not transforming people; rather it is being transformed by the people. It is not raising the moral level of society; it is descending to society's own level, and congratulating itself that it has scored a victory because society is smilingly accepting its surrender."

Israel's situation in those days had slipped beyond our own familiar place of stubborn, self-serving sinfulness, into a set period of God's judgment for their sin. It is interesting by definition of the word that "Israel" was a "prince who had power with God!" Yet, they were serving seven years under the hand of the "Midianites," a people whose name meant "strife." They were reaping what they had sown and were given into the hands of what they had become!

Today, the church is heading toward this same outcome. When Israel finally cried out to the Lord for help, He chose Gideon whose name meant, "a tree-cutter" or one who destroys. He was a simple solution to a simple problem! God sent Him to cut down the idols Israel had erected in their rebelliousness, so the spiritual way would be cleared for Him to restore their freedom. In the end, the people of God were stirred to action by a courageous remnant. Their enemies were destroyed more by the new "images" God created through the leadership of one man than anything else!

Like Gideon, it is so important to get a word from God for your life! God's Word is the key to living for him, and leading for Him...it is truly wielding the sword of the spiritual realm! Only when we begin to understand the mind of God, will citadels of evil be cut down, so that strongholds for God can be built back up. The Church's last-day cry will be, "The sword of the Lord and...YOU!"

DECEMBER 21...DAY 355
GO OFF THE DEEP END

"But as it is written: Eye has not seen, nor ear heard, nor have entered into the heart of man the things which God has prepared for those who love Him (Isaiah 64:4; 65:17). But God has revealed them to us through His Spirit. For the Spirit searches all things, yes, the deep things of God."
1 Corinthians 2:9-10 NKJV

If you really want to follow God, you have to get into the deep end of His pool.

When I was young I liked to swim. In my hometown all the girls were at the swimming pool in the summer time, so it was the place to "display." If you really wanted to get a girl's attention, however, staying in the shallower parts of the pool wasn't going to get it for you. You had to get to the deep end of the pool, where all the "advanced" people were. Both low and high diving boards were located there, and if you wanted to make an impression you had become proficient on the high dive. The "king" of the deep end of our local pool was this sandy-haired college age guy with a "ripped" body. When he "strutted" out to the end of the high dive everyone watched! Of all the dives in his arsenal, the coolest by far was the one where he would turn around, put his toes on the end of the board, stiffen his body and simply fall backwards into the pool...with no splash!

One day I had a life-changing thought, "If he can do it at eighteen or nineteen years old, how cool will I be if I dive that way at twelve?" I mustered the courage to ask him for his secret, and I've never forgotten his advice. He said, "You can do exactly what I do, IF, in that moment you are about to fall backwards, you do not fear...because everything in your mind will tell you that it won't work. You have to believe me that if you stay straight you will go in head first, but if you flinch and bend your back, knees or waist you will experience nothing but pain and shame!" To make a long story short, I was eventually able to summon the public bravery to walk out on that high dive in front of all the prettiest sixth, seventh and eighth graders in Kirksville, Missouri! Because I remained focused on an expert's advice, my knees didn't buckle under the pressure and I came up out of that pool a different "man!"

Now, you are not trying to impress as believers, but we are aiming to obey God and take our ground. So, use the same basic approach in stepping out for Him. His Word tells us everything we need to know to follow His Spirit into the deep end of the

Christian pool...where we can fearlessly trust Him to advise us how to accomplish the highest leaps in life!

DECEMBER 22...DAY 356
REVERSING THE CURSE OF REJECTION
#1 FOLLOW A GODLY EXAMPLE

"If anyone hears what I am saying and doesn't take it seriously, I don't reject him. I didn't come to reject the world. But you need to know that whoever puts me off, refusing to take in what I'm saying, is willfully choosing rejection."
John 12:47-48a, The Message

We have all experienced the pain that accompanies rejection. Emotionally honest people know how the effects of this kind of pain can last a lifetime, unless something is done to stop it. Even though it is often extremely difficult to examine such issues, it is well worth the effort required to take a closer look at rejection in our own lives. In order to do that, we sometimes need a little help from someone who knows what we are going through. My pastor is a man by the name of Neil Miers. After building a large church He pastured, Neil and his wife Nance also had the responsibility of planting and overseeing thousands of churches on six continents throughout a span of seventeen years. They are a very unassuming couple with humble roots. But I have watched as God has made them equal to His calling for their lives, many times using the rejection of others to temper and strengthen them. Whether ministering in large crusades or small churches around the world I have often heard Neil use the phrase, "Most of us are like the rest of us!" In spite of situations going on behind the scenes that could have made him bitter, this expression is his way of always bringing others back to a place of hope. Having often experienced the sting of rejection in ministry myself, that kind of spiritual example has certainly helped me to remember how to overcome rejection and remain in a frame of mind to encourage others.

Choosing the Word of God despite difficult circumstances always helps us to retain our identity, while firmly holding onto our acceptance in Him. When people know that they are just like everyone else, struggling with common problems in life, they also begin to realize that the same doors of opportunity can be opened before them that have opened for others!

On the other hand, when people do not know this simple truth it opens the door for more rejection. This leads to a never-ending cycle of conjecture and misunderstanding about their future, which never allows them to see the things around them as they really are in God's eyes. In this way Satan often hinders the progress of individuals, families, churches, businesses or teams, obscuring the Lord's vision from them, robbing them of all confidence and thereby delaying His blessings.

I pray every reader would have the opportunity to be influenced by a godly spiritual mentor like Neil Miers. In any case, always remember God is your supreme Father and you can choose to embrace the spirit of His Words. They will reverse every trace of rejection and keep you ready to overcome every challenge you face...until Jesus returns!

DECEMBER 23...DAY 357
REVERSING THE CURSE OF REJECTION
#2 THE FLIP SIDE

"If anyone hears what I am saying and doesn't take it seriously, I don't reject him. I didn't come to reject the world. But you need to know that whoever puts me off, refusing to take in what I'm saying, is willfully choosing rejection."
John 12:47-48a, The Message

The Bible has a lot to say about rejection. It also contains plenty of character sketches illustrating the importance of overcoming this spiritual obstacle in the lives of those who have walked with God.

Jesus Christ was unfairly rejected more than any person in history. Since no one suffered the effects of rejection more, He is our ultimate example to follow. The flip side of this issue is that no one has His present place of honor either! The biggest temptations carry the biggest rewards, if overcome.

Notice in the scripture above, Jesus made it abundantly clear that He is not the author of rejection. Rejection is something that is an automatic outcome of this human experience, everyone runs into it. Instead of being avoided, it must be responded to properly. If it is, spiritual rewards will follow.

In the context of this passage, Jesus was responding to the failure of the people to accept as true what He was telling them. Unbelief, or not exercising faith in what God says, is the greatest form of rejection man can display toward Him. It is never a good thing, and this kind of response to His advances can ultimately carry dangerous effects! Look closely at Jesus' words here. He tells us something about rejection that we must never forget. When we reject the truth we will automatically open ourselves to absorb rejection. Built and fortified through past rejections of our own, our hurts can cause us to live in that cycle of conjecture and misunderstanding I spoke about yesterday...which can lead us to reject others, even God, sometimes without fully realizing what we are doing! Rejection works like a thief, blinding us to who we really are by continuing to subtly but surely influence the decisions we make, until we sabotage our own personal success by denying the truth in any situation. It can lead us to become someone we really are not, and end up living a kind of alternative spiritual lifestyle. The reality we experience there is a mere by-product of our perception, tainted by that "alternate Christian world" of offenses and unresolved hurts. Even though God chose King Saul, he continually opted to reject what God directed him to do! Ultimately Saul was the one most affected by his own rebellious heart, being replaced by a mere boy with an open heart to the will and way of God.

In the same way, when we stand before Jesus we will be accepted or rejected by Him then based on our own acceptance or rejection of Him now! So, flip your heart like David and get God's full rewards!

DECEMBER 24...DAY 358
REVERSING THE CURSE OF REJECTION
#3 STEPS TO REVERSING REJECTION

"If anyone hears what I am saying and doesn't take it seriously, I don't reject him. I didn't come to reject the world. But you need to know that whoever puts me off, refusing to take in what I'm saying, is willfully choosing rejection."
John 12:47-48a, The Message

I believe we can overcome the effects of rejection and unlock our future if we can find the courage to do three basic things Jesus spoke of regarding this issue.

First, SEEK THE TRUTH. Jesus calls Himself the Truth in John 14:6 when telling His disciples how to walk in spiritual realities. In John 8:32 the Lord said something equally important to a group of new converts. To paraphrase, Jesus told them the secret to spiritual freedom was to continue listening to His Word and as a result they would know the Truth, which would make them free. Sometimes rejection contains portions of truth that we need to recognize about ourselves, but because of the pain involved we fail to grasp the 'gift,' which has come wrapped in such ugly paper! We must learn to love Truth regardless of its appearance and use it to continue walking with God. If we can, rejection will come to mean more to us...another occasion to let God liberate and elevate us!

Second, FACE THE PAST. Everyone has a 'closet' with 'skeletons' inside. But not everyone has opened the door, identified the contents, and removed the shame. Paul tells us in Philippians 3:13 that the 'one thing' he did above all in his quest to fulfill his destiny in God was letting go of the past. We can only remove the failures found there by willingly disregarding the success we have attained as well. Yesterday must have no hold on us if we want to achieve God's best today, and build a solid foundation for tomorrow. Those who face the pain of past rejections can release the promise of what God has spoken over their lives!

Third, BE YOURSELF. Just before our text in verse 46 of John chapter 12, Jesus said He came into the world to be a light. He explains the way things really are and then works with those who want His help to reveal what/who they really are.

Mankind tends to hide in the darkness from God like Adam and Eve after their fall into sin (John 3:19). Most people naturally avoid having their deeds exposed, yet it is the very test we must pass in order to receive true enlightenment. The real you is hidden in Christ. Lay down the fear of rejection for the hope of a greater revelation of God in you! Break free from the rejection and be the real you today! Truth and transparency will be precious commodities in the last days.

DECEMBER 25...DAY 359
SPIRITUAL CALIBRATION

"So it was, when the angels had gone away from them into heaven that the shepherds said to one another, 'Let us now go to Bethlehem and see this thing that has come to pass, which the Lord has made known to us.' And they came with haste and found Mary and Joseph, and the Babe lying in a manger. Now when they had seen Him, they made widely known the saying which was told them concerning this Child. And those who heard it marveled..."
Luke 2:15-18 NKJV

"And behold, there was a man in Jerusalem whose name was Simeon, and this man was just and devout, waiting for the Consolation of Israel, and the Holy Spirit was upon him. And it had been revealed to him by the Holy Spirit that he would not see death before he had seen the Lord's Christ. So he came by the Spirit into the temple. And when the parents brought in the Child Jesus, to do for Him according to the custom of the law, he took Him up in his arms blessed God...Now there was one, Anna, a prophetess,...and coming in that instant she gave thanks to the Lord, and spoke of Him to all those who looked for redemption in Israel"
Luke 2:25-38 NKJV

"Now after Jesus was born in Bethlehem of Judea in the days of Herod the king, behold, wise men from the East came to Jerusalem, saying, 'Where is He who has been born King of the Jews? For we have seen His star in the East and

have come to worship Him.'" Matthew 2:1-2 NKJV

Someone once reminded the Church of the secret power of spiritual unity by using the analogy of many pianos calibrated to the sound of one tuning fork. Regardless of the number of instruments, if they all bow to the same individual standard, they are automatically tuned to each other. In other words, true Christian harmony originates not from trying to tune ourselves to each other, but by conforming to the voice of Christ.

Perhaps this is a facet of meaning Jesus had in mind when he said, "I am the good Shepherd; and I know My sheep, and am known by My own...My sheep hear my voice, and I know them, and they follow Me" in John 10:14, 27. His life is the thing that gives the proper resonance to His voice, which in turn is the instrument used by God to tune every believer.

Notice in our texts for today how the voice of the Lord in its various forms (words & unction, angels, prophetic signs) gathered diverse people from such a wide range of places to the baby Jesus! Nothing else was needed to create the proper unity on the purposed occasions to welcome God in the flesh...so what else will be needed for the unification of the Church of the Lord, in the last days?

DECEMBER 26...DAY 360
THE OUTLINE OF FAITH

"Now faith is the substance of things hoped for, the evidence of things not seen. For by it the elders obtained a good testimony. By faith we understand that the worlds (during the successive ages) were framed by the Word of God, so that the things which are seen were not made of things which are visible...These all died in faith, not having received the promises, but having seen them afar off were assured of them, embraced them and confessed that they were strangers and pilgrims on the earth."
Hebrews 11:1-2, 13 NKJV

How many faithful men and women have accomplished great things throughout the ages to promote the eternal plan of God, even though they did not live to see final completion? This chapter of the Bible highlights the accounts of those believers who changed history by putting their faith in God's word. In the process it gives us an outline of ways to use our faith to be world-changers in our own generation.

There are more than eighteen specific uses for your faith listed here. Abel OFFERED acceptable gifts. Enoch displayed unusually faithful DILIGENCE. Noah meticulously PREPARED for a cataclysm. Abraham patiently OBEYED the Lord's personal direction. Abraham's wife Sarah RECEIVED strength to conceive. Abraham also PASSED his ultimate test in his willingness to offer his son (all). Isaac prophetically BLESSED his sons. Jacob also blessed his sons and INSTRUCTED them about the future of the nation they would become. Moses' parents CONCEALED him against the law of the land of Egypt. Moses himself made a major CONTRARY CHOICE in walking away from the royal court of Egypt. In this process he REFUSED reputation , PREFERRED the Lord, LOOKED FORWARD to His rewards, FORSOOK the world, ENDURED the suffering, AUTHORIZED and INSTITUTED the process of judgment and redemption as a the Lord's chosen leader, and DEMONSTRATED God's miracle power in delivering His people! Israel SHOUTED down the walls of Jericho under Joshua's leadership. Rahab the harlot HELPED the spies and SURVIVED.

Beyond these, Joseph, Gideon, Samson, David, Samuel, the prophets and others are mentioned for their world-changing acts of faith in God and His promises. They walked through fire, escaped danger, exhibited strength and courage in battle, defeated their enemies and even saw their loved ones raised from the dead! Then there were those who were exposed to all sorts of trials, tribulations and the ultimate suffering of martyrdom...successfully enduring all these things by the power of faith! The Bible depicts these people as ones "of whom the world was not worthy" and as those with whom we are connected in the eternal plan of God. They were "the just" who lived by faith in expectation of the Messiah's first coming. We are the faithful torch-bearers, following in their footsteps, until Jesus returns. These have shown us the way of faith...let's learn from the legacy they have left us and overcome all for Christ!

DECEMBER 27...DAY 361
SPIRITUAL DEPTH PERCEPTION

"And in that day you will say: 'O Lord, I will praise You; and You comfort me. Behold, God is my salvation, I will trust and not be afraid; For YAH, the Lord, is my strength and song; He also has become my salvation.' Therefore with joy you will draw water from the wells of salvation. And in that day you will say: 'Praise the Lord, call upon His name; declare His deeds among the peoples, make mention that His name is exalted. Sing to the Lord, for He has done excellent things; this is known in all the earth. Cry out and shout, O inhabitant of Zion, for great is the Holy One of Israel in your midst!'" Isaiah 12 NKJV

Because my grandfather was a Northeastern Missouri farmer, when I was a kid we used to go for long walks in the "woods." Since I reared along with my brothers by our single mother in the rougher side of a town about thirty miles away, this trek was a kind of escape for us on many weekends.

Our scripture for today makes me think of one of the things we used to do during those rural adventures. In addition to the Native Americans, others such as French explorers, European immigrants or "old world" Americans who had come from the east in the westward expansion of this nation, had left their mark on that land. We would often find remains of old wells and mine shafts that people had dug long before our time. Then we would imagine that these mysterious holes in the middle of nowhere were entrances to other worlds or portals through time! In order to test our theories we would drop a rock in a well, or shaft to conduct a "fool proof" experiment. We learned that depending on the length of silence before you heard the "plopping" sound of water, we could guess its depth. Sometimes though, we would drop a rock and never hear anything! Then you would drop another and another until...well, that would lend itself to wildly embellished campfire stories of "bottomless pits" and haunted parts of the woods!

Recently, the Lord reminded me of how sometimes the church in these last days is just like that. He drops revelation, blessings, graces and gifts in us, listening for the response of faith, of praise, of joy and honor to His name...and judging our spiritual depth by what He hears! The truth is we can draw everything we need from Him if we remember that WE ARE God's wells. Believers must remember that God is their source and they are the outlets He has dug in order to contain and release the water of life! Jesus was the biggest rock ever dropped into the vacuous spiritual condition of planet earth...let your life echo the sound of the deeply mysterious yet abundant Rock of our Salvation, Christ our Lord!

DECEMBER 28...DAY 362
YAH-SHUA SAVES!

"And in that DAY you will say: 'O Lord, I will praise You; and You comfort me. Behold, God is my salvation, I will trust and not be afraid; For YAH, the Lord, is my strength and song; He also has become my salvation.' Therefore with joy you will draw water from the wells of salvation. And in that day you will say: 'Praise the Lord, call upon His name; declare His deeds among the peoples, make mention that His name is exalted.'"
Isaiah 12:2-4 NKJV

"On the last DAY, that great day of the feast, Jesus stood and cried out, saying, 'If anyone thirsts, let him come to Me and drink. He who believes in Me, as the scripture has said, out of his heart will flow rivers of living water.' But this He spoke concerning the Spirit, whom those believing in Him would receive."
John 7:37-39 NKJV

The "day" mentioned here in both Isaiah and John are one and the same. By using the reference to "waters," Jesus was technically saying that He WAS the "God of salvation" predicted by Isaiah!

Throughout the four Gospels, you clearly see how much trouble this kind of candor created for Jesus (see John 10:22-39). In fact, His own people killed Him because He called Himself the "Son of God." The Jewish religious leaders finally conspired with the civil Roman authorities to crucify Him, but they could never escape the evidence of who He really was. In the end, Pontius Pilate even posted a sign above Jesus on the cross announcing that He was the "King of the Jews!" In their stubbornness they rejected the obvious. They could have just as easily accepted the obvious indicators God had arranged throughout history for them.

As we approach the Lord's second coming we can make the same unnecessary mistake. Today, please see that believing on Jesus is the secret to drawing the living waters of salvation from God's wells. I find it more than a little interesting that Israel could not honor "Yashua," whose name literally meant "Yahweh saves," in the way that Isaiah taught them to honor Yahweh, the "God of salvation!" Everything about Jesus screamed, "He is the One, True and Living God, and He saves...through Me, His offspring in human form!"

If they had they would have been able to draw life from His Spirit through praising, trusting, and exalting Him! They would have also been able to declare Him to the world instead of having to have the world (saved Gentiles) be of assistance in saving them! If the Jewish nation missed their Messiah we can miss Him again, too. Submit yourself to Jesus as the Lord of your life today...then His strength will make you ready for anything the end times hurls at you!

DECEMBER 29...DAY 363
WHAT TO DO IN CHURCH AND WHY

"What then, brethren, is [the right course]? When you meet together, each one has a hymn, a teaching, a disclosure of special knowledge or information, an utterance in a [strange] tongue, or an interpretation of it. [But] let everything be constructive and edifying and for the good of all...but all things should be done with regard to decency and propriety and in an orderly fashion."
1 Corinthians 14:26, 40 AMP

"His INTENTION was the perfecting and the full equipping of the saints (His consecrated people), [that they should do] the work of ministering toward building up

Christ's body (the church), [that it might develop] until we all attain oneness in the faith and in the comprehension of the [full and accurate] knowledge of the Son of God, that [we might arrive] at really mature manhood (the completeness of personality which is nothing less that the standard height of Christ's own perfection), the measure of the stature of the fullness of the Christ and the completeness found in Him."
Ephesians 4:12-13 AMP

There are many different kinds of things that we can do and are supposed to do when we meet as a body of believers. In a traditional church setting or a more open type of service, a home group, just two or three Christians getting together to fellowship around the Word and prayer, there are specific things we should be attentive to.

This scripture lists singing and teaching, as well as the exchange of divine revelation, unknown tongues and their interpretation. It seems the Lord likes to use His people in more variety than we have become accustomed to being used!

This is not to say that the Church does not need spiritual leadership from those God has called to equip and build it up. The fourth chapter of Ephesians makes that perfectly clear, but we should keep track of who is supposed to be doing what and why. When the body of Christ comes together it is supposed to be a flowing, living, moving thing. When churches discontinue moving in the direction of God, they stop touching people's lives in meaningful ways. When a believer goes to church he should prepare himself to receive something from God by first bringing something to Him and His people. The Lord reveals His intentions so that believers, churches and working ministries can become active, growing, capable, experienced and mature representatives of Himself. If the people up front aren't using their authority to develop and release the abilities of others, as did Jesus, the direction probably isn't true and precise!

Before you blame someone else for the deficiencies you will find in all churches, first hold yourself responsible. Then try working with others to create an environment in which God will work through you. No church is perfect, but the closer we come to doing things in the church God's way, the more prepared we become for His return!

DECEMBER 30...DAY 364
HOLD YOURSELF UP AGAINST THE WORD

"I charge you therefore before God and the Lord Jesus Christ...Preach the word! Be ready in season and out of season. Convince, rebuke, exhort, with all longsuffering and teaching. For the time will come when they will not endure sound doctrine, but according to their own desires, because they have itching ears, they will heap up for themselves teachers; and they will turn their ears away from the truth, and be turned aside to fables." 2 Timothy 4:1-4 NKJV

The words, "teaching," "doctrine," and "teachers" in this passage are the same basic word in the Greek language in which the New Testament was originally written. It simply means "proper instruction" or "a proper instructor," depending on the various forms that are used. Both Timothy and Titus were the Apostle Paul's personal disciples in the faith. In his writings to them you will find the word "sound" combined with "doctrine" several times. He did this for the same reason God placed these same words inside the entire Bible. "Sound", "healthy", or "safe" teaching in your life serves to lay a foundation upon which the Lord can build. Unless you have a doctrinal foundation you may not discern if the more subjective, supernatural revelation that often comes through other members of the Body of Christ (the Church) is authentic or not. Only by running such information through an expansive and objective process can you discern whether a tongue or a prophetic word spoken in your presence is legitimate. This is why although we are told in the Bible not to despise prophesies, or to forbid tongues, or to quench the movement of the Holy Spirit, we are also told to let all be done in decently and in order.

The influence of solid Bible teaching and the accountability to proven spiritual leaders are not meant to remove our own ability to discern spiritual sources, but to help us build responsible boundaries. These two things help us learn how God has done things in others' lives and test this against what we think He is doing in ours.

Notice how one of the most effective schemes of the devil in the last days will be to lure believers away from the objective into the subjective! It is similar to the way a wolf isolates a lone young or weak sheep from its fold in order to devour it. Many people today listen to what they want to hear when it comes to Christian teaching. Their ambition and self-will leads them to find those who teach the fiction they prefer, instead of the pure "Word of God" which, if implanted in them, is able to take root and save their souls (James 1:21)! Notice, you have to "endure" the real thing....that means to "hold yourself up against it" until it changes you!

DECEMBER 31...DAY 365
FOUR STEPS TO STAYING READY

"And they steadfastly persevered, devoting themselves constantly to the instruction and fellowship of the apostles, to the breaking of bread [including the Lord's Supper] and prayers. And a sense of awe (reverential fear) came upon every soul, and many wonders and signs were performed through the apostles..."
Acts 2:42-43 AMP

"Every Scripture is God-breathed (given by His inspiration) and profitable for instruction...so that the man of God may be complete and proficient well fitted and thoroughly equipped for every good work."
2 Timothy 3:15-16 AMP

We need to study the Bible because it is a spiritual document, and better men than us were inspired by God to write it! We don't just read it for the sake of gaining knowledge; we immerse ourselves in it to touch the underlying essence of the One Who wrote it. Natural knowledge will come in handy at times for connecting informational dots, but if you are going to have truly "sound doctrine" you must desire an understanding of the "spirit" of the book.

The Word of God is a perfect blend of practical and mystical writings, meant to help us live a "supernaturally-natural" life. So if you are serious about Christianity, try reading your Bible with a few basic tenets in mind.

First, consider how Jesus and other writers practiced what you are reading. In the New Testament look at how Paul, Peter, John, James or any one of the people mentioned in their writings put into action with what they learned. Observe Bible characters in the Old Testament practicing their faith in God, and compare them with your own circumstances and choices.

Second, think about how other faithful believers currently live out God's truth around you. Most of us know genuine, godly people we can "look up" to. So put the scripture into your own "real-life" context by learning from the faithful believers and leaders surrounding you.

Third, consider what may keep you from practicing God's Word. Choose to ask yourself probing questions, and answer them honestly. How does this affect me? How do I feel about this? Is there anything in me that does not want to do this? Where does this issue from, and what does God tell me to do about it? Then, bring your fears, hesitations and weaknesses to the Lord personally, seeking His assistance. Do it while it is "hot" and when the faith springs up inside you, go with it!

Finally, try to sense what is underlying in the text. Revelation knowledge is what you are really after, the spirit of the Word. Dig until you begin to hear God's still small voice for yourself and experience the transforming renewal it brings into your everyday life.

Do these things and your Bible will come alive. You will stay free from deception, recharged by doing what you hear and remain ever-ready for Jesus return!

BIBLIOGRAPHY

Arde, Benjamin. The term, "Supernatural Technology" is borrowed from the comments of Prophet **Benjamin Arde**

Clark, Adam, "Reprinted by Permission. Adam Clarke's Bible Commentary, Thomas Nelson Inc. Nashville Tennessee. All rights reserved."

Alcorn, Randy. "A. W. Tozer: Pastoral Ministry". EPM Eternal Perspective Ministries official website of author Randy Alcorn. http://www.epm.org/resourcespastoral-ministry/

Coke is a registered trademark of The Coca Cola Company

Conn, Charles W. A Balanced Church. Cleveland, Tennessee:

Dr. T.J. McCrossan, Bodily Healing and the Atonement 1982], p. 91. Used with permission. www.rhema.org.

Fenelon, Francois. The Best of Fenelon, Spiritual Letters/Christian Counsel/Maxims of the Saints. Gainesville, Florida: Bridge-Logos Publishers, 2002.

Fenelon, Francois. The Seeking Heart. PO Box 285, Sargent, GA: The Seed Sowers Christian Books Publishing House, **1992**

Flynn, David. Temple at the Center of Time. Crane MO 65633: "Official Disclosure" A division of Anomalos Publishing House, 2008.

Gimbutas, Marija. *The Language of the Goddess*. Thames & Hudson, London, 2001.

Gladwell, Malcolm. Outliers. Little, Brown and Company, 2008.

Johnson, Buffie. *Lady of the Beasts*. www.InnerTraditions.com Harper & Row Publishers, New York, 1981.

Miles, Robert. Term, Provision vs. Promise borrowed from him.

Missler, Nancy. Be Ye Transformed. PO Box D, Coeur d'Alene: Koinonia House, 2003.

Nee. Watchman. Sit,Walk,Stand. Copyright © 1977 by Watchman Nee. Used by permission of Tyndale House Publishers, Inc. All rights reserved.

Olson, Paul. The Distinctively Christian Marriage. Scott Publishing, 1991

Oxford Dictonary. Copyright © Oxford University Press, 2011. All Rights Reserved

Pepsi is a registered trademark of The Pepsi-Cola Company, a division of PepsiCo, Inc.

Pontiac and Pontiac GTO are registered trademarks of the Pontiac Corporation and General Motors. All rights reserved.

Plymouth and Plymouth Valiant are registered trademarks of Chrysler Group.LLC. All rights reserved.

Renner, Rick. Sparkling Gems from the Greek. Tulsa, OK: Rich Renner, 2003.

Strong, James, "Reprinted by Permission. Strong's Exhaustive Concordance of the Bible, 1995, Thomas Nelson Inc. Nashville Tennessee. All rights reserved."

Superman is a registered trademark of DC Comics, a general partnership composed of Warner Communications Inc. and E.C. Publications Inc.

Tolstoy, Leo. A Confession.

Frank Viola and George Barna. Pagan Christianity? Tyndale House Publishers, Inc., 2008

Yarnall, Judith. The Transformation of Circe: The History of an Enchantress. University of Illinois Press, 1994.

INDEX

C

214, 248, 252, 258, 265, 295, 297, 319, 325,
326, 331, 349, 359
circus, 340
cities, 15, 147, 201, 211, 220, 239, 243, 248,
250, 253, 269, 326, 346
citizens, 168, 230
city, 1, 2, 17, 24, 43, 45, 68, 104, 147, 157, 182,
212, 214, 230, 238, 240, 242, 245, 250, 252,
253, 256, 259, 263, 264, 265, 312, 323, 324,
325, 339, 340, 341, 345
clean, 107, 113, 218, 316
cleaner, 218
cleanse, 104, 127
cleansed, 45, 97, 109
cleansers, 323
clearly, 10, 11, 37, 50, 56, 70, 106, 114, 128,
129, 152, 161, 171, 185, 189, 215, 220, 263,
292, 309, 332, 356
clever, 178
climate, 71, 153, 254, 264, 305
closeness, 100, 137
closer, 8, 26, 29, 46, 60, 63, 68, 75, 82, 106,
111, 126, 137, 147, 153, 159, 183, 192, 213,
226, 227, 251, 257, 262, 313, 335, 349, 357
clothing, 40, 81, 307, 308
cloud, 10, 177
codes, 136
coerce, 76
coin, 216, 337
cold, 51, 195, 202, 250, 307, 312
collect, 30, 160, 191, 237
collection, 125
collective, 239, 271
collectors, 90, 91
collusion, 57
Columbine, 94
combination, 82, 99, 133, 204, 267, 295, 303,
323
comfort, 15, 22, 48, 51, 82, 87, 133, 136, 137,
147, 158, 222, 249, 256, 263, 319, 337, 354,
355
comfortable, 15, 22, 48, 51, 82, 87, 133, 222,
249, 263

command, 38, 46, 52, 81, 93, 100, 173, 180,
199, 222, 224, 229, 232, 255, 274, 276, 287,
291, 298, 299
commander, 276
commanding, 37, 38, 207, 209, 219, 222, 270,
276, 291, 315
commandments, 132, 138, 158, 171, 172, 184,
185, 284, 285, 319
commando, 208
commandos, 207, 208
commands, 69, 92, 123, 128, 157, 201, 249,
255, 270, 297, 298, 319
commentators, 176, 250, 256, 294
commerce, 14, 250, 251
commercial, 14, 224
commission, 216, 244, 269, 326
commissioned, 131, 140, 163, 171, 199, 222,
272
commitment, 299, 300, 312
commodity, 71
common, 12, 19, 29, 95, 128, 164, 181, 230,
249, 256, 257, 258, 283, 301, 311, 314, 335,
345, 349
communicate, 25, 164, 165
communicated, 129
communion, 16, 138, 192, 310
company, 87, 90, 112, 135, 232, 327
compare, 11, 28, 173, 258, 301, 335, 337, 359
compared, 34, 38, 43, 57, 71, 131, 190, 220,
304, 338
compassion, 37, 46, 49, 107, 203, 336
compatible, 60, 252
compete, 80, 232, 245
competitive, 80, 232
complacency, 288
complacent, 241
complete, 11, 60, 62, 92, 95, 109, 111, 131,
132, 146, 147, 153, 173, 175, 181, 195, 212,
256, 260, 269, 283, 284, 300, 301, 312, 323,
327, 337, 341, 359
completing, 68, 196, 216
completion, 185, 186, 353
complex, 29, 30, 97, 182, 183, 185, 193, 316
compliance, 208
compliant, 38, 153

decision, 95, 98, 101, 102, 105, 116, 262, 293
decision-making, 303, 310
decisions, 58, 65, 86, 95, 96, 97, 98, 101, 103,
    126, 134, 351
decisive, 96, 97, 101, 104, 113, 180
decisiveness, 96, 97, 104
declarations, 108, 176
declare, 127, 128, 129, 130, 138, 145, 354, 355,
    356
decrease, 235, 236, 334
deductive, 97
deep, iv, 13, 23, 28, 40, 86, 112, 116, 126, 129,
    138, 139, 140, 149, 150, 190, 203, 275, 289,
    304, 342, 348
deep end, 13, 348
deeper, 50, 96, 111, 117, 119, 137, 144, 161,
    185, 188, 288, 317, 337
defeat, 44, 221, 274
defeated, 142, 180, 181, 220, 229, 232, 233,
    252, 273, 276, 295, 354
defeats, 200
defended, 50
defense, 125, 137, 246
deficient, 2
definition, 34, 50, 51, 60, 75, 126, 138, 162,
    195, 196, 197, 231, 251, 277, 290, 317, 318,
    325, 347
degree, 64, 71, 78, 86, 92, 103, 120, 136, 140,
    194, 277, 281
degrees, 197, 240, 341
deliberate, 193
deliver, 70, 82, 167, 197, 237, 238, 239, 273,
    322, 343, 345, 346
deliverance, 16, 77, 93, 215, 234, 237, 284, 344,
    346
delivered, 54, 147, 179, 214, 237, 238, 239,
    270, 284, 322, 347
delivering, 1, 143, 216, 237, 238, 354
delusions, 8, 33
demand, 37, 49, 133, 141, 144, 185, 192, 195,
    216, 271, 289, 304
demonic, 46, 98, 149, 176, 183, 201, 204, 212,
    213, 217, 233, 247, 283, 284, 294, 341
demonic forces, 176, 284, 294
demons, 46, 110, 127, 203, 245, 322

demonstrate, 25, 105, 146, 147, 148, 164, 209
demonstrates, 43
demonstrating, 26, 147
demonstration, 146, 147, 148
demonstrators, 146
denial, 35, 80, 82, 121
denied, 119, 193, 255
denomination, 91, 164
denominational, 183
denominations, 242
deny, 61, 72, 79, 109, 120, 121, 176, 252, 291,
    309
denying, 80, 81, 82, 309, 351
departing, 15, 127
dependable, 251
dependent, 21, 87, 88, 236
depth, 176, 267, 355
depths, 28, 31, 209, 253, 254
Derbe, 238
deregulate, 184
descendant, 42, 228
description, 13, 25, 35, 43, 79, 80, 94, 130, 131,
    145, 156, 165, 174, 302, 304, 313, 334
descriptive, 161, 185
design, 32, 103, 113, 199, 277, 320
desire, 11, 12, 14, 21, 22, 23, 44, 79, 121, 154,
    171, 192, 210, 221, 267, 289, 290, 359
desires, 33, 83, 117, 120, 121, 126, 133, 144,
    154, 158, 193, 198, 257, 290, 294, 314, 320,
    358
despair, 87, 89, 164
desperate, 87, 133
desperation, 5, 41
despised, 6, 7, 90
destiny, 83, 87, 89, 96, 102, 129, 131, 265, 312,
    352
destroy, 15, 33, 53, 57, 69, 70, 107, 111, 119,
    207, 214, 222, 223, 234, 269, 299, 310, 327,
    328, 341
detach, 13, 168, 233
detachment, 168
deter, 44
determination, 212, 274, 305
deterrent, 231
detour, 99

F

I

J

K

L

N

O

P

Q

S

supernatural, 26, 29, 48, 58, 82, 96, 98, 120,
125, 128, 136, 148, 150, 151, 161, 162, 164,
170, 202, 231, 236, 243, 248, 264, 265, 267,
276, 301, 358
superstitions, 68
supervise, 37, 274
supper, 179
supplications, 139
sure, 8, 21, 25, 29, 55, 56, 60, 66, 80, 84, 86,
87, 106, 107, 116, 123, 127, 128, 152, 153,
161, 192, 195, 212, 228, 232, 255, 276, 287,
302, 311, 319, 328, 331, 335, 338, 339
surface, 31, 32, 182, 187, 215
surprise, 19, 22, 75, 97, 237, 264, 294, 319
surprised, 86, 141, 191, 239, 311
surrender, 314, 344, 347
surrendering, 191
survives, 62
suspicious, 54, 113, 183, 253, 289, 340
sustained, 192
swerved, 127
sword, 17, 177, 266, 275, 319, 320, 321, 325,
326, 343, 344, 347
symbolic, 182, 185, 196, 213, 215, 248, 317,
339
symbolism, 213, 304, 311, 333, 334, 338
symptoms, 109, 342
system, 12, 13, 14, 15, 50, 53, 54, 58, 59, 68,
71, 73, 98, 106, 124, 126, 158, 310, 320,
324, 338
systematic, 53, 183, 322
systematically, 96, 196, 247

T

tabernacle, 31, 32, 188
tables, 214, 233, 234, 262
tablets, 140, 198
tactic, 231, 232, 234, 238
tactician, 252
tactics, 168, 178, 222, 231
tailgate, 189
tainted, 14, 127, 194, 296, 351
talents, 29, 87, 247
tapped, 86

target, 59, 192, 236, 251, 267
taste, 11, 120, 156, 157, 327, 328
tastes, 118, 156, 338
taught, 28, 42, 44, 67, 106, 115, 124, 138, 140,
144, 148, 167, 214, 218, 232, 233, 236, 244,
261, 287, 356
tax, 7, 8, 89, 90, 91, 203, 335
tax collector, 7, 8, 89, 90, 91, 335
taxes, 89
taxing, 90
teach, 38, 46, 91, 96, 120, 127, 139, 140, 190,
194, 200, 206, 213, 241, 265, 277, 278, 281,
282, 287, 291, 292, 294, 297, 302, 335, 358
teachable, 115
teachers, 19, 83, 112, 165, 235, 239, 241, 242,
358
teaching, 2, 3, 6, 10, 31, 56, 83, 111, 118, 121,
139, 151, 161, 162, 177, 184, 196, 201, 205,
207, 208, 214, 215, 216, 249, 254, 271, 278,
282, 293, 318, 356, 357, 358
team, 7, 144, 239, 263, 323
tear, 24, 27, 39, 71, 73, 78, 174
tears, 43, 46, 88, 300
technician, 95
technologies, 125
technology, 125, 130, 267
temperature, 256
tempered, 171
temple, 6, 7, 27, 28, 111, 112, 113, 214, 215,
217, 218, 352
temptation, 93, 134, 168, 290, 309
temptations, 87, 93, 193, 200, 224, 255, 289,
291, 309, 320, 335, 350
tempted, 44, 67, 87, 131, 195, 198, 213, 225,
232, 255, 263, 298, 321, 332
tenacious, 46
tend, 4, 5, 37, 51, 70, 74, 91, 163, 166, 168,
172, 194, 242, 308
tendencies, 74, 133, 154, 155, 176, 206, 251,
278, 310, 320, 335
tendency, 11, 12, 142, 150, 171, 173, 210, 259,
300
tender, 2, 193, 208
tenth, 69, 70, 92, 237
terminology, 24, 36, 52, 156, 295, 305

U

Y

Z

MORE FROM THE AUTHOR

For more resources by Rocky Veach, visit his website and go to the resources tab at:
http://rockyveach.myshopify.com/collections/all

8 Ways to Recover ALL

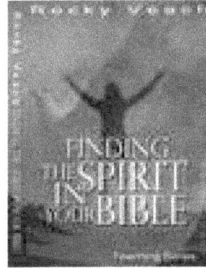

Finding the Spirit in Your Bible

Dead Man's Faith

One Thing

The Anointing

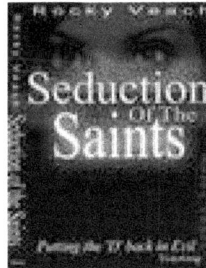

Seduction of the Saints

www.ingramcontent.com/pod-product-compliance
Lightning Source LLC
Chambersburg PA
CBHW072336090426
42741CB00012B/2809